Washington Wife

JOURNAL OF

ELLEN MAURY SLAYDEN

FROM

1897–1919

HARPER & ROW
PUBLISHERS
NEW YORK AND EVANSTON

WASHINGTON
WIFE

Journal of Ellen Maury Slayden from 1897-1919

This was written in deference

to an often expressed wish

of my husband,

James Luther Slayden;

and it is now tenderly dedicated

to his memory.

CONTENTS

(Sections of illustrations follow pages 134 and 262.)

[vii]

Contents

INTRODUCTION

In Mission Burial Park in San Antonio two monuments mark the last resting place of James Luther Slayden and his wife, Ellen Maury, the author of this book. The rough-hewn granite boulders contrast sharply with the polished marbles and slick granites of this fashionable resort of the forgotten dead. Since Ellen Maury outlived her husband by two years, it is a reasonable assumption that she determined what would be appropriate at this place. Two boulders, one large and one small, symbolize the towering height of the husband and the petite figure of his wife. They also reflect the relation between them, as far as the woman could determine it. Throughout her life she wanted J., as she called him, to be in the lead. Consciously she played the highly feminine and secondary role as the wife of Congressman Slayden, though her gifts were such that she must at times have found it difficult to keep out of the lead.

Ellen Maury was born at Piedmont, the ancestral home in Charlottesville, Virginia, in 1860. Piedmont, near the campus of the University of Virginia and now a part of the campus, was headquarters of the Maurys, one of America's famous families. The public is conscious of the contributions made by the Maury men to history and geography. Thomas Jefferson records in his memoirs that he was prepared to enter William and Mary College by the Rev. James Maury. Matthew Fontaine Maury's name is a byword, "pathfinder of the sea." But the public is perhaps not informed about the Maury women; surrounded by the culture and the youth of the University of Virginia, they were great record keepers and diarists, and among these Ellen is probably the most talented and assiduous of the lot. She relates in her foreword how she formed the habit of keeping notebooks, and it was this habit that served her well when she went to Washington.

Ellen Maury married James Luther Slayden on June 12, 1883. He was born in Mayfield, Kentucky, June 1, 1853. After his father's death in 1869, he moved with his mother to New Orleans. He was educated in the public schools, and attended Washington and Lee University at Lexington, Virginia. In 1876 he moved to San Antonio, Texas, to become a cotton broker and ranchman, and it was probably there that he met Ellen Maury, who was visiting her sister, Mrs. Jane Maury Maverick. In 1892 Slayden was elected to the state legislature, but did not seek re-election. His business career was brought to an end on August 21, 1896, when his firm of Slayden, Clarkson, and Robards, cotton brokers, went into bankruptcy due to the collapse of cotton prices in 1895. On the day following the assignment, August 22, 1896, he was nominated to stand for Congress from the San Antonio district, and was elected in November. This meant that he and Ellen went to Washington for the opening of Congress in March, 1897, and they returned each session for the following twenty-one years. Their experience in Washington was begun on the eve of the Spanish-American War and ended just at the close of World War I.

History will not record that James L. Slayden was a distinguished congressman. His career was honorable and his action intelligent, but no major legislation bears his name. He looked after the interests of his district in an acceptable manner, and often had the courage to cast unpopular votes. In his opposition to a reckless extension of pension benefits, Slayden said: "The Spanish-American War was not a great war. A large number of our troops took the hazard of watermelons in Georgia and Florida, and fought the malaria and mosquitoes, but very few Spanish. . . . The Spanish-American War yielded comparatively little in heroics, [but] paid the most marvelous dividends in politics and in magazine articles of any war in the history of the country."

Early in his career Slayden became interested in the peace movement, and he retained this interest to the end of his career. It finally cost him his seat in Congress. When he first went to Washington he was made a member of the Military Affairs Committee because of the heavy military installations in and around San Antonio. As his interest in the peace movement developed, his concern with military affairs declined, and he relinquished his place on the Military Affairs Committee. He was a delegate to the Hague Convention just prior to the outbreak of World War I. He was president of the American group of the Interparliamentary Peace Union which was devoted to settling international problems by talking instead of by fighting. He was president of the American Peace Society and a trustee of the Carnegie Endowment for International Peace. Mark Goodwin, writing from Washington on Slayden's death in 1924, said his most distinctive service was in drafting an amendment to the naval appropriation bill of 1916 directing the President to invite the nations of Europe to a world-wide conference to provide for a reduction of armaments and the preparation of a code of international law. "The Slayden amendment became the basic idea in the drafting of the League of Nations and was frequently referred to in speeches by President Wilson as 'the mandate of Congress' which was made a part of the covenant."

Then came the election of 1918. World War I was near its end, and the politicians knew it. In the meantime strong opposition to Wilson had developed in Congress, and Wilson decided, or someone decided for him, to purge those who were opposing him. James L. Slayden was a victim of that purge. Since his ideas of peace for the future coincided with those of Wilson, it is difficult to see why Wilson executed him politically. The records do not reveal that Slayden actively opposed Wilson or the war effort. He did keep his head in the midst of war hysteria which was very strong at that time. The real explanation of Wilson's act may be wholly personal, related to the Texas clique that E. M. House took to Washington during the Wilson administration. It may be related to Ellen Maury Slayden's disdain for Wilson and something bordering on contempt for House and his Texas entourage in Washington. Ellen knew Woodrow Wilson when he was a student at the University of Virginia. She did not like him then, and she did not like him any better when he became President and moved to Washington where she had been holding court among the famous personages for many years. She thought him narrow-minded, too much of a Presbyterian, and too much of the schoolteacher. She thought his attitude toward Mexico was entirely wrong. When his wife died, Ellen wagered a friend a five-pound box of candy that the President would marry before he left the White House, and she won. She almost wrecked Washington society by conducting a feminine war against Wilson's Cabinet when the Cabinet wives announced that they would return social calls from the wives of other Cabinet members, the Supreme Court judges, and senators, but could not be bothered with social obligations to members of the House of Representatives. The fact that she won this war may not have endeared her to the Wilson set.

Though evidence is lacking that Slayden failed to support the war effort, conditions with which he had to deal may explain why he refrained from war hysteria and clamor for revenge on the Central Powers. The first is that he had long been dedicated to peace. The second is that the German population is and has always been very heavy in his district. Such communities as New Braunfels and Fredericksburg are almost solidly German. These people had always been Slayden's friends and supporters, and it was necessary for him to retain their support. It was not in his nature to seek revenge, and to clamor for it now would have ordinarily been political folly.

But the circumstances were by no means ordinary in the summer of 1918. The war fever was at its height, patriotism amounted to fanaticism; the Germans were not numerous enough to elect a congressman, and were too intimidated by the tyranny of war to do so if they could. So by merely holding his position, Slayden lost. The opposition—in this case led by the Texas contingent in Washington—chose Carlos Bee. His qualifications were perfect. He had been in the Texas Senate, had a shock of gray hair, was a good speaker, son of Bernard E. Bee, of an old and respected Texas family. More important than all this was the fact that his wife was the sister of Albert Sidney Burleson, Wilson's postmaster general, a member of the House-Gregory-Burleson clique from Austin.

I have not been able to identify the person who sent Wilson a telegram inquiring as to whether Slayden had supported the war effort. The telegram was solicited not by Carlos Bee but by the supporters of Alva Pearl Barrett, but Bee was the beneficiary. The timing was perfect because Wilson had decided to make his purge of such members as Representative George Huddleston of Alabama, Senator James K. Vardaman of Mississippi, Senator Thomas W. Hardwick of Georgia, and Representative Francis Lever of South Carolina. The fact that the telegram had to be solicited indicates that Slayden had not already been marked for political execution.

It is interesting to speculate as to whether Wilson himself dictated the answering telegram. Did he really want to get Slayden out of Congress or did he want to get Ellen Maury out of Washington? Did the presence of this little aristocrat who had a social arrogance equal to his intellectual arrogance make him uncomfortable? Did the fact that she knew him, and didn't like him, when he was winning second place in debate at Charlottesville have any influence? Who knows? The telegram reads:

THE WHITE HOUSE WASHINGTON D.C.
JULY 24, 1918

YOUR LETTER RECEIVED   THE ADMINISTRATION AS
BETWEEN CANDIDATES EQUALLY LOYAL   NEVER
TAKES PART   IN THE LIGHT OF MR. SLAYDEN'S
RECORD NO ONE CAN CLAIM HE HAS GIVEN SUPPORT
TO THE ADMINISTRATION.

WOODROW WILSON

On July 25, the day after the Wilson telegram, James L. Slayden published the following statement:

For Twenty-two years I have tried faithfully to represent the people of this district and of the whole country in the American Congress. . . . I was not one of those who sought to plunge the country into war while expecting to remain in the security of private life. However, the President of the United States has said, in a telegram to a local newspaper, that I have not supported his Administration. No matter how false the statements made to the President that procured this telegram, my continued candidacy for Congress, in view of it, will appear to put me in opposition to those charged with the prosecution of the war, at a time when every good American must support the country regardless of his personal fortunes. I therefore announce my withdrawal from the race for Congress.

James L. Slayden[1]

It was March 3, 1919, that the Slaydens caught the train to Texas, knowing that a long political career had ended. There seems little doubt that he had been a casualty of the crossfire of politics. The harried Wilson had been guilty of an injustice. According to Mark Goodwin, Slayden "always thought that Mr. Wilson regretted having sent the telegram."

If James L. Slayden escapes the oblivion that shrouds most congressmen, it will be because of the diminutive Ellen—less than five feet tall—who had been his companion throughout his long service in Washington. As a Maury she had membership in one of the distinguished American families, a family that has spread the name Maury over the country. The Maurys were related to the Lewises, of Lewis and Clark fame. The Langhorne sisters, the Gibson girls, were cousins, and that includes Lady Astor. Ellen Maury's sister, Jane, married Albert Maverick, of another famous family. Jane was the mother of the late Maury Maverick, who went to Congress from Slayden's San Antonio district.

Since the Slaydens had no children, Ellen was free to write for newspapers and magazines, to serve as secretary to her husband, and to exercise her sophisticated charms on Washington society.

We have her word for it that she never attended a real school a day in her life but that she was highly literate from wide reading and good remembering none could doubt. Her early notebooks were studded with quotations from the best writers. She contributed to *Century,* to the New York papers, and was the first society editor of the San Antonio *Express.*

Never until she went to Washington had she had a real outlet for her born talent, that of a reporter with all the social graces, a keen hard

---

[1] It was the supporters of a third candidate, A. P. Barrett, who sent the telegram. Ironically, he was defeated by Carlos Bee. The decision lay in the hands of the German voters to whom Slayden's strength went. In the election of 1920 Slayden attempted a comeback. Both Bee and Slayden were defeated by Harry M. Wurzbach, a Republican.

intelligence, and apparently a complete awareness of the drama going on around her. Her background was perfect for the role she was to play in a great triangle from the Maury homestead of Piedmont in Virginia to the Maverick clan in Texas to the Capitol in Washington, where all the political and social forces of the nation met to engage in the great game of strut and compromise which is the art of government in a democracy. She was enough of a democrat to be acceptable in Texas, enough of an aristocrat to please the Virginians; and a combination of personal charm, wit, and design made her much sought after in Washington. There was just enough snob in her to make her intriguing and a little challenging in all three places. What she had above all else—and she was fully conscious that she had it—was social acceptance. She quickly mastered the Washington protocol, and the family legend tells that she taught many newcomers to Washington about napery, silver, calling procedure, and who sat next to whom at dinner. It is doubtful that she was ever caught in a social error.

It must be remembered that when she went to Washington women were supposed to be seen more than heard. She played this role as best she could, considering her nature and talents. She never intruded herself in front of J., but she built a background for him that would make any politician proud. The men—and perhaps the women too—had to go by him to get to her, and they did. It is a family story that they reached Washington with about $50, but even so she converted a rather dreary rented apartment into a place of charm and elegance. Her household effects, now distributed among the Mavericks and the Maurys, from Virginia to Texas, are distinctive, the brasses, the silver, the samovars, the braziers, and the furniture. Some of her comments on the coldness and lack of charm in the great houses of Washington indicate her desire to put some personality into these impersonal places.

Ellen Maury Slayden was all feminine, and she wanted other women to be feminine too. As a social arbiter, she was uncompromising. She could not endure the hackneyed social phrases. The formal speech of the Victorian age was breaking down, and she did not like what was taking its place. The stock reply of "just fine" in response to the common inquiry of "How are you?" she would not endure among her nieces. "Don't say that," she would plead.

"What should I say, Aunt Ellen?"

"Say 'Very well, thank you.' "

One niece recalls a trip on the San Antonio trolley. A young lady sitting beside Ellen began to make her toilet—in public. She combed her hair, touched up her lips, and powdered her face. Aunt Ellen looked at her appraisingly. "Young lady," she said coolly, "you forgot something."

"What did I forget?" asked the puzzled girl.

"You haven't brushed your teeth."

But Ellen was not all Victorian. She believed in woman suffrage but was irked by the bad manners and bad dress of the professional suffragettes. She did not favor prohibition, not because she was from the beer town of San Antonio but probably because she was from Virginia where they know how to drink wine and hold hard liquor. Though she was very fond of Mrs. Bryan, her strictures on Bryan's grape-juice functions in Washington and her description of the contempt of the imported European caterers for the stuff they had to serve is a masterly job of reporting, with the reporter's preferences showing.

What the public did not know about this little woman who knew everybody who was anybody is that she was a combination of Boswell and Samuel Pepys. For twenty-two years she kept cases on Washington official society, relieved now and then by some comedy or pathos from Texas or Virginia. While she was being gracious to a senator or congressman, a diplomat or scholar, she was appraising him with feminine realism. When she went home from some reception or dinner, she wrote down in her notebook what went on there. In some instances she did not wait to go home, but made her notes on the menu cards or programs. The notebooks were filled, and the stock of them grew to formidable proportions by the time she left Washington in 1919. She seems to have had no idea of writing a book, until she returned to San Antonio at the age of fifty-nine.

She had seven more years to live, but the lingering illness that brought her death took about two of these. She must have transmitted her notes into the book during the five years from 1919 to 1924. She did a chapter for each of the twenty-two years she was in Washington, and brought the story to a dramatic close with the scene on the train bringing the Slaydens home.

It is remarkable that her manuscript had to wait nearly half a century for a publisher. She did not have time to seek a publisher, and on her death she left the manuscript to Maury Maverick, as related elsewhere. Maury was just beginning his tempestuous career as an attorney and politician, and his life was too exciting for him to undertake marketing a memoir by a woman. There is evidence that he sent it to one magazine publisher, but it was the wrong one. In fact, many publishers might have shied away from it at the time. For one thing, her comments on people still living might have caused unpleasantness. For another, the people— and the publishers—were a little tired of what went on between 1898 and

1918. The Republican years had been relieved of unutterable dullness only by the antics of Theodore Roosevelt. Wilson brought some hope,
but his domestic program was blasted by a world catastrophe. The frenzy
of war and the ecstasy of victory—sardonically recorded here—were followed by disillusionment that was at its height when Ellen Slayden finished
her story, when the world she knew was falling down in the days of boot-
legging, walkathons, and flagpole sittings, when women were flappers instead of ladies, and men were exhibiting their egos in silk shirts. It was an
era of bad taste and bad manners, to be ended by the stock market crash
of 1929. During the depression following the crash, no one wanted to
publish a book and few wanted to read one. It is significant that when
this manuscript was brought to light in 1961, it was accepted by the first
publisher to examine it. The editors at Harper & Row have cut some of the
more trivial material from the original manuscript, and in a few instances
they have inserted entries from Ellen Slayden's original, hand-written notebooks—anecdotes which she evidently felt would be indiscreet to publish
in her time.

Readers of the journal need not, should not, expect to find their current political opinions confirmed or all their social views supported by this
daughter of a Virginian and wife of a Kentuckian residing in Washington,
Virginia and Texas in the first quarter of the twentieth century. The historic
value of her narrative is that it reveals an age as seen by a woman of awareness, sensitivity and amazing candor. When she gets through with Theodore
Roosevelt or William Howard Taft or Woodrow Wilson or "Colonel" E. M.
House or Porfirio Díaz, and many others of that day, there is no doubt as
to *her* opinion of them. She may not leave them great, but she leaves them,
every one, quite human.

Washington Wife is among the best contemporaneous records of
the period between the Spanish-American War—which announced that the
United States was a world power—and World War I, which defined the
duties and fixed the cost of holding first place. Ellen Slayden not only
recorded the social life of Washington, Texas, and Virginia, but she took
note of almost every historical event of importance in the nation. Though
her touch was light, her observations were intelligent, and always personal.
Five books have portrayed this period, or a part of it, and all are indeed
notable. They are *The Autobiography of Lincoln Steffens, The Letters of
Archibald Butt, Only Yesterday* by Frederick Lewis Allen, *Our Times* by
Mark Sullivan, and *42 Years in the White House* by Ike Hoover. *Washington Wife* belongs with this group, but in this distinguished company it is
unique. It is the only account written by a woman, it is the only view of

national and world affairs that gives the feminine point of view, the only one that deals to any extent with the feminine contingent in the national capital.

WALTER PRESCOTT WEBB

Austin, Texas

PREFACE

Ellen Maury Slayden had a major effect on my adult life. My first contact with her was in San Antonio, Texas, in the spring of 1920 when I made my decision to set up the date of my marriage to her nephew, Maury Maverick, from June to May.

Like most nineteen-year-old girls, I had dreamed of being a June bride. Alas, it was not to be. My new husband could not be honeymooning for a month in California because James Luther Slayden was a candidate for Congress again, and he wanted his nephew, Maury Maverick, to campaign for him. We would have to be back in San Antonio a few weeks before the Democratic primary election to be held on the last Saturday in July.

Since James Slayden was unsuccessful in that bid to return to Congress, the election of 1920, once it was over, was of no great importance to him and Ellen. It was important to me. It not only changed the date of my marriage to their nephew, it introduced me to the world of politics in which I was to live for many years. From that summer political activities in general and the Democratic primary elections in particular have dominated and enriched my life.

As a congressman's wife I lived the sort of Washington life that Ellen Slayden describes so vividly. Our house in the capital was the usual furnished place, and left something to be desired, but it was warmed by certain personal possessions—some of them Slayden items, paintings, brasses and copper, for which we shared a mutual delight. Like Ellen, I did my share of card leaving, and I stood in line, as she had years before, at White House receptions waiting to ascend slowly the great stairs leading to the East Room on the upper level. I also have been invited to arrive at the north entrance of the White House, which seems to be a special star in one's crown. The lovely wood paneling on some of the walls, especially in the great dining room that Ellen Slayden speaks of, I remember nostalgically. I believe that the walls have now been painted. And I, too, while waiting for our wraps, have felt that blast of icy wind coming straight from 16th Street.

Although the spirit and personality of Mrs. Franklin Roosevelt were independent enough to encourage many official wives to dispense with much of the unnecessary and completely routine "at homes," bulk calling, et cetera, there remained and will always remain a certain amount of purely official entertaining. Many times it is exciting and thrilling, but it can be both tired and tiresome. I have also drawn those uninteresting escorts at official dinners, but occasionally my card would have the name of some attractive personality who would make an otherwise stiff and formal dinner—caviar, guinea hen, truffles, and champagne notwithstanding—something more than a physical endurance test.

For all these reasons, and many more, this journal touches a responsive chord in me. But my involvement is even closer than I have indicated. In time I found myself the owner of Ellen Slayden's journal. This came about because Aunt Ellen Slayden called her favorite nephew, Maury, to her bedside and gave him the original manuscript. She included all the small pencil-written notebooks that she had started before he was born, with the remark that it was all his, and she also expressed the wish that her story might be published.

Twenty-eight years later, in 1954, Maury Maverick died of a heart attack. Those were strenuous and exciting years during which Maury met life head on. He served four years as a state and county officer, four years in Congress, was mayor of San Antonio for two years, wrote two books, many magazine articles, coined a new word for the English language, and engaged in every political controversy involving human rights and human freedom. In view of the sort of life he lived, it is not strange that he did not continue to seek a publisher for the Slayden story. A literary agent might have had trouble placing it at that time, when the depression was imminent and a world war not far off. Washington was making too much history to be much interested in a woman's observations on it in the twenty-two-year period bracketed by two wars. There is another reason why publishers might have shied away from the risk of publication. Ellen Maury Slayden's comments on famous personages, both men and women, are acute and revealing. These people were still living and quite influential —for she knew everybody—and some of them might have made a fuss at seeing themselves stripped of their pretenses. At any rate, the original manuscript and the many notebooks on which it was based remained in Maury's extensive collection of books, manuscripts, and letters.

In 1958 Dr. Richard Henderson was given permission to examine the Maverick papers in connection with a book he was writing on the political career of Maury Maverick. He came on the Slayden manuscript and the notebooks and proclaimed them "a historian's dream." I passed this word along to a historian, Dr. Walter Prescott Webb of the University of Texas, at about the time he proposed marriage to me. Before our marriage late in 1961 I transferred the Maury Maverick collection to the University of Texas for safekeeping, but not before Dr. Webb had extracted the Slayden story. He tucked the manuscript under his arm and drove off to Austin with it. He telephoned me a few days later and said he thought it was sensational, and that it should be published at once. For a while I thought the Slaydens, now dead for more than thirty years, were going to crop up again in my matrimonial plans, for until Dr. Webb had made transcripts of the original and placed the story with the publisher I seemed to take second place. Harper's quick acceptance of the Slayden story put things back in perspective.

There are several friends who have identified names and supplied important information concerning the Slaydens, and I am especially grateful to them. Mrs. Sondra Gray rendered invaluable service in making available her research on the political career of James L. Slayden. I also wish to thank the members of the Maury and Maverick families in Virginia and Texas who have hunted through family albums for photographs and contributed family lore.

Now, not as Terrell Maverick, my name for many years, but as Terrell Webb, I am pleased to share Ellen Maury Slayden's experiences, her wisdom, her incisive pronouncements—not always objective, fortunately, and certainly exciting. In her observations of the life around her, in Washington, in Texas, in the world at large, she revealed with equal clarity her own remarkable personality. You will remember her, for she is not easily forgotten.

TERRELL WEBB

Austin, Texas

FOREWORD

Long intimacy with politicians makes it natural for me to say that I have been induced to put my reminiscences into book form because of the "earnest solicitations of numerous friends," although the fact that my habit of keeping notes extends over the period of my adult life does justify the suspicion that I had long intended to do something of the sort. But really it was not until my husband's spectacular retirement from Congress after his long service that the idea occurred to me seriously. After twenty-two years of life automatically arranged for us, coming to Washington for the first Monday in November and every other year leaving early in March, we had a curious feeling of being adrift; we had almost forgotten how to make our own plans.

Before we actually left Washington my husband was deluged with letters, sympathetic, approving, applauding, and always indignant about a Democratic President's interference in a local Democratic fight. Among the letters were many to me personally begging me to write my experiences and observations, to tell all I knew, etc. To tell all I knew in the sense suggested would have made a brief story. Mysteries have never come my way; I knew no secrets, political or social, so there was no chance of my making a book of backstairs gossip to tempt sensation. But we had lived the ordinary official-social life rather fully, we had known the great and the near great, the outstanding figures of the time—and there were the notebooks! The idea of sifting the notes and putting the worthwhile incidents into readable shape suddenly took hold of my imagination as something with which to steady myself until we were fitted into another niche. They had been kept quite innocently, just from habit because a much-loved older sister gave me on my fifteenth birthday, after the sweet fashion of the Victorian age, a pretty commonplace book, with selections written into it here and there from her own wide and sound reading. She advised me to fill it with extracts from my own choosing, and I went about it with enthusiasm, cramming its clear pages with quotations from favorite sentimental or religious poets, and sometimes confiding to it outpourings of ado-

[xxiii]

lescent egotism after the manner of Marie Bashkirtsev but lacking her redeeming cleverness. A little later came views, theories and incidents too freely recorded and shared in by student friends at the University of Virginia near my home. In many parts of the United States there are elderly gentlemen, grown gray and conservative and now engaged in preaching down a daughter's heart, or setting an old head on a young son's shoulders, who, if their eyes should fall upon this page, may be relieved to know that long ago I had the moral courage to burn that particular book. It will never rise up to discredit the wise saws and fine social creeds they would have their children think they always lived up to.

But the notebook habit was fixed on me irrevocably, and after we went to Washington it settled down into an irregular record about people and events worth remembering. For these things, of course, Washington provided more material than any other place in America. It is of these notes that I am vain enough to believe I may make a book—a book which if not of lively interest today may be of use to future historians of the life of the American people of my time.

ELLEN MAURY SLAYDEN

San Antonio, Texas,
1925

Washington Wife

JOURNAL OF

ELLEN MAURY SLAYDEN

FROM

1897–1919

CHAPTER ONE

1897

San Antonio, January

This notebook has not been opened since the dog days. The novelty, excitement, and hard work of J.'s[1] brief and hectic campaign for Congress left me no time for recording personal experiences. I am sorry, because so many pleasant and amusing things happened that I would not willingly forget. One constantly hears that politics is an ugly game, but we have seen little but the kindly side of it.

The campaign brought such splendid opportunities to test the friendship of our friends, and of others who we had not dreamed were so much our friends. They were almost without exception loyal and helped us in many odd and unexpected ways. An appreciable amount of money from Republicans for the campaign fund was not the least of our surprises. Help of that sort was most opportune, for our cash in hand the day J. was nominated was little more than $100. My heart was touched to the depths by the fact that J.'s friends and neighbors, those who have known him best and longest, wanted him to represent them, and especially under the peculiar circumstances of his failing in business, making an assignment of all he possessed one day and being nominated for Congress the next morning. I doubt if I shall ever again feel the same thrill of gratitude and pride that I felt when hearing that the men who were thrown out of work by his firm's collapse just in the beginning of the cotton season were the first to organize a Slayden Club and to offer money for the campaign.

Wynne Andrews, not a rich man, offered his time, a pair of fine mules, and a strong buggy. He and J. drove hundreds of miles to places that cannot be reached by rail in this vast twelfth district—thirty-seven counties, and larger by 10,000 square miles than the state of New York. It was cold, wet weather, and stopping places few and primitive, but they made light of the hardships. After the first few days, they said, the mules could recog-

[1] Author's husband, James Luther Slayden.

[1]

nize a voter afar off; when near enough, they would stop abruptly, J. would stand up and make his argument, the voter would pledge his support, and the mules move on at once.

Of course J. was away almost constantly, and if sentimental people had not already convinced me that woman's sphere is in the home, the conviction would have been forced upon me by the exigencies of those ten weeks. We could not afford clerical help, so I spent many long days at the typewriter, addressing campaign literature, writing letters and sometimes speeches for supporters who wanted to speak and did not know what to say. I was flattered when a friend quoted her coachman as saying that my colored boy made the best political speech they had had at the Coachmen's Union.

Ed is the son of our colored cook, and when we employed him last summer, we little thought that his services would be so largely political and clerical. He is amazingly educated for his age—about sixteen years —and writes such a good hand that J. said reproachfully, "It makes me ashamed to see a colored boy write better than my wife."—"And spell better than my husband," I retorted, after which passage at arms we settled down to make use of his gifts. We found him unfailingly loyal, trustworthy, and best of all, cheerful under every trial.

Only once did he mope or neglect his various duties. The election was close, the result in doubt for several days, and during that time he let the house get very dusty, but one night the good news came that J. had won. When we went down to breakfast the next morning, Ed was waiting for us all smiles, and writ large in the dust on the tables and piano was the one word "Elected."

McKinley has let it be known that he will call an extra session in March, so we shall be breaking up, and I dread it, but except for that the outlook is pleasant. Sometimes I feel a little irritated by the idea some of our friends have that we must feel socially elevated by the new position. How could we be socially elevated? I cherish the good old American belief that if you are born gentlefolk, no amount of worldly honors can make you anything more, and only your own conduct make you anything less. There are others who seem to think that Washington is almost entirely peopled with diplomats and discuss my fitness for diplomatic society, or say, "When you get up there among those foreigners—" Happily, so much of my youth was spent in Washington that I have no delusions of grandeur as to the status of a new congressman's wife, but renewing old friendships and being so near my parents in Virginia are pleasant things I look forward to.

Our first experience of the obligations of congressional life was in entertaining W. J. Bryan, our defeated candidate for president. San Antonio thinks it the crowning glory of our hitherto obscure career, but it was really only a visit from a simple, cultivated gentleman of the kind—barring a few Western touches—that I have always been accustomed to.

Elected by Bryan's party, J. thought he should be our guest while he was here on his lecture tour, but when he accepted the invitation only two days before he was to arrive, I was a bit upset. We were dining at Jane's.[2] Good sister that she is, she offered to have mince pies, cake, and jelly made for me; and I drove at once to market to buy venison, quail and wild duck, so as to be prepared for much coming and going and feeding of hearty Democrats. Coming home through the back gate I ordered the killing of a big gobbler bought weeks before and named "W.J.B."; paused in the kitchen to put a Virginia ham in soak, and then sat down to think "What next?"

It was bitter cold, and this, like most Texas houses, all doors and windows, is a cave of the winds in winter. The largest fires are only ornamental. My good cook was away; Ed was gone back to college, alas!; the best long tablecloth was soiled, and the water pipes frozen. I wondered if our Virginian ancestors who entertained Washington and Lafayette ever had more to contend with. Bryan himself didn't appall me, but the people who would come to see him would look around to see how the new congressman's wife was doing things.

Besides Bryan, we were to have Governor Culberson, ex-Governor Jim Hogg, and several local magnates, and a later telegram, saying that they could not get here to dinner Thursday but would come to breakfast Friday and to dinner that evening, did not make the situation easier.

Snow was falling when they all arrived, but the house was almost warm. Bryan was easy to get acquainted with, and we had a pleasant breakfast and a good one—thanks to Mrs. George Maverick, who lent me her cook, the best one in town. Could such a simple kindness be thought of in any society more formal than our frontier?

I have always liked and admired Governor Hogg. For all his roughness (some of it assumed, I think) he is a stimulating companion, wise, kind, and sincere, and full of homespun humor. Among other hot breads, we had some very small biscuits, and apropos of J.'s asking him to take two at a time, he launched out in his tremendous voice, "When I was a gre't big water-jointed boy, used to eatin' at the blowin' of the horn, my

[2] Jane Maury Maverick (Mrs. Albert Maverick).

sister moved to town, and one day she had some o' these biscuits, and I'd take one and they wouldn't get 'round the table before I'd want another, and I felt so foolish, and got so mad that I never would let one be made in my house." I assured him there was a "free and unlimited coinage" of them going on in the kitchen at a ratio of "sixteen to one," and I think he ate his allowance. I had a plateful kept by him, but didn't know until that night that he had noticed it.

Before breakfast was over the gallery and front rooms were full of people waiting to see the lion, but Hogg was in some respects more the center of attraction than Bryan. Our biggest chair creaked under his weight, but he made Rena and Jessie Maverick sit on the arms and held little Mary Wilson in his lap. When I introduced him to my most punctilious friend, he reached around the children to shake hands with her, and said, "Howd'do, Mrs. Moore, I'm glad to know you," so heartily that she quite forgot his failure to rise.

The dinner party strained the capacity of our dining room. Bryan never insisted upon leading but followed any person who introduced a subject worth while. His talk was easy, unpretentious, and amazingly humorous for such a dead-in-earnest person. He discussed his defeat without embarrassment or bitterness, told funny stories of the campaign, and read newspaper jokes at his own expense. His hair is too long—the usual weakness of Western statesmen—and his clothes of smooth black cloth and eccentric cut are queer, but I didn't notice them until he was on the stage. I saw only his clear, steel-blue eyes with black brows and lashes, very Irish, his straight uncompromising mouth, and well-kept teeth.

From dinner we hurried to Beethoven Hall where the mass of people shouting for Bryan, Hogg and Slayden almost carried us off our feet. When Bryan began to speak, I realized for the first time that he was a big man, not just a pleasant one.

He has the most perfect voice I ever heard. The audience went wild. When he finished people swarmed around him, shaking his hands, touching his shoulders, almost kissing the hem of his garment. How can a man retain his sanity amid such adulation?

I was standing in a stage box looking down at the ovation when Governor Hogg, who was beside me, called out to a dignified-looking gentleman almost across the hall, "Jack Dunkin, Jack Dunkin, come here! I want you to meet Mrs. Slayden." When Judge Duncan came near enough, he went on, "She's little, but, I tell you, she's a whizzer. She kept me a whole plate o' hot biscuits to myself this mornin'." I felt as if I were being dangled before the crowd by the back of my neck.

Home again sitting around the fire, Bryan was only a quiet, genial guest, talking of his wife and children, of books and poetry. He repeated the "Ode to the Waterfowl" so beautifully that I felt as if I had never heard it before.

Privately Governor Hogg told me to prepare to stay a long time in Washington, giving some expert political reasons and some personal estimates of J. that almost brought tears to my eyes, but the future is in the lap of the gods. I shall not look too far forward.

Bryan was immensely taken with my sister and Albert Maverick and their eleven children. After his address to working men on Alamo Plaza at noon, J. took him to lunch with them, and the children hung around him with delight. My house is littered with queer presents people brought him, rare bits of stone, historical letters and documents, and old books of dubious interest. If he accumulates such stuff everywhere, I hope his house has an ample attic.

Washington, March 28

J. came up before the 15th for the Democratic caucus. I spent a few days in Virginia and arrived here late on a cold, rainy night. I have rarely felt so profound a sense of homesickness and depression as when we came splashing up the gleaming avenue in a sprawling old hack to the Oxford Hotel where J. has found a place for us to live. We have left a pleasant way of life for a future full of turmoil and uncertainty, and sometimes my heart sinks, but I never let J. know it. We have four rooms on the first floor at the corner of 14th and H. They are a little apart from the rest of the hotel, fortunately, but woefully ugly and ill arranged. However, they are large and airy, with big gilt mirrors and marble mantels in the grand old-Washington manner, and since I have banished the folding beds and marble washstands from the front room, and put out my own belongings— table covers, books, and flowers (so expensive here compared to Texas)—it is quite presentable. The house was once the home of a Kentucky senator of philandering memory, and from the look of some fair ones in the dining room I think a few of his light o' loves must hang round it still, but on the whole it is dull and respectable.

Our first caller was a blond, curly-haired young man, "Governor" Osborne of Wyoming, newly elected to the House. He talked politics all the time. Art, literature, religion and weather were unconsidered trifles to him. We are inundated with cards of people we never heard of, and who, I strongly suspect, never heard of us until they saw our names in the Congressional Directory.

It is a distinct advantage to have known Washington before. An invitation came from a "Baroness" something, and instinct prompted me not even to send a card of acknowledgment. I have heard since that she took the title from the given name of a departed husband who made a fortune keeping a bar, and that new congressmen's wives are her favorite prey. Some Texas girls told me that I "missed a lovely time" at the tea; that the Baroness was "real elegant" and "was coming to call"—just as I feared.

My many sweet "cave dweller" Maury relatives have been most kind, and Mrs. Sayers of the Texas delegation, a pretty and graceful woman with twelve years' experience here, has led me gently in the way I should go officially. The Texas delegation is splendid. Thirteen of the fifteen men sworn in were over six feet. J.'s six feet two inches, and white hair (it grieves him no little, but I admire it), his strong, firm lines, a very Anak rejoicing in his strength, filled me with content. He has the chance now to do justice to himself and be a credit to his state.

The great debate on the Dingley tariff bill[3] ended today; the Republicans were more overbearing than ever; the Democrats hacked and harried. Bailey of Texas, Democratic leader, pouted and made no speech worth mentioning. He had a scornful air as if he might do wonders but didn't choose to. If any Democrat led, it was McMillin of Tennessee or Sayers of Texas—the "Watchdog of the Treasury." Sayers is a handsome man, heavy and swarthy with fluffy, white hair and a big mustache, but rather careless in dress and carriage. He is to be our next governor, and will make a good one, they say. McMillin is florid, bald headed, and has humorous watchful eyes with none of Bailey's contempt for the enemy.

Except for luncheon with J., I was in the gallery from ten till five. The speeches were short and some were amusing. Hartman of Montana urged prompt passage of the bill so as to get to the "real issue, the financial question," which threw a gentleman from Michigan—undoubtedly the original of the picture on Quaker Oats—into a fine frenzy. Professionally he defended the gold standard, but as an enthusiast he dropped into poetry and shouted:

> If you clip the eagle's wings so it cannot cross the sea,
> It will cease to be the emblem of a country proud and free.

Then he sat down hard and mopped his forehead.

Dingley of Maine is ill, querulous, and resentful of any criticism of

---

[3] The Dingley Act, passed in 1897, remained in force until 1909.

the bill bearing his name. He is a pathetic figure of an old man with narrow, sloping shoulders and the features of an aged rabbi. He sits huddled down in his seat but rises halfway out of it every few minutes to gasp, "Mr. Chairman," then settles back again, drumming his long fingers nervously on chair arms or desk.

The comedy of Bailey's coat fills the newspapers and promotes the gaiety of many dinner tables. He, with the other members of the Ways and Means Committee, was invited to dine at the White House, but declined, and sent another note to explain that he did not have an evening suit, never had worn one, and was "too old to learn." The last clause set the chamber in a roar, because few men in this country have ever attained such political eminence as his so early in life.

We are in the diplomatic circle at last. The Chilean Minister and I take lessons in bicycle riding at the same hour, and he has an incorrigible tendency to ride up the walls of the houses on either side of the yard. When he falls off and fairly claws up the earth, he rises with perfect gravity, has the darky boy brush him off, remounts the wheel and charges the wall again with the intrepidity of Don Quixote at the windmill.

Everyone rides now. J. and I have beautiful wheels, and I hope I shall learn to enjoy it, but the divided skirt, for all its modesty, is so hideous and uncomfortable I feel as if I were in a bag. The streets swarm with cyclists, and they are especially pretty at night when clubs, sometimes of hundreds, go out for a spin. There is no sound but the faint chatter of the riders, and each wheel carrying a light, they look like a parade of will-o'-the-wisps. All the big shops, theaters and churches have rows of stalls where you can stable and lock your wheel while you go about your business or pleasure.

Representative King of Utah is in this hotel, and we see him often. He is a Mormon, the first I have met, so I am enjoying the chance of studying what is, no doubt, a choice specimen. He is good-looking, with clean, strong teeth, wavy black hair, and manners almost too gracious. He talks well, though he is too rhetorical at times, especially about his church, for which his admiration is boundless. He even defends polygamy and says that before they all began scrupulously to obey the law against it it was practiced by "only the very best men"—those who had been so good to one wife that they were thought worthy to have another. I listened with credulity until he said that second marriages were nearly always entered into at the request of the first wife. It will take more than the unsupported evidence of one male Mormon to convince me of that. He is a son-in-law of one of the twelve Apostles, and I long to know how many mothers-in-law he has, but J. won't let me ask him.

May 6

Mrs. Maxey is here for the Council of Regents of Mount Vernon which begins this week. Tuesday afternoon we made our visit of ceremony to Mrs. McKinley—an experience more pathetic than pleasant. Mr. Handy of Delaware got our cards, and a friend with profound reverence for the proprieties wanted to order our carriage, said one *must* ride to the White House, but we preferred walking, and nothing frightful happened. It was a heavenly day, all sunshine and bloom and delicate green; the three blocks did not exhaust us, and the man at the door asked no credential but our cards. After a wait in the Red Parlor we were summoned upstairs, but turned back because a flock of schoolgirls had gone ahead of us, so we went on a tour of the bleak Blue and Green rooms. Later an obviously bored young officer met us at the elevator, led us through the dreary gray corridor to where Mrs. McKinley sat enthroned, introduced Mrs. Handy and left us to our fate.

The first glimpse of Mrs. McKinley made me ashamed of coming. She sat propped with pillows in a high armchair with her back to the light. Her color was ghastly, and it was wicked to have dressed her in bright blue velvet with a front of hard white satin spangled with gold. Her poor relaxed hands, holding some pitiful knitting, rested on her lap as if too weak to lift their weight of diamond rings, and her pretty gray hair is cut short as if she had had typhoid fever. She shook hands with us lightly, but didn't speak until the words "Mrs. Maxey of Texas" seemed to strike her and she then said in a faraway tone, as if talking to herself, "That's a long way off." Mrs. Maxey murmured some commonplace about her kindness in receiving us, and she went on, saying "I've had a great deal of experience." I expressed the hope she felt no ill effects from the cold at the Grant memorial parade in New York last week and again she said, "No, I've had a great deal of experience, my husband was in Congress a long time, and then he was governor of the state." She was rambling on in the same strange tone when we saw other visitors coming and slipped away as gracefully as we could. We all shrank from being there with a poor, suffering woman who ought to have been hidden from the gaze of the curious. Her voice was gentle and refined, and her face almost childishly sweet. There were two stiff females, much dressed up, standing on either side of her like the wives of Ham and Shem in a Noah's ark, but they never said a word to us, and we hardly knew how to include them in our leave-taking. This morning's society news—so important here—says they are relatives from Ohio and that they "were graceful assistants at the charming reception." My provincial eyes are opening to the value of newspaper accounts of the great.

And my provincial prejudices also must be revised. A heavy senatorial couple from the Southwest called on us—a very kind thing for them to do, as by all the rules we should have called on them first. The weather was stifling. The lady was stout, and as I looked at her dress of red velvet with a ruffled train, a rich bonnet to match, and soiled white gloves split down the palms, I thought to myself, "Now isn't it like a woman from a small Western town to wear such finery?" And just then she said, "Mrs. Slayden, I have been so anxious to meet you since I heard you were a Maury of Virginia. You know, I am a Virginian too." And so she was, of the actual "first families," the Jamestown colonists of 1607, who look down on the Puritans—latecomers of 1620—as mere parvenus.

It is getting dreadfully hot and sticky here, and I long for the clean, fresh air of Virginia and Texas. It will be hot enough in Texas, but there the heat is dry and stimulating, while here one feels parboiled.

Washington, November 17

After the fashion of new congressmen, J. was obsessed with the idea that we must live on Capitol Hill "near his work," so I left him to his political chores in Texas, came on here alone and spent some weary days hunting a house to suit our means and my taste. When I wrote him that I had taken one near enough to Mrs. Leiter for me to "exchange pies with her over the fence," he was horrified at my getting into such an expensive district, but he doesn't yet realize the sharp contrasts of this overgrown and underdone town. The house is two rooms deep and three stories high, the dining room is a half moon, the back yard a triangle about eight feet at the base, but there are possibilities of comfort and prettiness.

That matter settled I went to Piedmont and while there Father[4] gave me a farm of one hundred acres, rough mountain land, but good for apples, and the craze for Albemarle pippins now is almost equal to the Klondike fever. Whatever the success of the orchard, it will never bring me happier

---

[4] Jesse L. Maury, whose home was "Piedmont," Charlottesville, Virginia, now a part of the campus of the University of Virginia.

days than those spent riding over it with Father, eighty-six years young, and the surveyors. We had two good fresh horses, the autumn air and coloring were glorious, and our hearts were full of that inexpressible love of the good brown earth, and of one special part of it, that most Virginians have. Father was full of reminiscences, showing me places where "pa," "grandpa" and even "great-grandpa" had builded and planted, and remains of the house where Mrs. Bartley Dedmond lived, who was tried on the charge of being "a common scold." A prudent neighbor parried the lawyer's questions by expatiating on her good qualities until, pinned down about the sharpness of her tongue, he answered, "Well, please your honor, women will be women."

I acquired "Aunt Frances" for cook, and her daughter Maggie, a black but comely damsel, for maid, and came back here to begin Washington life in earnest. With my pretty things from Europe and Mexico the house is getting quite a little air. At least there's nothing downright ugly, which isn't true of all M.C. homes. One I recall where the greenery-yallery chenille curtains are tied up in knots—to give the smell of cabbage free play, I inferred—and another where the marble center table is piled up with all the badges, red, white and blue ribbon, gilt fringe, and buckles, that the Congressional master has acquired at every county fair or national convention in the last twenty years.

We are fortunate in our next-door neighbors—George Vest, son of the old Senator from Missouri, his wife and two children—all agreeable and very good to look at. I never lived in a cramped little town house before, and sometimes feel suffocated by it. Hearing voices through the walls is irritating, and would be unbearable if they were loud or ill-bred ones.

CHAPTER TWO

1898

The Lord has tempered the wind to the shorn Texan so far, but there is a blizzard today and for reasons of manners and politics I had to go out in it to call on the wife of a Western senator. Half-frozen, I was ushered into a drawing room with white walls, a grass-green rug, gilt chairs and mirrors, and a vase of white carnations. Madame wore a dress of transparent linen over green silk that crackled like icicles, and the ladies receiving with her were just as cold, which perhaps accounted for the general stiffness. We sat around like nymphs in a grotto until invited into another frigid apartment and given iced lemonade and "boughten" wafers. My teeth were chattering, but I stayed long enough to get even by playing on their credulity about Southern women. So many Northern people betray their belief that we are self-indulgent, incompetent, and dependent upon servants. One of the "receiving ladies" was the literal, capable, bread-alone type of Westerner, evidently studying me as a specimen. Somehow the limitations of my back yard got into the talk, and from across the room she asked, "Well, Mrs. Slayden, *ha*ow do you get your washing done?" It didn't seem the place to discuss our soiled linen, so assuming an air of imbecile ignorance I said, "Why, really, I don't know. My servants attend to it." Her eyes widened with astonishment: "But don't you look after it? Don't you kna-ow, really?" I, still guileless, "No, but I think they do it in the furnace room." She followed me to the door, warning me that the clothes would get yellow, and protesting that "You Souther-rn women *are* so funny." I ran home to get warm, and while taking a hot drink told the story to Aunt Frances, who commented, "What dem white ladies got to do wid you washin', I wonder? Dat's *my* business."

February 10

One of our Sunday callers was Stephen Bonsal, writer, traveler, diplomat, and editor of *Munsey's*. He is fresh from Cuba and has written a sane book about it. People who know Cuba are in demand now, and I smiled to think what a lion had strolled in on us when others are beating the bush to find one. We met him in Madrid four years ago. He is classed with Richard Harding Davis and Frederic Remington, but seems to me to pose less than they do; and he certainly writes less cant about war. S.B. said that Davis's and Remington's craving for blood was insatiable; that when he was in the diplomatic service in Madrid, at the time of the little Melilla incident, they cabled him, "Can you promise us big fighting?" He replied diplomatically, "Can promise you some Maryland Club whiskey."

For two, three, or even four women, arrayed like Solomon in all his glory, to get into a big, closed carriage and roll solemnly around to call on others of their kind is, if not the whole duty, the chief pleasure of the Congressional set, and some of our Texans excel in dress and equipage. Aunt Frances, who never before dreamed of a town bigger than Lynchburg, is so excited over the company that Tuesday afternoons she runs a race with Maggie to get to the front door. She is dreadfully fat and unsightly, but I can't bear to make her stay in the kitchen where she belongs. The basement is dark and cramped, and she longs for the open country houses as I do. Yesterday she burst into my room, breathless from climbing two flights of stairs, and gasped, "Miss Ellen, come on down an' see dem ladies! Dey's got silk an' satin trailin' dis far on de flo' "—she spread out her arms—"an' you kin smell 'em clean up here."

The Washington Smart Set, like others I have glimpsed, is too much concerned with smartness to be interesting. I went to a ladies' luncheon where twelve overdressed and overfed women, with not even one little man to leaven the lump, sat down to a table beautiful and expensive but too much beribboned for my taste—ribbon and gravy are so incompatible. Broad pink satin strips ran diagonally across, with big bows, like a little girl's sash, at each corner. There were pink-shaded candles and a center piece of Battenberg lace over pink silk, beautiful china, and four wine-glasses at each place. We were offered ten courses, all wonderful to behold, especially the ice cream—pink roses falling out of a pink sugar umbrella into spun-candy snow. But the company! It was selected without regard to acquaintance or congeniality—just people. And the talk was worse than nothing. Mrs. Heistand,[1] unknown to fame until the McKinleys adopted her, was most deferred to, and she never let us forget her intimacy at the White House. She was short, stout, and upholstered in a large pat-

---

[1] Mrs. H. O. S. Heistand was a friend of the McKinleys from Canton, Ohio. Her husband, Captain Heistand, was attached to the Adjutant General's Office.

tern of velvet brocade like a hotel sofa. All through the luncheon I could hear her saying stuffily, "The President just threw down his cards," or "There was a jackpot, and the President—" and "The President and *dear* Mrs. McKinley"—*ad nauseam.*

We dined at the Mexican Legation lately—a great compliment, Mrs. Vest tells me, for newcomers—but we have known the Romeros before. The Mexican government, too, has unofficially expressed satisfaction at J.'s being in Washington. He has so often, through his commercial relations, helped to promote good understanding between the two republics. The other guests were the Secretary of Agriculture and Miss Wilson, several senatorial couples, two superannuated army people, and a young couple from the Chilean Legation. J. took Miss Wilson in, but sat next to the great, deep-chested, blonde Chileña; and her oiled and curled young husband next to me was in an anguish of jealousy at their gay conversation. He spoke no English and his thick "gullah" Spanish was hard to understand. I tried to reassure him about J. by appearing not to share his anxiety, and giving my attention to Senator Warren, who brought me in. The Senator is said to regard women as necessary evils, but he was very nice to me, as well as to a high official dame on his other side who wore a gown of red velvet, with rabbit ermine around a chest rock-ribbed and bare as her native Sierras.

Mr. Romero is scholarly and grave, "a man of sorrows" as the intellectuals of Mexico nearly always are, feeling the potentialities of suffering and shame in their strange, uncertain people. Madame is an American, gentle and refined in a misty sort of way. I never quite get at her. The dinner was fairly good and well served, but flowers and candles were so thick down the center of the table that the people opposite you seemed in ambush. The champagne was sweet, as usual under the Mexican flag.

The Romeros have enormous receptions every week—all sorts of people, chiefly women. They say the apple woman on the corner goes sometimes. I went one afternoon and found it deadly, though Mrs. Vest made merry over the fact that the only man present (a decrepit old general) devoted himself to me. I glanced into the big ballroom and saw dozens of pretty girls dancing together; not a man in sight, and such lovely music!

February 17

Yesterday I was giving a little dinner and facing some domestic problems. My dining room seats only eight and I had had to telegraph an impending guest not to come till later. I was up early; J. had gone to breakfast, and when he called out excitedly, "Now we *are* in trouble," I thought only of another complication about the dinner. He came running upstairs with the *Times* and read to me the brief telegram: "The battleship Maine blown up in Havana harbor." It was some time before I realized that one of the high notes of history had been sounded and that it would be long before we heard the last of it. We thought it meant immediate war with Spain—dear Spain, where we have received so much kindness and know and love so many people—no more to blame for this horror than we are. I believe I have a prenatal terror of war—a child of the sixties—and my knees trembled and I felt sick all day. We were at the Capitol by eleven o'clock expecting, like the rest of the excited crowd, to hear the event discussed in the House, but except in the chaplain's prayer it was not referred to, and all day we waited in vain for more news. Our dinner was pleasant enough, but spirits were low; the President's and other big receptions were abandoned because of "the nation's mourning." Flags are at half mast and everyone is nervously expectant.

February 20

The story of the *Maine* disaster grows more ghastly. The country on the whole is behaving well, and people of importance withhold opinions, as Captain Sigsbee[2] begged that they should do "until more is known." This is especially creditable in the face of a frantic and mischievous press. The New York *Journal* prints Cuban news in blood-red letters; the Washington *Times* is as bad in a smaller way, and still makes much of the de Lôme incident.[3] An Arkansas paper wires the *Post* for news of the Council of War supposed to be sitting here, and a Texas Yankee offers to raise a company of ex-Confederates and go himself as a private. Congress goes on discussing the Bankruptcy Bill.

The Chinese Minister and Madame Wu called on us in full canonicals. He sat in a large chair, his yellow robe hanging loosely about his wadded legs, and a glorious ruby flashing from the front of his cap as he talked agreeably about war, politics, and progressive euchre. She perched on the edge of a

[2] Charles D. Sigsbee, commander of the *Maine*.

[3] Señor Enrique Dupuy de Lôme, Spanish Minister to the United States, had written a letter to a friend in Havana in which he abused President McKinley and made sneering remarks about the autonomous government in Cuba. The letter was stolen from the mails in Cuba and released by Cuban revolutionaries to Hearst's New York *Journal*, where it was published on February 9, 1898. De Lôme immediately resigned.

chair, her little feet planted helplessly, and her hands, loaded with diamond rings, lying stiffly on her lap. She has a terrible, toothy grin, but her
face is pleasant for all it is so broad and flat. She said she liked "loman
fleedom" in America—freedom for women I finally guessed—and was
proud of learning to "splick lil bit Englis," and she went on grinning kindly
and splicking the same Englis over and over. When they left, the Minister
said we were all "American Beauties," took madame by the hand, tucked
his queue into a loop of his yellow jacket, and toddled down the steps and
away.

March 20

My days, and almost nights, are spent in the gallery listening to war
talk. I keep house by calling to Aunt Frances down the dumb-waiter.
Women who usually boast of taking breakfast in bed stand with the rabble
at the Capitol doors at 8:00 A.M. and are glad of a seat on the steps of
the aisles in any gallery.

We talk of war and taffeta ruffles (very fashionable now) during the
long wait before fat Mr. Hobart and fatter Mr. Reed call the two Houses
to order at noon. Most of the women are for war—"to the knife, and the
knife to the hilt." It is so safely glorious when only men are killed. In
the streetcars and shops, even within the church doors during Lent they
declaim about the dying reconcentrados, and the *Maine*. Senator Proctor
sobbed aloud while telling the Senate what he had seen in Cuba, Mrs. Vest
told me; I was not there to see.

One woman I talked to offered a striking contrast to the general
softheartedness. She is an intimate friend of the Mark Hannas. We were
discussing Spanish atrocities, the butchery of children and outrage of
women, and she said with the sweetest baby stare, "It seems a pity to
keep up this agitation; it has already disturbed business interests so much."

April 12

Yesterday ended the long uncertainty as to what the President was going
to suggest. The message had been put off from Thursday to Monday and
from Monday till Thursday and then over again, and then at last it came,
so long and vague and weak that hardly the most bigoted Administration
follower could find anything to applaud. If he has a definite policy, he
managed to conceal it under a stream of weak English.

"Czar" Reed holds the House in such slavish subjection that the discussion of the message there amounted to nothing, but I heard the Senate ring with denunciation. Gray of Delaware defended it in exquisite English, really worthy of a better cause; and the Administration Republicans snarled, except Mark Hanna, who sat slumped down like a huge ruminant animal and flipped his big ears with his finger as if the whole Cuban question was nothing to him.

April 19

We went early to hear the resolutions from the committee conference, but at ten the House met and adjourned till noon. The Senate refused to concur, and Dingley offered a resolution to which Bailey objected and in the debate Reed addressed Bailey in a sneering tone that would have been met with a blow, I'm afraid, if he had been on the floor or in Texas. Bailey behaved better than usual while Reed was an intolerable bully, as he often is. The galleries were stifling, but few risked losing a seat by going out to lunch, so there was much surreptitious passing of sandwiches and candy from innocent-looking handbags. It is against the rules to eat lunches in the gallery, but we are getting adept in concealing it. The national habit of chewing gum no doubt helps to avert suspicion.

It became so dull that Agatha[4] and I went off to F Street for some urgent shopping. I bought emergency blouses and she a bright red lawn called "Cuba Libre." We went home for a rest and bath and hurried back to the Capitol determined to stay to the bitter end. But just as we arrived the House took a recess till 8:00 P.M., "and so home for dinner," as Pepys would say.

April 20

The vote was not taken till 3:00 A.M. and J. came home too tired and nervous to sleep. He has no sustaining enthusiasm for the war; thinks we might try other means without loss of dignity or prestige. It does seem rather like a bully to fight such a poverty-stricken and small country as Spain. J. says we will dictate our terms eventually, and we might do it now so judiciously as to save Spain's face and our own men and millions. Two hours before we were up the troops from Fort Myer and Washington Barracks marched through the city, and war had begun. If it comes to nothing, as still seems possible, I shall be glad to have had the opportunity to see the war spirit in a nation. But if it should be a real war—! I feel a chill of terror.

[4] Agatha Maverick, author's niece.

The President signed the resolutions at 11:24 this morning, and Polo de Bernabé, the Spanish Minister, may leave at any moment. Society holds its breath except in the Hanna-Administration inner-circle, which tries to act as if nothing unusual was going on. Shop windows are full of pictures of military and naval heroes, and of battles long ago, even to the Spanish Armada. Everyone wears a little American flag—they are peddled at five cents—and street boys whistle "The Star-Spangled Banner." The rest of us sing it as far as we know the words—first and last two lines of the first stanza. Almost forgotten are the two recent favorites, "There'll be a hot time in the old town tonight" and "My gal is a high born lady; she's black but not too shady," though the latter would be singularly appropriate to our chivalrous rush to the rescue of Cuba.

Senator John Daniel—always "Major" to Virginians—lives near us, and the old negro woman who looks after him is often in our kitchen. Today quite a party of us were at lunch, all talking war, of course, when Aunt Frances came puffing in and said, "Miss Ellen, *is* you got a couple o' breeches buttons? Aunt Mary say Major Daniel do need 'em *powerful*." No doubt the Senator had burst some buttons in his forensic efforts on behalf of Cuba, so I gladly went upstairs, robbed a pair of J.'s trousers, and I hope saved the situation.

Postmaster General Gary resigned yesterday "on account of ill-health." He is a Catholic; Rome considers this a religious war, and the inference is that the Pope ordered Gary's resignation. The Cabinet doesn't seem substantial. Sherman's being in his dotage made no special difference in the Senate, where there are others, but he is certainly not fit to be secretary of state.

There are resounding scandals about Alger's[5] appointments of generals to command regular troops. They say Merritt[6] is left without a command because he approved the findings of a court-martial that sat on Alger during the Civil War. Miles[7] is accused of being strongest on millinery. The *Post* hurls squibs at him every day: "The situation is serious enough to warrant General Miles in getting a new uniform" and "When in doubt, Miles has his photograph taken."

The town is aflutter with flags, and the sound of cheap, stay-at-home

[5] Russell A. Alger, Secretary of War, 1897–1899.

[6] Wesley Merritt, Major General U.S.A., assigned May, 1898, to command U.S. forces in the Philippine Islands.

[7] Nelson A. Miles, Lieutenant General, senior officer commanding U.S.A., 1895–1903.

patriotism is deafening. The cant about "Old Glory" makes me sick. Why can't they say the "American flag" or the "Stars and Stripes"? Most people talk as if the war was to be a gigantic picnic.

April 28

This morning it snowed for two hours—big, soft flakes like real winter —but the news from Key West is that the fleet has beautiful weather "too cool for white uniforms." How important! It is hard to think of dear, sleepy, shabby, sunny Key West as a war base.

May 2

Last night at 12:30 we were wakened by loud shouts of "Extra *Post*" from boys running madly through our usually quiet streets. It was indescribably startling, terrifying to me, but J. was skeptical of real news and refused to get up until the noise of opening windows and voices calling for papers made sleep impossible. Then we read how Admiral Dewey had attacked the little Spanish fleet at Manila, and how the poor Spaniards went down with their wooden ships and our fleet was practically uninjured. It was all very fine, no doubt, and we should be jubilating, but one little sentence at the end made my heart stand still: "The American fleet withdrew to the west side of the bay to land their wounded."

The phrase "during the war" suggests only the sorrow and adversity that shadowed my childhood. I cannot realize that comfortable and comparatively serene as we are now it is also "during the war." I remember Sheridan's raid, the terror, the destruction of all food and comforts— only pictures, but very vivid ones on the mental retina of a child of four years. General Weyler[8] cannot reach us; there is no change in our way of living. Having to stay here all summer is the worst danger confronting us. Many think that Manila will practically end the war, and we devoutly hope so, but if it does, there will be many a brokenhearted militiaman. The people are getting in the notion of war—a fight or a frolic. J. is snowed under with telegrams asking for everything from a general's commission to a book of tactics.

The papers are frivolous as only the American press can be. The New York *Journal* says that "the little King of Spain will be no more than a ten spot in future" and advertises in huge letters "Several rich

---

[8] Valeriano ("Butcher") Weyler, Spanish general, who established concentration camps in Cuba where revolutionists, sympathizers and neutrals, including women and children, were confined and subjected to ruthless treatment.

islands for sale. Address Uncle Sam." Maps are searched to find the Philippines—few people ever heard of them before. I am sure I never did. There is a general impression that they are the subject of one of St. Paul's epistles; indeed, a wise-looking old Presbyterian preacher told me so.

San Antonio, October

The summer has been a nightmare. I apologize daily to J. for my folly, my lack of imagination about the necessity for this war. The money it is costing is the smallest of the evils, but we might have bought Cuba and made a present of it to the patriots less expensively, I believe, and saved the lives of thousands of American boys besides. Sampson and Schley[9] destroyed the Spanish fleet and ever since have been trying to destroy one another's reputations. I think the only real hero of the event is Captain John W. Philip of the *Texas,* who silenced his men when the Spanish ships were burning and being beached or sunk by saying, "Don't cheer, men, those poor devils are dying."

Coming down from Washington we were often delayed by troop trains, those going south filled with gay, shouting, often drunken boys, thinking of "glory"; and those northbound carrying more boys, sallow, dispirited, ill, or wounded. A few had been to Cuba and got what glory there was (the little left by Colonel Roosevelt) but many more had been clearing millionaire Flagler's[10] land in the swamps of Florida, and living on spoiled beef and canned tomatoes supplied by our government. In every camp now they are dying like flies of typhoid fever. Charges and counter-charges are made of incompetence, rascality, and plain carelessness by officials providing for the army, and it seems as if each would prove the other guilty. The quarrel between Quartermaster General Eagan and Miles is too nasty to write about.[11]

[9] The rival supporters of the American Admirals William T. Sampson and Winfield Scott Schley have been arguing ever since about which deserved the real credit for the naval victory at Santiago, Cuba, which virtually ended the Spanish-American War.

[10] Henry M. Flagler, Standard Oil executive, and builder of Florida East Coast Railway, promoted Florida real estate.

[11] General Miles testified before the Dodge Commission, appointed by the President to investigate the War Department, that "embalmed beef" had been supplied for soldiers' rations. The press took up the cry, demanding General Charles P. Eagan's resignation, and the rumor spread that Eagan had profited financially from beef contracts. Goaded by the charges, Eagan, in turn, made violently intemperate statements about Miles before the commission, which led to Eagan's being brought to trial for conduct unbecoming an officer and a gentleman. A verdict of guilty called for his dismissal from the service, but the court recommended clemency. President McKinley commuted his sentence to suspension from duty for six years, the time remaining before his retirement.

We found San Antonio in such a state of exaltation at the honor of having the Rough Riders mobilized here that the ladies, particularly, were ready to swear that Roosevelt was a Chesterfield and Wood[12] an Adonis. They fail to see anything amiss even in Roosevelt's ridiculous insubordination in sending a round robin (like a spoiled schoolboy complaining of his food) over the heads of his superior officers. We have been hearing lately that the negro troops saved the Rough Riders from annihilation at San Juan Hill, but I get the impression here that Wood and Roosevelt took the blockhouse singlehanded. But however it is, everyone wants to get out of the army now. It is a stampede and while J. is campaigning I am at his desk for hours every day listening to anxious relatives giving good reasons why their own particular Johnny should come marching home immediately. They nearly all think that a congressman has only to turn a crank or drop a nickel in the slot and get out any soldier called for, and I am weary of repeating that it must be done "through military channels." I have had one compensating compliment. A young Irishman who came to see me about his brother told a friend that the only way to defeat Mr. Slayden was for the "Repooblicans" to nominate Mrs. Slayden.

Washington, December 17

It seems almost as if death had had the victory in the case of General Calixto García.[13] After thirty years of alternate fighting and imprisonment, he came here with the Cuban commission for his triumph's evidence in being received as a citizen of a free country—and died of pneumonia. It has been bitter cold, with sharp and sudden changes, and his vitality, reduced by three years of constant fighting and starvation, was not equal to the strain. García was my favorite Cuban patriot, so I went down to the avenue to see the funeral procession. Two or three companies of soldiers, blue with cold, were standing around the side door of the Raleigh guarding a caisson draped with Cuban and American flags. When the coffin was brought out it had a little Cuban flag spread over it like a table cover. A bunch of red roses and a laurel wreath were the only flowers. The streets were gleaming with ice, and it was so deathly still and cold that all the flags, usually snapping against the hard blue sky, hung down limp as if in sympathy with the sad little ceremony. The

---

[12] Leonard Wood, Major General, U.S.A., who was Roosevelt's superior officer in Cuba.

[13] Calixto García Iñiguez, revolutionary leader in Cuba.

soldiers were glad to get in motion, but just as they turned the corner one of the caisson horses fell flat and there was another long delay. The lure of "mournful, martial music" was too much for me, so I followed the soldiers, only stopping a moment to buy a pencil from the old man who hobbles along F Street singing "Ladies, ladies," so sweetly and who looked so pitifully cold.

There is grave doubt if García was a Catholic, and no doubt that he was a Freemason, but Father McGee, who absolved and anointed him, testified that he died in the faith, so there was to be a military High Mass at St. Patrick's with Archbishop Ireland officiating.

In the crowded door of the church an usher took me in charge, and escorted me to a platform almost in the chancel, and another came to ask if the seat suited me and said I might take any of the several vacant chairs. I was thoroughly mystified and ready to jump down and run away when several other women and some men came up and I found it was the space reserved for the press. A flat package like a paper tablet in my hand and the new pencil had done the trick, so not being an intentional impostor, I enjoyed my post of vantage, borrowed paper from one of my colleagues and wrote diligently. The service was long, the choir vile, the Archbishop's voice unpleasant, and his remarks on the annexation of Cuba ill-timed. Generals Miles, Wheeler, Lawton, and others in gorgeous uniforms sat beside the coffin, and a crowd of sad-faced Cubans hovered near. Senators Mason, Proctor and Money were among the pallbearers. As the coffin was carried out, someone sang "Nearer, My God, to Thee" very badly, the band outside took it up; people stood up on the seats to see, and we could hear romping and screams of laughter as the indifferent, merely curious crowd slid down the icy embankment to get away in a hurry. It was all crude, rude and pitiful, and must have hurt the Latin Americans. They do such things with a difference. They may not be more sincere, but such an exhibition of bad manners would not have been permitted in their country.

CHAPTER THREE

1899

Washington, January 7

Think of getting $50,000 just for the asking! We have had a desperate time keeping up a public library for San Antonio, and Andrew Carnegie, dispenser of libraries, ignored an appeal from our board sometime ago. Last month J. helped me to concoct a personal letter that we thought might move his Scotch heart. We sent it only a week ago, and this letter came today:

New York, January 6, 1899

Dear Madam:

Mr. Carnegie has been interested in your letter touching San Antonio Public Library. If the city will furnish a suitable site, so that a detached building can be erected thereon, lighted from all sides, he will give $50,000 for the purpose, provided the city will agree through its Councils to maintain the Library free to the people at a cost of $5,000 per year which he thinks it will require to provide for the wants of a city of sixty thousand inhabitants.

Very respectfully yours,
James Bertram

We wired the good news to Mrs. Ainsworth, the chairman, and wish we could be there to jollify with those who have almost given their lives and fortunes and sacred honors to the cause.

January 11

I have written and asked Mr. Carnegie to put the money into the hands of trustees who know something about libraries so that the building (and the money, alas!) may not be left to the tender mercies of the city authorities, "reformers" though they be at present.

My request was refused in accordance, it seems, with Mr. C.'s invariable rule, and with the reminder that if we did not have an intelligent and honest city administration, it was in the people's power to get one.[1]

January 12

Society has made several false starts, being turned back each time by the illness or death of some high official person. During the holidays we were entertained with a rare assortment of funerals. Grippe prevails to the confusion of everything from the Police and Fire Departments to the Cabinet and Diplomatic Corps. But the President's first reception came off successfully this week, and society hopes now to keep its gait.

During Cleveland's administration the evening receptions became just free-for-all jams. McKinley has wisely adopted a rigid censorship of the invitation list and, what is more important, a closer inspection of people who come to the door. But even with these changes you take your life in your hands to go to the White House on a cold evening. It is strange that in all these years no way has been devised to prevent a blast of north wind coming in with every guest.

As the crowd increased Tuesday night it became impossible to close the door at all, so the gale, with a spray of fine snow, was continuous. The front hall with rows of coat racks and a flock of women with bare arms and shoulders looked like a municipal bathhouse. The time spent getting wraps checked and ourselves into the double line moving almost imperceptibly to the right seemed interminable, but it was a good-tempered crowd, full of apologies for the crush which no one could have prevented except by staying at home. It began to get warmer too as we got into the

---

[1] Rereading this after twenty-six years, it is tragic to record how our worst fears were realized. Through the papers at the time I suggested a Spanish building like the Murillo gallery in Seville, plain outside and initially only one story, enclosing the site on three sides, to leave open the end next the river for a wall and embankment. This would form a large patio with three corridors open to the southeast breeze where almost the year around people could sit out of doors. The blessing of such an indoor garden and outdoor reading room—especially to those who worked in shops and offices downtown—would have been incalculable. A "noonin'," as old Texans say, in such a place would sweeten the whole day. There were excellent plans in the so-called "competition," but for reasons best known to "reformers" the plan selected was suspected of having been foreordained from the beginning. Instead of a beauty spot, we have a monstrosity, bad material, badly constructed, without deference to books, readers, light or air. It is now ready for the junk pile. It reminds me of a story about the Pension Building in Washington—perhaps the ugliest on the continent. The architect took old General Sherman all over it and then asked his opinion. "Wonderful," said Sherman. "Never saw anything like it; there is only one objection." "And what is that?" asked the proud architect. "Why," answered Sherman, "they tell me the damned thing is fireproof."—E.M.S., 1925.

family dining room. Through the long corridor there was a nice warm view of the conservatory where the red-coated Marine band sat playing the Wedding March. In the Red Parlor, enlivened by the portraits of Andrew Jackson and Mrs. Hayes, a quiet but compelling voice said, "Single file, please," and before I knew it I had shaken hands with the President, bent down a moment to hear Mrs. McKinley, who was seated and spoke very softly, the Cabinet ladies had smiled at us across their barricade of blue velvet sofas, and it was all over. In the East Room, for the first time in a trifle more than an hour, we thawed out and began to enjoy ourselves. The ceiling and the crystal chandeliers were veiled with gleaming smilax; the national shield done in flowers occurred at intervals around the room, and every mirror, mantel and window was banked with fern and poinsettias. Also, ambushed in every corner, was a detective in plain uniform. I don't see the use of them.

It was a more than usually distinguished company, many of the faces familiar from frequent appearances in newspapers and magazines. General Shafter took up more room than is usually allotted to one person, but General Wheeler[2] took less than the country thinks him entitled to, so the average was maintained. General Miles towered like Saul a head and shoulders above his fellows and was always surrounded by admiring ladies. Commodore Schley and his wife were kept shaking hands almost as constantly as the President. They were barely able to move from their places the whole evening while government officials, the judiciary, foreign diplomats, and citizens filed past them. Lord Herschell of the Anglo-American Joint High Commission looked innocent and Lord Fauntleroyish in full court dress with black velvet knee breeches and a ribbon around his collar. Sir Wilfrid Laurier[3] wore plain evening dress and moved about briskly as if he felt at ease with American ways and people.

There were a great many foreigners and an unblushing chase after them by the young girls—and their mothers who joined in the view halloo. Mrs. Colgate, heiress of all the scented soaps, has just married the Earl of Strafford, and it seemed at the White House as if our young women seeing had taken heart again and were in full cry after anything in foreign uniform, no matter how insignificant. A tiny Chinaman was surrounded by pretty girls fairly hanging on to his words, and Turks, Hawaiians, and even the dark-brown Minister from Haiti had more attention than his charms called for. Only one group baffled them, the Koreans. As we say

---

[2] Major General William R. Shafter, who commanded the American Army in Cuba, was noted as the fattest general in the army, while "Fighting Joe" Wheeler, the ex-Confederate, who served in Cuba, was one of the scrawniest.

[3] Prime Minister of Canada.

in Texas, there was quite a "bunch" of them. They were fat and oily and each one seemed to have been rolled in cotton batting and stuffed carelessly into a blue satin bathrobe. Standing together they looked as helpless as a group of rag dolls—and they smelled horribly of *tallow*. Perhaps that was what kept the girls away.

Getting away from the reception was worse than getting in. The wraps were hopelessly confused, pulled and hauled about by hurrying, freezing people, not always polite or considerate, and the sleety gale had increased till it cut us like knives. It does seem as if something might be done to make the place more comfortable. J. vows in unseemly language that he will never go there again till the Fourth of July.

The body of Ambassador Matias Romero starts today on its long journey to the City of Mexico, where it is to have high honors well deserved. The embassy was still draped in mourning for his wife when he died. They will be a loss to Washington, and he, I am afraid, an irreparable loss to his country. He was dean of the Diplomatic Corps but had been created an ambassador only a short while ago. With the exception of two brief absences on duty in his own country he has served here since 1859—nearly two years under President Buchanan! And he was the first Mexican to ask Lincoln's aid in getting rid of the French invaders. I rarely talked to him at length, but he and J. had frequent interviews, and J. was always impressed with his goodness and his sadness. His whole soul was devoted to fostering peace and commerce between his country and ours, and making the two peoples understand each other—an uphill task. It is not customary, I believe, for diplomats to write for publication while on duty in foreign countries, but Mr. Romero published a great many magazine articles, always, however, refusing any pay for them because he felt that everything he wrote was just a part of his duty as minister. He brought J. a copy of the first volume of his book *Mexico and the United States* just a short time before his death.

January 27

The world is wearing a path to the door of the Navy Department to see the Dewey sword. It lies in a large wood and glass case in a dimly lighted room and the atmosphere of a first-class funeral is heightened by the frequency with which you hear people remark on "the elegance of the casket." The inscription in gold letters runs almost the length of the blade —"The gift of the Nation"—and the hilt is a cunningly contrived eagle in gold. The scabbard is decorated with Toledo work, wreaths of laurel enclosing stars, while tiny dolphins frisk along the edge to the point finished with two dolphins in heavy gold. (What would artists and poets do without dolphins? They have petted them from time immemorial. Venus rises from the foam driving them four-in-hand; they grin at you from every marble fountain, and figure in many poems. There are many just as pretty and just as good fish in the sea and yet custom lies upon us so heavily that the Dewey sword would lose something of romance if it were adorned with herrings or sardines.)

There is a Spanish flag in the room with the sword, so fresh and clean and cheap that it might have been bought on F Street yesterday instead of being "taken," as the legend tells, "from the Spanish ship *Santo Domingo* on the twelfth of July." A government card serves notice on the ubiquitous relic hunter that a fine of $5,000 or ten years' imprisonment is the penalty for mutilating it, but no one here would be surprised to see the yellow castle or the red lion cut out and carried off under the very nose of Secretary Long.

The Washington Monument—five hundred perpendicular feet of stone—is the only thing proof against the souvenir maniacs. Last spring a policeman arrived just in time to save one of the high relief figures on the bronze doors of the Rotunda from a head-hunting savage from Indiana; and in the last fortnight the statue of Père Marquette in Statuary Hall has been mutilated by vandals. In the bas-relief of Marquette preaching to the Indians the most striking figure was a warrior leaning forward resting his hands on a strung bow. The bow was stolen, and the warrior is left in a foolish attitude leaning on space. One of the heaviest expenses for the women who have supported Mount Vernon so many years is for policemen to keep American patriots from slipping off with the Washingtoniana collected by the regents at a cost that often entailed serious personal sacrifice.

The Rotunda of the Capitol lately has been a gruesome or a laughable place according to how you were affected by seeing the statues of Jefferson, Hamilton, Lincoln, and a person named Baker[4] standing on rough sleds, their arms and legs bound with ropes and a noose over their heads as if awaiting a quartet lynching. It would be better to hang some of the sculptors who perpetrated the statues, especially the one who no doubt told poor Mr. Baker to "look natural" in a frock coat and a toga. If he could divide his superfluous raiment with George Washington, left by Greenough out

---

[4] Edward Dickinson Baker, who became acquainted with Lincoln when they were both lawyers in Springfield, Illinois. Later he was a senator from Oregon. He was killed in action during the Civil War.

on the plaza naked and ashamed, both would be more comfortable. Someone learned in the law discovered that only statues presented by states are entitled to a place in the grim circle of Statuary Hall, so these four gentlemen were trundled out. The law not indicating any place for such windfalls of art, the government was embarrassed until Congress decided to make the Rotunda—heretofore just a place for the wind to blow through—an asylum for homeless marble statesmen.

J. estimates our expenses in the following order: House rent, fuel, and visiting cards. This is the calling season, and in the afternoon from three to seven flocks of little one-horse coupés, some shabby with a slovenly negro driver and an old horse with ill-kept feet, others highly polished and with "two men on the box"—the acme of elegance—and a high-stepper with nickel-finished harness, fairly swarm around the big hotels and fashionable streets. Of course, there are many grander equipages, but the little ones predominate, and usually carry two women, one holding a list while the other does visiting cards up into little packs with a rubber band around them. To an untutored Texan like myself it seems a foolish waste of cardboard and an insult to the intelligence of the person called on to leave so many. There is one for every adult female in the family called on from every adult female in the family making the call, which, with a scattering fire of them to and from the gentlemen, makes an appalling quantity. Sometimes I get packets of a dozen or more. Insatiate caller! Would not one suffice? One would make it perfectly clear who had called and save me the trouble of burning the others. As official position regulates society, those who, like myself, live in houses twenty feet wide with a maid at the door have the same visitors as the neighbor in a palace with a dozen lackeys to guide you from the carriage to the upstairs drawing room. The entertainment, except for richness of equipment, is about the same in both places. A number of women stand about in semi-evening dress and pass you from one to another with an aerial handshake (at the level of your nose is the latest fashion) as each one remarks, "So good of you to come." One gives you an ice with a rumcake, and another some sizzling tea, and after agreeing with all of them on the state of the weather and the prevalence of grippe you go out with a fugue of cheery "good mornings" following you into black night and rain or snow. Officially it is morning until you have had dinner, and there is also some social distinction in having your dinner very late, or even being like the young man in *Patience* who "frequently breakfasts at five o'clock tea, and dines on the following day." The "good mornings" give me much inward satisfaction when I hear them come trippingly from the tongue of the lady from Nebraska or Alabama who never saw dinner later than two o'clock before in her life.

We are to be uplifted socially and intellectually by a visit from Gertrude Atherton—the erotic, epigrammatic damsel who has achieved distinction by a real gift for writing and notoriety by the things she writes about. She must be treasure trove for reporters. There is one on every corner here and she confides in them all. She starts off at a rattling gait talking about herself and never pauses except for "a coquettish shrug to her shoulders" or "an arch glance from her steel-blue eyes" until she has told all the secrets of her heart. She declares that she has "letters to many prominent men, and will go much into society" and then will go away and write a novel about us "from an Englishwoman's point of view." Though in four years in England hunting big game she has not achieved a British husband, she wonders "how a woman can bring herself to marry anything but an Englishman" and "unconsciously looks at everything from the true Britisher's standpoint." Of American men she says that "there is so little courtesy among them, so little of their boasted chivalry." She doesn't know Southern men, but supposes "they are windbags too," and describes "the homebred youth" of her unhappy country as "a compound of alcohol and tea cakes." (Perhaps she objects to the tea cakes—wants them all alcohol so as to conform more closely to the British standard.) A chip off the old block, too, she says that the greatest pleasure of her childhood was to watch from a distance "the line of carriages and buggies bringing Momma's admirers to the ranch"—one pictures whole caravans of forty-niners trailing Mommaward. An admirer was always sent to "hunt for Gertrude," and then, "I got a spanking every day." Momma must have done her darnedest for her daughter with what success time is showing.

In marked contrast to this lady of emotions and egotism is Washington's own cherished resident novelist, Molly Elliot Seawell. It is a cruel word to use, but Miss Seawell (pronounced Sowell) is an old maid, and prim—with a straight-laced, flat-backed primness that makes her *con amore* style of writing about dashing cavaliers seem almost improper. She is from "lower Virginia" where "first families" prevail and where the chief product for generations has been ancestors for the rest of America—an industry in which the Cavaliers and the Pilgrim Fathers seem to have been about equally ambitious and successful. Miss Seawell's youth was fed on traditions of the glory of Virginia's colonial and ante-bellum days, and she reflects them in her writing with not only literary but financial success. She is able to keep a pretty home and has something very like a salon. She is polished and clear-cut in her talk, sometimes a little sharp and never quite of today. She reverted to antiquity in becoming a Roman Catholic and remarked in my hearing lately that the Episcopal Church had "lost everything but its social prestige," to which Father Lee, a fashionable abbé, whose good looks and good clothes give distinction to many tea tables, raised his eyes in pious assent.

Miss Seawell, Mrs. Phil Sheridan, and Mrs. "Silver Dick" Bland's names were on the list of distinguished people who invited us to hear Bishop Spalding talk on "Higher Education for Women," and incidentally ask endowment for a Catholic woman's college in connection with Trinity. There was a big crowd. Cardinal Gibbons, Martinelli, the Apostolic Delegate, Bishop Spalding, and Dr. Harris, Commissioner of Education, were en tableau on the stage with a background of palms and roses. Dr. Harris, friendly and homespun, was a proper foil for the dark, exotic, subtly intellectual Martinelli. These Latin ecclesiastics always look to me as if they wore their faces to conceal their thoughts. Spalding was handsome and buoyant, and treated his subject with common sense and wholesome humor, very refreshing after the stock arguments and platitudes commonly used to defend a position no longer assailed. The dear old Cardinal gave a blessing or a prayer, but mostly sat beaming on the company with a wise, sweet smile as if he had an inward assurance that "God's in His Heaven, all's right with the world," whether women were highly educated or not.

J. was sitting in the Senate with George Vest. They saw Gertrude Atherton's red head (she wears the straight-cut bang of the early eighties) up in the gallery and Senator Proctor leaning over waggling his long beard as he whispered to her. Mr. Vest said, "Now, look at old Proctor up there with Gertrude. Doesn't he look like a goat hovering over a carrot?"

February 16

During the blizzard last week I never thought to make a note about it though we were shut up for two days shivering and wondering at a veritable inferno of cold more intense than any of us had ever known before. Perhaps my forgetfulness was due to the subconscious terror I feel whenever the elements swerve far from their common track, and never having seen a cyclone or an earthquake this is my worst experience. As a child my spirits rose and fell with the weather, and like Elaine (but not because of any dallying Lancelot), I "mixed my fancies with the sallow-rifted glooms of evening, and the moaning of the wind."

They say that the temperature went as low as 22 degrees below zero. Sunday Frank Yoakum came to dinner, and after a long wait everything came up half done. Aunt Frances was humiliated but said, "De stove jus' wouldn' git hot." That night it began to snow, and by morning we were wrapped in the strangest silence, no newsboys, no milkmen, vehicles, or pedestrians except one man who looked as if he were fighting his way.

J. started to his office, got as far as Connecticut Avenue, and finding no streetcar, not even the track, came back bewildered like Noah's weary dove. The few men who reached the Capitol had to stay there twenty-four hours. The snow kept falling, the silence deepening until the sound of the servants rattling the furnace in the basement was a welcome interruption. From the window we saw all the familiar street lines smooth over, steps leveled by drifts, and even railings and shrubbery disappear. We began to be sorrowful over the inevitable suffering of the poor and to fear for the old folks at home in Virginia, not knowing for a day or two afterwards that Washington was the center and bore the brunt of the storm.

Next morning we opened the front door only to meet a wall of snow, but from the upper windows we could see men opening paths along the sidewalks and at last one signaled from the foot of our steps and began to work up as J., with the furnace shovel, worked down. It was a good half hour before they met. In the afternoon I walked down Q Street through white corridors I could not see over and just wide enough for one person, but spreading out here and there so another could pass. The next afternoon I went through the corridors, sunken a little but not thawing, to O Street and saw drifts that reached the second stories of several houses. The nights were eerie with the sound of doleful negro voices calling "Co-o-al"—it sounded like cold—that they were peddling from sacks on their backs, and sometimes the sobbing of negro children as their mothers dragged them along to a little grocery near us to buy provisions.

The suffering has been terrible and there were many near catastrophes of women from the departments rescued and given shelter at police stations or sent home on trucks. The poor D.A.R.s making their annual "demonstration in force" are so discouraged that I hear they will change their time of meeting to April or May.

CHAPTER FOUR

1900

1631 R Street, May 28

This morning, nine o'clock exactly, the much-heralded eclipse of the sun is in progress. I have enough to do and no scientific knowledge to help me enjoy eclipses, but I cannot go about the trivial round and common task until it is over. With my opera glasses wrapped in a black chiffon sash I risked my life leaning out the front window, but it is too cloudy to see any of the wonders that the newspapers said would be revealed to the eye of faith aided by smoked glass. Heretofore my interest in an eclipse was chiefly in seeing the superstitious terror of the darkies, but the Washington colored gentry are too sophisticated and even my cook, who is singularly ignorant for these days of higher-colored education, is not impressed. Passing me she remarked, "I b'lieve the sun is clip," and went on with her work. The sun is a terrible crescent of fire, the light is portentous and depressing, and birds are twittering in their soft twilight voices. The noise of a passing vehicle jars upon me strangely.

Mrs. Robert Hill invited us to the Unitarian church to hear Dr. Edward Everett Hale. The day was so lovely I feared a crowd, but the church was only comfortably full, and General Chandler was good enough to take us into his pew along with Representative G—— of Pennsylvania whose unction irritated me. He said the Lord's Prayer as if he had invented it, and put three coppers on the plate.

There has been so much talk of Dr. Hale's age and infirmity that I was unprepared for a voice like a sailor's and thoughts so vigorous and hopeful. He made me feel that there was so much to do in the world that I ought to go out and get to work at once. He wore the old black Geneva robe, but he wore it like a sou'wester. It was not the awe-inspiring garment our clergy used in Virginia when I was a child—perfectly suited to the hell and damnation they preached. No orthodox home there was complete without a steel engraving of Bishop Meade in that gown and another of John Knox arrayed in it as he hurled unchristian denunciation at poor terrified Mary of Scotland. I was afraid of both pictures in the twilight, but no one could be afraid of Dr. Hale in any garb.

West Point, June 2

We are here for the annual meeting of the Board of Visitors, and I find it pleasant being with army people who know that Texas is a part of the United States, and not inhabited exclusively by Indians and cowboys—a knowledge apparently denied to the average Easterner. One of the young ladies attached to the board (called facetiously "Splinters") asked me if I didn't find the social restraints of Washington very trying after the freedom of Texas. I asked her gravely, "Which ones?" and she was driven to some queer explaining.

So far the board doesn't interest me except old General Vielé, a veteran of the Mexican War and a classmate of my dear old cousin, General Dabney Maury, and Mrs. Church, wife of the editor of the *Army and Navy Journal.* They all say "boar-rd" except David Houston of Texas who doesn't say anything. He seems awed but is well dressed and has an irreproachable leather hatbox which should go a long way toward proving the civilization of our state.

The Cranston where we are domiciled is a quaint little tavern with antiquated furniture and small crinkly mirrors in which I can see as far as my chin, and there is a basement dining room where we have dinner at one o'clock. We have a group table presided over by a general. He was obviously afraid some of us might take the seat to his right reserved for his wife, though she looks able to maintain her rights, being massive and having a mustache that any cadet might envy her.

Our days are filled with reviews, parties, and displays of the work or play at "the Point." This morning we were taken on a drive. Senator ———, always aggressively polite, hustled me into a carriage with his wife, Mrs. C. of Chicago, and Mrs. McCook (one of the "fighting Mc-Cooks") of New York, where I realized quite helplessly that I was as much in their way as I was out of my element. They made no effort to include me in their talk, and when I put in a word, listened politely, then went on discussing the price of gloves, "Your little milliner," "A *dear* little dressmaker," and things that were "*simply* awful" or "just too perfectly sweet." Going through Pierpont Morgan's place they forgot the glorious masses of rhododendron and the bland curves of wood and meadow in wondering how much money they had cost. One of them, as if trying to impress a moral lesson, kept telling "Lovey," her small boy, how good and generous it was of *rich* Mr. Morgan to let us come through and see it all.

Admiral Philip, late commander of the *Texas,* is here to address the Y.M.C.A., and I find him and his wife more companionable. He is not handsome, nor distinguished looking, but likable and even jokable—not always the case with men in uniform—and I don't think they have any money; at any rate they don't talk about it. No one pays them any attention, so I took one of the carriages that wait our bidding and asked them to go with Captain Harry Davis and me on a trip over the Point. Unrestrained by the seriousness of the boar-rd, we had a good time, and the Admiral was like a big, kind boy. But he is abrupt and direct on occasion. He called Captain Davis, who was walking with me, and said, "Captain, I want to speak to Mrs. Slayden," and began without preface, "I want Congress to appropriate some money for the Y.M.C.A. here. The boys need it, they have a miserable little room. I'm going to speak to Slayden, but if he doesn't agree with me, you press it." I promised, and he never referred to it again but I foresee the snubbing I shall get from J.—"Spending the taxpayers' money for sectarian institutions," etc.

J. shows signs of becoming a "Watchdog of the Treasury," anyway, and tells me privately that these board meetings are extravagant nonsense, bringing people here from all over the country for a week's gaiety at the expense of the taxpayers. He means next winter to introduce a bill to abolish the board and all its "Mommers" and "Splinters" and substitute a Congressional committee to come in the winter and see West Point at work instead of playing.

I think the officers stationed here are more heavily burdened than the taxpayers. They overwhelm us with dinners, luncheons, and receptions that, I fancy, they can ill afford. Mrs. Church and I had the happy thought of borrowing Cullom Hall, and, with the other ladies of the board, giving a luncheon or tea in our turn. We broached the subject to the chairman and his wife, saying we thought it would be nice to show our appreciation that way. They looked at us vaguely at first, the Senator saying loftily, "Oh, yes! You return their visits, or send cards," but she said quite positively and tartly, "Oh, no. We never do anything." (It is not their first service here.) "These people expect favors of the boar-rd, and it is to their interest to pay us attention." Mrs. Church and I faded from view as soon as possible but looked at one another in mild amazement.

The board certainly expects every officer to do his duty. Every

woman attached to it, however casually—grandmothers some of them, too
—expects to have her card filled for every dance as if she were a debutante.
When two handsome officers came to see about mine, I pictured my fat
and fortyness dancing while crowds of light-footed girls stood around the
door of Cullom Hall without partners, so I said I would not dance at all
and they could give those numbers to whom they pleased. They displayed
the most graceful regret, but one evening J. and I were unexpectedly guests
of honor at a bright little dinner at their club, and when I came back to
the hotel with four young men in attendance, the fat ladies on the veranda
stared through their lorgnettes, not guessing that it was gratitude and not
my *beaux yeux* that attracted them.

The night of the final hop I was a happy wallflower watching my lady
colleagues tripping as lightly as their bulk permitted with those same young
officers. General Francis Greene, a vice-presidential possibility this year,
was much in evidence dancing in the whirling fashion of the seventies.

But, verily, the young men have their reward! The river is dotted with
private yachts from New York, and millionaire mammas are trotting their
daughters around the track continually. They seem to think any lieutenant
an eligible. Very funny it looks to us who know for what occult reasons
congressmen make these appointments and that the boys are as often the
sons of Judy O'Grady as of the colonel's lady. But there is a saying, and
an honest belief, among army people that "four years of West Point makes
a gentleman." Perhaps, but I think three generations is safer; turns out a
more durable product.

CHAPTER FIVE

1901

Piedmont, February 6

Father's birthday—a brilliant, clear, cold day with high wind. Looking out at the fairly well-kept old place I try to see what it must have been when he was born here ninety years ago: a small stone and timber house in a recent clearing, primitive and perhaps comfortless (except for the dubious comfort of slaves to serve you) and surrounded by oak saplings, such giant trees now. He is sound and well, and sitting by the big log fire he loves reading the Washington *Post* without glasses. He tells me he is the only man left in the county who voted for Andrew Jackson and he is still a Democrat, nourished with "the pure milk of the word" by his father's friend and neighbor, Jefferson, whom he remembers well. He hates the injustice of the Boer War and wants the Philippines freed. He is interested in the Marshall Day celebration and tells me how he remembers the great Chief Justice, "tall, thin and gangling," walking up "Random Row"— there were no carriages for hire here then—"after a game of quoits with Pa and others. He was very fond of pitching quoits."

We had no company for dinner, but when the family was seated he said with quaint, old-time formality, "I am glad to see you all here." It made my heart ache. "All" means so few now. It is a place of ghosts for me, and I hear their trailing garments and see the old familiar faces in dreams day and night. What must it be for him after ninety years! The table was drawn up near the fireplace in the big basement dining room, the oldest and best chimney in the house, built by a Hessian soldier of the Revolution who told my grandfather that he deserted the British army when he saw a stream choked with dead.

Father told me today of Thomas Jefferson's part in building the Episcopal church here. He resents the cheap statement that Jefferson was an atheist, says he was just ahead of his time, no one would criticize him now. "Previous to 1820 there was no church or place of religious assembly in Charlottesville. Services were held in the courthouse and Mr. Jefferson came on horseback, brought a folding seat under his arm, and, as I remember, sat very far back." Jefferson's fancy was taken by a suggestion of some Presbyterians to build a hall to be used by all denominations, but when he found that it was to be called the Presbyterian church he and all the Episcopalians withdrew their subscriptions.

They decided to build their own church and Mr. Jefferson subscribed $300—a tremendous sum for those times. "He and my father, Reuben Maury," Father said, "were on the building committee, and many letters passed between them. In one of these Mr. Jefferson urged that the pews should be 'benches without doors, and free, so that people may be seated pell-mell as they shall lie in death.' "

All these letters and many others, chiefly from Andrew Jackson to my Father's uncle Tom, were properly docketed and stored in the office. During Sheridan's raid when General Custer had his headquarters in this house, he permitted his soldiers to throw all the family papers out in the mud and run bayonets through them to make sure there was no gold in them. They would be worth much more than their weight in gold now, but invading armies are not given to considering historical values. I asked Father rather naïvely if he couldn't have saved just a few of them, and he looked at me queerly and said, "With your mother and other ladies in my charge at the mercy of that drunken little Custer, and straw piled around the house ready to be fired, I had no time to think of Mr. Jefferson's letters."

He loves to tell how, when a boy of fifteen, he was one of a militia company that met "Mr. Lafayette" at the county line and escorted him to Monticello on his last visit to Jefferson.

February 25

It is being borne in upon me that a state of uncertainty is the one certain feature of Congressional life. We are invited to go to Cuba on an inspection trip with General Miles and some old army friends, but no one but Mark Hanna knows if there is to be an extra session, and he won't tell.

Wednesday, March 13

We sailed today at two o'clock with snow falling on us at the pier, but it made the beckoning of the tropics even more alluring.

Matanzas, Monday

It looked as if it might be mansions in the skies for us until Saturday when we emerged from the worst storm we ever experienced at sea. And on a little transport with her load line way up out of the water! I am bruised black and blue. There were some pleasant people on board but lost to sight till the last day of the trip, and then old General Daniel Sickles of various kinds of fame monopolized the little deck and everyone's attention claiming his rights as the ranking officer on board, and demanding all sorts of extras for himself and two uninteresting women traveling with him. One of them, youngish and handsome, usually sat on his steamer chair in the place where his other leg would have been if he had had two, gazing rapturously at his wisps of hair and mustache, brown when we left New York, but suffering a sea change into a shade of green too vernal for his seventy-six years. American officers with yellow skins and bilious eyes met us at the landing and have shown us the strange and beautiful country beyond this town very comfortably from army ambulances.

Havana

Coming into the water slips here was a breathless experience of warmth and color and tropical life, but on land it is disappointing. Everything is gummy with heat and moisture, and the flowers and trees all look out of season and less luxuriant than I expected. Some are blooming, some withered or leafless like an ill-kept greenhouse. I wish they would all bloom or fade at the same time.

At the Hotel Florida—home of some noble family of the old vice-regal days—we have a big room, floored with glorious dark-red tiles, and a balcony of marble and wrought iron hanging over a noisy street like a bit of Spain itself. Our clothes are disposed in armoires of rich red mahogany with silver trimmings, built into the wall with many shelves, mostly inaccessible. An elevator, or at least a hook and ladder device, would be invaluable when I try to dress in a hurry.

April 1

The army here doesn't impress me as suffering any hardships but the climate. Havana is not without its attractions. There is the allure that many forms of gambling have in Spanish countries, and Americans soon drop into lazy irresponsibility when removed from Puritan social codes. Old friends showed us all the sights before we went with General and Mrs.

Ludington, two most lovable people, on an inspection tour practically around the island, and I am still wondering at its lack of beauty of line and vegetation. I wanted the fierce tropics, jungles, vines, and snakes. Steaming cane fields and silly old crabs stumbling sideways everywhere are a poor substitute. The wooded hills rising from the water at Santiago are very fine, but seeing battlefields and studying battles required too much effort in such heat. Living on the transport anchored in the harbor, shut in by primeval forest, was like so much time spent in a teakettle. Sometimes I wondered why the water around us was not bubbling.

The great Spanish warships, beached on the wooded shore or half sunken, rotting where they fell near Santiago, were a heartbreaking sight. Perhaps I should have been waving the flag and swelling with pride over our victory, but I could not. Why should we, in the vicious pride of youth, rejoice at the suffering and humiliation of a country like Spain as great and glorious as our own in her time?

Certainly we are doing wonders for Cuba. No American here ever lets you forget it. But a still small voice keeps asking me, "But what is Cuba doing to us?" Is it good for one country so completely to dominate another —especially a poor and weak one—even benevolently? Are not nations, like individuals, apt to become intoxicated with their own generosity and let it degenerate into patronage or even tyranny? J. and I have both noticed that many of our officers, especially the younger ones, have an arrogance, a sort of swagger, that they did not have at home, and there is a distinct tone of condescension toward "these people down here, these Cubans," as if they were all inferiors. Going with us to places of interest they do not conceal their impatience of the little delays caused by Spanish etiquette, though, Heaven knows, they have leisure enough to practice it.

Leonard Wood, Governor General, Viceroy, or whatever he is, could take a few lessons with distinct advantage. His wife invited me to the Arsenal garden to a party she was giving (at United States expense) to the Cuban orphans in honor of her own child's birthday. I went with several army ladies and at a pretty place on the shore found the company assembled, the General, I believe, the only man. He was seated with some ladies, nearly all Cubans, on a pile of lumber, there being no other seats of any kind. Mrs. Wood, with some difficulty, dragged him up to speak to us, and the instant afterwards he lurched back to his place as if afraid some of us would get it, and left all of us and old Senator Cockrell standing until the boats came in with the children. He had to stand at last when the little Cubans—under American orders—began to sing hymns of praise to him for his benevolence.

And, oh! the schoolma'ams! They have flocked here like birds of prey, each one talking Pecksniffian disinterestedness as if the enormous salaries our government allows them had nothing to do with the case. One day watching hundreds of little Cubans, shaded from black to cream color, being drilled into machines by some inconsequential American women I expressed a horror of the bullets for men and concentration camps for women that had left them orphans. One of the teachers rolled her eyes to heaven and startled me by saying, "But, *really,* they are better off as they are. If their parents had lived they would never have had this training."

Saltillo, Mexico, September 8

While our baggage was being examined at Nuevo Laredo, a rumor came that McKinley had been shot. No particulars, the news seemed to come from nowhere, just dropped off the wires, and the same rumor said a woman had done it. J., always a doubting Thomas, insisted it was only Mexican sensationalism, but before we reached Monterrey the story was repeated, "shot by an anarchist, and the assassin torn to pieces by the mob," which again made J. incredulous. "Mobs are bad anywhere, but not that bad in America," he said.

We are staying with dear Jennie Wheeler at the Presbyterian Mission and had the first cool night in weeks. Today there is no doubt the President was shot, and we are so sorry and ashamed. Anyway the wild stories of the mob were untrue.

September 15

We had a beautiful and tender little memorial service for the President at the "English church," all Americans, regardless of creed or politics, taking part in it with real feeling.

McKinley was a gentle, refined nature, suave and peace-loving, and his poor ill wife's state must be pitiful indeed. And above all looms the question of Roosevelt. What will it mean for the country to have him roughriding over it preaching war and the strenuous life?

CHAPTER SIX

1902

To the scandal of precise friends and advisers I have never made the Cabinet calls. One pompous ex-senatorial dame at West Point exhorted me to edification about it, said such failure to observe the rules would injure my husband, but as she had kept her husband in the Senate for only one term, I doubted the efficacy. The custom of calling is greatly abused here, for the Cabinet especially, so I determined to wait until some of the Cabinet heard I was in town and asked me to call. This has happened in only one instance, so meantime I argue like Sairy Gamp when she robbed her unconscious patient of his pillow that "He is just as comfable, and I am more so."

All of which leads up to the fact that I do not know Mrs. John Hay, who is under fire at present for allegedly drawing freakish and undemocratic social lines. The *Post* published a society notice purporting to come from Mrs. Hay who, it says, has "once more taken up the reins of leadership" and "has cards prepared requesting certain ladies to call on Madame Cambon at the French Embassy." Also, "the ladies to whom the notices, which are virtually commands, are to be sent include the wives of justices of the Supreme Court, the Cabinet hostesses, the wives of senators, certain matrons of the army and navy, and in some cases the wives of assistant secretaries. The line is said to be drawn absolutely at the House of Representatives, the members' wives not being expected to visit the wife of the Ambassador." To say that it has made the devil to pay is putting it mildly. One "colonel's lady" almost sobbed when she spoke to me of "the insult to the army."

Mrs. Hay contradicted it as soon as she could, but the contradiction never got beyond Washington and a lie can put a girdle round the earth in twenty minutes. The papers around the country are hurling rather rough fun at her.

That snobbish twaddle about invitations to the White House and elsewhere being "virtually commands" is having quite a vogue lately, chiefly, of course, among those just "arriving" socially. I wish I could reproduce the savage humor with which old Senator Vest treated the subject when we discussed it before him. He said he had been declining invitations to the White House for fifteen years because he didn't want to go and had not been threatened with impeachment yet.

San Antonio, Texas

We have had a happy summer, spent partly with Judge and Mrs. Maxey visiting the City of Mexico and little Cuernavaca. When "the glory that shall be" is revealed I know one spot of this dear old earth that surely is worthy to be compared with it—daybreak at Cuernavaca, the clear-cut peak of Popocatepetl "apparelled in celestial light," all alone in the sky, and framed by the black arch of the upper corridor of the Bella Vista Hotel. As the light spreads downward, it gradually reveals a scene of vast and almost unbelievable beauty but those moments of breathless splendor at dawn make the day a fading climax.

We sat on a low roof one night as if in an opera box looking down into the tiny Plaza Mayor with its moving crowd of languid native women and men with the biggest hats in Mexico, and enjoyed the daintiest exhibition of fireworks imaginable. We had seen the Indians making them that morning out of newspaper and rags and strings. In the evening they sizzled through the orange trees, wriggled up and down the walls, and flashed in spirals over our heads while the band played music that drew your very heart from your breast. And all to celebrate the Governor's safe return from the capital (it is 35 miles away)—and his "almost miraculous recovery from a stomach trouble"! I was gladder than anybody. If he hadn't recovered, we should have missed the most perfect opéra bouffe ever staged. It almost gives one a respect for Cortez to remember that this was the place he elected to bring his Indian light o' love after he had disposed of Mrs. Cortez in a well up at Coyoacán.

J. and Judge Maxey, whenever not studying Spanish or hunting another cigar store, disputed over Schley and Sampson. The squabbling of those heroes has been a conversational boon to their jaded countrymen. In the city Mrs. M. and I wandered about the Alameda and the Zócalo and the pretty shops, even haggling now and then with "Opal Joe," but we bought almost nothing. The Judge has to try smugglers from El Paso to Brownsville, and he and J. sternly forbade our risking criticism by bringing in anything. When we were met at the border by an order from the Secretary of the Treasury to waive examination of our baggage, the Judge laughed heartily at my moral obliquity when I exclaimed, "Don't I wish I'd brought a trunkful!" He said I was honest only by compulsion, but even so it is more credit to me to be honest than it is to him. He is too sound in heart and clear in head to be anything else. I have to *try* to be good.

Southern Pacific train, November 19

One of my favorite amusements is to read the signs of the times by listening to what people talk about on the trains. They cannot discuss their private affairs—not quite all of them—so the subjects must be those of prevailing interest. Everywhere women's talk is of things they call "progressive," or "altruistic," certainly strenuous. They seem to me to have an exaggerated sense of the importance of their undertakings—what Herbert Spencer describes as "morbid intellectuality—a small brain in a state of intense activity." I cannot remember what we used to talk about, children and servants perhaps, but there was more of fun and sweetness. Now it is "Chapters" (of organizations, not books), "Amendments," and "Federations." From Houston our car was full of women on their way to a meeting of the Federation of Women's Clubs at Beaumont, fine, intelligent-looking women, but aggressive and self-conscious, full of would-be-wise saws and "shocking instances," and an undertone of antagonism toward some undefined enemy—men, I suspect. At New Orleans a no less intense but more sentimental crowd discussed a meeting of the Daughters of the Confederacy, sometimes with voices angrily tearful as if all had not been peace at the gathering. I wish they were not all and always so desperately in earnest.

December

I am driven to make the original remark that life is full of surprises. In Dixie we grow up thinking that all Northern people are cold and unapproachable, just as firmly no doubt as they believe that all Southerners are gushing and insincere. J. and I have always found the Northeast most kind and hospitable, around Boston especially, but there is a difference and they rarely have our "terrible gift of familiarity." But there are sports in every garden and Miss Lilian Whiting must be a rare one in the "trim parterre" of New England. I never cared for her books. A steady diet of sweetness and light is cloying to a nature like mine in which the elements are so mixed that I enjoy an occasional bitter herb in my bouquet. But I wanted to meet her and was immensely flattered when the Washington Club asked me to talk on Spain the same morning that she was to give personal reminiscences of the Brownings. It was snowing hard, the audience was composed of middle-aged women in serious suits and "sensible" hats and shoes. My first shock came when the star blew in, late and flustered, arrayed in light gray with many loose ends of drapery, a big "picture hat" with pink flowers, long white gloves and many strings of beads. Her manuscript was not fastened securely and on the platform she dropped a good part of it, producing endless confusion, but her talk was well worth hearing. Her enthusiasm over my little paper left me in a state of wonderment, for she seemed sincere and could have had no purpose in just flattering me. She insisted so upon our "spiritual kinship" and her desire to know me better that later I sent a note asking her to tea on Saturday and this is what came back:

Yes, Fair Enchantress—with delight.

Lilian

Saturday—at four—or a little later I will materialize before you.

Something called her out of town, so she did not materialize. I set another date and she sent this:

Dear Love—You "presumptuous"! You, the flower of Southern sweetness, grace, loveliness! At this moment (7:45 A.M.) I can only say this for I have to be at the Colonial Hotel to see Sen. Teller at nine, and at the Capitol by appointment with Sen. Warren at 10, and I'm writing to prepare before. I will tell you the story later on.—In outline I am trying to assist a tragic, stricken woman.

I will write you by noon today—a little fully—With ever-increasing and ever-loving appreciation.

Lilian W.

She did come to the tea, late and breathless, and with one sleeve of a black lace jacket so nearly ripped out that I called down my sewing woman to make repairs on her while she protested. Then came this return invitation quite cold and formal:

Dear Mrs. Slayden,
Will you give me the pleasure of seeing you (with your paper!) this Saturday—at four—when Mrs. Rolfe (Anna Katherine Green) and another friend or two will be with me

And make happy
Yours
Lilian Whiting

She was called away again, so the symposium did not assemble, but this plan was substituted:

                                    The Dewey, March 2, 1902

Dear Mrs. Slayden, I count every day lost that I do not see you. I have been submerged beyond my power—but now—Could you—Friday, April 4, give me the great pleasure of seeing you here for lunch at one P.M. and I may or may not invite anyone else. I am a little selfish in seeing you—alone * * * I think of you and dream of you. Believe me. Most affectionately,

                                    Lilian Whiting.

I took lunch with her, and we had an hour or two of serious and pleasant enough talk watched over by several "spirit" photographs of Kate Field and others. She seems to be a convinced spiritualist and implied that her ministering angel, or familiar spirit, or "control" had directed her to me, and she made me a tentative offer to go into some sort of literary work with her in Boston. As I have a love of a home and a husband—neither of which she would comprehend—I declined, and the intimacy languished, but not before she had sent me at least a dozen notes as tropical as those I have given. Her dot and dash style I am too lazy to copy exactly, but I must give this one received after I had been away from town for a while:

Hasten the happy day—dear Mrs. Slayden, of your return—that I may embrace you—contemplate you—listen to you—meditate on you! . . . Will you come to me—for an evening . . . and have Mr. Slayden come later for you? . . . With unforgetting devotion and affection.

                                    Lilian Whiting.

I need hardly say that J. did not come for me; he is too cool, too calm, too normal to breathe in such an atmosphere. I have had no experience like it since my earliest girlhood when Southern students at the University of Virginia, trained in the florid tradition of ante-bellum literature, used to write me valentines.

December 14

The chiefs of bureaus were summoned by Secretary Root to hear the government's side of the new hoped-for General Staff bill before the Military Affairs Committee, and General Ainsworth said it was Root's way of letting them know what his opinion was and serving notice on them to keep their mouths shut, so he just decided not to go so he could remain comfortably ignorant of the Secretary's opinion. General Breckinridge was there and talked all the time that was allowed him. General A. says it is true of

Breckinridge as was said of Joe Blackburn in the House that he "would borrow time to talk from a man on the gallows."

Mr. and Mrs. Jackson Ralston are always interesting, but never more welcome than this rainy Sunday when they came in to tell us of their experiences in The Hague where he was representing the American Catholic Church in the "Pious Fund" before the Hague Court. Mr. R. thinks the work there made a great step forward in the cause of world peace and sanity and may be the beginning of an actual, permanent World Court. J. admires Mr. R. tremendously, thinks him so large-minded and impartial and often seeks his help and advice in the international questions that he has to work over in the House. It is astonishing—and a pitiful evidence of our parochial-mindedness—how few people realize that a congressman's work means anything but a pork-barrel watchfulness for the district, and many of them actually resent his concerning himself with our relations with other countries.

December 20

Met J. down at Brentano's to buy Christmas cards and books. General ————'s wife was there, and I was surprised to find how well we knew each other. J.'s work to save her husband's place on the General Staff has advanced our acquaintance by ten years.

CHAPTER SEVEN

1903

January

If Roosevelt had never done anything else, the metamorphosis of the White House from a gilded barn to a comfortable residence that he has accomplished would entitle him to his country's gratitude. Still, there is a howl of outraged sentiment from many quarters. One would think that every battered bracket and what-not had been the cherished possession of Martha Washington and must be kept forever sacred.

Some Western temperance women presented a "handmade" sideboard to Mrs. Hayes in token of their approval of her firm (and provincial) stand against serving wine in the White House. It was a "hijjus" thing (as Mr. Dooley might say), the worst of a bad period, all jigsaw rosettes and vari-colored woods, but selling it—and by the irony of fate to a barkeeper—was thought such a desecration that the matter was brought up in the House, where Uncle Joe Cannon, who keeps alive the torch of American humor, laughed it out of court. Ridiculing the idea that everything in the White House must stay there forever, he said, "When Adams was President, the family washing was hung to dry in the East Room." Then, raising his hands to heaven, he exclaimed, "My God! Where *are* those clothespins?"

Entering on the ground floor through a warm, spacious corridor is spoken of as "coming in through the cellar," and putting the portraits of Presidents' wives down there is another "desecration." It seems to me it has rescued those admirable females from oblivion. The light is good, there is plenty of room and anyone who wants to gaze at Mrs. Van Buren's bobbing curls or Mrs. Hayes's blue velvet dress "all buttoned down before" can do it at leisure without incommoding other people.

One thing I do regret is the loss of a large china hen on a china nest bulging with eggs. In the old "glacial period" when we came in from the north porch, and stood sometimes for an hour with the wind sweeping over us from the open doors, that hen sat on top of the Hayeses' sideboard, the very incarnation of bourgeois complacency; the only suggestion of comfort in the whole place. We called her Patience smiling at Pain, and I would like to have bought her, but no doubt she and the sideboard went together.

The new dining room is a triumph—good paneling, some good tapestries, and superb heads of moose, deer, Rocky Mountain sheep, and the bear that the President did not kill on his recent hunt in Mississippi— all finely American. I hope he will leave them to his country when his term expires.

The last reception was tiresome as usual, the slow-moving procession about as inspiring as the grand march at a drummers' banquet. The East Room is white and bare yet, but seems more spacious except for the big candelabra that rather crowd the entrance. In that deadly period when you stand on your own and other people's feet indefinitely before going through the line, I felt something like marbles on the floor, and several people spoke of it. Once when there was room enough to see, we found they were camphor balls. Senator Blackburn, who was jammed in with us, began to laugh and whisper to his wife, and finally confessed that he had found his pockets full of them and rather than carry them around with him all the evening, had been surreptitiously dropping them ever since he came in. His wife, a comparatively recent venture, is bright, handsome, and a Roman Catholic. He is a dyed-in-the-wool Presbyterian but says he had tried "Rum and Rebellion" and had to add Romanism to prove his democracy.

My gown ("gown" is la mode now, but I say it wi' deeficulty) was a new one from New York, a trailing white satin with cream lace overdress sweeping down from my shoulders, and a garniture around the bust of exquisite little pink chiffon roses with quantities of "baby" ribbon streamers with more roses at the end. With the rope of pearls that Rena[1] brought me from Paris I was more gloriously appareled than ever before in my life and must have made an impression, for the very next day Mrs. ———, a social Tarquinia Superba, dropped in to renew acquaintance that I thought had died forlorn some three years ago. She told me all about her father's having been secretary of state, lectured me on how to keep my visiting book, and said that "the diplomats are so exacting—Mr. ——— has to return their visits in twenty-four hours or they just *will not* come again." I must train my Texas Colonel a bit and see that he makes his obeisance "with hindward feather, and with forward toe," and maybe they will come to see us sometimes. I have often watched poor old Mr. ——— scurrying about with gloves and cane like the White Rabbit in *Alice* and never knew what was

---

[1] Rena Slayden, Mr. Slayden's sister.

the matter with him before. With only twenty-four hours between him and social extinction, how could he help being flustered!

At a smaller tea at the White House Mrs. Roosevelt was receiving alone and stopped me to talk awhile. I can only think of inanities at such times so just commended the changes in the White House—perhaps the three hundredth person who had done so that afternoon—but she seemed pleased and said she was planning to change the garden too into something like that at Mount Vernon. She is such a sweet "gentlewoman." There are a few people that only that fine old word describes.

I wore my new calling dress, black crepe de Chine, very long and clinging as to skirt and with a deep yoke of white satin covered with fine black Chantilly lace. My large black hat, lined with white and with a sweeping black feather, came from Paris, and my coat of black zibelline, like a well-combed Angora goat, is lined with white satin and down to my heels. It is a white-lined elephant, I'm afraid, but the other women are wearing them and I must try to bear my burden as gracefully.

At the tea the head of one of the scientific departments, rather noted as a climber, found himself stranded with me, and though talking agreeably, his eyes were roving like a shipwrecked sailor's looking for a sail. Suddenly they lighted up and I saw the "sail" was a skinny, countrified little man who called out with a strong nasal twang, "Why, how do, Mr.— I ain't seen you— Oh," as if trying to swallow back his words, "I haven't seen you in a long time." And I was presented to Mr. Secretary ———.

J. told me a funny incident he witnessed in T.R.'s private office. He was seeing the President rather informally when Senator Burton of Kansas, a most unprepossessing person, came in with a young constituent, presented him hurriedly, and said, "Now, Mr. President, my young friend is just passing through, and I want you to make him an epigram." J. says Roosevelt fairly snorted, "What! Make you an epigram to order?" and later remarked, "Did you *ever* see such a damned fool!"

The American Association for the Advancement of Science, meeting here this week, certainly deals with a variety of subjects. We had several guests to dinner and they hurried off, some to hear Remsen's address, and J. and Mr. Roth to hear Professor Louis Haupt on harbor engineering, every Texan being interested in Haupt's scheme for Aransas Pass. When they got to the Columbian University Building, they met a gentleman leaving and asked him if Haupt was speaking in a certain room and he said, "Oh-h-h, no! That is a lecture on cottontail rabbits. I am hunting the philosophical branch."

Piedmont, May 20

Besides being a place to spend all we can spare from J.'s salary, our orchard in the Ragged Mountains is promising an unexpected road to fame.

The family name Sprouse is almost a generic term in this neighborhood, and our manager, "Ole Burrell," is the finest and purest of the type. He thinks that congressmen are the richest and greatest men in the world, and that among them J.'s name leads all the rest, and he occupies a superior position in the mountains because he works for us. He usually dresses up to come to see me, but yesterday when he called for me to see him "on a matter o' business" I was surprised to find him in working clothes and a battered hat. He was evidently much hurried and excited, too. I expected the usual request for another work horse or more fence wire, but he burst out with, "Miz Slayden, I jes' come down to tell you thet thar's a buzzard nes' up in the hollow en it's got two aigs in it." Not knowing what was expected of a landed proprietor under the circumstances, I waited to hear more and he went on, "En I jes' come down to ast you to ast Mr. Slayden to sen' me two bells—jes' common turkey bells will do—so I kin bell the little buggards when they come, en then they'll be our buzzards." He was so happy that I had to express some sympathy, so I said, "That would be very nice, Mr. Sprouse, for you know I never owned a buggard before in all my life." "That's jest it, Miz Slayden! En I want Mr. Slayden to put his name on the bells and then people will know whose buzzards they is. They say a buzzard in his lifetime goes a far ways, and I reckon a cong'ssman would be proud to know thet his name wuz bein' carried wherever a buzzard flies." Alas, good old Burrell doesn't know that in the strife of politics a congressman's name is often carried where buzzards might scorn to tread.

Washington, December

Thank heaven at Christmas there is surcease of the social eternal feminine. Many of the Southern people give eggnog parties from which women in general are excluded. It has been my good fortune to be asked to several. The one at Justice Seth Shepard's was the biggest and best this year, with a huge bowl at either end of the table and Southern fruit cake, olives, and salted nuts between. Mrs. Benton of Missouri is the Congressional beauty and looked lovely over one bowl, and I did my best to make good at the other one. With all the Supreme Court justices not too decrepit to appear, the leading Court of Appeals justices, and members of the bar, choice selections from Congress, and quite a number of the worthwhile diplomats, it was decidedly stimulating. Justice and Mrs. Shepard received everyone in the drawing room and passed them on to us, so I don't quite see what fun they got out of it—the dining room was much gayer—but they seemed more than pleased with mine and Mrs. Benton's administration and invited us to do the same again next year.

CHAPTER EIGHT

1904

Piedmont, February 13

Waking to find yourself famous is not always a pleasant sensation. J.'s letters that beguile my sad vigil here with Father have for three days been concerned with a letter of mine that got unexpectedly into print. I wrote my sister an account of a White House reception. She gave it to an old friend, a society reporter, expecting her to make some extracts from it for her column, and she printed it in full from "Dear Jane" to "Aff. Ellen." J. writes, "After I got through my business the President said, 'By the way, Mr. Slayden, Mrs. Roosevelt and I enjoyed a letter written by your wife more than any description of the White House receptions that we have ever seen." He went on to ask J. why I had never called on Mrs. Roosevelt. J. knew nothing of the letter, so he said, "I don't know what she has written, but, of course, I stand by her," and was completely mystified until he heard from me. Then he divined that the same good Republicans at home who used to send my letters in a St. Louis paper to the McKinleys, hoping to make trouble for us, were at work again. (I always laugh when I meet those people. They think we don't know it and are so cordial.)

J. had to see the President again the next day and he reiterated his enjoyment of "the style and descriptive power," and I think the approval of Roosevelt the writer more than compensates for any trouble it might make. I am pleased, too, and having crept in favor with myself, I shall maintain it at the little cost of copying a part of the document to read over someday when my *amour propre* is not so robust. The stuff has been copied into many of the Texas papers and may have dire consequences for me yet, because I said, "Not all the Texas women are beauties." Here it is:

The White House reception has been the burning question for a week, and has created serious domestic differences. The most extreme views are held. One ponderous Member declares that a person base enough to accept an invitation from Roosevelt would sit at table with negroes of any shade, and that he, for one, means to rebuke him by staying away.

Some of us frivolously suggested that it was not our mission to discipline the President, and that in welcoming the select three thousand, he might even fail to notice if the Texas delegation stayed away "like one man" and a lot of disappointed women.

J. flatly refused to go and predicted that I would be trampled to death, die of fatigue, and certainly take cold. The invitations had "Not transferable" printed on them in very black ink, but Nan[1] went as "Miss Slayden," and we were escorted by Chester Harrison, J.'s new secretary, a very nice young fellow from Brownwood. I am always proud of the way young Texans fall on their feet here socially. Eastern people have such a way of looking, if not actually asking, "Can any good thing come out of Texas?" that we cannot help being pleased to see young men from our small towns come here as well dressed and often with better manners than those who believe that west of the Blue Ridge is the great American desert.

The new east entrance to the White House is opened at eight o'clock on reception evenings and long before nine I saw many smiling Texas women nodding triumphantly to others who had sworn they would not come. There are many booths from floor to ceiling, and at each one was a polite negro maid who took the wraps, handed them to a polite negro man who ran up a ladder and put them away and brought back the check. You may be glad to know that these were the only negroes, and they were certainly the right people in the right place.

White House receptions are always badly managed, but this was the worst. Perhaps it is impossible to make fifteen hundred to three thousand people comfortable in a house meant for five hundred, but Secretary Cortelyou and Colonel Bingham, the military major-domo, had been there so long that they had almost accomplished the impossible. Their successors, Secretary Loeb and Colonel Symons, were trying their 'prentice hands, and everyone hopes they will do better next time.

The corridor is a far cry from the Blue Room. It was jammed to suffocation, and all we could do was to hold on to our clothes and our tempers, either of which might have been lost by the pressure of the crowd. There was no order to walk two abreast and keep in line as there used to be, so we were at the mercy of the least considerate. I still bear the mark of General ———'s epaulette upon my damaged cheek. We would stand in one spot for ten or fifteen minutes, then be carried forward for as many steps and wait as long again. One had to have easy shoes and the calm mind of a Christian Scientist to enjoy that part of it. The broad shoulders of Representative Gregg of Texas made an effectual bulwark for me most of the time. His wife, the acknowledged beauty of the delegation, was with him in a charming dress of ecru lace, but he seemed not to appreciate his blessings. One of our fellow sardines spoke sadly of a lady who had wanted to come and could not, and Mr. G. said fervently as if to himself, "How I wish she had my place!"

The staircase to the drawing-room floor is divided like Jacob's ladder to accommodate the angels ascending and descending, and long before we reached

[1] Author's niece, Nan Lemmon, later Mrs. John Lightfoot.

the top many people had given up the fight and were going down. I was tempted to slip under the ropes and do the same, but George Bailey, a mighty good-looking and bright Texas newspaperman, said scornfully that no Texan would be a quitter, so we pushed on. It was cheering to hear the music tootling upstairs, and the sight of the big front hall rewarded us for all our trouble. The walls and columns are radiantly white, lighted by a maze of gold-branched electroliers. There were big palms here and there and in the center the Marine Band in scarlet coats. We moved slowly through the family dining room, a greater part of which was concealed by deep red curtains, and you would have laughed to see how many people stepped out of line to lift them and wonder at the chairs piled up and the table pushed back just as in the houses of ordinary mortals. At the door of the state dining room we were ordered into single file, and our troubles were over. We had spent an hour and a half getting there and my arms were almost paralyzed from carrying my train.

From that point there is a policeman almost every step of the way until you reach the President. Not a big, blue-coated "cop" but a man in plain clothes and often very keen and intelligent looking. Mr. Wilkie, chief of the secret service, stood nearest the Blue Room, and the President. He is an awfully nice man and his wife is a friend of mine, so he shook hands with me as I passed and said, "Where is Mr. Slayden tonight?" I called back in my usual high-pitched voice, "Oh, he had too much sense to come." Mr. W. turned several colors, and while I was taking in that I had said something "I hadn't ought to," Colonel Symons leaned over and said, "What name, please?" and I had to tell the truth. The President took my hand in both of his and said, "Mrs. Slayden, I am dee-lighted to see you." Mrs. Roosevelt, who is the sweetest sort of a woman, smiled prettily and said, "Good evening, Mrs. Slayden," and all the Cabinet ladies, in light dresses and white bouquets like pretty (old) maids all in a row, bowed like mandarins, except Miss Wilson, who leaned forward and said, "Good evening, Mrs. Turner," as if we were intimate friends. That is all there is to it as far as the President is concerned and after that your fun begins.

The first reception of the season is given to the Diplomatic Corps. Not quite everyone is invited, but there are usually more strangers, especially the rich and great from New York. Every official of every foreign legation comes, and wears his best suit of clothes, his medals, decorations, and all the military cutlery he is entitled to. His wife wears a few clothes and all the family jewels and it is the most brilliant thing of its kind to be seen in this country. Most of them were fenced off in one room the other night, and those who wished could stand by the ropes and stare at them. That, somehow, is a thing that I rather shrink from doing, so I went on to the East Room. The new Chinese Minister was there, a combination of a rainbow and a "Rising Sun" quilt. He is tall and broad like the figure of Buddha, and wore a flat red cap with a little red button on top, and a black satin kimono embroidered in life-size peacocks. He shed a glow around him as he walked. I haven't met him yet, but a woman told me that he "seemed really a gentleman, quite unlike Mr. Wu," his predecessor. I confess to having liked Mr. Wu very much, but then he never asked me my age as he did most women.

There was the usual array of overdressed Austrians, Germans, and Russians attended by underdressed ladies, a swarm of little off-color South Americans and a few Orientals, but Mrs. Whitelaw Reid "paled the ineffectual luster" of all of them. If Gus Houston had been there he would certainly have thrown out a line, she glittered so like a tarpon. Among the interesting people was "the good gray head that all men know" of Dr. Edward Everett Hale, who is now chaplain of the Senate. His face is as wise and kind and humorous as old Dr. Herff's, and he shows the same gentle deference to the most insignificant acquaintance.

Texans were on every side. The President must have felt complimented instead of rebuked—that is, if he noticed that we were there. We got in so late that the receiving hours were soon over and we were still in the East Room when the presidential party left the line and marched upstairs to supper—a performance that always makes me mad and hungry. We had a good view of the whole Roosevelt family. The President has innumerable relatives, and some of them are so tacky that it really makes me like him better to see how frankly he parades them on occasions. Alice Roosevelt is getting to be almost pretty, but she has not quite arrived and still has bumptious, awkward manners.

There was no supper in sight for us, so we hurried away, and at the corner of the Treasury Mr. Gregg bought bags of hot popcorn from the little wagon that stands there. We ate it as we went home on the streetcar in the same inexpensive way that we had gone down. Everything is still covered with a smooth sheet of ice, and we had a regular lark from the car to our house, leaving popcorn bags in the vestibules of houses and doing silly things like children at Hallowe'en.

I suppose you noticed that Mr. Slayden had introduced a bill authorizing the President to offer his services in effecting arbitration between Russia and Japan. There is great interest in the matter here, and there is to be a mass meeting at one of the theaters tomorrow afternoon when Cardinal Gibbons, Andrew Carnegie, and Dr. Hale will speak. It is my day at home, and I had asked several friends to receive with me, but I have a suspicion that Washington society will not be paralyzed if I shouldn't be on hand, so I have un-invited the ladies and we are going to hear the speeches instead. I am fortunate in having friends with whom I can take such liberties.

April 18

The White House letter will not down. The President asked J. again to have me call on Mrs. Roosevelt. I sent a note explaining that I had not come because I was in mourning and had a note from Miss Hagner saying that Mrs. R. had gone to Groton to see one of her boys who had the mumps, but she would make an appointment for me as soon as she returned. I went this afternoon at 2:30 and to my amazement found T.R. himself on hand, and though it kept a number of other people waiting in line, he took time to catechize me thoroughly about the letter. I thought it questionable taste in his own house to call me to account for personal opinions obviously not intended for his eyes, so I decided to be as frank as he was. He expressed his admiration of my "style" again, for which I thanked him, and said Mrs. R. had read the letter to the Cabinet ladies, and went on, "But I don't like your saying that my daughter is 'bumptious.' " I had said it, there was no retreat, so I looked at him quite seriously and said, "Yes, Mr. Roosevelt (I never can remember to say "Mr. President") but I have had a great deal to do with young girls and feel sure it is just a stage in her evolution. Perhaps she will get over it." His teeth snapped with a Grandmother Wolf expression. I don't remember his exact words except that they were not unamiable, and we parted friends. He was rather funny over my having said it made me "mad and hungry" to see them go off to supper, and told me that he would see that we were asked to go with them another time.[2]

The Interparliamentary Union for the Promotion of Peace by Arbitration (what a name!) is composed of members of the parliaments of fifteen sovereign countries, our own included. Founded in 1887, it has met in most of the great capitals of Europe, and this year is to be the guest of our government. We have appropriated $50,000 for their entertainment and there will be two special trains to take them to St. Louis for their business conference, and then on a tour of the West and back to Washington. J., with the rest of the Congressional committee, meets them in New York. I think I will die if I don't go.

May 7

J. is having a private view of the St. Louis Exposition. He writes: "The Exposition is not ready and I am afraid will not be for a month. The only exhibit at all in order is the Japanese and that is enormous and of surpassing beauty. The freak, star-shaped Texas building has one virtue; it is the best ventilated house on the ground, and if there is any cool place here in August, it will be in that hall. Except for oil, nearly the whole exhibit from Texas in the Mines building is from West Texas, and forty-five per cent of it from my district, which makes me proud, of course. You must see it all with me while we are here at the meeting of the Interparliamentary Union in September which will be quite the most interesting gathering of people that you and I have ever seen. It is not yet decided if you women are to go all the way with us, but I will wire you in time to join me here."

   [2] But he never did. I was told he was offended at an article of mine in the New York *Evening Post* in which I criticized rather severely the poverty and indifference of the entertainment of the Interparliamentary Union at the White House the following September.—E.M.S., 1925.

Southern R.R. en route to Texas, June 9

Leaving Charlottesville yesterday very tired I lay down in the empty section opposite my own rather crowded one and went sound asleep. Waking up hours later I apologized to a gentleman on the other seat for my intrusion and found myself acquainted with ex-Secretary of the Interior Hoke Smith, rotund of figure, orotund of voice, and very kind and courteous. I must be a better listener than J. admits for he talked till dinnertime and found my company so much to his liking that he asked me to dine with him. I declined and in his absence enjoyed my basket lunch of bread and spring chicken from Piedmont, which was well, as he came back and talked till 11:00 P.M. He is a hero worshiper, and his hero par excellence is Grover Cleveland and his life's ambition "the guidance of the Democratic party back to the sound doctrines of the gold standard and free trade"—and Presbyterian Sunday schools, I inferred. He says G.C. is "the only man that can win" and as he knows that no one can possibly differ with him and be right, I held my peace.

San Antonio, September 5

J. is campaigning in New York and writes me a hopeful account of the Democratic candidate. "Judge Parker and I sat on the porch and talked for an hour. He has light, sandy gray hair, and an undeniably red mustache. His manners and style generally are those of a well-to-do, educated Southern planter, which is good enough for me. He is sound on the Philippine question, the negro question, and militarism. Later we walked around the grounds and garden and the place is wonderfully like Mount Vernon—a good omen? Be ready for my wire to come to St. Louis, and go on the trip afterwards with the I.P.U."

October

Of the dozen congressmen appointed to escort the Interparliamentary Union on the western trip only five came. Mrs. Bartholdt and I were the only ladies. J. met them in New York and went the rounds of West Point, Philadelphia, and Pittsburgh. I joined them at St. Louis and from that moment to this I have had no chance to write more than a few headlines in my notebook.

My first sight of the party was in the lobby of the Southern Hotel, and their plight was pitiful. Many of the women had not learned that lace blouses, diamonds, and white-feather boas are not suitable for day and night travel in America in September. Others, especially the English, complained bitterly of the heat with their heavy cloth suits augmented by more or less "light topcoats."

The floor was piled with the weirdest baggage—little yellow tin trunks, leather hatboxes, and linen laundry bags, and a pyramid of fat brown canvas roly-polies called "holdalls," which the negro porters and bellboys were eying with profane glee. Their handbags had linen covers and many foreign statesmen were wrestling with a tape-string in a hard knot. Poor things! They spent seven purgatorial hours the day before looking at glowing forges and caldrons of molten metal at the steelworks in Pittsburgh, followed by a night on the unfamiliar Pullman cars with no chance for a bath or change. (But the experience had one good effect: every discomfort thereafter was anticlimax. Whenever we had to apologize for heat or dirt, they said consolingly, "Oh, it cannot be as bad as the steelworks.")

Rooms, baths, and luncheon restored their equanimity and confidence in our good intentions, and they were ready to accept the deluge of invitations that fell upon us from the foreign commissioners at the Exposition. The party included distinguished citizens or subjects from fifteen European countries, so there was a round of really brilliant receptions at the national buildings and many others given in their honor by the Exposition management. The mornings were spent in conference at the Hall of Congresses, and I was taken strongly with a suggestion made first by our own Representative Theodore Burton and followed up and elaborated by Count Apponyi of Hungary (an incarnated prairie fire sort of man) for an International Congress to convene periodically to discuss current questions and secure "amity by understanding" among nations. No doubt wise people have thought of it often before, but it opened a new vista to me.

With much social foregathering and informal sightseeing the party got acquainted with itself, and figures of special distinction stood out from the crowd. Count Apponyi was easily first to me; his great height, mobile face and glowing eyes compel one's interest. But next to him was little Mr. William Randal Cremer, carpenter and plasterer, labor unionist, Chevalier of the Legion of Honor, and founder of the Interparliamentary Union. John Lund, ex-premier and Norway's greatest orator, Dr. Tydeman of Holland, and the Marchese di San Giuliano are all men I shall look forward to hearing about in future. They seem so charged with interest and energy for the world's work. Philip Stanhope and Sir Howard Vincent were my special friends, and a delightful old gentleman, Ritter von Gniewosz, Court Chamberlain of Austria, who wore several deep scars of battles long ago on his kind old face and was profoundly in earnest in the cause of peace. Some of the party thought they had a great joke on me when they caught him kissing my hand in a dark corridor of a hotel, but he really owed me the courtesy, for he was running around hopelessly lost, and I had caught him and shown him to his room. There were a number of clever Englishwomen who made excellent speeches when occasion required—a thing so few American women can do—several lovely young girls from Sweden, Belgium and Norway, and some exquisite young matrons from Hungary, but I saw little of them as our train ran in two sections, and I was with the English, Scandinavians, and Germans.

We went at a family-nag gait out to Denver and back, stopping at several large cities, and everywhere were met and entertained with exuberant hospitality. Unfortunately the receptions were generally in the hands of Chambers of Commerce whose excuse for being is to "boom the town." We were shown too many skyscrapers and fine corner lots and too few places of historical interest. There were no potential settlers among the Parliamentarians, and it gave them an unfair impression of our social atmosphere. Never was American boastfulness more in evidence or more ill-timed. A little Belgian girl told me, "I am learning American. I know 'sho-r-re,' and 'bigges' in the worl' "—the way Americans describe everything." Sir Howard Vincent told me that when he spoke at St. Louis he really wanted to praise the Exposition and its management, "but President Francis spoke first and left me nothing to say in the way of commendation."

Many of the visitors spoke English, but many did not, and our ineptness in foreign languages made many awkward situations. Kansas City, however, was equal to the emergency. As we were ushered into a luncheon of barbaric splendor one young man, obviously selected for his knowledge of French, greeted each of us, regardless of nationality, with "bon jour," and when we left wished us all "bon voyage" with the same, fine careless rapture. John Lund of Norway disappeared for several days after leaving Kansas City and explained that he had been made ill by a drink they called a "foxtail."

Rounding up the strangers for the train after one of these stops was the time that tried the souls of the American committee. A difference of thirty minutes in a schedule was an unconsidered trifle to many of them, and one old Norseman we christened "the missing link" he was so invariably late. After runners had been sent out for him, he would come up beaming and unashamed bearing his picture postcards with him—a mania he shared with all the party. Our official badge, Mr. Bartholdt's artistic flight, was so flamboyant that we shrank from wearing it, but the hemisphere of brass with four inches of tricolor ribbon back of it soon abundantly justified itself. It could be seen afar off, and a description of it to a policeman often resulted in the prompt capture and return of straying statesmen.

J. and I made regular visits through the train and had formal engagements for luncheon, dinner, and afternoon tea. It was not possible to prevent what Mr. Dooley and all the Europeans called "poleetickal" talk, and keeping the peace between representatives of nations and factions was not the smallest part of our duty. One day driving about Detroit I was the unhappy fourth in a party with a Swede, a Hungarian and a Norwegian. The two latter sympathized volubly over their mutual woes oppressed by Austria and Sweden. The Swede overheard them, and ignoring my amiable chatter, growled out, "I understand you, sor-r-r." The Norwegian retorted sharply, "I hope you do, sir-r-r," and the air became electric. I plunged in with a question about Jókai's novels, the only subject I dared to hope they had in common. The Hungarian responded with some charming scandal of Jókai's last days, but the others went at one another's throats on the question of taxation in Norway.

Our guests sometimes expressed themselves a little more freely than they would have done if there had been more Americans in evidence, but their criticism was generally kind and judicious. They found much to praise that we never think of—the cheerfulness of the crowd on the streets and the lack of brawling or drunkenness. The closing of the Exposition on Sunday was a piece of religious tyranny they could not comprehend in a free country. An English M.P. was astonished (as I was, but I didn't admit it) when he enquired about ores to a fireman on the train that took us to Cripple Creek and was answered by a discourse on the value of the discovery of radium. I was laughing in my sleeve at another who was quoting Wordsworth to a hotel clerk in Denver and could hardly adjust my mind fast enough when the clerk supplied the missing lines.

One of our national weaknesses much in evidence was the feverish anxiety of some Americans to meet the titled men and women. Some young girls in Colorado Springs spoke loudly of their joy at meeting a "real live marquis" and gladly ran several hundred yards to catch up with and be introduced to a prince and a count. It gave me gooseflesh when I thought how those foreigners must be laughing at our "republicanism." Most of them, even the titled ones, were of liberal politics and had been idealizing Americans and our freedom from Old World superstitions, and these things showed us to them in the light of very common day.

Later they had a lesson in the simplicity, not to say rawness, of our democracy that I think would have done credit to "Oom Paul" on his African farm. They had been surprised, even a little chagrined, at not going first to Washington to be welcomed by President Roosevelt, and there was more than a shade of sarcasm when they said, "Of course, he is too busy with his campaign for re-election to think of foreign visitors." Still, Washington was to be the climax of their visit, and they asked many questions. They didn't hope to be met by a troop of calvary such as attends a secretary of war and other civil officers nowadays, but they did expect an evening entertainment like that always accorded them at European capitals; to meet some representatives of our government, and such of their own as were here. The women especially were concerned. They could understand the President's shaking hands—that was a sacred symbol of democracy that must be observed—but surely some divinity must hedge about the President's wife. Would she stand on a dais? Would there be ladies in waiting? Must they bow or only curtsy, and above all, would the evening gown each one brought be the proper thing to wear? I avoided the subject, and tried to divert their thoughts to the sights of Washington, for my prophetic soul foresaw one of those early afternoon "cake and death" teas for which the White House is becoming rather celebrated.

Still, there was a flutter of expectation when the time came to go to the White House—at two o'clock in the afternoon, as I had feared. Staying at the Arlington, it was only a pleasant walk through Lafayette Square, and we were ushered into the East Room without even the delay of a much-desired peep into a mirror. Countess Bethlen of Budapest, the beauty of the party, came up to me anxiously to know where she could go to take off her veil, and, seeing no dressing room was to be offered us, I diplomatically suggested that her veil was so pretty I thought she ought to keep it on. "But," she said, "are we permitted to wear a veil when we meet Mrs. Roosevelt?" and I learned for the first time that in Europe or even England one cannot be presented to even the youngest royal princess with a veil over one's face.

It was rather tiresome to stand about idly while the President received the spokesmen of the Union and promised to hasten the millennium, so I asked an Englishwoman, who I knew was ill, to come and sit down by one of the windows that commanded a pretty view. "May we sit while the President is in the room?" she asked with astonishment. I suggested trying it, and seeing it was not followed by a convulsion of nature several others joined us and waited comfortably.

I looked around for the people our visitors expected to meet, but the Interparliamentary Union was still alone except for Mrs. Belva Lockwood in a rainy-day skirt and a little knitted shawl around her shoulders. Where was Dr. Mary Walker? Why could she not have been there in her weird trousers and little top hat to complete the foreigners' impression of the official circle of Washington!

Some master of ceremonies had carefully separated the women from the men, and it looked like a children's party. After the speeches the President went to the Blue Room, where he was joined by Mrs. Roosevelt and, the men going first, we filed past them and they shook our hands with all the ceremony and elegance usually accorded to a visiting Elks Convention or an excursion of schoolgirls. We passed immediately into the state dining room where there was an inviting little "school spread" of sandwiches and punch, and cigars for the men, but nobody to do the honors for the house except some waiters and two or three young army officers. The President and Mrs. Roosevelt had disappeared, and the company roamed at will. The windows were wide open, the Marine Band playing outside, and the visitors said the house was "quite pretty and homelike." Very few comments were heard afterwards except about the President's speech, and they were generally, "Do you think he meant what he promised? Is he sincere?"

That night at the Arlington we had a farewell banquet, though many of our guests had taken earlier trains. I wished that all of them had fled and I alone been left to tell the tale when among the speakers was one from the Treasury who gave them a detailed account of the money appropriated for their entertainment, how judiciously it had been spent by the committee, and what a rich and lavish nation and people we were anyway.

Mrs. Thomas of Wales, such a clever woman, saw my lowered head, and whispered to me quizzically, "Don't mind, Mrs. Slayden. We have vulgar people in England, too."

San Antonio, October 6
When I came home I felt rather like Cinderella when the chariot and horses reverted to pumpkin and mice. J. is away going the hard round of the campaign, driving many miles every day in the dust, and speaking at all hours. Today he writes of the account I wrote for the New York *Evening Post.* "I am glad your 'piece was took.' If it had not been good the *Evening Post* wouldn't have printed it, and in the present state of our finances the check ought to make you feel rich. I speak at Brookesmith at 'early candlelight,' at Mercury and Richland Springs tomorrow. Everyone wants to hear Teddy abused, and it is easy to do the trick."

Washington, December 1

Dreadfully cold, Aunt Lucy not here, and a basket of flowers from Dr. Gerritson of Amsterdam and his wife, "Dr. Aletta Jacobs," friends left over from the meeting of the I.P.U. Of course I must have them to tea and find some intellectuals to meet them. I shall have to get the kind that will not be scandalized by the different names of this perfectly good and loving married couple. We hear they had trouble in explaining at the hotels, but the Shoreham finally took a sporting chance on them.

Thursday

No man servant yet, so I brushed walls and pictures myself. There is heavy snow and sleet, but the tea was a great success. Clever people are so easy to entertain; they do it for themselves. Mrs. Hill helped me to get dear Miss Alice Fletcher, Mrs. W. H. Holmes, and Dr. Irving, so, with Dr. Rosalie Slaughter, we made quite a showing of clever titled women. Some of J.'s scientist friends and some from the House and Senate gave the foreigners an opportunity to see a creditably representative American company. The blatant Chamber of Commerce type drowned out everything else on the Parliamentarian trip. I was so glad to let these two clever people meet some of our compatriots who could see beauty not represented by skyscrapers, and success not estimated in dollars. There are no people in Washington more agreeable and cheery than those connected with our scientific departments. In a simple, unpretentious way they entertain a good deal too, which is greatly to their credit for they are wickedly ill paid. Our government loves to spend money on things it can see, hear, and touch like battleships. The fairy tales of science and the long result of time but moderately interest the average lawmaker. The cost of one battleship would advance our scientific work by many years if spent on better salaries to attract more young men and give better housing and equipment. The departments are sheltered in all sorts of old rookeries, hampered by lack of room and danger of fire. The Geological Survey camps in an old building on F Street that was antiquated when I was here as a young girl.

Judge George Clark of Waco is here, an agreeable man, but a gourmet, and his wife a notable housekeeper, so it took some courage for me to ask him to dinner. I had a pair of fine ducks, and Aunt Lucy cooked them so well last year that I trusted her to do it again, but this time the ducks came in looking as if they had died in a free fight. Mixing the salad I found that Thomas, the new butler, had given me paraffin instead of the disguised cotton seed of commerce. That was followed by a stone-cold mince pie. But an old Confederate soldier knows how to starve gracefully, and the Judge stayed him with flagons and comforted him with olives and almonds at the same time that he diverted me from my humiliation by good stories and clever talk. He described Stonewall Jackson as "the Blind Tom of military science" and told how "Shell" Hogan, one of our old acquaintances in Waco, when defeated for mayor lately, addressed his supporters and said, "You can't keep a good man down. Sphinx-like I will rise again."

CHAPTER NINE

1905

January 5

Our usual eggnog party went well. There was a trifling embarrassment when Postmaster General Bob Wynne arrived late, in morning dress, and several people inquiring tenderly for his wife, he had to admit that she had not been asked. J., in his artless, casual fashion, had said to him, "Come up tonight and get some eggnog," and told me afterwards that he "didn't know Wynne had a wife." If Mr. Wynne was hurt he drowned his sorrow, and I don't think it was chagrin at his social deliquency that put J. to bed with a bad attack of grippe as soon as the last guest left the house.

January 11

J. remained too ill for us to accept an invitation to meet the delegates to the American Forestry Congress at Mrs. James Pinchot's. I was much disappointed as Mrs. P. is one of the few grandees that I especially want to know. Her son, Gifford, is so interesting and genuine that I was sure she must be the same sort. However, we went to her next Monday at home and found her very *grande dame*, in dark-purple silk, Irish lace, and long amethyst chain, but so easy and humorous that I was not surprised to find myself sitting on a sofa beside her laughing over the queer thick under-clothes we used to wear and wondering what had become of our flannel petticoats. Mrs. Walcott, who was assisting, told her what a "brilliant literary talk" (I wish people wouldn't use the word "brilliant" so recklessly) I had made at the Washington Club, which rather upset me. The talk was sensible, I hope, but not scintillating.

Mrs. P. asked us to come again whenever we could, because she was "too old to make calls," and I shall take her at her word. We met Gifford down in the hall, very cordial, and regretful that he hadn't been at home too. I like the house better than any I have seen in Washington. It doesn't glitter, or jingle with money, and the furniture belongs to no period but that of good taste and comfort. There is nothing artistic in the strained modern sense but everything pretty and restful. The library where we sat is very large, with bookshelves practically all around it and from floor to ceiling. The books look as if they had been read and might be read again at any time. There was an open fire, and over the mantel a picture built into the wall that kept me saying to myself "Where the quiet colored end of evening smiles, miles on miles"—just the hour when you would like to sit in a room like that and read old books that you haven't had time for since you were young.

January 20

J. was to have taken me to Mrs. Roosevelt's at home this afternoon, but came in bland and smiling so late that I was ready to leave without him. He had to dress, so many carriages were rolling away as we drove in. We had a few minutes with Dr. E. E. Hale and Miss Nellie downstairs before going to the East Room where Mrs. R. was receiving with only one of the aides to introduce people. We had some pleasant talk, but she said she couldn't go to San Antonio in April with the President, because the last time she went on a trip the children had measles. I tried to persuade her, saying measles couldn't happen again, and I am grieved that she can't go. Accustomed as the country is to thinking of Roosevelts as explosive, her gentleness would be such a pleasant surprise.

We passed through the Blue and the Red rooms with the usual remote, unfriended sensation, until we met Mrs. (Justice) Harlan and Miss Harlan. Mrs. Harlan was ponderously cordial; Miss Harlan, leaning back on both her hands, brought one out reluctantly and put it back as soon as it had served its mission of a limp shake. The state dining room was not crowded, and the tables rather long and bare. A huge tea service was at one end, Miss Hagner presiding, a punch bowl at the other, flowers and bonbons intervening. The punch bowl is hideous—heavy china with a dark-maroon band, and the American eagle screaming on one side. I would like to lend them my Spanish brazier—brass and mahogany—and blue Japanese bowl.

Our old friends Drs. Rannie Kean and Edie (U.S.A.) and their wives looked as glad to see us as we were to find them, and we had punch and three-cornered sandwiches together. Miss Alice Roosevelt was among those present but took no notice of anyone but some young officers. Bob Wynne rose above circumstances and was actually gay; and young Ulysses

Grant, handsome and intelligent, was pleasant to meet again. When leaving we blocked a doorway exchanging sweet nothings with Justice Brown and his pretty new wife. Growing serious, the Justice said he was weary after fourteen years of Supreme Court duty and meant to resign soon and make way for a younger man. I hope he will hold on till there's a chance of appointing a Democrat—though what difference does it make? Such prejudices are just a habit of mind, I believe, not reason. J. says I am the most contemptible of political hybrids, a mugwump, and that there must be parties, but Republicans and Democrats individually are Tweedledum and Tweedledee to me.

January 22

Last night a note from W. J. Bryan said he would like to come to breakfast if it could be early enough for him to go to church afterwards. He arrived, large and benevolent as ever, little changed except that his hair is woefully scant on top. He shows growth in things spiritual and fewer signs of fanaticism than I thought he had years ago. Chicken was just what he liked, and when Aunt Lucy sent in late reserves of corncakes, he helped himself again, remarking, "All their lovely companions are faded and gone."

I told him with what interest Jane and I had read his speeches for Parker last summer, and he said they had demanded "more mental athletics" than anything he had ever done. My own opinion is that Parker's defeat was due more to his provincialism than his politics. His point of view was so entirely Eastern. How can a man essay to lead a vast country like ours without knowing something of all parts of it? I understand that he had never seen the Mississippi River.

January 24

The afternoon round of Congressional calls was enlivened by the sight of three ladies from widely different sections of the country making their first plunge into society. It was from a bo'din'house parlor with big figured wallpaper, green chenille curtains, and red carpet, a large lithograph of "A Winter Scene" over the mantel, and a table of fruit punch and wafers. They all clutched at their trains when crossing the floor as if they were on their way to the hen house, and were so exercised over "receiving" that they forgot to be hospitable. There were plenty of chairs, and though I wasn't asked to sit down, I did it anyway, and one of the ladies had to sit with me and by the action relaxed into a natural and pleasant person. They were good material, just inexperienced, and Montana will learn from North Carolina, and rural New York from both, and none of them will ever be as provincial again. Washington is a great school for us country folk.

That kind is far more hopeful to me than the stout and serious mistress of the next house I went to early, hoping to miss the charge of the six hundred that I heard were invited. It was a veritable "Tom Tiddler's ground" where one might be "picking up gold and silver" from gilt mirrors, gilt furniture, jingling portieres and tables blazing with candles and cut glass. The Midas touch was so obvious that had I dared to risk any of the cakes and dainties I am sure they would have hurt my teeth. There were roses, roses everywhere, chucked into grotesque pieces of bric-a-brac, and withering under glaring electroliers. There were twenty woman in the receiving party "bunched," as we say in Texas, on one side of the room back of madame, who answered exactly to a late newspaper description of her as a "large machine recently wound up, but not yet in good social running order." But if she wasn't in running order, I was. Suddenly, overcome with longing for my 'umble 'ome, I escaped from the heat and glare into the soft gray peace of thickly falling snow. I had given the cabman a long list, but I said, "Take me to 1631 R Street," and here I have been reading a blessed book until J. came in powdered with snow like Santa Claus caught out in a silk hat.

January 26

It is clear today with wind like knives, but J., Mrs. Ash, and I braved it to go to an auction at Sloan's ("Grandpa" Sloan's from whom strangers and sojourners here, like ourselves, "inherit" our old mahogany). G Street was blocked and the side streets packed with carriages for the wedding at Epiphany of Senator Warren's daughter to a Captain Pershing.[1] I expressed surprise that we weren't invited, the Warrens have always been our friends, and J. said, "Why, an invitation did come to the office but I forgot to bring it home." I gave him a proper scolding, not because I wanted especially to go, but for his dropping into the habit *assumed* by so many Texans of being indifferent to society. One can forgive them when they don't know better, but I hate the heavy democratic pose.

January 27

I usually dislike people who screw up their mouths and say "hooray" instead of a good honest "hurrah," but when President Taylor of Vassar at

---

[1] Later General John J. Pershing, commander in chief of the American Expeditionary Force in France during World War I. Helen Warren Pershing and their three daughters died when fire destroyed their home in San Francisco in 1915.

Mrs. Walter Weed's this afternoon said "Hooray for Texas," it was so warm and hearty that I forgot my prejudice and enjoyed a talk with him. He said in lecturing to his seniors on the Platonic method he used a book of Dr. Mezes' (University of Texas) as his example. Vassar talk predominated, of course, but it seemed to me a shade less self-conscious than in gatherings from other colleges, and there was a little less slang.

Sunday, January 29

The Hulls of Iowa dined with us today, and after dinner, while J. and Mr. Hull smoked, we ladies, Miss Hull, Rena, and I, sat with our toes to the fire and gossiped. The Hulls betrayed a bitter dislike of the President and quoted Mr. H. as predicting that he would split the party. I hope so, but that prediction is always made about this stage of an administration and fades into nothingness as the campaign year approaches.

February 4

Thursdays I made senatorial calls. In a spirit of adventure, and being in the neighborhood, I called on Mrs. Clark, the copper queen of Montana, but a blowsy Irish waitress said, "The missus is nawt resaivin'," and what I saw of the house through the wide-open door made it seem just as well that she wasn't.

The weather has been unusually cold, dark and depressing, which makes Colonel Cowart's latest story on C. of Texas all the funnier. C. had been on the water wagon, but slipped off yesterday, and in the evening his wife was troubled by his red face, and feared he had a fever, but he told her not to worry, it was just because he had been "sittin' 'round in the sun all day without his hat."

February 8

Rena and I went to see the electoral vote counted, but had poor seats. The doorkeepers play favorites on such occasions and swear that certain galleries are full. Democratic remonstrance now, unless made by a member in person, does no good, but I stirred up a ponderous Republican dame from the Northwest to go for them, and I was sorry for those doorkeepers when she got through.

The counting was exactly as uninteresting today as on the two previous occasions that I have seen it. Republics are colorless in their official functions, but there seems no middle ground between this and the fuss and feathers, the men-at-arms, the Black Rods and heralds, and expensive and meaningless millinery of royalty.

There was loud Republican applause when Missouri was read into their column and clapping from both sides when Senator Bailey gave the magnificent Democratic returns from Texas. Mrs. Benton of Missouri, whose husband was defeated, sat near us and leaned against the wall dead white as if she would faint, her pallor not relieved by the glow of the deep-red velvet hat and dress in which, like Mary Queen of Scots, she had arrayed herself for her execution. Her absence will sadly reduce the average of good looks in the House, and Mr. Benton is a sound, earnest man who will be missed.

February 11

Congressmen with the most lofty scorn of afternoon teas are apt to find they can go when the Speaker's family is at home, and J. agreed to take me to Miss Cannon's today, but, of course, "a bill came up" and I went forth alone. Mr. Tittmann—aristocrat and scientist, head of the Geodetic Survey—was on the herdic[2] bound for the same place. Mrs. T. was ill; so we made common cause of our grievances, and he made a charming understudy for my Texas Colonel. Neil, the Speaker's colored messenger, opened the door. I had not seen him since last summer when his good manners and true kindness saved so many situations on the Interparliamentary trip, so in my artless Southern fashion I shook hands with him. The hall was full, and I saw some Northern friends making big eyes at me, and one said a little later, "An old servant of yours, I suppose?" "No," I said, "only an old friend," which still further mystified them. Northern people even yet are unable to comprehend our taking negroes naturally. They think we must either accept them socially or pursue them with Simon Legree's blacksnake whip.

New Braunfels, Texas, April 6

We came over at one o'clock to meet the President and to save Herr Banker Clemens from nervous collapse. He was to make the address of welcome, and I know Teddy's inaugural didn't cost half as much conscientious effort. We sat in the bank and studied it until four, when young Mr.

2 Horse-drawn cab.

Clemens took us driving to see one hundred and forty acres of satiny green onions—a new and astonishing crop here—and the ever lovely park with wild flowers repeating the color of the sky from our feet to the distant mountains. Is any country more beautiful than Texas in bluebonnet time?

After a good supper at Frau Platz's, we went to the station. School-children all in white were drawn up on each side of the track, the public schoolteachers in charge on one side, some Catholic sisters on the other, and all inflated and ready to burst forth into singing the verse composed for the occasion, and dedicated to "Unseren Präsident":

> *Heil Dir O Präsident.*
> *Roosevelt roll achtung nennt*
> *Nun alle Welt . . .*

to the tune of "America."

Herr Banker Clemens stood ready on a goods box. Little Melitta Faust, the village beauty and heiress, in accordian pleated chiffon and topaz necklace, with a cataract of crimped yellow hair falling down her back, held a bouquet of roses as big as she was and a parchment copy of the song to hand to his majesty. A troop of girls in Rough Rider costumes with real guns and pistols but not mounted "because they couldn't ride already, and besides it was so dangerous" marched around singing a martial tune and waving a nondescript banner.

At last the engine roared in, covered with flags, and on the rear plat-form "Unseren Präsident," teeth and spectacles gleaming. The song was sung, the speech was made, and the flowers presented exactly according to program, and his response was apropos as always. I don't remember his claiming a German grandfather—he has a polyglot collection to bring out on occasions—but German citizenship and thrift, Germans' part in the making of Texas and the United States were dwelt upon until the listeners almost burst with enthusiasm and their chests swelled visibly as they sang again:

> *Wog' unsere Nation*
> *Woge die Union*
> *Ewig bestehen.*

They do take their love of country and *"die Union"* so seriously and musically.

Now they are at the beer gardens talking it over with their wives, and while J. confers with some politicians and I sit under a tree waiting for him, I can hear through the soft warm darkness renewed strains of the song mingled with "Hochs" of satisfaction. This is the sweetest, Germanest town—shining clean windows, with stiff white curtains, polished doorknobs, well-swept walks, and borders of gay flowers and herbs, and every bit as humdrum as Germany. Once the jail was empty for two years. The city marshal has served since 1882. Lately another ambitious citizen ran for the place and defeated the incumbent. He was sworn in, and invested with the insignia of office—a steel badge and a pistol—but his wife and children were so tortured by the thought of his being out at night and carrying fire-arms that after three days he resigned and returned the job to the former officer already inured to the strenuous life.

San Antonio, April 8

T.R. made his visit "with music waiting on his steps and shouting of the throng." When he spoke on Alamo Plaza to a multitude of his admirers, he paid J. a tremendous compliment, turning and speaking directly to him on the platform. He congratulated the people on having a congressman so alive to their interests and so capable of accomplishing what he undertook. It was very fine and generous of him, too, for he and J. have frequently differed.

At the banquet that night, J. tells me, an awkward thing occurred, but it greatly increases my respect for Roosevelt. The toastmaster was a loud, flamboyant man who often mistakes coarseness for humor, and in his speech he took occasion to allude to the President's views on race suicide with a rather nasty verse. When he sat down Roosevelt quite pointedly turned his back on him, did not address him again during the evening and when making his own address omitted the customary thanks to the toast-master.

May 20

It begins to look as if we might, after all, get off to the meeting of the Interparliamentary Union at Brussels this summer with time for the "cure" at Carlsbad which J. needs and I enjoy. The North German Lloyds are running very good boats from Galveston. They are rated second class and are slow, but class rarely disturbs my self-esteem, and the long, dull journey—seventeen days to Bremerhaven—will be just to our taste.

Leipsic, July 25

After a dreary walk through grand new "places" and dark alleys of the old town, we found Auerbach's Keller. Ten minutes in such a hole in the ground in America would be intolerable, but here I am quite happy dividing the limited oxygen with a dozen other people, and waiting to divide a chicken and a bottle of white wine with J. Behind us is a compensating little carved figure dated 1529, and some low, black wooden doors shut slantwise on an underground passage where we might find the *alte Barbarossa* if we looked in. Arching over us are dim pictures, the very same that inspired Goethe's version of the Faust legend.

German women would be so pretty if they carried themselves instead of dropping their weight on their hips and did not neutralize the lovely tones of their hair and skin by wearing sickly shades of pink with cream and green with tan. This year they have a nauseating combination of blue with bronze. Dress reform has invaded the country and they are wearing Germanized Empire gowns low in the neck and loose in the waist, but there the reform ends and they carry a bedraggled and skimpy train. The only real reform is in their bare heads. The absence of a German hat necessarily improves any woman.

Carlsbad, July 27

So many changes since 1894. The streets are full of fashionably dressed people, and rooms on the Schlossberg are at a premium. We pay thirty-five gulden a week at the Villa Klenun for a small room and the services of two red-cheeked maids, besides Anton and Fräulein Anna to make pleasant remarks to us on the unpleasant weather when we go in and out. King Edward is to stay next door at the Savoy next month, and I would like to see him, but we shall be flitting before that time. J. persists in studying the questions on the agenda of the I.P.U. when he ought to be resting. We have found pleasant friends, Ernest Kruttschnitt of New Orleans, who was at Washington and Lee with J., and his lovely sister, Miss Alma, and we have had some pretty excursions with them to nearby villages for supper.

Our program leaves room for nothing but the "kur" though it begins at 6:30 A.M. In fine weather we breakfast at the Jägerhaus and read the Paris *Herald* with its six inches of news and six columns of gossip about foreign nobility, America's "Smart Set," and automobile accidents. There is yellow fever in New Orleans, the Russo-Japanese Peace Conference is in session, and an extra session of Congress is predicted, but the first page of the *Herald* today has, under large headlines, a detailed account of "Harry" Lehr and "Jimmy" Hazen Hyde (of Equitable fame) in Newport yesterday throwing balls at nigger babies.

We ran across the Bartholdts at Cologne and came on with them. They had the "Programme des distractions" for the conference of the Interparliamentary Union and I have already marked out many of them. Steel plants and agricultural expositions would distract me especially. When there are agreeable people to talk to, why seek other distractions? There are to be enough balls, "raouts," and banquets to keep me quite happy. We are comfortably placed at the Flandre; we could not get in at the Belle Vue, where more of the I.P.U. people will foregather.

In our first day here the coiffeur downstairs was to wash my hair at 8:30 and I went promptly. He kept me waiting a long time, then came into the little box and waited with me till the water was hot, then slowly and awkwardly began his work while I could see in the mirror the lobby I had to go through filling up with people—J. with a rose in his buttonhole looking for me, Count Apponyi, the Bartholdts and others. I grew desperate, snatched my hair from the little Flemish rat, put myself into what order I could, made a dash for the lift and ran plump into Mr. and Miss Bouman. She seized and kissed me, and it was pleasant to hear her gurgling Dutch laugh again, but we were standing in the very front door. People I knew were coming in every minute, and I was painfully conscious of the combs and brushes under the blue negligee on my arm. Later, when properly gotten up, I came down to find the place empty, but Colonel and Mrs. Roosevelt (he is consul general) called and were very pleasant. He is cast in a smoother mold than his Rough Rider cousin, and she is a pretty and vivacious Georgian. We returned their call in the afternoon, and hurried home to dress for dinner at the Grand Hotel with dear old Mr. Cremer.

We found him in the lobby, a quaint, sturdy little figure with short stubby hands, and dressed in a badly made suit and a black velvet skullcap. Roland, M.P., another Labour member, dark, somber, and heavy, was with him, and Mr. S——, whose two "sets" of teeth clicked as dryly as they did last year. The group looked as if it had been written by Dickens and illustrated by Peter Newell. Our dinner was interrupted by Mr. ———, M.P., a florid person who patronized our simple friends and betrayed social intentions toward us, making me promise to go up to see his wife, who was ill. We sat at table two hours and I thought she might have died or recovered, but when we went out, there he was waiting for me. The fat and well-looking wife was in bed, smothered in pillows, her head stiff with curlpapers, and not ill at all, "only a bit seedy, you 'now, from the crossing." I felt silly, and would have escaped even more promptly than I did, but was detained to talk to the daughter, a rosy, *Ladies' Pictorial* young woman who expressed surprise at my small feet, and kicked up her own to show me that she wore *sixes*. Obviously I had been called up for inspection, and the next morning we received an invitation to an "International Luncheon" at the Café Helder. I hear there are to be people from every country represented at the conference, and we are the Americans— flattering, no doubt, but promising onerous service for our country.

Mrs. Roosevelt took Mrs. Bartholdt and me to the conference at the Palais de la Nation. I was overcome with the array of lackeys in the vestibule all in black dress suits with big gold chains around their shoulders. Masses of lovely fresh flowers followed the sweep of crimson carpet up the broad stairs. Mrs. Roosevelt had brought the wrong card, but her fluent French smoothed the way and we were soon seated in the Hall of Delegates under the gallery in the rather dark place reserved for women and strangers. Miss Bouman joined us and we enjoyed some of the speeches, but it was evident there were to be too many of them. Beernaert, Minister of State, presided. He is a wise-looking old man with a large coarse mouth and nose, and very small keen eyes. In the amphitheater I saw many familiar faces and was glad to find that I remembered most of the names. At the recess quite a number came to speak to me, which pleased Mrs. Roosevelt, and we had a gay half hour.

Sir Howard Vincent had asked us to lunch with him, and soon afterward Philip Stanhope, debonair and cordial as ever, always with that we-have-a-joke-in-common air, also came to ask us, and said he had tried to find us the day before. He is a person one can be really fond of; he is such a genuine friend of all the world. Sir Howard walked back with us through the park and then we decided that it was too late to do downtown with him, so he stayed with us. Old B. of Boston, quite uninvited, sat down with us and took the conversation and ran away with it, exploiting his pet hobby of prison reform. The lunch was bad, but Sir Howard takes hot milk and toast with bits of anything else in sight, so I didn't care. He is an amazingly careless feeder, handles his knife and fork as if he had forgotten them, as I think he has, he has so many more absorbing interests.

Whenever old B. permitted, we talked of the Portsmouth Conference,[3] which is reaching a nervous crisis, and agreed that peace seemed farther off than ever.

When we went back to the conference, J. made a short speech to

[3] Negotiations to end the Russo-Japanese War were held at the navy yard at Portsmouth, New Hampshire. A peace treaty was signed September 5, 1905. For his work as mediator, President Roosevelt was awarded the Nobel Peace Prize in 1906.

which they listened attentively, which was more than they did to the spread-eagle oration that another American was bugling through his nose when I left. Count Apponyi had spoken earlier or I should not have come away. To me no one approaches him; his voice is so full, so charged with soul and energy, and he has no mannerisms, no oratorical tricks, just speaks "as the spirit gives him utterance."

He is six feet four inches and slender, his face is extraordinarily mobile, and the flash of his eyes and roll of his voice always make me think of him by his sobriquet "The Soul of the Hungarian Revolt." I can see how the European press holds him responsible for the pandemonium that has reigned in Hungary for years, though he is still under sixty. As minister of public instruction he has authorized a special Peace Day in the schools to interest the youth of the country in the idea.

I am always forgetting how these Europeans hate one another. Among our pleasant acquaintances of last year are Mr. and Mrs. Brandt of Norway. She has been ever affectionate to me, witty and quizzical, but bitter about the troubles between Norway and Sweden. She told me blackening stories about John Olson, from whom I had just had a letter, and her hatred of all "the dirty Swedes" is an obsession. There is a tiresome smallness about the Norwegians, a sort of Irish tendency to be "agin the government," though one cannot help being sorry for a people who want a republic and are threatened by England and Germany with, as Mrs. B. says, "an old deef Bernadotte" for king. This morning at breakfast she came toward us, but seeing Baron Bonde of Sweden at our table talking rather gaily, she flounced off and has not looked our way since. Baron Bonde is one of the most interesting men here, a statesman who takes time to lead in art and letters, and we could hardly forgo his acquaintance for the sake of Mrs. B.'s prejudices, sorry as I am to lose her.

Later

When J. had gotten himself up in "habit noir et cravatte blanche" as requested, for the reception the King was giving the conference, I went to the palais with him to see how the others looked. They had fairly blossomed into decorations, orders, and ribbons; only the Americans were ostentatiously simple, wearing their evening clothes "with a difference," conscious of sinning against one of our cherished conventions by putting them on before 6:00 P.M. Some also betrayed a more tremulous nervousness at the prospect of meeting a king than was quite consistent with democracy. Mr. Cremer and a few other British radicals were not going because they were too indignant about Leopold's part in the Congo atrocities, and when I said he was a "mean old thing not to have asked the women," several of them exclaimed, "I am glad *my* wife is not to meet that old roué!" with a fervor calculated to shake one's faith in the obdurate virtue of the British matron. "Filthy old beast" was a pet phrase even with some of those who drove away to the palace while I, who had no conscientious scruples—in fact was dying to go—was left behind. I went off to the lace stores and consoled myself with one of the long appliqué scarves that are so much the fashion, to wear to the reception tonight.

When I came in J. was too busy interviewing himself for a London paper to tell me about the palace, and besides had no standards by which to judge royal tea parties, so I waited till that evening at dinner with Sir Howard Vincent to hear the story. He has been received at every court in Europe, and said, "The Czar could not have done it better." The King had brought in a retinue of two hundred and fifty people from the Summer Palace, and everything was in perfect order, fifty footmen on the stairs, and lavish refreshments. I mentally contrasted it with the "cold swarry" for these same people at the White House last year with the furniture pushed back, the floors bare, and the President and Mrs. R., after a formal hand-shaking, leaving us to seek a sandwich in the dining room unattended except by two army officers and negro servants. J. says that Leopold moved about among his guests and stayed until they left. It seems that we have something to learn from kings in the way of simplicity. Some Belgians told me that Leopold had expressed great admiration for J. on account of his height and good looks, but I think he must divide the praise with Little-field of Maine and Barchfield of Pennsylvania, who are both as tall, if not so comely.

The "raout" at the Palais de la Nation was a great experience. The lighting was exquisite, and my especial joy, the Palace Guard, had been fattened for the occasion, I'm sure, and given their gold chains an extra polish. There was a refreshing absence of that recent American invention "the receiving line," whereby the forlorn stranger is passed from one cold handshake to another until turned adrift in a roomful of people as lonesome as himself. Mr. Beernaert and his pretty wife received us, and then we were impercept-ibly taken in charge by people whose pleasure it seemed to entertain us. Sir Howard Vincent presented to me—"Captain" was the only word I caught—a square, dark little man in a uniform only a shade redder than his face, who offered his arm in a predestined sort of way and took me on a regular Cook's tour of all the great rooms. When I found that he spoke almost no English I was aghast, but said to myself, "Let me like a soldier fall!" and brought out all the French I knew. Our guardian angel must have inspired J. and me to reread *The Dutch Republic* on our long trip from Galveston to Bremen. I was fresh on the historical subjects of the pictures and tapestries, and the Captain and I parted an hour later with mutual thankfulness, and respect, I hope, but not before he had brought me back to the buffet and fed me on engaging little sandwiches and champagne. I did not realize the honor of being escorted by the "Captain of the King's Guard" until my mentor, Mrs. Roosevelt, told me today with obvious pride. "Belgium's Capital" was not gathered there—the female portion of it is largely out of town at this season—but there were numbers of distinguished men, with decorations to indicate, from all over Europe, and some picturesquely dressed women. Here as at home the provincial woman seems timid about evening dress, and there were many dark stuffy frocks and not a few bonnets. My Norwegian friend was one of the stuffiest and was scandalized by a beautiful Swedish girl in a brilliant national costume that delighted everyone else. Mrs. Bartholdt had explained to me that she "could not wear low neck" because her father was "a very strict church member," so she was quite ready for Wednesday night prayer meeting.

September 6

The real highlight of the conference, and the most dramatic historical incident that most of us will ever witness, was last night at the "raout" given by the municipality of Brussels at the Hôtel de Ville. Outside, every arch and turret was gay with electric lights, but twentieth-century illumination cannot cope with the gloomy vastness of medieval interiors. The vestibule and stairs were dim and solemn, and for me crowded with a company of ghosts more real than the living people—poor Egmont and Horn, Margaret of Parma, the lean and cruel Alva, William the Silent breaking his heart for his "poor people," and such swarms of knights and ladies, heretics and persecutors that when the Burgomaster, in a costume rich with medieval signs of office, held out his hand to welcome us, he only seemed another of that gray company. Not quite all the three thousand guests had arrived, so we lingered in the large room overlooking the entrance and were talking to the Boumans and Sir Howard Vincent when Senator Houzeau de la Haie came up, his sweet old face illumined with pleasure, and calling for silence, read from a telegram in his hand that peace had been agreed upon at Portsmouth! The band had stopped playing, and there was an instant's stillness, and then it was as if the company had been electrified. They did not exactly cheer, but they exclaimed, they laughed, shook hands, and the Europeans embraced and kissed one another. It was so utterly unexpected that it seemed too dramatic to be true. Everyone expressed admirable Christian sentiments, and I hope they were all as glad as they professed to be, but I could not help a little cynical incredulity when I thought how much to the interest of Europe it might be to have Russia crippled. The Americans had a superior tone: "Of course our President never fails," etc. Sir Howard hoped it was true, but gave the best possible reasons why it could not be—"It was not yet three o'clock in Portsmouth," and I would see. He wanted peace, I believe, sincerely, but he didn't expect it, and he likes to feel that he is in the secrets of the great powers. He was not quite himself the rest of the evening.

Antwerp

Yesterday at Ghent we said good-by to all our pleasant friends after the happiest, most informal and carefree day of the conference. The Russo-Japanese peace has lightened every heart, and the Belgians are so gay, anyway. Under the guidance of Burgomaster Braun and other jolly Gantois, we almost romped through towers and dungeons and the stock sights, and ended at a banquet in the Hôtel de Ville where the mirth was fast and furious. Perhaps it was our sheer frivolity that saved an unpleasant situation. Mr. Bartholdt had asked J. to take his place at the speakers' table and speak for the United States—a difficult thing to do on short notice, but the happy discovery that the room was the same in which our treaty with England was signed after the War of 1812 gave him a text and he did well. After that I lost interest in the speeches. I was a long way off with a merry party of English and Belgians and did not notice when the time came to drink the toast to King Leopold. My glass was empty when old Mr. Cremer addressed me from a distant seat, and said, "Mrs. Slayden, I see that you are displaying your usual good sense." Unaware that I was displaying sense of any kind, I asked, "In what way?" and he said, "Why, in refusing to drink the health of that filthy old beast." I recalled the crime of lèse-majesté, and also the dungeons of Ghent, and saw myself shut into one with only the Englishman for company, but the Belgians were opportunely deaf and nothing came of it.

I shall miss Mr. Cremer. Not many people are at once so fine and simple. We had many pleasant talks, and he always speaks of himself as "a workman." Though he received the Nobel Prize last year as founder of the

Interparliamentary Union, he shows no elation, only hope for what the I.P.U. may do for humanity. He told me that the medal "weighed a pound and cost twenty of 'em." He is so poor—Mr. Stanhope tells me his income has never been more than $2,000 a year—that I cannot help regretting his giving all the prize money to the Union.

London, September 11

How fortunate it is that we forget the ugly phases of travel! Fancy retaining a vivid recollection of a September morning at Liverpool Street Station with a London fog through which the people moved, as Carlyle said "like spectral flies in a spectral glue-pot."

But somewhere the sun is shining. Our English friends, as they themselves would say in a similar case, are being "f-rightfully kind" to us, and we have many pleasant things ahead. Tomorrow evening we dine with Mr. Cremer at the Liberal Union Club. He writes, "Our party will be small, but *very* select. Madison is ill, but Mr. Stanhope will join us. Will you allow me the pleasure of showing you over the Houses of Parliament tomorrow? I will meet you at three o'clock at the Palace Yard entrance."

September 14

The trip through the Houses was a rapid-fire performance just tantalizing. So many things we wanted to see, Abbey's pictures for instance, we passed in a hand gallop. No doubt our dear big Capitol has less of history and mystery, but it has space, and sunshine, and unafraid folk. You can stroll through it and enjoy the pictures of the Battle of Lake Erie, Lincoln's Cabinet of bearded ladies, and Trumbull's three-handed girl and six-toed Indian without being treated like a suspicious character.

The dinner was jolly and simple. I sat between my two partners, Mr. Cremer and Mr. Stanhope, the only woman with eight men. There was some good talk, the usual speeches about "the festive board" of course, interrupted by "Hear, hear" when pretty things were said about England and America's undying love for one another. My contribution at Mr. Cremer's earnest request was apropos of some old statesman's eleventh-hour conversion to the cause of world peace.

King David and King Solomon led very wicked lives.
Their goings on were awful with their various kinds of wives.
But when old age approached them, they felt some horrid qualms,
So King Solomon wrote the Proverbs, and King David wrote the Psalms.

We didn't see Mr. Cremer again. A note from him today says he was caught in a heavy rain and missed us at Paddington Station. He sent some little presents about which he spoke with deep feeling, and J. and I are touched at his selecting us, of all his friends, to give such close personal possessions. He sends J. a cane made by "an old friend, a workman, and Member of our International League, from a piece of the training ship 'Eurydice' that went down with nearly three hundred boys within a mile of the Isle of Wight." To us both he sent two exquisite little Crown Derby cups bought at the factory thirty years ago when he spent a rare vacation in a walking tour. He and his wife used them for their coffee until her death not long ago. He asks, "Will Mr. and Mrs. Slayden accept them as a little token of my great regard for them both?" The tenderness and delicacy of this great little man "in his simplicity sublime" goes to my heart and compels me to walk humbly.

We are disappointed that we cannot accept an invitation from Mr. Stanhope and his wife, the Countess Tolstoi, to visit them at Dingley. Her note was kind but stately; his, like himself, full of warmth and gaiety. "We shall of course send to meet you, and not be alarmed at any amount of American baggage. On Monday we can do Warwick Castle. I am coming to dine with you in London tomorrow. How nice it would be if we could all come back together."

Sir Howard Vincent writes from Bad Ems to J.: "The rain brought down by the Bartholdt oration has continued until today. Alas! That I am not there to show you and Mrs. Slayden that London and not Texas is your home. The bright talk and bright face of Mrs. Slayden will remain among the pleasantest recollections of the Peace Conference." How warmly hospitable English people are! I wonder if it isn't a habit of mind induced by the confidence of good service in their homes? I am just as instinctively hospitable, but my invitations are all sicklied o'er with a pale cast of doubt as to whether my servants—most uncertain of mortals—will give us three meals a day.

On the 16th we sail for Galveston on a frightfully unpleasant-looking boat.

CHAPTER TEN

1906

January 24

A New Year's letter from our good friend Philip Stanhope says, "I have read with infinite interest and pleasure Mr. Duval's book *Early Times in Texas*. Times have changed, of course, but I should like to see Texas again. I had only a glimpse twenty-five years ago. We are in the midst of a general election, in which, however, I have no active part, as I have been raised to the other House, and you will find me changed in name to that of Lord Weardale of Stanhope, but not in any other respect. *Mes hommages à madame."*

As if out of habit, he signs his old name, and I know the title will not change him, but it will worry me when we meet again. I have that incorrigible American diffidence about titles. Our own Texas brevet of colonel is the only one that comes trippingly to my tongue.

We are having a visit from Bishop Johnston of West Texas, which would be an unmixed pleasure if my cook had not taken occasion to make the corn bread he lives on the very worst we ever had. I have invited to a tea party people he said he wanted to meet and some who have said they wished to see him, the Hales among them. Dr. Hale is a great admirer of our bluff old soldier-bishop whose prayer for peace was discussed at the first Hague Conference. He has asked him to take his place and pray for the Senate one day next week.

February 7

The President is always devising new ways to uplift and manage us. His latest fancy, to create the office of "Commissioner of Social Relations" for his friend "Jimmy" Reynolds, is getting a lot of ridicule from the papers.[1] Miss Hale is giving me a chance to meet Mrs. Reynolds at tea, where I hope to guess what Jimmy is and perhaps find out what are the duties of a position that no one is able to define.

Miss Hale writes: "Mrs. Reynolds is the wife of the new Commissioner on—what do they call it?—Social Relations in the District, I believe. Her appearance suggests the relations prevailing at teas and dinner parties, but in reality they are of a much more serious sort, the condition of the poor, schools, and so on. My dear Eliza Orne White, whose books you may know, is one of my oldest friends, and I want them both to know you."

I shall have to refresh my memory of Miss White's books though I used to enjoy them.

March 28

Anne Warner French, author of the Susan Clegg Stories, and I established a heart-to-heart intimacy almost at first sight. It was "Anne" and "Ellen" in an hour. I really like her but would enjoy her more if she were better balanced. She is so intense—often about nothing at all—that I feel as if she were burning up her scrap of a body in its fantastic clothes before my very eyes. The wet blankets I throw over her don't put her out one way or another. Her husband may be as black as her fancy paints him, though I doubt it as I see more of her powers of imagination. Even so, it would be better for her to stay with him awhile—during Lent, for instance—and get wound down, or even "called down" occasionally. A husband, even if not a model, has a steadying effect on a woman, abbreviating her flights and keeping her feet on the earth though her head may be in the clouds.

There is something elfin about Anne. Her eyes are big and round, her skin and hair very dark. As she strings her paradoxes together, her whole tiny body quivering with mischief, it seems as if she might at any moment fly away singing

> *Merrily, merrily shall I live now,*
> *Under the blossom that hangs on the bough.*

If she kept to the standard of "Susan Clegg," her name might live among the best American humorists, but she writes too much. She has a fatal facility in writing, does her voluminous magazine work without a typewriter, and challenges me, a new-found friend, to a correspondence with a letter of twelve pages and a short story of three sheets as a postscript. There

[1] James Bronson Reynolds, lawyer and social reform leader, had been appointed by the President as adviser on municipal affairs in the District of Columbia.

is not a blot, an erasure or an abbreviation, thirty lines to a page, and so fine that her pen might be a hummingbird's quill. And alas! my answer will look as if I had written it with shoe polish and a toothbrush. I gave a tea for her that had two unexpected features—one, her mounting the little landing on the hall stairs and reading two short stories that made each particular hair of my modest company to stand on end; and the other I think could not have happened anywhere but in Washington. A newspaperwoman whom I barely know by sight came early and uninvited. She took possession of the company, introduced herself and other people, pointed out things of interest in the rooms, and was so aggressively at home that Mrs. Gregg slipped in from the dining room to ask, "Who is the strange lady receiving with us?" Of course I was helpless then, but later I sent her a note saying that I hoped she would not make use in her newsletters of my small party for a personal friend, for when I wanted my affairs reported I would *invite* someone to do it. There was no answer but she saved her material so cleverly I almost forgave her. Her next syndicated letter told of a tea for Anne Warner, described the house, endowing it with "palms and floral decorations, and spacious rooms," gave the names of distinguished people present—the usual society stuff—but skillfully contrived not to say whose house it was. I wrote Anne about it, and she replied—she always replies in the most incredibly short time: "Be gentle with newspaperwomen. I used to snub them, and now one is a book reviewer, and says that Susan Clegg is the coarsest creation foisted on the public for years!"

My dearly loved Mrs. Rixey called for help yesterday—one of the exigencies of Congressional life—a formal dinner on hand and an important constituent dropping in unexpectedly to stay for a few days. She said, "I need you more than anyone else. I am sick and cannot *talk*." For that fling at my besetting sin I should have refused, but I went and had a good dinner and a pleasant time, and some mixed emotions at sight of a Virginia congressman with a long, colored "four-in-hand" tie obscuring the front of his perfectly proper evening shirt. I wish he had come from the West, or even from farther south. J. is so glad it was a Virginian.

April 15

The cornerstone of the new House Office Building, Uncle Joe Cannon's great conception, was laid yesterday to the sound of the rolling drums and much oratory. The Marine Band and the Engineers' tried to drown one another out, and Teddy laid down the law more emphatically than ever. It will be a magnificent addition to the plaza, and most of the congressmen expect it to facilitate their work, though habit compels them to make vocal protest against "that awful squandering of the people's money."

Many a congressman's wife whose husband has an office at home will rise up and call Uncle Joe blessed. I never get my small establishment in order for company that a truck doesn't rumble up to the door and one or more big porters—sometimes very rough and insolent—come in with dusty sacks of documents and garden seeds. Then rugs must be taken up, furniture moved, and servants mollified as they mop and brush away the marks of muddy feet. I am sorry for the dear people who must pay a few millions for the building, but am I not one of them?

April 24

Last night I had a comical experience, or it would have been if I had had one sympathetic soul with whom to exchange a wink. Miss Virginia Miller, the most toploftical of F.F.V.s—hasn't she the blood of all the Lees and Washingtons?—asked me to give her and the Society of Old Washingtonians "that most charming talk on your visit to Spain." If she had asked me to walk a tightrope for their delectation, the urge of my Virginian blood would have made me try it, but if I had known how old "old Washingtonians" were, or how volubly they slept, I wouldn't have accepted so lightheartedly. The assembly in the high, ill-lighted ballroom of the Rochambeau was like one of those ghostly scenes in Maeterlinck's plays, twenty or thirty very old ladies feeling their way about, talking of their symptoms and their ancestors. At last they were seated in a wide half circle of large, soft chairs while poor little I stood with my back to the wall to "speak my piece." The room was warm and the sound of my voice evidently the last touch of comfort they needed. One by one they fell asleep while I became almost hysterical wondering what I should do if not one of them was awake when I finished. But Miss Virginia was game, *blood will tell*. She blinked bravely through it, and her cordial thanks waked the others. They coughed, wiped their eyes with ancestral point-lace handkerchiefs, straightened the colonial miniatures on their fichus, and assured me that they had enjoyed themselves so much. They did, I am sure, but I had the most fun.

Lake Mohonk, New York

We rode here from New Paltz with the Jackson Ralstons to attend the annual Conference on International Arbitration. There is a great crowd in which the distinguished people are submerged, even Cardinal Gibbons' red hat bobbing up only a little above the others. Slept all afternoon and dressed in white princess frock for supper which was announced at six o'clock by a bugle that set the wild echoes flying from the theatrical crags above the lake. It is good scenery in miniature, the little bridges and summer houses and other artificialities making it seem like a stage set for an opera. Later the sunset over the Catskills was far too grand to leave for the eloquence outpouring in the auditorium, but there was no escape. Bartholdt was backing and filling, trying to explain the apparent disparity between his votes in Congress and his talks at arbitration meetings. J., called on unexpectedly, was almost as frightened as I, but he did himself proud, and I unlocked my fingers and breathed freely as the approval and interest of the company became evident. His talk was alive and sincere, which could not be said of many of those that followed, and he has a real genius for knowing when to stop. We sat late in the smoking room having a pleasant talk with Colonel Church and Oscar Straus, and listening to old General Wilson, who has known everyone worthwhile in England and America. He showed us a ring in which he had entwined the hair of George Washington, Alexander Hamilton, Napoleon, Wellington, Lincoln, and Grant, and accounted quite reasonably for his possession of it. I wondered how those worthies would have endured getting their heads so close together in life. We had a heavenly night's rest with the stillness of the lake and hills enfolding us.

The morning session could hardly have been held anywhere but here, and under the management of our Quaker host, Mr. Smiley. He opened it with a psalm, we sang "Lead, Kindly Light," and our giant bishop, Mc-Vickar, said the Lord's prayer and some collects. Cardinal Gibbons followed with a sweet, human plea for peace and arbitration, and a Unitarian preacher drew a clever picture of what the English dreadnought would be doing in case of our getting into a foreign war.

The $10 million cruiser is the theme of many of the speeches though no names are called, all criticism of the Administration being barred "by order of the management." Oh, canny Mr. Smiley! Many of the speakers urged an enlarged army and navy, and preparedness for war, and a sincere desire for peace and arbitration did not impress me as the dominant note of the meeting. Later I found that J. and Mr. Ralston agreed with me.

The Cardinal is a lovable old gentleman, more truly Christian and tenderhearted, I think, than intellectual. His frequent quotations from the poets are trite and not always correct, but he knows his Bible. He wore his robe of glorious moiré silk, and laid his red hat on the table as indifferently as if it had been a golf cap. I have seen many a small-town clergyman more conscious of his ecclesiastical importance.

June 1

Oh, what a mixture of sweet and bitter this Congressional life is! This is a campaign year, and if J. doesn't sit tight at home, some other worthy Texan might get his place—there are always plenty of them ready and waiting—but the Interparliamentary Union meets in London in July, and such alluring letters are urging us to come. Mr. Cremer writes:

It having been practically decided that the next Hague Conference will be held in May 1907, the British Group will hold the I.P.U. conference this year in London, with the view of shaping the program to be considered at The Hague.

Our government is quite sympathetic; has promised a subsidy, and we look forward to a splendid gathering, which, of course, will not be complete without the presence of Mr. and Mrs. Slayden. We hope to have a goodly gathering from the U.S. Congress. We are also trying to get a representative from the newly founded Russian Parliament, the Duma.

To think of actually knowing some members of the Duma, that triumph over czarism and tradition, of London and the meetings in Westminster Hall, and the clever people we would meet. How proud I am of the way they like and appreciate J. and how I enjoy being the tail to his kite! But, alas, we must fix our minds upon the district, and the opposition of "the city ring" which never heard of the Duma, and would "guess" that the I.P.U. was something like a Shriners' convention. Parochial-mindedness is the worst enemy of any congressman who aspires to serve his country as well as his bailiwick.

June 25

Charles Francis Adams' article in the *Century*, "A Reflex Light from Africa," is like another millstone on the necks of those who are losing hope of solving the bitter negro question. J. wrote to Mr. Adams and had this reply:

I this morning received your favor of the 21st, which, it is needless to say, I read with considerable interest. In it you exclaim—"But what are we to *do*?" The same question has reached me from a good many quarters. It was put to me last evening in two columns and a half in the Boston *Evg. Transcript*. I have never met the writer of this communication, the temper of which was excellent, but today I felt moved to write him a reply. I enclose you a copy. It is not so long as to weary you, and it covers the whole ground so far as I am able to cover it. The other letter, a copy of which I enclose, addressed to Prof. Kelly Miller, you may take the trouble also to look over. The two together set forth the solution of the problem so far as I have been able to approximate a solution.

I freely confess the progress thus far made is like the progress apt to be made in a committee of the whole;—"the committee rose and reported progress."

I remain, etc.

Charles F. Adams

J. asked Mr. A. if he might publish the letters, and he answers:

"I have no objection to your printing them. My sole object in writing the *Century* article, which led to your first letter to me, was to stimulate discussion. The subsequent letters were in exactly the same line. . . ."

They are tremendously interesting but too long for me to copy more than a few extracts, giving the general drift and his conclusions which are to the last degree inconclusive, hopeless. This to Kelly Miller, professor of mathematics at Howard University:

Your contribution deserves most respectful consideration. The race problem in this country is one of the largest magnitude and the greatest complexity. . . . Philanthropy has nothing to do with it; the feeling of common humanity has nothing to do with it, the patronizing spirit which would raise an oppressed race has nothing to do with it. It requires matter-of-fact, cold, scientific, historical investigation.

With my present lights, it [the race problem] seems to me insuperable. . . . That the African can be assimilated to the white American even partially is yet to be proved. That he should ultimately be absorbed into the American is scientifically most undesirable. . . . The result would be a bastard and mongrel race. The process would be in its result good neither for the white nor the black. . . . Now, if the African had anywhere in the world evinced a self-sustaining and self-developing power, the solution of the problem would be comparatively easy; but such is not the case. There is no instance of it in Africa, the home of the race; and Haiti, San Domingo and Jamaica are not encouraging. . . .

When some years ago Mr. John Morley, statesman and author, was here, he remarked that he considered our race problem as on the whole approaching as nearly as anything conceivable to the insoluble.

Frisco train, Indian Territory, November 15

The last days at home always try our souls and make us wonder if the game of Congress is worth the candle. No doubt a brief rest will restore our taste for it, but today there is just heartache at leaving family and friends, and the physical weariness of doing the myriad things polite or politic or both that have to be done at the last moment. Yesterday there was a big, jolly luncheon at the Golsteins' and an equally gay dinner at Reagan Houston's which we left to come to the train. All night it was too hot to sleep, and at Dallas this morning there was raging wind carrying clouds of hot dust. Indian Territory appears to be burning up, forest fires on both sides of the track, and the cars scorching hot and filled with smoke. What must the engineer and fireman be suffering if it is like this in the Pullman. It is a gorgeous spectacle as night falls, rings of fire high up around invisible mountains, trees blazing to the very top, and a wild wind whirling showers of sparks.

The smoke is too dreadful to admit of reading, so I have been listening to the talk around me. Two women in the next section are discussing Christian Science, amicably, of course, because they are "perfectly in rapport." One had been so ill that she "did not know her environments," but she sent for her healer and in fifteen minutes was "calm and tranquil." I wish he was on this train. Because of her "mortal mind" she has not completely "overcome error." Her mind doesn't impress me as being of the insuperable order, either, but she must "conquer it someday," for "really, all the *best* people, the very nicest people in Joplin, Missouri, are in science." I like better the sweet stillness of an old lady near them in drab Shaker dress and bonnet, sitting with slightly bowed head and closed eyes, clasping a little black Testament in her withered hands. I don't think she is "in science," but I could easily think of her in heaven.

St. Louis

Missing connection here was pleasant, though J. had to go on to Chicago. Mrs. Jackson came for me and we paddled home in the rain, both, I think, talking at once. She first took a car going exactly the wrong way and excused herself on the ground of heredity—the usual scapegoat—because her father (Senator Vest) after thirty years in Washington only knew his way "from home to the Capitol and back, and always took a cab for that." I am glad that two people as clever as she and the old Senator lack the sense of locality as hopelessly as I do. The compass in my head, if there is one, has no preference for any point. When I go indoors, streets and buildings seize the opportunity to turn around; and as for hotel corridors, they are broad ways to lead me to destruction. J. has an irritating infallibility about directions. I never saw him lost but once, and that was in Tangier where an alley cat might have been puzzled. When I go in the wrong direction, he doesn't stop, but calls back, "It is twenty-five thousand miles that way."

Mrs. Jackson's home is sweet; Philistine, no doubt, the high artists would call it, but so comfortable, and with an atmosphere of old-fashioned religion that goes with mixed furniture, and is rarely found in houses "done" in dull greens, art glass, and dim religious Copley prints. One of the little books of piety on the "candle stand" by my bed restored my soul before breakfast this morning.

November 28

I am still haunted by regrets that we could not go to London this summer, but, no doubt, our going would have defeated J. for Congress. How strange that even in an enlightened community like San Antonio an appreciable number of people resent their representative's participation in anything out of Texas, even out of the district. They don't realize that he must deal with all matters that promote our commerce and friendly relations with other countries, and that it is his moral duty to inform himself so as to work and act intelligently.

Mr. Cremer writes: "At the Conference lots of people enquired after both you and your wife, expressing great regret that you were not present. I the more regretted your absence because of the numbers attending, the historic building in which it was held, and the whole proceedings of such an extraordinary character."

It must have been a great sight, the Mother of Parliaments with so many of her offspring around her, but Count Apponyi disputed England's claim to having the eldest self-governing body. These sentences struck me in his address and I can imagine the fire and grace with which he made his point: "No heart animated by the spirit of liberty can think of it without experiencing an almost religious emotion. . . . I represent a parliament of which the destinies have been less brilliant, but of which the age is as great and the youth as indestructible." It is hard to realize that he means Hungary, that fickle and inconstant firebrand among nations.

House Gallery, December 3

The opening of Congress is rather dingy. It always is for the short term. Defeated members regard the last three months listlessly and fewer men bring their families, so our gallery is less gay and sociable. Mrs. Mann of Illinois and I came up together, and on the House floor we saw a man carrying the mace, bird downward, as if it had been an umbrella. It rather shocked me to see the emblem of the majesty of our government swung about so familiarly, but it proves that we are still a republic. The floor of the House suggests a hotel lobby, but the ladies from the country who usually swarm about the members' seats and the Speaker's desk are conspicuously absent. I can see an imposing group of Texans, Judge Seth Shepard, Judge Hare, Slayden, Burgess, Henry, and Stephens, all over six feet. John Wesley Gaines's ambrosial curls, longer and more ambrosial than ever, are a striking contrast to "Nicky" Longworth's shining bald head, a target for opera glasses. Everyone around is whispering, "There's Alice's husband." I wonder if he will ever live down that title. J. says he will, as he is a really high-class man. He likes him very much. Alice herself strode into the President's gallery (she always strides) dressed in a light-brown suit, long white gloves, hat with a white cock's breast and plume, and a big red bow at her throat. John Sharp Williams is as unkempt as ever; his whole figure drawls like his voice.

As the hands of the clock touched twelve, Uncle Joe tripped briskly up to the chair, the Sergeant at arms raised the mace to the pedestal, every man went to his seat, and the House was in order. Mr. Couden prayed a longish prayer and after a few minutes of vociferous talking, the gavel fell with a peremptory thump, the roll call was ordered, and routine work began.

December 23

Yesterday it rained, hailed, snowed, and beamed sunshine by turns, and Aunt Lucy said, "Dey say dat de Lord is de same yistiddy, today, an' forever, but He sho is changeable about de weather."

CHAPTER ELEVEN

1907

The President revels in sound and fury. Failing the roar of cannon or Tillman speaking in the Senate, he turns on the Marine Band and at the diplomatic reception, the pounding of drums and braying of brass horns nearly gave us concussion of the brain. Many people stood with their ears covered while they watched T.R. shaking hands with those ahead and saying, "Dee-lighted," like Job's war horse that "paweth in the valley . . . and saith among the trumpets, Ha ha!"

There were more plainclothes men than usual. Perhaps they were to guard Mrs. Cornelius Vanderbilt, whose diamonds blazed like a prairie fire. She is rather a pretty woman with reddish hair, but a cold smile and hard eyes. Her dress, what there was of it, was cloth of gold in the Empire fashion as most very elegant dresses are just now, and as she and the Persian Minister stood together they were a startling pair. He is tall and thin and wore a red fez and a black robe embroidered all over with gold. His poor chest had caved in with the weight of jeweled decorations. The most conspicuous of them was a portrait, as big as a saucer, of his master, the Shah, who, we know since, was at that moment dying in Oriental splendor on a gilded throne in a room lined with mirrors and lighted by a myriad electric globes. Strange antechamber to the Valley of the Shadow!

There was another woman who represents as many millions as Mrs. Vanderbilt but did not wear the outward and visible signs of them, the wife of Senator Clark of Montana. She is small, timid and apologetic, and her clothes the triumph of a village dressmaker. Clark himself is so thin that in evening clothes he just seems the handle for his yellow mop of curly hair and whiskers. Someone said if you took away the whiskers and the scandal there would be nothing left of him, but, however he has used his money, he came by it honestly, which is more than is said of some other senatorial millionaires. And I know several people down in Virginia who have been saved from real want by his disinterested generosity.

The Vice-President and Mrs. Fairbanks give the only entertainment at which the Senate and House are asked to meet one another, and it is the only big official affair that seems to give real pleasure. Maybe it is because the supper is so good! There are few people with souls so dead that they don't glow a little over creamed oysters, boned fowls and aspic, and real honest punch in place of grape-juice and W.C.T.U. concoctions. The house is large, and spacious, not decorated nor cluttered up with furniture, and one moves about with ease. Last night the President and Mr. and Mrs. Longworth came in late making a little stir, but without parade or formality, and today the papers are gurgling over it as something astonishing. "The President came and walked about in the most democratic manner," etc. What did they expect? If he had walked in on his hands or been borne on a golden palanquin with slaves to fan him with peacocks' tails, they might have remarked on it. When did it become amazing for an American President to behave like an American gentleman?

January 23

Dr. E. E. Hale sat in his big chair and talked to Mrs. Butler, Mrs. Philip Hale and me. The rooms were full, but Miss Nellie's "Dear Papa, here is so-and-so" failed several times to divert him from his theme. He told the story, for which he has good authority, of the influence Bishop Johnston's prayer for peace had on the Kaiser during the Hague Conference. The American Secretary showed it to Hohenlohe, who took a copy to the Kaiser to show how earnestly the Americans desired peace when the Bishop of West Texas, "a country where the wolves bid the foxes good night (how German!) had written this prayer for the use of his people." A few days later the Kaiser's covert antagonism to the Czar faded away.

As I was leaving Dr. Hale called me back to send his regards to J., and said, "Tell him to go on fighting the battleships. I detest this draw poker policy of going nations one better." He laughed when I said, "The President doesn't let his right hand know what his left hand does. He blesses peace conferences with one and builds battleships with the other."

Every winter I have a reception for the Texas schoolgirls, but their numbers increase so rapidly that I shall soon have to get a larger house or "hire a hall."

It is a lot of trouble to get their names and send an invitation to each school. Knowing only a few by sight I instructed "Lonzo"—Mrs. Gregg's superb Texas butler borrowed for the occasion—to ask their names and announce them. It was a new bit of style to Lonzo and he was delighted, but it was too new for the young ladies, and they refused to co-operate. They looked at him blankly and passed on, and after a while he slipped up to me and said, "I ax 'em dey names, Mrs. Slayden, but dey won't tell 'em to *me*." They trooped in bubbling with pleasure or stiff with self-consciousness—some with paint and feathers like their predecessors of the plains, but more, I am proud to say, with clean, intelligent faces, well dressed and sweet mannered.

It was a dreadfully difficult party to entertain. They had a tendency to "bunch" around the few young men I had corralled to help me, and they stayed bunched, charmed I never so wisely. They ate pyramids of sandwiches and swamped themselves with chocolate, and each one as she left assured me that she had had "a perfectly lovely time," or "the time of her life"—the new slang phrase that threatens to supersede perfectly lovely.

I wonder if teachers in these schools advertised as "fashionable" or "finishing" and boasting of the "social advantages" never advise the girls what to say on certain occasions or how to avoid such parrot phrases. Sometimes I wonder if they are taught at all, there are so few surface indications. I am old-timey enough to think some elegance of speech as important as long gloves and trains for the evening about which, I understand, they are carefully instructed.

Certainly the methods by which some of the schools give them "social advantages" are abominable. I have received—and no doubt other congressmen's wives have also—lists of the girls from the district with a note, which is almost a threat, saying that unless they are shown some social attention their fathers will be told of it. Hospitality on compulsion is not to my taste and it makes me so angry I can hardly force myself to invite them, but Mrs. Gregg and I, with fine impartiality, ask all of them from the Panhandle to the Gulf. I know so many dignified, well-bred parents in Texas who would be sick with shame if they knew how their daughters were being dragged about in flocks to any official house that is open regardless of whether or not they have a claim on the hostess. Not long ago my little drawing room was awkwardly crowded, and my proper guests driven away by an inroad of young ladies from South Dakota, marshaled by a raw-boned woman who had better have been roping cattle. This was, I think, an extreme case for people not higher up officially than we are. I understand that the Cabinet hostesses find it a serious problem. The schools do not *give* the girls social advantages, but show them how to *take* them.

February 21

It is really tragic to record the absolute rout of the delegation from the Federated Women's Clubs assembled to prevent the seating of Senator Smoot of Utah.[1] Terrible as an army with banners, they marched to the gallery and sat in impotent silence while the Senate "shook the foundations of the American home" by seating a Mormon. Applause or expression of disapproval is unheard of in the Senate gallery, so the poor ladies marched down again breathing out threats and slaughter against these men who had "betrayed their country." I heard one rolling woman's-club voice declaring, "It was treason, the rankest treason!" With the ignominious defeat in the Senate, with Roosevelt complaining that woman suffrage has not purified politics in Colorado, and with Grover Cleveland advocating a marriage qualification for the suffrage for men and women, we pretty maids hardly know where we are going this week.

Harvey's Restaurant, March 7

A stern regard for truth prevents my saying that I never had such a dreadful time and never was as tired in my life. I have just this sort of time and am just as tired twice every year—when we come in December and go away in spring or summer—and the average citizen thinks that congressmen's wives are being "carried to the skies on flowery beds of ease."

An Ioway lady camped on my trail and compelled me to put my house into a state of unprecedented tidiness at breakneck speed. I was rewarded by having her look me critically up and down, and say, "Well, for a Southern woman, I say for a Southern woman, you have more snap and

[1] On February 20, 1907, the Senate voted, 42 to 28, not to unseat Reed Smoot, Mormon senator from Utah. The effort to oust him was based on the allegation that he, as an Apostle of the Mormon Church, had taken an oath "which implied disloyalty to the United States." Though Smoot himself was not accused of the practice, there was also objection to him on the ground that his church countenanced polygamy.

go than any I ever-r saw." The secret of it was I wanted to rent the house and get away, she offered a fair rental and I snapped her up and went. Now, thank heaven! we are on our way to the train. Our lunch is fried oysters and coffee for J., smelts and beer for me, and they are both good. The snow is blinding outside, and I am shivering from sheer fatigue.

3:45 on train to New York

General Fred Grant has talked to me ever since we left Washington. He is one of the kindest of men, but I am so tired I could think of nothing but the pillow on the opposite seat. He has had charge of the military display at that fizzle, the Jamestown Exposition, and told me all about it, also about the Philippines. He has gone now to the smoker "to buzz old Slayden for a while." A woman near me has a lace veil of the latest style. It has deep black points and one runs up and makes her look as if she had a harelip. I hope I won't dream about it when I seize my pillow and go to sleep.

Piedmont, April 15

Such a nice jolly letter from Lord Weardale today:

My dear Mr. Slayden:

I have been waiting to write to you in order to send at the same time the official report of the London Conference. Alas, I am still unable to do so. Our excellent friend, Cremer, is not as young as he was. . . .

I cannot, however, wait longer to send you the note of introduction to Mr. Bryce[2] which contains all the bad things I would naturally say about Mrs. Slayden and yourself. You will find Bryce and Mrs. Bryce agreeable people. He is somewhat of a professor in manner, but a thoroughly reliable and able man, while she is a very amiable lady.

I am afraid you will not be coming to Europe this summer. There is no conference to tempt you, but you must, at all events, make up your minds to come in 1908 to Berlin.

You are having high old times in America with your President on the war path, but it looks as if you were beginning the presidential contest a bit early, for you will now have to keep it up until 1909.

I am fairly well, but *no* younger. Our friend Cremer has aged a good deal. He is, I believe, 79, but as shy as a lady about confessing it.

Please say everything and anything which is respectfully tender and which you will allow me to say to Mrs. Slayden, and believe me always to be, my dear Mr. Slayden,

Yours sincerely,
Weardale

[2] James Bryce, British Ambassador to the United States, 1907–1913.

Mr. Cremer's signature to a dictated note written at the same time as Lord Weardale's is sadly changed and wavering.

Dear Mr. Slayden,
    Lord Weardale is sending you a letter of introduction to Mr. Bryce. If it were customary for two men to sign such a letter, my name would have been added to his.
    I have reprinted a portion of your excellent speech in "the Arbitrator," and had space permitted I should have used more of it. Kind regards to Mrs. Slayden, the Merry Cricket (who has never been forgotten by the British M.P.s) and yourself.

Faithfully yours,
W. Randal Cremer

The "Merry Cricket" at my age! "Lord preserve me from becoming young when it is too late!"
    J. is too busy to enjoy the letters praising his arbitration speech, but I treasure them in my heart.

San Antonio, April 30

It was intensely hot when we came five days ago, but a wet norther brought the temperature down to 47 degrees, and I got into my best "tailor made" for a reception this afternoon, only to find I had worn the wrong thing. Invited by telephone, to "a very informal afternoon," I found the house elaborately decorated and lighted with multitudinous pink candles. A string band was doing its best to be heard above the din of a hundred voices. The hostess and the "honoree" (a new word much prized here) were in full evening dress, elaborate refreshments were dispensed by quite correct waiters, and withal—the hostess' own little son and daughter stood at the door holding silver card trays just like servants! My dark suit was looked at askance by my fine friends—something more glorious evidently being expected of "the lady from Washington" as many of them call me—and yet I felt so correct in it at receptions in Washington a month ago.

On train to Brownsville

We have been in Corpus Christi at a bankers' convention with gay asides of fish fries and lawn parties. It is such a serene, refined old place, conscious of its colonial dignity. I pray it may escape a "boom" and "boosters" with their "improvements" and loud vulgarity. As we left today we heard of a hailstorm in San Antonio doing frightful damage to glass and tiles and even to wooden houses. Here we have strong, raw sunshine, blue thunder clouds in the east, and a fresh wind whipping our faces through the car windows. It is my first trip over this new road. As far as we can see either way is a straight line of track with telegraph poles marching beside it. The rest is vast green pasture, a part of the great King Ranch, mesquite bush, wire fences, red cattle, and here and there reassuring tanks of clear water from the new artesian wells. They tell a story of how Mr. Kleberg wept when the wells gushed out and he thought of the age-long suffering of men and cattle in this drought-cursed country with water so near. Kingsville rose out of the prairie like a bed of mushrooms on a lawn, and we had a nice fresh dinner at the new King's Inn, set round with a nice new palm garden. Palms are getting acclimated all over Southwest Texas. I remember when there were only one or two in San Antonio, and now they are tiresomely frequent, such stiff, dry things giving neither shade nor greenery where both are so needed.

Brownsville, June 1

It was quite dark when we arrived last night and stepped out into a grove of willows with ghostly whitewashed trunks. There was a soft twanging of guitars, the smell of shuck cigarettes, and a murmur of sleepy Spanish around the station. In a dimly lighted street our picturesque old friend, Cobolini—Rockport fisherman, and eternal Garibaldino—loomed up, took our bags and escorted us ceremoniously to the Miller Hotel where we found a decentish room and a good breeze. This morning it doesn't seem such a lorn Mexican town as I thought. It is quite green and near our windows are two quaint papaya trees with necklaces of green fruit up under their chins exactly as they looked in the geography book.

J.'s object here is to see for himself the stage of the negro soldier outbreak that made Brownsville famous last August.[3] He wants to give a firsthand opinion in the Military Affairs Committee next winter, so we went thoroughly over the ground, examined the old barracks (nearly falling into the river), measured the distance, the direction of the shots from the wall they scaled, and were convinced beyond doubt that the colored guardians of our liberty planned and executed a nasty attack on the town.

Cobolini has sent me a pyramidical bouquet of Cape jasmine that

---

[3] On August 14, 1906, Negro soldiers at Brownsville rioted, resulting in death or injury to several citizens. After an army investigation President Roosevelt discharged every member of the three Negro companies involved although many informed persons felt that they had been provoked by local racial antagonism.

must weigh ten pounds. It won't sit up in the water pitcher, and I have nowhere else to put it. What am I to do with it when we go away tomorrow?

June 2

I sneaked off from the bouquet this morning before dawn, and in the musky,
tropical darkness, didn't Cobolini slip out of a black doorway to say
good-by and ask me where it was.

C. P. Díaz, June 27

One of the joys of coming to Mexico is that the moment you cross the
border it is as insistently and typically Mexico as if you were a thousand
miles in the interior—the same riot of color, crowds of men in striped
blankets, women in red skirts and blue rebozas, chocolate babies in pink
camisas or just nothing rolling in the dust around the man with a tray of
purple and yellow candy. The wail of kids pervades the air blended with the
familiar smell of mesquite wood, cigarettes and goats. Why do I love it all?
Was I once an Aztec princess? People who admit these atavistic yearnings
always claim to have been of the blood royal, so why not I? My little friend,
Keen Foo Wah, is here, but isn't as full of fun as she was at the mission
in Saltillo. She is studying Pekinese with an imported tutor, and when she
learns it she goes to Vassar, and then to China as a reformer. I asked what
reformation she planned, and she said in her artless, pidgin English, "Get
rid of emperor, make China republic, make Yuh Weh president." It sounded
so simple and easy as she outlined it, but remembering the fate of other
reformers in China I could almost see Keen's pretty little head with a
smile well bred, bowing three times to some Lord High Executioner, so I
begged her to stay where she was, and let China go unreformed a few
thousand years longer.

Kerrville, September, 1907

How little Eastern people comprehend the charm of the West, except the
largely artificial "wild West" of Roosevelt and melodrama. Washington
friends commiserate us for having to spend our summers in Texas but
would anyone who knew exchange it for the boardwalks and barkers of
the Jersey coast? Texas is so varied, its population so vivid and uncom-
monplace, at least in our part, and I always feed my imagination on
what it is to be in time. Outside the larger towns, which here as elsewhere
try to copy New York, social conditions are full of surprises. We are just
back from a Confederate reunion in a town that sent more men to the

Union than to the Confederate army. It is so Old Worldly that it was like a visit to Saxony. Fredericksburg even has a history and a birthday. It was settled on the 8th of May 1846 by a colony of Germans led by Baron von Meusebach. Discontented with kings and militarism at home, they bought the land from the Republic of Texas and with it the privilege of protecting themselves from the Comanches and Apaches around it.

Landing on the coast they brought their families and all they possessed across country in ox wagons, blazing their own trail, fighting Indians, and often suffering hunger and distress on the way. They also brought their songs and poetry, their flutes and horns, and even a piano or two. These stouthearted Teutons startled the wilderness with songs of Fatherland and danced when the camp afforded a piece of greensward. The story is a pretty one to hear from old Mr. Nimitz who, as a boy, dashed forward on his pony, the first to reach the site chosen for the town.

They were sustained by the love of freedom and the hope of material prosperity, and their faith has been amply justified. The county is playfully called "the Free state of Gillespie." There are no millionaires, no paupers and no delinquent taxpayers. They have kept their cheerful hearts, too, and singing and dancing prevail especially on Sunday. This, of course, is a scandal to their puritan neighbors, but they balance their nonobservance of unwritten Sunday laws by such scrupulous respect for the civil laws that their jail is empty and their criminal docket blank. In the Nimitz Hotel we propped our door open at night to get the breeze, and traveling about here for weeks I cannot remember having turned a key in a lock. Generally there is no key to turn.

We drove across the mountains, passing many picturesque family parties camping on their way to the reunion. Big white wagons were drawn to the side of the road, the women cooking supper over a blazing fire, while the men staked out the horses. Children and collies romped on the grass where they would all sleep safely with no shelter but blankets. Jokes and greetings were exchanged in broken English.

The white glow of electric lights guided us to the village, and when we arrived at midnight the hotel doors stood wide open and we had to wake the proprietor, who told us to go upstairs and take any room we liked. The big assembly hall had the oddest combination of public and domestic utilities. Past a stage with well-set scenery and two grand pianos we had a good view of the kitchen; and a prompter's box and a washing machine were in friendly proximity. Our severely clean bedrooms opened into the peanut gallery.

By daylight the town displayed one wide street nearly a mile long; big stone houses far apart with thick walls and small windows. Each had a well-kept garden where stout hausfraus sit under the trees and knit as their grandmothers did in Germany. In many yards there is a little stone or log cabin of the bitter pioneer days kept standing as a matter of sentiment. One of the unique features is the "Sunday house"—a substantial cottage where prosperous farmers bring their families to spend Sunday, going to the Lutheran or Catholic church in the morning and dancing the rest of the day in a beer garden.

There was more than a suggestion of German militarism in the flags, the brass bands and the resplendent mounted marshals that met the streams of visitors arriving in every sort of vehicle from a prairie schooner to an automobile. There was food in barbaric plenty from barbecue trenches, free to every comer.

But there is nothing sadder than a Confederate reunion. Among five or six thousand people there were only three hundred veterans, all of them old, most of them poor. As in the days of the Civil War, some had fine gray uniforms, the majority were in blue shirts and jeans trousers, but each wore proudly on his breast a picture of his old commander, Lee, Jackson, or Forrest.

Whether in jeans or uniforms they had the best of everything—the best places in the big green-brush arbor, at the fireworks, the pageants, the dances, and all absolutely free. The singing societies had learned the old war songs, and concerts and historic tableaux, wonderfully well done, were especially designed to please them.

Meant for a festival, it was too often a time for memory and for tears. As the veterans followed the national and Confederate flags carried side by side, many of them fell out of line, too feeble to go on. In the pavilion I watched a gaunt old grandmother with the austere, heroic face of the frontierswoman stand erect and unmoved through bursts of eloquence from the Governor and Senators Bailey and Culberson, but when the band played "Dixie" and men cheered the white head bowed over work-hardened hands, tears fell on her shabby black dress, and the strong old shoulders shook with sobs.

One ceremony of a reunion is the roll call of the dead, when the names of those who have died within the year are solemnly called three times. When thirty-five names had been called, the tension became unbearable. The chaplain, a skilled conductor of revivals, prayed fervently, and then exhorted the veterans to prepare to meet their God. In a fine dramatic voice he reminded them that their time was short, that many were past the threescore years and ten. He exclaimed, "The grass withereth, the flower fadeth" and called them by name, saying "Brother, will you be here next year?" Men who cheered as they rode with Pickett at Gettysburg and gaily followed Pat Cleburne into the jaws of death at Franklin sobbed; they shook hands and embraced each other. There would have been general hysteria if a woman had not struck a few chords on a piano and begun to sing "Nearer, My God, to Thee." Voice after voice took up the song until it rolled far beyond the pavilion and made the camp of merrymakers for a time one vast religious meeting. It relaxed the tension, but when they should have played "Dixie" to introduce the next speaker, even the jolly Teuton bandmaster felt it would be a false note, and played the solemn German "Salutation" instead.

In the evening the veterans danced, hobbling through quadrilles and reels with pretty girls who were only too proud to dance with them. They enjoyed talking with one another, dwelling on their victories and rarely referring to defeat or suffering, and best of all, treasuring no bitterness in their hearts toward anyone. Hatred, I believe, is exclusively the part of noncombatants.

A shaggy old mountaineer, pleased to find a compatriot, told me eagerly how he had been a scout for Jackson and Rosser, and "Could go over every foot of the Valley now in the dark." He had married in Texas, and never been prosperous enough to take his family back home. "But," he said, "I done the best I could for 'em." Calling up two bouncing daughters with red cheeks and black curls, he said, "This one is 'Stonewall Jackson' and this is 'Valley of Virginia.'" Could state pride go further?

At sunset after all the speeches had been made and the dust had subsided somewhat, a tired party of us was sitting in the flagstoned porch of the hotel when a gaily decorated float drove up with the Concordia Maennerchor in all the regalia dear to their hearts. They were big, blond-headed men and as they exchanged "Prosits" and drank their foaming flagons of beer the whole scene might have been labeled "Made in Germany." Later they sang for us the sweet and tender Volkslieder that German hearts and voices remember wherever they may make a home. It soothed and rested us to listen long after daylight had given place to burning stars. There is no twilight at this season.

The sun's rim dips, the stars rush out,
At one stride comes the dark.

Bellevue Hotel, Boston

This place is full of students and friends of Yale and Harvard who came to see the game yesterday in which Harvard was defeated. The elevator boy told us, "Ef they'd a been playin' croquet, they'd a been champeens."

Mr. Erving Winslow called before we went to breakfast, so we had to be excused, but he sent up a box of roses for me. I was sorry to miss him. I can only think of him as an embodiment of Anti-Imperialist League stationery and a fine, flowering handwriting through which I have known him for years. He was here again when we came back from service at Trinity.

He is pleasant to look at, tall, slender, and a little lame, just the refined, delicate type one would expect of a person so entirely altruistic. His talk was steady rather than incessant and always about his soul's desire, to free the Philippines. I forced in a few conventional remarks, but enough for him to report to his family that I was an Englishwoman! Dinner with them that evening was very pleasant, his handsome daughter-in-law doing the honors, and his son, a teacher at the "Tech," agreeable but not idealistic like himself. Judge Blount, who divides honors with J. at Faneuil Hall tomorrow night, was the other guest. I expected the big, florid, pompous type of Georgian, but instead he is a skinny, dry little man. He wore a long-tailed coat, light-gray trousers that didn't fit, a starched white vest of ancient cut, and a red bow tie. His voice was crackling and nervous as if he needed to relax mind and body.

He was a judge in the Philippines for some years and writes well on the subject. He talked well, too, and under a light banter of modesty managed to tell us some of his most vivid exploits—having twenty-one natives shot was one of them—and that he was thought to resemble Alexander H. Stephens.[4] I can't see why he is proud of it. A.H.S. was not much to look at, and I always suspect arrested development in a man who, with gray hair on his temples, is proud of being the counterfeit presentment of some dead and gone worthy.

Later

It rained furiously today but the Anti-Imperialists were undismayed and the audience at "Funnel" Hall was large enough to stimulate J. and the desiccated little Judge to their best efforts. They both spoke well. Afterwards a crowd came up to commend them and to meet me, and I am sure they were the choicest Bostonese, they looked so refined and talked so gracefully.

Washington

I am so tired of the Brownsville incident I wonder why I write about it. J. said in his speech, "It is chiefly important as a symptom," but it colors

[4] Congressman, Vice-President of the Confederacy, Governor of Georgia.

the talk in drawing rooms, and you hear it on the streetcars and between acts at the theater, and even from the pulpit. John Sharp Williams intruded it in his speech at the beautiful Lee Memorial service and was much criticized. It was a pity, for Justice Brewer's address had touched a high plane, calling Washington, Lincoln and Lee the greatest Americans. Williams brought us down with a thump.

J. tells me that Nicky Longworth had a twinkle in his eye when he asked him if he had received a copy of a song written by one of his (Longworth's) constituents, called "You Will Miss the Colored Soldier." It was sent by Longworth's care to ensure J.'s getting it and being made to feel bad about his bill to exclude negroes from the army. J. said that "missing the colored soldier" was exactly what he wanted, but he saw no prospect of the bill passing this session.

The front page of the song has a lurid picture of the negroes charging up San Juan Hill while the white men behind them are being shot all to pieces. The number of vile anonymous letters about the bill that come every day do make me uneasy, and I beg Mr. Harrison to keep the shutters of the office closed at night when he and J. are working there. The letters are full of threats.

CHAPTER TWELVE

1908

January

The longer we stay here the more I feel detached, an observer rather than a part of "Official Society" as it figures in the headlines. The families of congressmen of long service gradually find that because of their staying qualities they make their friends more among residents than official people. I dare not love a Congressional family, my fond gazelle is so likely to fade away in the next election. Charming people who meant so much to us in the nineties have vanished from our horizon, gone back to Oshkosh or San Francisco, or just Delaware, like the dear Irving Handys who raised the standard of wit, good looks and good breeding in the far-off nineties.

There are so many pleasant people, so many possibilities of a richly interesting society, and yet it falls far short. I am trying to think out a reason for it, to see why things are so.

First, I think it is because in the Congressional world we do not so much act as we are acted upon. Everything was this way before we came, and it would not become strangers and sojourners to defy the rules or try to change them. About the time you get bold enough to suggest innovations, you are likely to be relegated to the district and another take your place to go through the same experience.

And that makes a damnable iteration of each social season; every winter the same thing, nothing changed but the names and the clothes— and not always the latter. The Congressional salary upon which most of the Southern members, especially, depend does not admit of new frocks after a campaign summer. Mrs. Gregg is telling a story that recently when she appeared at a reception in an old gown she thought successfully disguised, I looked at her dreamily and said, "I *always* liked that dress." The Congressional calling season is at its height now, women whirling "like midges in the sun," getting nowhere, accomplishing nothing except making hundreds of calls, at least one half of which might just as well not be made.

Every afternoon the streets are crowded with cabs, big old four-seated hacks or queer little herdics that open at the back occupied by two or more women who, to judge by the faces, are on anything but pleasure bent. Now and again they stop and go into a house and come out so quickly that it seems impossible for them to have exchanged the regulation futilities with the people inside. It is a matter of pride and rivalry how many times you can go through this motion in an afternoon.

This "dance of death" is not just foolish love of going; it is the urge of the stern, unhumorous American conscience that dares not to think for itself, nor risk criticism by varying a hairsbreadth from the beaten track. These women believe it as much their duty to pay the calls as to pay their taxes. Before they come to Washington the idea is impressed upon them by syndicated "society" columns in the Sunday papers—which I believe have done more than any other one thing to standardize us and destroy the local charm of American society. We are just copy cats of New York and Washington without regard to climate, tradition, or conditions in our own parts of the country.

When the Congressman's wife gets here the hotel clerk, or even a new-found milliner or dressmaker, gives her a list of official days and persons that she *must* (not *may*) call upon. The hotels turn an honest penny by furnishing the carriages and make the list longer and more compelling. It comprises first the wives of justices of the Supreme Court, the Cabinet, the senators—if your husband is a member of the House—and whether in the Senate or the House, the wives of men whose service antedates your husband's. When they add to that the wives of foreign ambassadors and ministers, it results in a curious life and a still more curious perversion of the common-sense standards of good society. The callers are guided usually by the rank of those to be called upon, beginning, of course, with the Supreme Court, above which no true-born American looks for worldly eminence or governmental authority. Some do it geographically, taking certain streets or parts of town, but most of them take the Congressional Record, make an alphabetical list and try to go through it.

They keep their books with businesslike frankness. Mrs. Gregg, receiving with me one day, was trying to hand a cup of coffee to a brand new M.C.'s wife who was engrossed with a paper in her hand. Looking up from it she said, "Are you Representative Gregg's wife? Have I called on you?" and before Mrs. Gregg could answer, went on, "No, but I'm going to. You live on Corcoran Street. Are you at home?" Mrs. G.'s bright eyes twinkled at me as she said, "*Always*. Have you made many calls?" The lady ran her eyes over the list and answered, "Yes, two hundred and fifty-seven. I have forty-six more to make, though I've been calling quite assiduously. Soon I'll have a day at home. Ought to have a good crowd, don't you think?"

And when the day at home comes, what an occasion of tremulous excitement it is; what a putting to use of all the new ideas of cake and decorations that you have gathered in your rounds! In the hotels all the Congressional ladies receive together, and there is much sifting of questions of precedence and often heartburnings about who comes first in "the line." The scene is usually set in a vast gilded parlor furnished with many overfed velvet chairs and sofas in all colors. There is a glorious refreshment table, and in the three hours hundreds of people come, and, as Dr. Holmes so aptly describes it, "gabble, gobble, and git."

It is a little better in your own house with the touch of individuality in your own belongings, but the intellectual atmosphere is the same. There is a silver service if you possess one, or a rented Sheffield "set," or gleaming brass and copper like my own. The tables are pretty enough, with sandwiches and rainbow tinted cakes, strange candies and cherry bounce —if you aren't a prohibitionist. You have all the flowers you can afford, and the glow of pink-shaded candles envelops everything. At three o'clock, with a group of your best friends in their best clothes, and often a visiting lady constituent, who takes it as a great occasion, you stand and wait, rarely in vain, for a stream of *just women*. The crowd increases steadily, voices get higher and higher, there is laughter out of all proportion to the humor of the talk, and for three mortal hours or more there is a fine imitation of an uproariously good time.

About 7:30 they are all gone and "silence like a poultice falls to heal the blows of sound." The table is a litter of cake crumbs, leftover sandwiches and soiled teacups; the candles sputtering; the little pink shades scorched and brown. The chairs are at sixes and sevens about the rooms, the fire smouldering and untidy in the hearth. In my own case, I look around and wonder why I did it all. Aunt Lucy comes in, and says with a mixture of sympathy and contempt, "Ain't it time for you to rest after all dis racket? Go 'long to bed. I'll give Mr. Slayden his dinner." All night with nerves too tense for sleep I say, "Behold it is altogether vanity!" But custom is a force that science has never reckoned with, and the very next week—four in succession usually—I get up and do the same thing over again, as all the others do.

The reasons for the vapidity of these gatherings are several. The rooms are crowded and the seats few—Madam de Staël and Sydney Smith could not have sustained their reputations standing up with a shrieking crowd around them—and there are practically no men. Not that the men are so very much cleverer, but their presence does for some occult reason sharpen women's wits and compel them to talk less of the infinitely little. Many of their dearest ideals are actually antagonistic to men and men's plans and purposes.

J. never ceases to deplore his disappointment about the houris and sirens he was led to believe would be everywhere waiting to lure political secrets from him and bewitch him into voting for things he never intended to vote for. He finds a singular dearth of such fair ones. So far the only ladies who have waylaid him are Charlotte Smith, a grenadier of some fifty summers interested in woman's rights, and Dr. Mary Walker, a veteran of the Civil War who wears weird little trousers, high hat and Prince Albert coat, often finished off with a white crocheted shoulder cape. In spite of her manly garments she is the most pathetically feminine little figure. Her face is small and has a thousand wrinkles like the dolls we used to make of peanuts, her shoulders are narrow, and her hands almost shriveled out of sight. Not quite the figure to lead a politician astray.

March 16

J. has his social innings at dinner parties which he enjoys more than any other form of entertainment and the fact that I am quite frequently not included in the invitations does not distress him as it should. He has gone to one of them tonight at Secretary Root's to meet the Committee on International Conferences of which Root recently appointed him a member. They are a pleasant lot of men, Andrew Carnegie, L. S. Rowe, Robert Bacon, General Bates, and others whom he enjoys working with. Tomorrow night we go together to a dinner given by the Argentine Minister in honor of the International Bureau of American Republics. I love these big South American affairs, they are done with such a flourish.

I am gathering my roses while I may as the summer promises little besides the usual campaign round of the district, but I'll see the people I love, and the fig and watermelon crops and fishing at the coast all beckon pleasantly.

San Antonio, June 9

A letter from A. W. Drake of the *Century* today says, "Mr. Luis Mora, who is part Spanish and part American, has made the illustrations for your article on Barcelona, and has taken great pleasure doing it," and several other things of a pleasant nature. How I wish I could take Mr. Johnson's advice and devote myself to writing instead of being, as he said, "a card-leaving biped."

July 18

The Republican convention is over and I wrote to congratulate Mrs. Sherman on Jim's nomination as the Republican vice-presidential candidate. J. and I like them both very much, though she has the reputation of being "difficult." I remember a kindness she did me once last winter. She and I were sitting in my drawing room gossiping comfortably when an unexpected crowd of visitors came, and kept on coming. The tea was there, but no one was there to serve it, and things were getting awkward when I looked around and saw Mrs. S. had slipped off her gloves and was seated at the table pouring tea and dispensing bread and butter as if she had come o' purpose. Not many women have such helpful common sense. They would wait to be asked. She writes: "Thank you for the kind wishes. November will tell who will be installed in the chair in the Senate end. The House and its members (and wives) are my first love, and we have at least one session of that left. I shall expect nice hot biscuits and tea when we talk it over in December."

Tarpon Inn,[1] August 8

We are having a heavenly week "close to Nature's heart," as New England writers say when they go out of doors. This morning, so early that the morning stars still hung in the sky, we went into the surf, utterly alone with the sea. After our romp with the waves I wanted to stay and pick up shells, but J., who always hurries to the next pleasure, kept calling me to come around the point where our boatman waited. As we ran for it we saw the large undulating form of Bryan Callaghan, descendant of Irish and Aztec kings and for many years dictator of San Antonio, going in for a plunge, though we thought ourselves the very earliest birds. We had crackers and hot coffee from that recent invention the thermos bottle while the launch sputtered over water strangely brown and gold in the half-light. We went out on the Gulf with the mackerel fishers and caught seven beauties, and I am glad of every minute of it though I've spent the afternoon cold-compressing myself to cure a raging sun headache.

[1] Port Aransas, Mustang Island.

This is a raw little place that thinks it will be a city someday. The "drudge," as everyone here calls it, is slowly boring a ship channel to Corpus Christi through a pass where our boat scraped on the mud and chewed up the sea grass yesterday. The beautiful curved jetty, designed by our friend Lewis Haupt, is deepening the way to Rockport, besides making a welcome haven for seasick fisherwomen to sit and catch sheeps' heads when tired of mackerel.

I am reading Gosse's *Father and Son,* but J. doesn't agree with my estimate of it and returns joyfully to his Froude. Today Benson's *From a College Window* is giving me the comfort you get from a book that expresses your opinions better than you could express them yourself—indeed, reveals to you that they are your opinions. Now I shall refresh my soul with my ten-cent *Selections from Browning* (Browning's own selections from himself) bought for my handbag in case we should be cast away on a desert island.

"Oh, that the desert were my dwelling place!" But J. has to be in Goldthwaite 500 miles away on Monday, and back in San Antonio for the state convention Tuesday—two hard nights' travel for him, and one for me.

August 13

For two days I looked on at the state convention in Market Hall—a rough, sordid place and a rough, spitting, shirt-sleeved crowd. It represented the brains of Texas in a way though. Many of the leading men were absent, but I wished that those who were on hand had been as clean in person and dress as I believe a majority of them to be in life and character. Is it our climate or the traditions of the frontier that makes us careless of everything beautiful and refining around our political meetings? Cheap bunting in crude colors and badly hung is the limit of our aesthetic efforts. The American flag floating against our flawless sky is a beautiful and inspiring thing, but the same flag hung on a sagging string across a wall of cracked plaster with a painted tin cornice makes me wish I was anything but an American. The reign of the broom and the suppression of tobacco chewing might have a distinct influence in promoting clean politics in the state.

The women were confined to a dusty gallery with board seats without backs, but when I looked around and saw that many of them were chewing gum and others sucking soda water through a straw stuck in a bottle I thought it quite as much as we deserved. Most of them were well dressed in the freshest, daintiest white, and took an intelligent interest in the proceedings, but why chew gum?

Saltillo, Mexico, August 27

It was so frightfully hot in San Antonio that Jane and I ran down here for a week to get cool. It was rather eerie arriving at 3:00 A.M. with no one to meet us. A ramshackle coche, fit to wake the dead as it rattled over the cobblestones, brought us to the Presbiteriana Normal. We slept on sofas in the sala until the rest of the house was stirring. The change in temperature is life-giving but we do little besides seeing our friends in the day and listening to the music on the plaza at night. Our one excursion has been to the battlefield of Buena Vista and the lovely ranch nearby where some hundreds of American soldiers are buried. They lie in a typical old Mexican garden, acres of flowers, vines and long shaded walks with no sound but of water rippling through the acequias and the song of birds; the high, solemn, deep blue mountains keeping watch above it all. There is a plan afoot to move the bodies back to the United States. Of course I am expected to get Congressional influence for it; I never escape that sort of thing. But I cannot sympathize with the idea. The place is so heavenly beautiful, and they have been there so long. If I were a dead soldier I would hate to exchange it for a stiff American cemetery with a "ready-to-wear" tombstone and tin-plate poetry about "Fame's eternal camping ground" and "So sleep the brave" stuck around as it is at Arlington.

Kerrville, September 5

The life of a campaigning congressman's wife is not always cakes and ale; sometimes, disastrously enough, it is champagne. Today I am in bed trying to classify and account for a varied assortment of miseries, and have decided that champagne was, so to speak, the last straw.

After a noon dinner at Boerne yesterday, we drove up here, stopping on and off the road to call on friends and constituents, and were received everywhere with substantial hospitality—fruit, ice cream, or just plain ice water. Long ago it became evident that eating at odd hours and of strange dishes was my share of the political work—I have a good appetite and an iron digestion, J. just the reverse—so I nibbled at all the nice things and had had quite enough when we arrived at Dr. Nooe's. The unexpected is always happening in Texas, and I wished some of our Eastern friends could have seen us sitting on a gallery furnished with rugs, cushions, and easy chairs like Newport, drinking iced champagne and eating cake that would have graced the window of a Parisian pastry shop. But it was my Waterloo. The heat, the dust and the bad roads no doubt contributed to the tragedy. Lying in bed here at my good friends the Locketts', I have time to meditate and to philosophize on what it means to be a Texas congressman's wife.

This flimsy little yellow cottage of the Locketts' is typical of the surprises and inequalities of our part of the country. In the tiny drawing room with spotty wallpaper and poor furniture are eighteenth-century books and beautiful portraits that any collector would be proud to own—remnants of ante bellum grandeur in Alabama. In the dining room, flanked by the poorest china, is a magnificent silver pitcher and tray engraved "Robert Treat Paine." I wonder what family connection there is between them and the present bearer of that proud name whose square-cut face and stiff white mustache I have seen so often at Mohonk and other peace gatherings.

Mrs. Lockett lives up to the pictures in her gentle elegance and dignity. She does all the work, and there could not be more delicious cooking, but she never discusses it. I think the theory that Southern women are "thriftless" gained credence because they rarely parade their thrift. When they come out of the kitchen they shut the door behind them and enjoy their leisure gracefully.

There is one burden of campaigning very real to me but hard to put into words. Maybe I take it too seriously, but it is a feeling that I must always be a "shining example," always accessible and, if possible, pleasant. Fortunately I like most people and never lose my interest in Texas and Texans for their own sake, so it is easy enough to be amiable. But many of J.'s constituents live so far from main-traveled roads that I am the most "prominent lady" who ever comes their way. With that universal human interest in those who by official position are a little distinguished from their fellows, they observe what I do and say as closely and with far more interest than I would fasten on a roomful of first ladies of the land.

It is especially true of the young women and girls who have dreams of the great world—dreams that so often "go by contraries"—and consult me on questions of etiquette and style that tax my experience and sometimes my gravity. One fine, old gentleman asked us to visit his home because he felt that to have his daughters know me would be "a liberal education in social elegance." It was sweetly archaic and sincere, but what overwhelming responsibility it puts on me. And, then, in trying to be a paragon it is so easy to become a prig. I can only pray for grace.

What would we do without our great daily, the San Antonio *Express?* It has an obituary today of a Texas lady "whose sister lives in El Paso and

belongs to the Country Club and the Episcopal Church and often enter-
tains the social set." What more can St. Peter ask of her fitness for the
Kingdom of Heaven?

San Antonio, September 26

This morning after rolls and coffee in the stuffy little dining room of the San
Antonio Club, I followed J. to the reading room, and among the new
magazines on the table found the *Century,* and beheld, on the very first
page, my article, "Mid Pleasures and Palaces in Barcelona." I had been
thinking for months how it would look somewhere far back in the
volume with Luis Mora's dainty picture to commend it, but though Mr.
Johnson had praised it above its deserts, I never dreamed of his giving it
such prominence.

November 27

Just as I was finishing our trunks to get off tonight J. came in and said
we would stay over to help entertain W. J. Bryan when he stops here
tomorrow on his way to Mexico.[2] Another day at home is always welcome,
so I left off packing and began to get ready for lunch, to which I had
invited Jane and Allie.[3] Then J. remarked casually that he had invited
Reagan Houston, Captain Lindsey and Judge Reinhart, and I saw the
small loin of venison I had ordered reaching a vanishing point. I hurried
to the café and my good friend Henry came to the rescue with some fine
trout, a pair of wild ducks, and a couple of bottles of wine, so the day was
saved, but I wonder if J. will ever learn not to expect miracles of loaves
and fishes.

November 28

Before nine o'clock we found a crowd on the streets and at the Menger
waiting to see Bryan. Senator Culberson was the first person to greet me,
and gushed over my *Century* article, perhaps to drown the memory of
some insolence about the Episcopal Church in a cheap political speech of
his which had brought on a passage at arms between us last summer.

Mrs. Bryan sent for me to come to her room. I found Bryan seated

---

[2] Bryan had just been defeated in his third and last campaign for the Presidency.
[3] Mr. and Mrs. Albert Maverick.

in a big rocking chair reading the morning paper, but Mrs. Bryan was so nervously tired that her lips were quivering and tears were in her eyes. She is usually so calm, almost phlegmatic, that her state of emotion was much more distressing than it would have been in me, for instance. Bryan jumped up to welcome me, his wide smile, bright eyes and clear skin showing that physically at any rate the campaign and his defeat had not hurt him.

I apologized for coming so early and said I hadn't expected special privileges. He remarked on my getting stouter, said I was better looking, and I replied that nearing the fifty mark it was a compensation for never having been a beauty. We both talked very fast to save Mrs. Bryan from trying to join us.

There was a knock at the door and Culberson's face appeared and a series of expressions ran over it that make me laugh even to remember. He doesn't like for anyone to be closer to the great than he is, and finding me in the bosom of the Bryan family disturbed him. He first looked puzzled, and then annoyed, but soon his habitual suavity fell over him like a mantle, and his interest in me increased visibly.

We all met again in the big reception room of the Menger where the Daughters of the Confederacy loomed large in a "receiving line" in which they asked me to stand. I said, "Nay, nay," and enjoyed myself as a free lance. I don't know why I hate receiving lines, but I'd rather be a dog and bay at the moon than to stand in one. I suppose it is because the dog can stop baying when he gets tired, but in a receiving line one must stay "till the last galoot's ashore." Mrs. B. was delighted to renew her friendship with my sister—"On the common ground of motherhood," she said—another line in which there is no place for me. I wore my rajah silk with a tiny wrap covered with fine white Cluny lace and a big black hat, though it was small compared to the cartwheels worn by most of the women. The clothes were amazing, rich satins and lace, almost evening dress, and the company all sorts and conditions of men, women, and babies in arms.

An immense crowd on the plaza called for Bryan and he went to the balcony, J. introduced him, and he made a charmingly friendly and humorous little talk. Far back in the room behind him I heard every word, and people in the Alamo Flats across the plaza also heard him distinctly. There never was such a voice.

Tonight we go to Waco, tired, tired. And if I am tired, what must Mrs. Bryan be with her disappointment, her heartache for her husband, and the political compulsion to look as if she didn't mind. Some distressing news she had just heard of her daughter's domestic affairs made her so nervous this morning, but she proved herself a good sport this afternoon.

November 29

Through the Pullman window early this morning I saw the high, level prairie line against a copper sky and knew we were near Waco. When we lived here twenty years ago that line and color, and the prairie lights at sunset, comforted me for the day-long ugliness of the crude little town, greatly improved now and dreadfully rich.

There is some talk of J.'s being nominated for governor next, and through two receptions this afternoon (at Bob Henry's and the Prathers') and at dinner at the Rotans' I was sustained by that stern joy that candidates feel when playing the game. The parties were pleasant too, with many good things to eat. At the Prathers' they had those dear, big, thin wafers baked between two disks of iron that I thought had vanished with the Confederate flag.

Washington, December 29.

We went to an interesting party at the British Embassy given to the Association of Historians and Scientists last night. As J. and I are neither, I don't know why the Bryces invited us, but I am much obliged to them all the same. We were also the only Congressional people present. There was a lack of introductions, but learned people are easier to approach than fashionable ones, and they were especially so. The talk was scientific, the clothes historical, and the supper was good as always at the Bryces'.

I heard someone ask Charles Francis Adams if the people of Richmond were "polite" to him when he went there this summer, and he replied in a peremptory tone, "If they didn't feel kindly, no people ever concealed their feelings with such success." I was so proud that he could say it when I have heard him tell how he rode through the streets during the war with the houses blazing on either side. To forgive and forget gracefully is such an essential part of good breeding, and Richmond people possess it to a high degree.

New Year's Eve

When young, and much farther from heaven in fact than I am now, I used to be solemn with myself at the end of the year, sit up till midnight by a dying fire, sentimentalizing and making resolutions which I am afraid did not get me up in time for breakfast or make me more considerate or kind even the next day. Perhaps I have only grown callous, but at any rate it seems to me better to face forward and make every night a New Year's Eve and every day a new birth to joy and usefulness.

J.'s eggnog party is impending, and I am going to bed early and hope not to be wakened by the pandemonium of whistles, bells, and wooden rattles with which the young people see fit to usher in the new year.

CHAPTER THIRTEEN

1909

Sitting on steps of members' gallery in the House. Such a crowd no seats to be had. Diplomatic, executive and press galleries are full to hear a special committee's reply to President's annual message in which he insinuated that Congress withheld appropriation for Secret Service because they were afraid of being investigated themselves. Cannon is in the chair, Miss Cannon, in panoply of war, in her gallery seat. Every woman I know in the Congressional circle is here. When the President is criticized there is applause from both sides of the chamber. After the first two speeches two clerks came stiffly down the middle aisle, presaging, "Mr. Speaker, a message from the Senate," but instead, it was a "message from the President," and the House roared; it was so opportune. There is nothing so rare as a day without a message from him. Mrs. R—— of Massachusetts sits by me and applauds with vim. Talking of T.R.'s being metaphorically "thrown to the lions," I said a friend of mine had a lion staked out in Africa starving into an appetite for him, and her lips tightened as she expressed the pious hope that he might be lost in the jungle forever. When Herbert Parsons kept interrupting Tawney's attacks, I asked her how the Parsons stood at the White House, and she said, "Oh, very well, no doubt! You know they are *very* rich."

Later

Yesterday Mrs. Butler and I sat around the small tea table at the Hales' with a delightful party of New England spinsters—Miss Susan Hale, spinster *par excellence,* Miss Nellie, Miss Clement, and Miss Putnam—and talked about CATS. If it had been the Oversoul or the Subliminal Self, they couldn't have been more in earnest.

I had heard of Miss Susan's unusualness from friends in Mexico, but the half had not been told. When Miss Nellie asked her to pour the tea, she thumped down in her chair, and gave a little extra bounce before she began to pull up her sleeves so hurriedly that I thought her next move would be to pound the teacups into atoms. But what a wonderful old woman she is—and not old either. She is so free from prejudice, social, political, sectional. She said it cost like the devil to stay at the Grafton and you couldn't keep a cat. She was going to Pass Christian because she boarded there with "two mousy little widows" who fed her on canned oysters, but the women were so hard up, what else could she do? She said she "listened quietly" (I doubt it) to people who spoke of "the most beautiful place in the world." It was in the eye of the beholder, of course, but she always saw those two clear peaks of the volcanoes from Cuernavaca, and she put up her great hands to form a pyramid. I could have embraced her, I agreed so entirely.

Miss Nellie let us go in to shake hands with "Papa." The doctor was seated in a long chair with a very ugly pillow back of his shaggy head, but his grip and his voice are always surprising. He had enjoyed my answer to his note some days ago asking if I could get him some data about the earthquake in Mexico in 1838. Books failing me, I had rung up Mr. Godoy at the embassy and gotten an excited reply, "No! An earthquake in Mexico? No, I have not heard of it! When?" News travels slowly there.

I told Dr. Hale how J. thought that voting $800,000 for the earthquake sufferers in Italy was too precipitate and too lavish, and I maintained that it was not. I said that if we had had the least little cause to go to war with Italy we would have voted ten times the amount in half the time, and this was buying peace and good will very reasonably. The old man laughed aloud and applauded my argument.

January 12

Another letter from Charles Francis Adams this morning. They always come to the house so I read them before J. does and he pretends to be displeased by it, but he does the same with my letters. It is fortunate we have no secrets.

Mr. A. says:

Herewith, under another cover, I send you a copy of the speech I made at Richmond during the last presidential canvass.

The speech in question was by no means "purely political," nor did it deal only "with topics of interest at the moment." On the contrary, I therein re-

motely tried my hand at what I regard as the most serious question now confronting the American people, to wit: the great Afro-American Problem. . . .
I regret extremely to say that, according to such light as I am at present
enjoying, the outlook for the Afro-American Race is far from encouraging. I
greatly fear that emancipation will prove to be by no means the benefit which
we who brought it about once anticipated. On the contrary, I fear that the
figures of the coming census will reveal a condition of affairs the reverse of
hopeful.

However, in taking this view of the subject, I may be borrowing trouble.

How wise and big and modest, too, Mr. Adams always is! Not many
men who, as he says, "brought emancipation about" are willing to admit
the possibility of its being a mistake; though, heaven knows I am grateful
to them for doing it! How horrible slavery would be today. Mother always
says it was the white people of the South, not the negroes, who were
emancipated. Father belonged to the earlier period, and always took the
slaveholder view. Once he was called as a witness in a case where a negro
woman was bringing suit for damages to the amount of $10,000 for her
husband's being killed. When Father's opinion was asked, he replied,
"Why, nonsense! He was a bandy-legged negro, and they never were
worth more than fifteen hundred dollars!"

January 17

Mrs. Brown gave me the use of her pew in St. John's while she and Justice
Brown are in Cuba, saying she would like someone she loved, her "sunshine friend," to occupy it. I went this morning and enjoyed the quiet
service. Coming out, Miss Virginia Miller said she was glad to see me
there, and I told her of Mrs. B.'s kindness and said it was pleasant to have
"a sort of permanent seat in church." "Prominent, you mean!" said Miss
Virginia tartly.

January 19

We are reading a quantity of Poe centenary stuff, but I cannot get enthusiastic over him any more than I could as a child when I was afraid
of the "Black Cat" and couldn't make head or tail of "The Raven," though,
of course, I was early made to learn it by heart. I used to peep uneasily
into his room on West Range at the University of Virginia and wonder
how he put the bust of Pallas over the door where there wasn't any shelf.
Father made him seem real by telling me how he remembered hearing old
ladies speak of him as "a poor dissipated boy."

The memorial ceremonies at the University of Virginia were not impressive except for the innovation in that supposed school of democratic simplicity of a procession of dignitaries in caps, gowns, and flamboyant hoods. Barrett Wendell's address will probably be better to read than to hear. He has an English voice, with occasional lapses into nasal New English, and a dreary delivery that let my mind and eyes wander to the pretty foot that peeped beneath his gown.

The Vice-President's reception to Congress was even brighter than usual this year. Mr. Fairbanks seems an icicle and Mrs. F. is not especially prepossessing, but the atmosphere of their house is hospitable—more than can be said of some of our "great houses," as our Anglicized fashionables are beginning to call them. We had an amusing glimpse of "Alice." We were in the hall talking with the Bryces when she and Mr. Longworth came up. We stepped back but because of the crush had to remain quite near them. Alice looked very handsome, her clear white face, with irregular but pleasing features, rising from a low-cut dress of chiffon the color of blue tobacco smoke. She and Mrs. Bryce were evidently conferring about the ball for Ethel Roosevelt the next night at the embassy, and Alice inquired, "You mean after supper?" To Mrs. B.'s quiet "Yes," she called back as she passed down the stairs, "Oh! all right. That'll be *bully*." Mrs. Bryce's stony British stare made it funnier than if she had looked surprised or shocked.

They are not a polished family. Mr. Harrison told me of seeing the President keep Ashbrook of Ohio waiting at the Executive Office for ten minutes while he talked, in full view of them, to John L. Sullivan, the pugilist. As John L. said good-by, the President slapped him on the back and said, "Well, good-by, old fellow! You are certainly the finest that ever wore the mitts."

Members' Gallery, February 10, 10:30 A.M.
Everything crowded already, and we have to wait till one o'clock to see the electoral vote counted. I wonder why I came? It is always a dull performance.

Later
The ceremony was uninteresting but satisfyingly republican in its lack of fuss and feathers, just the Senate coming in two by two. Fairbanks, in a very long-tailed coat, led the way, and two men carrying polished ma-

hogany boxes walked behind him. The counting lasted exactly forty minutes. Afterwards the members crowded around Sherman, whose face was very red, and sang "For he's a jolly good fellow," which he really is, and his wife is another one.

February 18

Clubwomen, the "earnest" kind, tell me that a club fills a real need in every woman's life. I am convinced of it. I was appointed to receive and entertain from 3:00 to 6:00 P.M. yesterday at the new Congressional Club, but 3:30 caught me leaving my own door, and I reached the club (the old Gorman house at 15th and I) almost breathless. The maid's welcome was gratifying, but when I asked, "How many are here?" she looked puzzled, and said, "Dey ain't nobody here." "What time," I asked, "do they usually come?" "Dey don't come, 'less sometimes dey has friends."

The reading room was sunny and quiet and I read the restful *Delineator* for a while, then sat by the big window, but I got to feeling like the dummy of an exclusive tailor shop, so I lay down on the sofa. Soothed by the regular creaking of the satin lining of my best frock, I fell asleep and didn't wake till after five when the bell rang. I jumped up, put on my best receiving and entertaining manner and met my good friend, Mrs. Fairchild, with a visitor from New York who wanted to see "our quarters" on her way to the train. I came home a convert to the need of a club for a tired woman.

Whether the new club is to fill a long-felt want or be just one more burden of Congressional life is still a question, though the reception rooms are furnished (scantily), sandwiches and tea are on tap, and frilly little curtains, mirrors, comb, brush and powder upstairs. Mrs. ————'s already expansive chest grew broader as she swelled with indignation about it. She thought the "doos" too high. "I have some dear little friends in the House (her husband has been in the Senate about a month) who can ill afford it," she said. "I only joined to show I was not antagonistic, but saw I could not avoid accepting an office, so I let them put me on the 'Advisorary' Board."

February 25

J. has a letter today from Oswald G. Villard thanking him for his speech about the West Point dismissals and the President and Secretary Wright using their authority to force the cadets' reinstatement though they were dismissed on rather serious charges, "found deficient" in conduct and in studies. Evidently the President doesn't consider manners or mind necessary for an officer. Villard, after praising J.'s speech, says, "I hope some good will come of it. I am sure that a change for the better will be made when the inconsistent Mr. Roosevelt retires from office, and Mr. Taft comes in." The *Evening Post* has an editorial on J.'s speech and the subject in general, and says, "Mr. Slayden has done excellent service to the country in calling the attention of Congress and the country to the manner in which the discipline of West Point and the authority of its officials are being steadily undermined by politics."

March 2

Rain has poured all day, getting ready, no doubt, for the proverbial inauguration weather. I am glad we are leaving, J. for Texas and I to see Mother. The town is at its worst, crowded and ugly. Every space on the avenue from the White House to the Capitol is filled with scaffoldings for seats, most of them crude and unsightly, but every year they improve a little. The "Court of Honor" in front of the Treasury is well done—big white columns garlanded with green, and festooned with colored lights at night. The 15th Street side is cluttered with machinery for hoisting the new columns into place.

On Southern train, March 3

The grand new railroad station is justifying itself. The inauguration crowd is already immense, but there was room to spare in the cavernous concourse, and we got through the gates with ease. The weather is frightful. It rained all night, and this morning the poor bedraggled flags and bunting are whipped into rags by a savage east wind. This train is late, and I never remember a darker day. We cannot see fifty yards from the track. Poor Washington and the holidaymakers!

Piedmont, March 4

It is bright here but bitter cold, and we hear by telephone that Washington is almost cut off from the world. Trains from Baltimore were eight hours late, and those from the north and west never arrived. I hope J. is well on his way to Texas. Sitting here by the purring wood fire it is hard to realize such cold and confusion. We are making merry, too, over the fact that the jungle is yawning for Teddy, and we shall hear no more of him for a while. Everyone is so tired of the din he makes.

Later

About dusk J. came limping in almost frozen and tired to death. The night of the 3rd he spent in the station unable to get a train or to get home. The vast place was packed with people, mostly negroes trying to keep warm. He says it has not been so cold since the blizzard of '99 and yesterday he saw thousands of troops standing for hours in slush nearly to their knees. He finally caught a Southern train and came down here to escape the discomfort.

March 15

The opening of the extra session drew a crowd to see the fight on Uncle Joe and the rules.[1] Admission was by card, and our seats were in the gallery facing the House, so we could not see the Speaker. Miss Cannon occupied her "family pew" with Mrs. Dalzell, Mrs. Boutell, and Mrs. Longworth, who came in late, and stepped over the little gate instead of waiting for it to be unlocked.

Mrs. Busbey, wife of Cannon's secretary, sat by me. She said she was glad to be near a woman who didn't let party politics disturb her and wouldn't mind if she gave way to violence during the voting. Her face was crimson and often she controlled her voice with difficulty. One handsome Republican dame became hysterical when the vote was unsatisfactory, put up her hands and sobbed and shook till Mrs. B. and I christened her "Niobe, all tears." The galleries were crowded till adjournment at six o'clock.

Later we went to a bright dinner at the Anthonys'. Of course Teddy was discussed, and I asked Major ———'s wife how she liked him. She looked at me astonished. "My husband went on that walk," she said. I had never quite believed the story, but she told me that the Major came home wet to the waist, and the weather at freezing. They had been led over hill and dale, rocks and bushes and slippery banks, and finally into Rock Creek, one officer going in up to his chin. Across the creek the "dead game sport" of a President stepped into his waiting carriage, wrapped up comfortably and waved good-by to the officers who had to get home as best they could.

[1] Joseph Cannon, as Speaker of the House, exercised partisan and arbitrary control of procedure which became known as "Cannonism." Under the leadership of Champ Clark of Missouri at the opening of the first session of the Sixty-first Congress an unsuccessful attempt was made to break his power. It was not until the second session, in March, 1910, that a resolution was passed enlarging the Committee on Rules. It provided for the election of the committee by the House and excluded the Speaker from membership.

When we left cards at the White House Saturday, a nice negro footman in colonial livery came down the steps and received them on a silver tray— a pleasant contrast to the surly policeman who took them with rather dirty fingers in the Roosevelt regime. This afternoon Mrs. Hitchcock and I went together to the first tea, and from the very door of the east corridor the atmosphere was different. We went to the dressing rooms just as million- aires and diplomats used to do, only a few policemen watching us, and the crowd, passing upstairs two by two without regard to rank, was in high good humor—all except Mrs. Sherman, whose dignity seemed to be hurt someway. I heard her say sharply, "I don't see why *I* should be kept waiting," and I don't think she went up at all, nor did Miss Cannon. It was a little too democratic for the latter lady, especially, who is accustomed to being a preferred guest. Her back was like a gray chiffon-velvet thunder- cloud as she rolled grandly away.

At the East Room we fell into single file, but didn't have to go far as the President and Mrs. Taft stood near the door. One officer presented me to Mrs. Taft, who received me with a reassuring smile of recognition, and another to the President. A lady from Oklahoma was just ahead of me, and I heard him say he had been there and "it was great." So when I was presented, I said, "You have been to Texas, too, and you *know* that's great." He laughed and said, "It *is*. And didn't your husband get a lot out of me for Fort Sam Houston, too?" I agreed and told him Texas thought he was great.

I sent Dr. Hale some roses from our San Jacinto Day party, and he sends thanks, and says, "I suppose you know who San Jacinto was. I wish I did."

Mrs. Champ Clark set a syndicate letter writer on me. The woman was pleasant enough, but took up a whole morning, as she practices the leisurely psychotherapist method of trying to find out what she wants to know by apparently abstract talk. Everything went well until I refused to let my picture go with the letter, and then she became angry and threatened to leave me unhonored and unsung. But syndicates must be served, and the letter came to me in the San Antonio *Express* today with no picture, but my name in boxcar letters at the top.

I had given the plain facts for my autobiography, but she made it what she thought my biography ought to be. She represents me as a patron of the arts, a contributor to "the best magazines and newspapers," with "social gifts that suggest the salon," besides "the breezy nonchalance of the semi-Western type," whatever that may mean.

How I do hate that meretricious personal exploitation, and yet sometimes I wonder why I don't submit to more of it and encourage J. to do it, though he detests it as much as I do. It is certainly the easiest way to acquire merit with a credulous public. I know so many men and women here of the commonest clay who have achieved nationwide reputations for wit and grace by just such methods.

My aversion to having a picture of myself in a newspaper is a mild form of mania. Perhaps it is only self-consciousness, and so many refined people do it now that I cannot criticize them, but to prevent it has become a game that I play just to match my wits against photographers, newspapermen and -women, or just advertisers who want your picture and a testimonial for laundry soaps or patent medicines. No official's wife is too obscure to be asked for a picture, and most of us are coaxed, offered bribes or even threatened on an average of once a month. So far I have given mine to only one publication, the New York *Independent*, during the meeting of the Interparliamentary Union in this country in 1904, which, as a flippant friend remarked, was like having it "carved on the north side of a tombstone." My horror of the custom was fixed for good and all one muddy wet day on F St. when I saw on the pavement a piece of begrimed, torn paper being kicked about and trampled upon, and looking up from it the face of a sweet refined acquaintance of mine. It made me a little sick.

April 23

The tide of battle rolls on in the D.A.R. convention. Of all women they are the most bellicose, and I can't see why. The militant suffragists in England are fighting for what they think is a vital principle of human rights, but the "D.A.R.ters" have nothing but elections and an occasional relic or corpse. The Dolly Madison Chapter has buried one old man three times, I hear. (The government is doing something, too, in the undertaking line. They dug up the remains of L'Enfant lately—a few scraps and coffin nails, the papers say—and will reinter them in Arlington next week. Only two years ago we gave John Paul Jones his belated deserts in the form of a first-class funeral in three installments.)

The Congressional Club gave the D.A.R. a reception this afternoon. All those able to leave the firing line came—"some in rags, and some in tags, and some in velvet gown," but mostly very modish in high-waistline frocks, peach-basket hats, and generally a miniature of a distinguished ancestor on their manly bosoms. But they fought their battles o'er again around our tables, and not all our piety and wit or frappé and cake could make them talk of anything else. They forgot that they owed their humble hostesses any consideration. I am "nobody's child" and mean to remain orphaned of my country until these patriotic organizations mend their manners.

I telegraphed J. to ask if he would be here to take me to dinner at the White House the first of May and am much pleased to have his answer in the affirmative.

May 1, 11:00 P.M.

Comfortably in bed, and all the pomp of the White House dinner is "one with Nineveh and Tyre" or Belshazzar's feast, which it didn't in the least resemble.

As usual the cab company raised its prices when they found we were going to the White House, so we took a humble herdic, a "backer," and arrived at the east entrance with the other guests who had prancing horses, roaring automobiles, or were just walking. The party was almost entirely Congressional—the Dollivers, Johnstons of Alabama, Guggenheims, Stone, Sutherland, and a lot of friends from the House.

The diagram of the table was at the foot of the stairs so the men drew their little envelopes and knew their fate before we went up. J. drew Mr. McCall, and Tawney and Foster of Vermont also did duty as ladies. We were shown to the Blue Room and stood around rather stiffly until the President and Mrs. Taft came in. I think it would be more graceful for them to receive their guests, but far be it from me to cavil at the customs of the great.

When we went to the dining room the President gave his arm to Mrs. Dolliver (Ossa escorting Pelion) and we got quite gay and informal hunting for our place cards. Senator Dolliver was with Mrs. Taft, and my pleasure was assured when Senator Burton came for me. The President and Mrs. Taft sat at the center of the table opposite one another in bigger chairs than were allotted to the rest of us. There were four large silver candelabra the length of the table, and at the center an immense arrangement of the loveliest pink flowers and maidenhair fern. Little silver dishes of salted nuts and green and brown candies broke out everywhere just as they do on all tables nowadays, and in every way it was a comfortable, unpretentious meal, not as handsome as several I have seen in the houses of the merely rich. Senator Burton and I talked about books and arbitration. He advocated study of Shakespeare, the Bible and the Book of Common Prayer for the sake of their good English, deplored the cheap and slovenly stuff the young people were reading, and hoped for a renaissance of Dickens. Tawney on my other side joined us now and then excoriating the principle of armed peace. He said that 71 per cent of our income was spent on past wars and preparations for more. He consumed a whole dish of large soft caramels, taking one or more after each course from caviar to ice cream, but always found time to revile Roosevelt. It was a congenial theme to all the men near us but made me uncomfortable. Teddy's is such a persistent and intense personality that I couldn't help feeling that he was somewhere about, and that his teeth, like the grin without a cat, might suddenly appear among his moose and goat heads on the wall.

When the gentlemen went to smoke we sat about the drawing room in little groups rather far apart. I was with Mrs. Taft, Mrs. Johnston, and Mrs. Guggenheim, the last-named very beautiful in a rich, Oriental fashion. She wore a dress of cloth of gold, a dog collar of pearls and diamonds, and a long string of matched pearls with an emerald pendant as big as a filbert.

Mrs. Taft's dress of white satin with bands of cut-steel beads around the low neck showed wear. She was direct and sincere as I have always found her, but she looked dreadful and spoke of not being well. I thought the inauguration had tired her, but she said she had suffered of nerves all through the campaign while Mr. Taft was so constantly traveling in crowds where there was danger of accidents and bombs.

May 16

This has been a week of almost sacred pleasure in a visit from Mother and Jane. Living as far apart as we do it is not likely that we shall ever be together again, so I treasure every moment. Mother at eighty-two is well enough to go about with us, so we have been to all the beautiful places and even to the new Speedway where the gay world gathers twice a week and tries to be festive. There is no shade; the automobiles hiss and snort and smell dreadful; everyone talks who isn't too tired, and the men who ostentatiously practice at polo inside the field of green divert one's attention. Only now and then one hears a faint note of music and sees poor Santelmann, in a fiery uniform, patiently beating the air in the bandstand. I wonder if Americans will ever learn to sit still out of doors and listen to music as people do in Europe and Mexico?

May 30

It's a delightful experience to rediscover a girlhood friend and find her just as clever and spiritual and charming as you thought her at twenty-two— an age when one is so easily mistaken. She, Annie Lee Sloan of Charleston, and I went to St. Thomas' today to hear Canon Henson of Westminster, and sat with General John Wilson and Miss Waller. James Bryce, and some English lady, whom I took to be Mrs. Henson, sat just behind us. It is conceded in Washington that an ambassador, especially one from Great Britain, can do no wrong, but I don't think they often sing. Bryce's vigorous participation in the doxology and a hymn was amusing, but when he made a joyful noise unto the Lord in an elaborate Te Deum it was convulsing. Miss Waller and I nearly broke down, as we did when the slim little canon darted down the chancel steps and ran to the pulpit, only to find that he couldn't get in from that side. It looked for an instant as if he were going to "skin up," he has such a dauntless air in spite of his slight physique and ascetic face.

Washington, June 26

A week of reeking humidity, the streets like hot rubber all day, and at night giving off heat and odor like a pitch kettle. J. keeps up the habit of going to the Capitol, but comes back to lunch and later goes to hear the debate in the Senate. I went one afternoon to see if it was less tiresome than staying at home. Beveridge had been speaking a long time, Frye was asleep in the chair, Bailey and Tillman conferring in their seats, but a crowd was gathering in the galleries. Mrs. Bailey was there in a white linen tailored suit with long coat and a lingerie hat, so I went and sat by her and found that the gay apparel was because her husband was to speak. When he rose there was an instant silence, and the crowd, and even I, listened attentively for two mortal hours while he talked on the tariff. Imagine making that interesting and dramatic—on a hot afternoon, too. No one need tell me that oratory, just in itself, hasn't some occult effect on all kinds of people. If I had been asked to come, I should have shrieked my refusal, and there I sat and actually enjoyed it. He denied that free trade is a Democratic party doctrine and proved it by many historical references.

Piedmont, August 2

It is cool and green and quiet here. Mother and I sew and read and make preserves and pickles, and late in the afternoon drive a very good horse.

Mother talks much of the past and told me today how Mrs. Bankhead (one of the Jeffersons) took her when she was a little girl to spend the day at Monticello during the time of old Commodore Uriah Levy (uncle of the present florid proprietor, Jefferson Levy), and when she came home she told her mother that she had had "wine in a silver tin cup." She says she remembers still the big silver cups with handles.

San Antonio, September 7

One afternoon last week at Sunshine Ranch when Allie came from town, we asked casually for the news, and he said the evening paper reported that a man named Cook had discovered the North Pole. The next day it was verified, but there was more to come. Last night at the hotel our old waiter, Henry, looked depressed. It was Labor Day and he had all the labor while the other waiters celebrated, so J. and I tried to cheer him up. We asked if he believed Dr. Cook had reached the Pole, and he shrugged his shoulders and said, "It looks like it, but I hear Peary has gotten there too." We laughed indulgently and said, "Oh, no! He hasn't had time, someone is telling that just to be picturesque." "Vell, maybe so," agreed Henry. "A newspaperman tolt me, but dot means not'ing." We never thought of it again till J. read it to me this morning at my first symptom of waking up.

How suddenly the discovery becomes a commonplace after four hundred years of human effort and suffering. Dr. Kane's *Arctic Explorations* was one of my earliest literary treasures, and I felt quite near to the adventure when Father told me what a delicate little boy Kane was when he went to school in Charlottesville and how he once found him lost from his companions and crying, and took him up on his horse and carried him home. With the North Pole disposed of, we can now consider the cause of earthquakes and the perfecting of aerial navigation. J. and I disagree about airships. I don't think the world morally ready for them; it promotes human intercourse too rapidly, brings nations too close together. What would become of the tariff, and how could we restrict immigration? They would certainly put an end to war as it is now conducted. Fancy our fat old army officers engaged with "airy navies grappling in the central blue"! When Major Dick Richardson and Colonel Marshall go up, I shall stand from under.

September 16

A letter from Miss Hale tells me of the death of my dear old friend. How I shall miss him!

"It was such a pleasure to my father to be friends with you and Mr. Slayden; he felt so much in common with you both," she writes.

Saltillo, September 28

The Escuela Presbiteriana Normal with Jennie Wheeler (there never was a missionary so full of fun and good sense) is a heavenly place to rest. The eighty Mexican girls in the house move and speak so softly that we hardly know they are here except as something pretty to look at. Rose Pollard came with me, and the trip down was hot and dusty. We could not realize the deluge that endangered Monterrey and the valley three weeks ago until, sitting on the rear platform to delight in the evening view of the Silla and the Sierra Madre, we heard the little Santa Caterina, that I have often stepped over, still roaring like Niagara. This is the fourth day without one tiny cloud in the sky. It is like living under a blue porcelain bowl, pale by day and deeper at night when Mars seems to be in visiting distance and we can read by the moonlight.

Americans here are taking revolutionary and anti-Díaz talk more seriously than I ever knew them to do. They think a revolution will be staged next year during the centennial celebration.

Dallas, October 14

On the train coming up here J. said, "Maybe we are starting out to make a president," and I added fervently, "I hope so." We came to meet Judson Harmon,[2] who will speak on Democratic Day at the State Fair. The Democrats are enthusiastic but it is almost too much to hope that the party could nominate anyone so sane, experienced, and *comme il faut* as Harmon. We have acquired such a taste for "idealists," "tribunes of the people," and other freaks. Mrs. Harmon is a handsome woman, eminently sensible and a good sport. She didn't know our climate and came down in a heavy cloth suit and a close turban that didn't shield her eyes, but she never turned a hair all day, and when her baggage failed to arrive she wore the same thing to a reception in the evening without complaining or explaining. The drought here is awful, even worse than San Antonio, as they have no water to sprinkle, and trees and shrubs are dying. English ivy that grew over the cathedral in quite an English way is lying in brown heaps on the ground.

[2] Governor of Ohio, 1909–1913.

October 20

Senator Vest's wife used to say that men with young families should be forbidden by law to go to Congress. She considered the moral effect on the children, but there are not a few hardships for the wives too. The wives have to go to Washington early to put the children in school, and that means going through the miseries of house hunting and settling without even the moral support of a husband. The "peepul" would never forgive "Poppa" for leaving the district twenty-four hours before he has to, and then they watch the papers to see if he answers to roll call on the first day of the session.

Mrs. Gregg writes amusingly of trials that our admiring (or jealous) constituents never think could cross the primrose path they believe we are treading. She says:

I am back at 1737 Corcoran, and you would be surprised to see how well the furniture scatters over the rooms. Only wish I hadn't returned all your things. Do hurry back and give them to me. We actually have a new kitchen sink and drainboard. You must see it to believe. I am alone at night with Will and Alexander. They would only be useful to throw at the burglar, they sleep so soundly, but I have a pistol as big as I am.

Washington and the country are perfectly beautiful in fall clothes. Of course you know it, but it is new to me. As to other clothes, hats are higher than ever—the price, I mean, with turbans in the lead. They are large, too. . . . Lots of the Texans are back, the Baileys, Culbersons, Bealls, and Burlesons. I met Mrs. Burleson at market one day when she bought a live rooster and took it home in a *paper sack*. She looked *so cute*. I mildly remonstrated, and she looked at me reprovingly and said, "Why, *I* am not ashamed to carry a chicken, are you?" I said, "No, I wouldn't be *ashamed* to carry a cow if I *had* to, but it wouldn't occur to me to do it if I didn't have to. . . .

Washington, December 4

We find the Cook and Peary question very much alive here, though clouds are gathering over Cook's claims, scientists of the sternly exact kind like Dr. Tittmann being more than suspicious of him. Both have lectured here, and one resident scientist says that Cook talked like a liar and a gentleman, and Peary didn't talk like either. The *Post* says, "If Cook didn't discover the Pole, he at least helped the public to discover the real Peary."

CHAPTER FOURTEEN

1910

March 19, 2:30 P.M.

For three days Uncle Joe Cannon has been like an old gray wolf at bay in the discussion over his power as chairman of the Committee on Rules. The "insurgents" have been bitter beyond expression, personal and cruel in a way that I can't believe they would have been if they hadn't felt that his power was really, if not nominally, at an end. I don't specially admire Uncle Joe. He is a flippant, coarse-natured, brazen old man, coarse of speech and profane. I have seen him drunk and rarely seen him out of the chair without a cigar set at a pert angle in his mouth, but today I am sorry for him. He is so old. The tyrannies he is accused of may or may not be true; his age, his trembling hands, his quivering lips, grimly controlled, are *facts*. When he came in at noon to take his seat, well dressed and shaved with a red carnation in his coat, he ran up the steps to the desk, and it had the painful effect of an old belle tripping through a dance. He is always such a spectacular old scamp. The night before last he was up all night, and yesterday evening telephoned his daughter that he would be home to go to a dinner with her. Of course it was for effect, but it was plucky all the same. Most of the men, none of whom could have suffered the vital strain that Cannon did, went to bed as soon as the House adjourned around 5:00 P.M.

Friday morning as we walked from the car to the House, everyone hurrying, the air so bright and quivering with sunshine, I thought I never saw the view more brilliant and beautiful—a sharp contrast with the over-used air of the Capitol, the sickening heat of the furnaces that had been going so long without any open windows, everyone jaded, nervous, tense, or just frankly sleepy. The room looked like a boys' classroom after a school riot. The desks were piled with untidy books and papers, cigar stumps, apple cores, and baskets full of waste paper littered the floor, and the gallery was as bad as the floor. Even at 9:30 the galleries were fairly filled and people coming in continually at every door.

Outside the Capitol Dr. Harlan, a big white jolly Kentuckian, son of the old Justice, stopped us and told Jim he had thought of having him telegraph me that morning: "Dear Wife, will not be home till late today. Haven't been home yesterday yet." He went on with another story of a friend of his who was a gentleman even in his cups, who meeting a lady on the street in Philadelphia made her a profound bow and said "Madame, would you be kind enough to tell me if this is Chestnut Street or Wednesday?" The two jokes served us well all the morning and brought a laugh to a good many tired men.

April 27

Last night Mrs. Porter and I went to hear Hamilton Mabie. I rather enjoyed it though I never liked his books. The talk was advertised as "Idealism in America," but might as well have been called several other things, as it was largely a stream of anecdotes illustrative of American character. I felt as if I'd heard them all before, but they were amusing enough and the audience of respectable married people with umbrellas was pleased. He belongs to the school of Rooseveltian cocksure philosophy without T.R.'s superfluous vim.

I enjoyed far more the Church Congress this morning with the discussion of the influence of woman suffrage on education and the church. The cause was championed by such a pretty woman, Mrs. Laidlaw, in a beautiful, comfortable dress of soft gray crepe and a reasonable hat. She had a real gift of graceful womanly talk and was smiling and appealing. She made a clever argument besides, but the reason and right of it are so self-evident to me that I can't see how a poor argument could be made. She was answered by a fine old woman, sixty-five, homely, ill dressed and uncomfortable, who couldn't see her notes and spoke thickly. She made the same old home and fireside argument, which she as an old maid school-ma'am had not been able to enjoy and should have known the futility of making it woman's *only* career.

Dr. Nash of Harvard argues for woman suffrage on the highest ground I have ever heard taken, as benefiting women themselves by increasing their sense of civic duty and individual responsibility. He said that women already had higher education, and to educate us like men and then tell us to stay at home and confine ourselves to housekeeping was like manufacturing dynamite and then sitting on it. Cyrus Townsend Brady spoke against, on the highly intelligent position that we were slaves to our hats, our dresses, our shoes. I inferred that he thought when we abandoned them for trousers and derbies we would be qualified to vote.

May 24

Last night Mattie phoned us to "go out and look west." We went immediately, and were rewarded by seeing the long-discussed Halley's comet. I have been saying that I did not expect to see it unless it came to R St., and there it was, apparently just over the corner of R and 17th, a pale, disappointing thing like a melted star with a yard of faint gleam behind it to the south—not half as interesting as the full moon hanging like a gold bubble in the east as if waiting scornfully for the total eclipse she was to be subjected to in two or three hours.

It is extraordinary how even educated and intelligent people have taken the comet's influence seriously, and as for the others, there is no limit to the occult powers they have ascribed to it. I am inclined to agree with Aunt Lucy, who tells me today, "That comit ain't *nothin'*."

One friend told us seriously that he could smell it the night of the 18th, when so many watched and it failed to appear on schedule time; and Mrs. Lucas insists that it was a strange day with an oppressive, portentous atmosphere. Professor Asaph Hall of the Naval Observatory told me some weeks ago of hearing some darkies around the observatory discussing the awful things liable to happen, and each had a more fearful presentiment than the other. They had worked themselves into a state of terror when one of them who had worked there a long time and imbibed a flattering confidence in the powers of science said consolingly, "Yes, it is pretty bad, but I believe Professor Hall will be able to control it."

That delightful Mr. Jeffrey Parsons has sent me a great big book of the Bayeux tapestry, and marked the pictured tapestries where Queen Maude and her maids are; while the ladies sew the stitches, the courtiers gaze out the window at this same Halley's comet. It is a curious linking of far-off generations.

San Antonio, August

Tuesday the 2nd we went on the early train to Marble Falls to the Mountain Remnant Reunion and such unspeakable heat! We were fortunate in being taken out to a camp on the river where we were at least free of the dust and glare of the little town. We had a good tent, with comfortable cots, and had a good nap in the evening. After supper I went with some young girls down to the river and had a long bath. The water was more than tepid and only about 12 to 18 inches deep generally, so we simply crawled around on the hard clean granite and sand most of the time, but it was cold enough when we rose up in the strong southeast breeze.

I think it was the first night I ever slept in a tent, but it was heavenly after the day. We heard that the mercury was 107 that day in the village.

A visit to the legislature in extra session showed a cleaner capitol than the last time I had seen it; fewer spittoons and more pictures, mostly dreadful. Men were busy painting the halls white toned with gilt.

The legislators, generally in shirt sleeves, wrote, talked and spat in desultory fashion. They did not impress me as being as strong a body of men (although somewhat better dressed) as in the old days when the old fighting, fearless, frontier Texans were there. Those men had ideals beyond the regulation of the length of sheets in hotels and such other stuff. Many of them would have thought a sheet of any length a useless addition to a bed, but they would have fought for the honor of Texas and believed in its greatness, I think.

J. has received a formidable sheet of parchment which but for its bearing the seal of the State Department instead of a blue ribbon might be a high school diploma or one of those framed certificates that you read over and over while agonizing in the dentist's chair. It declares that the President, "reposing entire confidence" in J. for several flattering reasons, designates him "as a Commissioner to represent our country at the ceremonies incident to the one hundredth anniversary of the Independence of our Sister Republic of Mexico."

Nothing could be more delightful for us. J. is intensely interested in the politico-international side of it, and the social and ceremonial part will be dazzling. We love Mexico and like Mexicans and both will be at their best. The city is so splendid, and no people know how to plan a fiesta better or enjoy it more. We hear that this is to be done on such a magnificent scale that Finance Minister Limantour has washed his hands of the responsibility and gone to France.

Nearing Laredo, September 4

I have had time to make only a general survey of the dramatis personae of the special embassy.

The special ambassador of the President, Governor Curtis Guild of

The Honorable
James Luther Slayden

Ellen Maury Slayden

Ellen Maury, 1879

Ellen Maury Slayden, 1888

Congressman's lady

Mr. and Mrs. Jesse Maury, Mrs. Slayden's parents, on their Golden Wedding Anniversary

"He [father] tells me he is the only man left in the county who voted for Andrew Jackson and he is still a Democrat, nourished with 'the pure milk of the word' by his father's friend and neighbor, Jefferson, whom he remembers well."

"Piedmont," the Maury ancestral home in Charlottesville, Virginia

"During Sheridan's raid when General Custer had his headquarters in this house, he permitted his soldiers to throw all the family papers out in the mud and run bayonets through them to make sure there was no gold in them."

Jane Maury Maverick, Mrs. Slayden's sister,
her husband Albert Maverick and their family

"Bryan was immensely taken with my sister and Albert Maverick and their eleven children. After his address to working men on Alamo Plaza at noon, J. took him to lunch with them, and the children hung around him with delight."

Sunshine Ranch, the Maverick home near San Antonio,
where the Slaydens were frequent guests

". . . while J. was off Chautauqua-ing I had two weeks at the ranch with children and realities, and Jane and Rose in what Allie calls our annual jabberwork."

Left to right: Representative (later Senator) Carter Glass of Virginia, an unidentified woman, and the Slaydens on a Congressional delegation visit to Hawaii in 1915

"On the dock we received the wreaths of welcome . . . and yet one more school of Japanese-Chinese, Portuguese-Hawaiian children rolled their eyes obliquely to heaven and sang with fine irony: Land where our fathers died/ Land of the Pilgrims' pride. *Once more the class orator bade us welcome and asked for a return of the tariff on sugar."*

Congressman Slayden speaking at Wailuku, Island of Maui

"J. spoke briefly and to my satisfaction, as he neither told an anecdote, made facetious remarks about 'my wife' nor promised impossible things to our hosts—a marked departure from the style of most of the speeches on this trip."

Congressman Slayden, center, planting a tree on the Capitol grounds

"If J. had done nothing else in Congress he would deserve his country's gratitude for getting the Lincoln Memorial in its present form, instead of a highway to Gettysburg, and for firmly establishing the Arts Commission."

George and Maury Maverick, Mrs. Slayden's nephews, in France during World War I

"... they ceased firing at nine o'clock this morning, they cannot kill any more. Selfishly I think first 'Maury and George are safe,' though M. is hideously wounded. ..."

Massachusetts, is large, handsome, full fed, with something of Roosevelt's ebullience.

Senator Crawford is a large man. His wife wears a black taffeta frock and a silver star on her breast which she told me was "the *Eastern* star," though I had not questioned its position in the spacious firmament on high.

Senator Overman and his pretty married daughter are unmistakably from North Carolina. Representative Foster of Vermont, chairman of the House Foreign Relations Committee and chief of the commissioners, is New England genial but jokes "wi' deefeculty." His wife hasn't joked at all so far. She is preoccupied with the heat.

Mr. and Mrs. Rook of Pittsburgh are young and bright, and look as if they are prepared to enjoy whatever befalls them.

General Harrison Gray Otis, California, is a fine, soldierly old man and has with him a pretty granddaughter, Miss McPherron. Judge and Mrs. Jimmy Gerard are from New York. No one could doubt it, he is so oblivious of the existence of the rest of the country. Mrs. G. is young and pretty with the touch of Irish that we expect from New Yorkers. I think I shall like her.

Representative and Mrs. Fairchild, our old friends from upstate New York, are "comfortable bodies," taking heat and other discomforts as part of the day's work. With ourselves from Texas we represent all sections. We are the only ones who know Mexico, and we are promising "airs from heaven" as soon as we sight the mountains. We have certainly had "blasts from hell" all day. About 100 degrees in this car.

Across the River

At Nuevo Laredo, escorted by the most lovely band, we walked through cheering lines of *pelados* to the customhouse. The hideous old shed, scene of many a nervous episode for me in the past, was completely transformed by flags and wreaths; and many a citizen's home had lent its proudest possessions of Smyrna rugs and curly rattan parlor suite to furnish it. We were greeted by officers in glorious uniforms and many sweet and well-dressed women. A young man made an address in excellent English, and Guild replied in well-intentioned Spanish. Castellot, President of the Mexican Senate, had come with a large staff to escort us to the capital, and he and Mr. Foster exchanged *felicitaciones*. We all cried, "Viva Mexico" and glowed with friendship and *mucho calor*.

After a feast of champagne, good ice cream and that gray, porous cake peculiar to the border, we came to this decorated and luxurious train and dropped into the lap of the Mexican government for better or for worse. Baron Uchida, the Japanese Special Envoy, and the Baroness have one coach, the Mexicans have one, and we have several.

September 5

The traditional gravity that should hedge an embassy is little in evidence with us. Governor Guild is what darkies call "sometimely." Usually dignified, he now and then lapses into Rooseveltian boyishness quite out of keeping with his present rank.

The station at Monterrey last night was a solid mass of people and the loveliest music was being played in our honor. We were asked to come out and be received by the Governor of Neuvo León, so we stepped off the car into hopeless confusion, with no dignitaries in sight. Then the order was reversed and we clambered back while the Mexicans brought in the smallest specimen of governor I ever saw in captivity. The space was limited, and most of us were standing on the steps and vestibule when the band began to play "America." From humming the air we got to singing it, and soon were all singing at the top of our voices. When Governor Guild finished his official duties, he took a front place on the platform, and he and stout old Senator Overman put their arms around one another and sang, now vociferously, now sentimentally, with heads thrown back like the March Hare and the Hatter at the Mad Tea Party. We asked the band to play "La Golondrina," the Mexicans cheered and Guild told us when he did his arms "so"—making the forward fisticuff motion in the Harvard rah-rah manner—that we must give three cheers for Mexico, which we did, and finally the band struck up "The Star-Spangled Banner." We shouted the first two lines, petered out pitifully on the next three or four, but spurted in grandly on the homestretch, and altogether seemed more like a traveling minstrel troupe than a Special Embassy to Our Sister Republic. J. was considerably scandalized.

At San Luis Potosí another crowd was waiting and great hampers of flowers —roses, gardenias, gladioli, jasmines—were brought in for us, besides grapes and strawberries. As we were leaving, Senator Castellot himself and his aides brought armfuls of bouquets—very stiff and Victorian—of tube roses and carnations, till we were almost overwhelmed with perfume. Our gentlemen went off for one of their periodical visits of ceremony and champagne to the Mexican car, and we took the flowers and hung them on hooks and electric lights, banked them on window sills and over the doors and made the place a bower of color and freshness. But the floor was a sight, and ambassadresses though we were, we longed for a broom but hadn't the moral courage to ask for one and betray our simple habits to our lordly hosts. The porters were asleep.

The gentlemen came in to admire our work and brought each of us a box of candy tied with red, white and blue ribbons. Luncheon was interrupted at San Miguel by offerings of the local crafts, blankets and baskets, and mangos.

It is now five o'clock and we have had no presents for two hours.

Senator Overman is quite ill, and I have contributed a hot-water bag. The only one in the party, I believe, though I know of two diamond tiaras. Senator and Mrs. ——— grow more opaque and sad. I wonder why they came on a trip like this, all made up of scenery and adventure, when they could get so much better pie and cereal at home.

General Otis has been telling them the story of the Argonauts. When he finished I heard the Senator thank him and say, "I never ran across that story before. I have often wondered what the Golden Fleece meant." He is the only one in the party who still takes T.R. seriously. He looks wounded when the rest of us laugh about his performances. Guild told me at lunch how after he had worked for him all over the country before his elective term, T.R. sent for him and begged him to run for vice-president. He protested that he was not geographically suitable, but T.R. said, "I will *make* you vice-president." Then two days later Guild found that he was offering the place just as urgently to Dolliver.

There is a trifle of friction about etiquette between Guild and Foster. G. represents the President and F. the people, and these are days when it is hard to tell which one comes first. We are climbing mountains and my head feels like a drum. The engine appears rounding the sharp curves ahead like a red, white and green striped dragon breathing fire through the dark clouds that roll around us.

Cobian Palace, Mexico City, September 6

It was pitch dark and raining hard long before we came into the city. We tried to smarten ourselves with hats and coats that had been stuffed in the porter's locker for two days, but at best we were dusty and badly creased. As the train rolled into the station we were greeted with music ("The Star-Spangled Banner," of course) from one of those glorious, full-breathing Mexican bands that sound like one great woodwind instrument.

Under Castellot's order the ladies waited while our dusty gentlemen filed out into a world of shining silk hats and frock coats. When we followed them, each of us armed with a huge brand-new bouquet, we must have looked like a row of superannuated bridesmaids. We were presented to the Secretary of State, Mr. Creel, the American Ambassador, Mr. Wilson, whom I had met years ago in Brussels, and Mr. Godoy and José Romero, old friends from the embassy in Washington.

The front of the station and buildings around the plaza were sheets of red, white, and green electrics, and the mass of spectators so quiet they hardly seemed to breathe. It was part of the infinite tact of our hosts to provide coaches for us instead of automobiles, and the roll of rubber tires and clean tapping of hoofs on the asphalt soothed our nerves after the roar and rattle of the train.

From far off the palace was a glow of white light, every door, window and line of roof outlined with electric globes. As we passed the guard and through the stately iron gates my sense of dust and travel stain became poignant, and when the inevitable frock-coated gentleman took me fairly racing up the steps to a brilliantly lighted hall full of people in evening dress I felt like Cinderella deserted by her fairy godmother.

Mrs. Creel, Mrs. Díaz—the President's daughter-in-law—and many others of the so-called "court circle" met us as if we had been old friends, their well-bred eyes never wandering to our hats and dresses as nervous American eyes are apt to do.

A long row of white-aproned maids and men in livery waited in the corridor, but the ladies themselves showed us to our rooms. I wondered if any of our stiff Cabinet dames in Washington could have done anything so simple and graceful. They usually feel such solemn deference to their "position."

We have a front room fit for a queen with a bath all our own. I would have accepted a closet under the stairs just as gladly if it had served to remind some of my compatriots that we were guests and not in a hotel. One of them loudly demanded a screen around the corner separating her from her bath when I should have gone like Lady Godiva rather than complain. Another did not conceal her annoyance when she was given only one room and had to face the possibility of sharing it with her husband. She finally got two and a bath.

We are waked by a drum and bugle corps playing the "Advance," and I enjoyed its fine spirit as I always do. It is now nearly eight, and J. has been trying to get our trunks, but the proud young porter outside shrugged his shoulders, turned his palms and said, "A la neuve o diez, possible" (at nine or ten o'clock, possibly), and we are due at the National Palace at 10:30.

I am negotiating for bread and coffee before I get up. One maid has come to ask what I wanted, another to ask if it was really so, and a third to bring a menu card a foot long. Still another has taken my shoes. They are dull kid, and I know they will come back stove-polished.

Except for the patio, which was marble and moonshine last night, I have little idea yet of the extent and beauty of the Cobian. There is a heavenly glimpse from my windows of a garden of rain-washed grass and climbing pink geraniums guarded by two rugged little Indian soldiers, and there is a company of soldiers around the gates.

A maid has brought a silver tray piled up with great envelopes addressed to "Excellentissimo y Excellentissima Slayden" together and separately and inviting us to *funciones* given by representatives of every country and for every hour of the day. Will my strength and my clothes stand the strain?

September 8

It was nearly nine when the trunks arrived. There was racing and chasing to unpack, and such creases and disorder, but this is a fairy palace. Hairdressers, tailors, laundresses appeared, and my ivory satin with voile tunic and Dresden ribbon came back as good as new. J.'s clothes, too, were perfect.

Of course we were not all ready on time, but about eleven we got together, and each of us with a nice little Mexican cavalier, stepped into an automobile and were fairly whirled past the Iron Horse and down San Francisco Street to the Palacio Nacional. Soldiers lined the whole way on both sides; San Francisco Street was packed with people, many Americans, and besides the flags and bunting overhead the balconies were hung with rugs in the Spanish fashion and crowded with pretty women throwing flowers to us as we passed.

The massive gray walls of the courtyard made a somber background for bright dresses and uniforms and shining automobiles, and as each envoy arrived, they echoed back the sound of crashing bands playing the inevitable national air. Some of our party, I think, are a bit contemptuous of the worn grayness of the buildings and think they should have been calcimined for this occasion to show that Mexico is up to date. They speak of Mexico, too, as if she were a young and unsophisticated nation, forgetting that many of these splendid buildings were here, and art and science progressing, when the breaking waves were dashing (not quite high enough for me) over Plymouth Rock.

We raced breathlessly up the dark stone stairs (it is dreadful to walk fast at this altitude), only dimly conscious of the rare plants that filled every waste space and the funny little Indian guards flattened against the wall in imitation of those gorgeous Jacks of Clubs that do duty in places of state in Europe. We passed through vast rooms and corridors lined with bowing officers in native and foreign uniforms. I dimly remember some very big Chinese vases, immense portraits of Hidalgo and Juárez and a terrifying battle piece, but we sped onward and, panting for breath, were ushered into the Hall of the Ambassadors. It is a long, long room with glass doors on the right side, almost from floor to ceiling, opening on iron balconies overlooking the Zócalo. There were rows of chairs on either side, and between them a broad strip of red carpet leading to a dais with a thronelike chair surmounted by the arms of Mexico in gold.

Mrs. Creel, very pretty and cordial, gave us seats in the front row of chairs to the right, and I was glad to rest and look about for a moment.

We were all talking gaily when the doors back of the dais opened and the President, with his son and Colonel Cuellar, came in, and everyone rose and every sound was hushed.

Díaz wore plain black evening clothes with the broad tricolor ribbon slanting across his breast. He came forward along to the edge of the platform, stood perfectly erect, right foot slightly forward, head up, hands at ease—a superb figure of confidence and courage. His face was inscrutable, but it must have been a thrilling moment even in his eventful life. Representatives of all the principal nations of the world are here to honor him and his country, all of them curious, some critical, some jealous, but none doubting the greatness of this man, who "tore the fruits of victory from the unwilling hands of Fate." For thirty years he has kept his steady progress upward, carrying his country with him. He has been glorified and reviled, represented as superman and superdevil, ignorant tyrant or genius of constructive statesmanship, but never forgotten or ignored in the world's scheme of things.

At the audience Governor Guild, special envoy of Mexico's best and nearest neighbor, came first. He was conducted up the red carpet to the platform, made a few choice remarks that I couldn't hear, and was then seated in a high place. The Marchese di Bugnano, in the reddest coat, did the honors for Italy. Three dazzling little Chinamen made wonderful bows, handed in their papers, but said nothing, while pretty Mercedes Godoy and Conchita Sepulveda just behind me made frivolous American-girl remarks about their "goo-goo eyes." I can't remember how many followed, but when the ceremonies were over we had been standing for one hour and thirty-five minutes! Díaz stood like a rock throughout and answered each envoy in a voice as clear and firm as that of a man of forty. It is impossible to believe that we are to celebrate his eightieth birthday on the 16th.

Another day

I cannot keep count of time. We are "ambassadors in bonds." The silver tray is still piled with cards to *solemnes funciones,* dinners, garden parties, unveiling of statues, laying of cornerstones, openings of schools, hospitals, and a national university. There is a banquet given by every special commission or resident embassy from Greenland's icy mountains to India's coral strand.

Such a comical thing has happened about Ruben Dario, the great poet of Nicaragua. He was coming to represent his country, but while he was on the high seas his government changed hands, and when he reached Vera Cruz he didn't know whom or what he represented. Naturally as both poet and patriot he was thrown into a fine frenzy, and though Mexico received him literally with palms and laurels, calling him the delegate from Parnassus with credentials from the Muses, he refused to play, packed up his laurels and went home. I am sorry. I wanted to meet him. His verses are hauntingly musical and amazingly modern. Most Mexicans take poets more seriously than we do, and a surprising number of their intellectuals write graceful verse. Several times men have been presented to me with the simple statement, "He is a poet," and it remained for me to discover that he was also a leading politician or man of affairs.

Sunday, September 11

This morning we dedicated the base for the statue of Washington[1] on Plaza Dinamarca, henceforth "Washington," and we American women were seated on the platform with the President. For a wonder it was not raining, and the flowers, flags and costumes were at their best. The escorts were in blue and white uniforms with much gold, but Díaz wore a plain frock suit, a gray tie without a pin, and tan gloves. He must be terribly tired, but his step was firm as he came up, bowed gravely to us, and stood while

[1] The statue, by Pompeo Coppini, was torn down and dragged through the streets by a mob after President Wilson's ill-considered assault on Vera Cruz during the revolution.—E.M.S., 1925.

the band played the Himno Nacional. He sat down only after an apologetic movement for having to turn his back to us.

With that foreign uncertainty about our National Air the band played "Dixie" and "Massa's in de cold, cold ground," which always reduces me to tears.

Poor J. is getting arrayed to receive the French Ambassador. I just *cannot* go again. We dine with the President tonight and later attend a gala performance at Teatro Arben. For this afternoon I have contrived an invitation for our party to take tea with Mrs. Nuttall[2] at Casa Alvarado. I hope the beauty and charm of this house that has been lived in for four hundred unbroken years may remind them of Mexico's age and quality, and stimulate their respect for her.

September 13

The dinner at the Palacio Nacional was charming. The President, Mrs. Díaz and Mrs. Creel received us, smiling and cordial through the same inane speeches and *felicitaciones* in bad Spanish that we have treated them to every day and night of this devil-driven week. I am having the best luck. Foutura y Xavier, Ambassador from Brazil, took me in and Gamboa, Introducteur des Ambassadeurs, sat to my left, both easy to talk to and worthwhile. F. y X. is a real novelist's diplomat, good-looking, and able to talk knowingly about everything, especially of our country and government.

Gamboa seems more than ordinarily clever, earnest and sincere. If only Mexico had more men like him. He spoke of the sorrowful political necessity of Maximilian's death and of the wise firmness of Díaz, and how difference in conditions and temperament of the races made it desirable to keep the same men in office longer here than is safe in our country. He called my attention to the fact that Mexicans had never destroyed their beautiful places nor robbed them as the French did in their revolution. All the furbishing of Chapultepec is accounted for, and most of the Maximilian silver was before us to speak for itself. Down the center of the table were ten very good candelabra alternating with massive bowls for flowers, and at each end immense platters holding tall urns, all of silver. For the sixty guests the first eight courses were served on silver plates, the last two on gold.

[2] Zelia Nuttall, an American-born archaeologist, was honorary professor at the National Museum of Mexico, author of numerous articles and books on Mexican history of the pre-Spanish and early colonial period and an authority on the Aztec calendar. She edited the *Codex Nuttall*.

After long hours of pomp and parade, and rain, the Cobian is a heavenly place to get back to at night—always softly lighted, fragrant with flowers, and many servants to look after us. We never hear the wheels go round, but even to face powder and quarts of cologne, and fresh ruffled pin cushions, no trifle is neglected for our comfort. A physician is at our call; our letters and telegrams are franked; and each couple has an automobile, except Governor Guild, who has an ambassadorial Victoria with prancing horses. Each lady has a maid, and sometimes their zeal outruns their discretion. Our gloves are cleaned so often that the smell of gasoline on the ambient air indicates the approach of the American Commission. Mr. Foster is a sweet and gentle person with the Vermont view of propriety. He speaks no Spanish, and just now he came to the door with Mrs. F.'s maid and begged J. to ask her to keep out of his room for twenty minutes, so he could change his clothes.

September 14

Spain's lofty tact in returning the uniform of the patriot Morelos—spoil of war one hundred years ago—gave occasion for the finest, most significant ceremony we have had. Bringing back a moth-eaten uniform seemed so childish that I couldn't see how it was to be done with dignity. I had a vision of dear little General Polavieja (the Spanish envoy and one of the pleasantest men we met) carrying it in on a clothes hanger, but it wasn't the first time that my imagination has failed to compass the pride and artistry with which Mexico can stage her patriotic tableaux.

We saw the procession from the usual balcony of the Palacio Nacional. The uniform, very brave and bright, in a polished wooden box with a glittering sun-shaped decoration back of it, rested on a gun carriage drawn by four splendid horses. General Polavieja walked behind, followed by the Senate and Congress and many other grandees of Mexico with bared heads. The sun was dazzling, drums and bugles sounded, a band played the Himno Nacional, the vast crowd cheered and wept, and humble women broke through the cordon to let babies in arms throw one more flower on the relic of the loved patriot.

We were hardlly seated in the audience room when the President darted into his place of state—he always seems to be propelled—and he never looked better. It was his apotheosis to have Spain herself do honor to Mexico and to him. His official family stood behind him, and soon the box, held very high, was brought in. Men in uniform crowded in bearing aloft the pathetic, tattered little flags of Morelos' army and other loved standards and, at last, even the most sacred flag of Mexico, the Virgin of Guadalupe, the actual Enseña de Inmortal Hidalgo.

They were so solemn and quiet they might have been Crusaders taking their vows. Polavieja made a graceful speech in presenting the uniform and Díaz replied with more emotion than I have ever seen him show. In the moment of silence afterwards a Mexican officer, with questionable taste, cried out "Viva España." There was a start of surprise over the room, but Polavieja proved himself diplomat as well as soldier by answering instantly and heartily, "Viva Mexico!" Then Díaz, in his deep grave voice, said, "Otra viva España"; it was given, and all was serene. It is the nearest we have come to an international contretemps. Later we poured the usual libations of champagne, Mrs. Díaz and Mrs. Creel themselves handing the glasses to many of us. They were a pretty study in color and type. Mrs. Díaz, slender, patrician and dark, in a dress of rich wisteria color, and Mrs. Creel, round, blond, and rosy in dusty green like a spring flower.

Mrs. Díaz is *really* lovely in mind and person. She is a typical high-bred Spaniard, cordial but unfailingly dignified and reserved. She never chatters all over, eyes, hands and feet, as so many Mexicans do, but talks well and with wide information. She speaks English fluently. Her manner to the President is perfection, always gently solicitous to spare him fatigue or from embarrassment by his slight deafness. At the same time her eyes twinkle with the humorous tolerance that all we loving wives show for our husbands' little personal foibles—as, for instance, his refusal to sit at table one minute longer than a certain time—forty-five minutes, I think it is.

I am not much of a hero-worshiper. "In the clothes of the greatest potentate there is only a man" is one of my favorite quotations. But about Don Porfirio Díaz there is something tremendous, cosmic, inexorable, that compels belief in his greatness. His carriage expresses his character. His head is always erect, his chest broad and full without the least embonpoint, his hands and feet are small and well made. He rarely smiles, but he never looks grim, and his eyes are kind and understanding. His unfailing courtesy shows him keenly sensitive to the people around him. In our almost daily contact with him and Doña Carmen I am impressed with their good breeding. They are never afraid to be natural. His is especially evident at Chapultepec where he will draw up a chair and advise you which is most comfortable, and she moves about shutting out drafts, bringing the right people together, and saying a pleasant word to the most obscure and humble of her guests. Don Porfirio is said to have more orders and decorations than any other man living (outside of Asia), and we are to see him invested with still another, the Collar of Carlos III. It seems that Carlos had only a few collars, but the death of King Edward, which has kept the British Legation in mourning through this gala time, left one without a wearer just in time for Spain to bestow it on Díaz as a pledge of friendship from the Mother Country.

September 15

In Saltillo last summer we were told that there was to be a revolution at the time of the Centenario. With the world there to see, Díaz would be "dethroned" and Mexico become a republic indeed. With Mexican love of the dramatic the revolt was to be staged on the night of the Grito, but J. and I have watched in vain for signs of revolution or even discontent. Don Porfirio goes about his daily affairs in coach or automobile apparently unguarded. He doesn't slip out of the back doors nor drive by unusual routes. A fanfare of bugles and the National Hymn and a spontaneous chorus of "Viva el Presidente," follows him. His still, inscrutable face is always set forward; there is no nervous glancing from side to side when people press close to him and even climb on the steps of his carriage. There are hundreds of opportunities for an assassin to take a pot shot at him, but no one seems in the mood to do it. Our Northern Mexican friends are not alone in misapprehensions and misrepresentations. We read in American papers— not alone in Hearst's yellow rags, either—that our party here has been repeatedly "insulted" and one even told how a bomb had been thrown at us. What type of journalist is it that is willing to make trouble between nations by such preposterous lies? Our only danger is of being killed with kindness.

San Antonio, November

The following letter has naturally given J. and me great pleasure and a feeling of honest pride as well:

Andrew Carnegie
2 East 91st Street
New York

November 14, 1910

*Strictly Confidential
for the Present*

Hon. James L. Slayden,
    San Antonio, Texas
Dear Sir,
    In virtue of my interest in the cause of International Peace, and in the belief that the present is an opportune time to inaugurate an organized effort

to advance it, I propose to convey to a Board of Trustees Ten Millions of Dollars in Five Per Cent Bonds, the income of which shall be devoted to the advancement and promotion of this cause by such methods as the trustees may find to be wise and feasible.

The following have already accepted as members of the Board: Hon. William Howard Taft, Honorary President; Hon. Elihu Root, President; Nicholas Murray Butler; Henry S. Pritchett. No one has declined.

All expenses incurd by Trustees in connection with the Trust are to be paid; and those of wife or dauter also to the annual meeting.

The others I am now addressing, yourself among the number, will complete the Board. Your acceptance will confer a great favor, and a prompt reply will be appreciated.

Very truly yours,
Andrew Carnegie

Headquarters will be Washington.

CHAPTER FIFTEEN

1911

Washington, January 16

There is the devil to pay in Mexico. Almost impossible for us to believe who have known it so quiet and humdrum for nearly thirty years. The little town of Cusihuiriáchic in Chihuahua had the first outbreak, and my niece,[1] wife of the manager of the Potter Palmer mines there, writes me some particulars:

> Your card came just before the trains stopped running. I wanted to send a line to say we were safe, but the mail *would not* go out. The trains were turned over to the Government on the 13th of Dec.—unlucky day—and the soldiers—live ones from Chihuahua and dead and dying going back there— are given the preference. Nobody else can ride. We couldn't get supplies, and the Revolutionists took Cusi and almost everything there was to eat. Luckily Murray had laid in provisions for a month, and we go on entertaining as if nothing were wrong.
>
> The Revolutionists had a good time here, and made some excitement for us. They removed all Govt. officials, and compelled them to sign papers expressing sympathy with the revolution. Then the officials got frightened and left. The Revolutionists put in their own men, and they got afraid, so we have no government of any kind, but lots of drunken serenaders, pistol shooting, sounds of breaking bottles, and yells of "Viva Madero."[2] The Potter Palmers should be grateful to Murray for staying through the trouble. The Maderistas tried to borrow everything from him, powder, guns, saddles, horns, even field glasses, but being a foreigner and neutral has saved us so far.

I dragged myself out of bed to go to the banquet of the Architectural League and was amply compensated for the effort. After many teas it was joy to talk to such men as old Mr. Post, so winning and *simpático,* and with Blashfield, as clear-cut and graceful in his talk as in his physique,

[1] Mrs. Murray Crossette, nee Virginia Maverick.
[2] Francisco Madero, President of Mexico, 1911–1913.

like one of his own painted figures. J. hadn't told me that he was to speak, but my guardian angel prompted me to wear my very best frock which made my soul serene when I found myself at the raised table with the speakers and notables. Mr. Post was next to the president, then J. and me, and next to me the president-elect, Walter Cook, and his wife, both of them clever and jolly. Senator Chamberlain spoke well, but too seriously for the occasion, and J. followed brightly, almost better than I ever heard him. Mr. Marshall told me later that he believed the advancement of art in this country was most marked in the West, that the *International Studio* had ten subscribers there to one in the East.

Later people crowded around to praise J. for his talk and for the good work he constantly does through the Library Committee for the cause of the fine arts. I had some gay talk with several men and a Mrs. Day of Philadelphia, who claimed me as "a good suffragist." She said she had lately been helping to elect "a reform and, I hope, a decent mayor," and I wished her good luck, but I have an abiding distrust of people who set out to reform their neighbors. They protest too much, and the holier-than-thou mental attitude is likely to be self-deception.

January 24

As chairman of the entertainment committee of the Congressional Club I thought I had achieved quite a little triumph for myself and the club when Mrs. Bryce wrote:

"If you can assure me that the occasion will be absolutely a private one with no reporters present I am willing to try to do what you wish. You are right in supposing that I cannot speak on any political question but there are many other aspects of public work done by our women that could be discussed perfectly safely. . . . Could you come in tomorrow morning and tell me a little about the kind of thing that is expected, and how long, and the hour. . . ."

I had a chance to tell the club that afternoon, and they all agreed to the terms—we really do not seek newspaper exploitation of our meetings— and I saw Mrs. Bryce and set the date. We propose, but Mrs. Champ Clark disposes sometimes; in this case without the least intention of doing wrong, but just because she cannot imagine anyone not wanting to be reported. A day or two later we found that she had invited every newspaperman or -woman of her acquaintance to come and hear Mrs. Bryce. It was then my painful duty either to uninvite the newspaper people—a thing almost impossible without in a way compromising Mrs. Clark—or to see Mrs.

Bryce and give her the opportunity to withdraw. Fortunately Mrs. B. has a deal of common sense and helped us out of the dilemma as gracefully as possible. She had also heard of Mrs. C.'s telling that her subject was to be "The English Woman in Politics"—"The very thing I was not going to discuss," she said.

Aggregations of women and clubs are not in my line. They made me chairman of this committee in spite of my protests, and I tried to make it worthwhile by a course of talks to enlighten us about the things our government is doing quietly while we only hear the vociferous lawmakers. Few of us know how the Agricultural Department with its many ramifications of work affects our daily life; how the Geological and Geodetic Surveys are widening our interests and commerce; what the Library and the Indian Bureau do, etc., etc. But to my chagrin I find that still fewer of us want to know about them. (Mrs. Herbert Parsons, a member of my committee, was enthusiastic over my plan to invite the head or a distinguished member of each department to tell us on club days about his specialty.) I began with Dr. Howard of the Entomological Department, who made a thrilling story of the danger of small things like flies, mosquitoes, and germs. Miss Fletcher did not do quite so well with the Indians, but I was going on with my program joyfully when I found that a great majority of the club members were bored to death. Friends advised me that I was criticized as high-brow, and the members resented my efforts to "educate" them, and said that such stuff was not meant for a social club anyway. And I was glad to get a little education myself! They want pink teas or nothing, and they shall have them without interference from me when my term expires. I never realized until I had been here some years that "the government" meant anything more than the legislative, judicial and executive branches. Now I think they might with advantage to the country shut up shop occasionally and let the Agricultural Department run things for a while. New vegetables do so much more good than new laws. If we would mind the laws we have we might do without new ones for a long time.

This note was in Baroness Uchida's own handwriting. I wonder if I could learn in a lifetime to write my name in Japanese. She is clever and interesting in several languages:

1321 K St., Tuesday

Dear Mrs. Slayden:

My husband and I are asking you and Mr. Slayden and your two daughters to give us the pleasure of dining here with us tomorrow night in order to meet Mr. Casasus. We have just heard that he is free only tomorrow night, and so it is a very short notice, but if you all could spare the time we shall be perfectly delighted.

Yours sincerely,
Masa Uchida

P.S. My husband tells me that he did not know of the Misses Slayden and the formal invitations for them are not yet sent. Please take this one and consider it as good as the formal one.

I wonder where she learned to say "you all." The two daughters she endows us with are a surprise, but J.'s niece Agnes will do for one, and I have excused the other and accepted the invitation. The Mexican delegation is here to thank us for coming and having such a good time in Mexico last summer.

Thursday

The dinner was good fun, many more men than women, a rare occurrence here, and all the Mexicans old acquaintances. Agnes, who is a real daughter of the gods, divinely tall and fair, dreaded going in to dinner with one of the little Japanese attachés, but she was entrusted to a handsome young Mexican, not quite as tall as herself but with a sense of humor that saved her from embarrassment. When about to move into the dining room he said quizzically, "Mees Slayden, will you take my leetle arm?" and their contrasting color and animation made them very good to look at.

The Mexicans present a brave front and speak slightingly of the revolution, but we get ominous letters from friends down there, American and Mexican. The old lion is showing his age, and the foxes and jackals are yelping around ready to tear him to pieces at the first sign of weakness.

May 27

J., Mrs. Nuttall of Casa Alvarado and I were not a vivacious trio as we drove in a jerky little herdic to the White House garden party yesterday. Mrs. N. is handsome and intellectual but as serious as the idols and pyramids she is digging up in Mexico. We were all depressed by the news from that most distressful country—the resignation of Díaz and the beginning of what we believe will be an era of anarchy, or at best paralysis of the civilization he has achieved in his thirty years' rule of people who need a *ruler*. Mrs. N. ascribed the condition to disloyalty of the army and a subtle clerical influence. An aged canon of Guadalupe told her five weeks ago when she went to say good-by to him that he was glad she was going away "for Díaz must fall soon." She expressed surprise and regret, and he said vehemently, "It is time, it is time!"

It is hard to believe that the old Lion of the Puebla left the city last night almost like a fugitive from the people he has so long been saving from themselves.

The garden party was pretty, but weeks of drought have taken the green from the leaves and the grass crackled under our feet. The President looked well in a gray sack suit but wasn't half as buoyant as usual. Helen[3] received with him in a girlish but dignified way. Poor Mrs. Taft is still too ill to take part in anything.

There were not many interesting people, and I had to prod my conscience with memories of glorious afternoons spent with Mrs. N. at Casa Alvarado as I dragged up my friends and even enemies to present to her. Angels could have done no more, but I am sure she didn't enjoy it.

The *Independent* sent me five copies with my article, "The Grace and Gaiety of the Mexican Centennial," covering four pages of it. It is cut all to pieces, but the amputations are skillfully done and it isn't so bad. But how I hate "thru." How can a self-respecting magazine adopt such a verbal monstrosity? Hamilton Holt was more than kind about my style, etc., when I met him in Baltimore, but I wish it had come out in the *Century*, where Mr. R. U. Johnson says it would have been if I had sent it "before our impending annexation of Mexico makes it unsuitable."

May 28

Francis D. Millet, the great artist, the tender and humorous friend, Mr. Townsend, the New Jersey Congressman and author, and Mr. Sharp, an Ohio M.C., took breakfast with us this morning. There were daisies on the table to suit the pleasant summer day, but I soon moved them off because they hid us from one another and interfered with the general conversation that I love. We had corn bread, broiled chicken, and fried tomatoes. That breakfast is my invariable rule. I shall patent it like Dr. ———'s Favorite Prescription.

Mr. Townsend rarely says anything to prove it, but you somehow take it for granted that he is clever. He has a genial and assured manner, as if he could dazzle you if he chose. Though he found us seated at table when he came in, he was gracefully unabashed. Having written some serious novels and essays that nobody reads, he is said to resent being remembered

---

[3] Helen Taft Manning, later dean of Bryn Mawr College.

only as the creator of "Chimmey Fadden." He determined never to joke in Congress because he thought it cheapened a public man to be known as a humorist. I don't agree with him. A good joke, like some of Reed's or S. S. Cox's, lives longer than many a bill bearing the same author's name.

Mr. Millet sat down saying, "This is what I like—*Christian family breakfast*." When handed a plate of Aunt Lucy's corn-bread sticks, he asked, "Do you have a thing made to cook them this way, or do you use gas pipe?" He ate such a lot of them that we all made it a joke, and he inquired if there were a cab stand near for he knew he couldn't walk home.

In the evening J. and I took our supper out in the back yard—a pleasant "out ovation" in spite of the ash cans, washtubs, and ugly board fences. My blooming grapevine had the fragrance of Virginia woods, and some of our neighbors have lovely ampelopsis. What a shame it is that all this good space in Washington is given up to "back yards"—the very name is an offense—with no approach except through the kitchen or a back alley. This amount of ground in England would be a place of beauty and joy to the household, or in Spain where the tall houses enclose a great space without cross fences or unsightly objects, beautifully kept as a common garden for the delight of all the people who look into it from the high balconies.

Saturday we went to the Kauffmans' to a garden party—an annual delight. The drive with the Porters in a big open landau through Rock Creek Park seemed as if it must be the best part of the trip until we reached Airlie—such a lovely garden enclosed in walls of roses, with beds of sweet old-fashioned flowers and women in pretty summer clothes strolling among the parterres and seats.

In three different places about the grounds were tables of refreshments, making it convenient for Mrs. P., Agnes and me to eat more than our share of sandwiches and cream without being conspicuous, much to the scandal of Mr. P. and J., who are marvelously proper men. Most of "high society" was there, but I recall no one especially striking except Mrs. Sherman in a white lawn dress and many diamonds and Mrs. John W. Foster in an entire costume, even to a dotted veil over her face, of Prussian blue.

June 1

J.'s birthday, and I had a little dinner to surprise him. He was at the wool schedule caucus all day and got in at 7:30 with barely time to get into fresh things. I was overpowered with gratitude from the men for telling them to come in summer clothes, and I think it made it an easy evening for all of us. I positively suffer when I see men in weather like this trying to look pleasant while preoccupied with a melting collar and surreptitiously mopping the back of their necks. The guests were the Porters, Senator and Mrs. Hitchcock, and the Lowrys, he of the New York *Evening Post*—all clever and cultivated.

Apropos of something hot on the table, Senator Hitchcock told a story of an Irishman who bit into a red pepper and then laid it by his place saying to the waiter, "Lave it be. I want to loight me poipe prisintly." We warned him against some fine little Brazilian point doilies in the dessert plates because another Western senator had eaten one when dining with us a year ago. The Senator had not actually eaten it, but he heaped his ice cream on it, and was just carrying it to his mouth when I rescued it as gracefully as I could. I don't think he ever forgave me. He has not been here since. The dinner was good—soft-shell crabs, spring lamb and asparagus, and maple mousse. After dinner we talked Mexico until J. had to go back to the caucus.

June 2

We have had a splendid storm today and lightning struck somewhere quite near us. We thought it was the Cairo which is so high and inviting, but just then the house sprang a leak, as it usually does in a hard rain, and the servants and I had to seize buckets and cloths to stem the flood that poured down from the third story. Tonight the air is fresh for the first time in weeks and Washington not such a grievous prospect, but I do long to get away. We talk trips all the time, generally Rome for the meeting of the Interparliamentary Union in October, but lately the Congress of Races in London, July 27. Tonight Mr. Porter drank to the party's meeting in Rome, and asked us all to dine with him at Frascati. Alas! it all depends on the wool schedule. Mr. Porter spent some years in Rome when his father was minister to Italy (under Harrison) and it will make our visit much more interesting to have him there.

June 4

Yesterday the Butlers, Porters and ourselves with Mr. Meade, Elena Calderón and Agnes went on a picnic to a gorge near Burnt Mills as rough and wild as a bit of the Rocky Mountains. We had a good supper on the grass. Agnes and Elena ate a great deal at the same time contriving to fill the pockets of Mr. Meade's beautiful white flannel coat with pebbles so that he carried weights when he tried to get up. We came home by moonlight, and I hated the hot breath of the town when we met it far out. Mr. Butler told us that Bryan was first nominated for President at Burnt Mills. While here in Congress, he went there to a picnic and, the speaker failing to appear, Bryan was asked to take his place and spoke so well that the assembled farmers then and there declared him their candidate.

June 6

"Forrest Lodge" suggests Robin Hood and the good green wood, but instead it is the most unwholesome, dusty old Civil War hall and barracks out in Georgetown which Mr. Millet is using for a studio. He is never too tired or preoccupied to spend himself for others, and we had a gay hour with him yesterday afternoon studying his series of panels for the New Jersey State House. We learned for the first time the story of the purchase of New Jersey from the Indians for so much red cloth and so many brass kettles. It makes a rich theme for the pictures but is not an inspiring genesis for a state—other than New Jersey.

Colonel Carson, a genial and clever army officer, came home to dinner with us. He talked some military shop but put life into it and used rarely good English. He told us a funny story of his father's traveling in the West with Carl Schurz and some other friends, and the mystification of a land-lady who, asking how many there were in the party, was told, "Seven with Schurz, and six without."

At the Tittmanns' Sunday evening we had lovely music, Charles and Agnes singing with Mrs. Hitchcock playing their accompaniments. Justice Brown was there, and Colonel Hilary Herbert with his sweet, ornate, old-Southern manners. Not many of his kind are left. My J. without actually belonging to that period has something of that manner—like one born out of due time— a gracious way of bowing over a woman's hand, for instance, acquired, no doubt, in his boyhood in New Orleans.

When my little entertainments turn out as intended I am always surprised. My luncheon for Mrs. Nuttall was very nice, but with Mrs. Porter and Mrs. Radcliffe to help, a party really can't go wrong. The other guests were Mrs. Whitman Cross, Mrs. Cushing and dear Miss Alice Fletcher, so motherly and warm for all she is a "leading scientist." Mrs. Nuttall is quite different. One feels the Mexican pyramids and codexes all about her, and she doesn't countenance levity. She asked in her beautiful deep voice if the earthquake in Mexico yesterday wasn't "too bad," and I answered frivolously, no, that I had been wanting to shake Mexico lately and was glad the Lord had done it for me so thoroughly. She said, "O-o-oh," and Miss Fletcher laughed all over, not, I know, at my little joke, but at the way it was received.

June 11

Today (Sunday) the mercury went over 100 degrees, and we had company from eleven o'clock A.M. till late evening. At dinner we had some new Texans, Representative Oscar Callaway and his wife. They are *very* promising, fresh, unself-conscious, and radiantly intelligent. Both are graduates of the University of Texas and she, on her first venture outside the state, has eyes open to see and enjoy everything without a bit of false shame at not having seen it before. She is well dressed, has a soft voice without any drawl; and all he needs is a good barber and a well-made suit to make him a striking figure in the House. Why doesn't Texas send more like these? We have them in all parts of the state, but men are being elected because they are prohibitionists, or Baptists, or Woodmen of the World. Our next senator, they say, is running on a platform of "Mother, Home and Heaven."

June 12

Little Mary Maverick[4] arrived today after a year in Europe, and a funny little figure she was as she waved to me afar trotting beside the redcap with her bags. Her Paris dress must be the latest glory—dark-blue serge trimmed with startling white striped silk, a lace collar around a Dutch neck, and a light mauve sailor hat. Her skirt cannot be a yard wide, and caught on her stockings at every step showing her legs alarmingly. In the afternoon I took her on a tour of the Capitol. The House was holding a stuffy session, a man from Georgia sawing the air on the subject of wool to some fifteen weary colleagues, so we went to the Senate and on the way met Uncle Joe Cannon. Everyone is curious about him, so I introduced Mary, and he was as debonair as if she had been a prized constituent—never had approved of "Mavericks," but liked this specimen, etc.—and she was charmed. The Senate had adjourned, only Root and Warren sitting with their heads together, so we took a ride in the subway in one of the electric perambulators that our paternal government provides to take decrepit statesmen to their offices. Every Texan wants to see Bailey, so we dropped in on him. He knew all about the Mavericks, of course, and paid Mary grandiose com-

[4] Author's niece.

pliments fit for a dowager duchess. Half an hour later she asked thoughtfully, as if to be reassured, "Uncle Slayden, does he say those things to every girl?" J. laughed and left her in doubt, but for all his superlatives, I believe Bailey is sincere. He thinks in large orotund phrases and can't help speaking in them.

Sunday, June 18

It is too hot to have people to dinner, so we had General and Mrs. Ainsworth to breakfast and discussed the White House silver wedding that comes off tomorrow night. There are four thousand people invited, all officialdom here, of course, and selected classes of people from all over the country. The San Antonio *Express* says that our Rabbi Marks is invited and all the other rabbis. It isn't exactly politics and is still less a social gathering of friends. It looks to me as if the idea had "jes' growed" instead of being wisely thought out, and now is beyond control. The Tafts have such excellent taste usually, and I am sorry to hear them criticized so sharply for accepting carloads of presents. All officials, from the Supreme Court to the postman, have contributed, and still the presents come from the ends of the earth.

June 20

The wedding was a prodigious affair, the company promiscuous to a degree. It was so hot that I wore a lingerie dress, and poor J. looked longingly at his beautiful new tussah silks, but, of course, got into "decent blacks" and on the lawn he didn't quite suffocate.

The occasion has been much heralded, but it fell so far short of the effects in Mexico last summer that I was disappointed. The crowd was far too dense for us to get near the President and Mrs. Taft, but we knew where they stood by the blazing 1886–1911 sign that hung in the sky above them. Search lights on the State, War, and Navy Building and the Treasury made the lawn as bright as day, but it was crude like a fair or a circus.

The grass was damp, and the women standing in line had to hold up their trains, and unconsciously, as women will, kept getting them higher until the effect of décolleté and gorgeously jeweled shoulders with bathing suit extremities was grotesque. I never realized before how ugly women's legs are—collectively.

Alice Longworth wore an electric-blue satin, flesh-colored stockings and gold slippers. She held the very scant skirt quite high, and when the band played, kicked about and moved her body sinuously like a shining leopard cat. She has a way of throwing back her head and showing all her teeth just like her father, but hers are very white and handsome.

The papers today say that the presents were shown, but I think that is not true. I saw nothing like presents except some enormous "set pieces" of flowers that must have been given, for no sane person could have included them in the scheme of decoration. I heard a good many rather vulgar *sotto voce* inquiries, "How much did you put up?" "Are you getting your money's worth?" etc., that made me sorry that presents had been permitted. Many of the Tafts' friends regret it and feel that it was a mistake.

July 2

It is typical, hot, dull Washington summertime. The days are long, bright and still. The thick green trees lie utterly becalmed between the burning sun and glowing pavements. There is a smell of hot pitch from the street repair work. There is little traffic, and in the morning few sounds but lazy negro voices calling "Fra-i-sh feesh," "Branch fruit." "Branch" is a general term, a survival of the tradition that fruits from the eastern branch of the Potomac are the best. Now it describes whatever is grown locally, like the word "Creole" in New Orleans.

Yesterday on the slow and dilapidated 16th Street herdic, Mrs. Borland of Missouri assailed me insisting that Mrs. Champ Clark "ought to" have free use of the Congressional Club for her receptions. She knew it was against the rules but thought "rules should be set aside for the Speaker's wife." I don't need any club myself and would be glad to escape it, and I am fond of Mrs. Clark, but as long as I am an officer the rules of the club are going to be kept. (When the "old Alcalde"[5] was governor of Texas, he was urged to take some steps that were expedient but not lawful and, when he refused, was told angrily that the state would go to hell. "That may be," he said, "but if this state goes to hell under my administration, it will go *according to law*.") Mrs. B. could not see my point of view. Her view is typical of that growing deference and the social concessions made here to mere official position. Brought up as I was in the shadow of Monticello and with Jefferson for our example, that sort of thing gets on my nerves. One often hears Northern and Western women in the club speak of the President as "Our Ruler." That and the unctuous phrase "Our beloved Presadunt," so dear to female orators, try my soul. I see no occasion to love

[5] O. M. Roberts, Governor of Texas, 1879–1883.

a President. It is quite enough to respect him—if he's respectable. To love a new man every four years is not seemly, and to say that you do is hypocrisy and cant.

July 9

A note today from Don Porfirio, just a friendly acknowledgment of the letter of regret J. sent at the time of his retirement from Mexico, but the signature seemed that of a man much older than the one who signed the large photograph he gave us last September. He is a larger figure now, even old, poor and in exile, than Madero, the nominal leader of a successful revolution. It does not look as if "crazy Pancho," as he is called, will be able to control the situation that his clever and unscrupulous family have created with him as a figurehead.

August 8

The reception at the White House for Admiral Togo was to have been held on the lawn but, of course, it rained that day. We had red tickets admitting us through the northwest gate and the front door with the truly great, and we appreciated the privilege for the scene was most beautiful, far finer and more artistic than it was for the silver wedding. Both terraces were hung thickly with soft-toned Japanese lanterns, and the full moon did the rest.

The formalities were in the East Room where the President and Togo stood together like the kind giant and Hop-o'-My-Thumb. The Admiral is a bristly little brown man about my height—that is, five feet. His chest was covered with decorations and his face dominated by small eyes as hard and sharp as gimlets. We passed on through the big doors opening to the East Terrace where cigars were being handed to the Admiral's numerous little brown staff officers and a great crowd of our officers, all, by order of General Wood, "full dress, mounted." (He must think Togo an admiral of horse marines.) The "boots, spurs and sabers" made a foolish clatter rather jarring on the lovely scene and soft summer night. Later we found the West Terrace not so crowded, and were served with ice cream and champagne punch, met many friends, and altogether enjoyed the evening. The Tafts have a gift for creating an easy, hospitable atmosphere.

A few evenings later we went to the Chevy Chase Club to dine with Jim Cox[6] and, sitting on the veranda facing the golf links at the loveliest

[6] James M. Cox, Ohio congressman and Democratic candidate for President in 1920.

time of the evening, we saw approaching us the most appallingly fat man in shirt sleeves. As we were wondering how he kept his trousers up without suspenders, he called out cheerily, "Good evening, Mr. Slayden," and behold it was the President. He ought to play more golf and perhaps laugh less, but his frequent chuckle is very pleasant to hear.

S.S. st. louis, *August 12*

There was no one to wave good-by to us from the pier, but a quantity of letters consoled our loneliness, and after the confusion of the last few weeks, there are worse things than the prospect of a sea journey with only sixty-six on the passenger list. Because there are so few and not entirely because of J.'s "rank," I think, we have three rooms, real beds, writing desks and a bathroom. We must make the most of it. We shall probably never travel in such state again, certainly not at this price.

August 15

We are having news by wireless and there is a little paper on our breakfast plates full of disquieting Marconigrams about strikes and riots in England which may make it wise for us to land in Cherbourg instead of Southampton.

How Marconi has changed the psychology of a sea voyage. We used to have eight days or more the world forgetting, by the world forgot, and there was a thrill of expectation and a rush for papers on landing. Now we know it all in advance. Of course it makes travel safer, but you pay for it in a certain flatness of experience.

Off Scilly Islands

Happy is the crossing that has no history. Only one passenger has disturbed me, a soi-disant preacher of the Protestant Federation, whatever that may be, who sits by me and eats and grunts swinishly and talks about "racial equality." Fortunately the captain is on the other side, and J. just across. Captain Jamison is a pleasant and cultivated man, which made all the funnier some stories he told us of his experience with the navy during the Spanish War. He turned over his ship to a youngish "hero" captain who offered to make him a lieutenant, saying that it would "give him a gentleman's position, and he would be received everywhere." Small wonder that our navy is sometimes described as an offensive rather than a defensive institution.

Hotel Dysark

We did land at Southampton after all, but England is not like itself. There is a drought of almost Texas severity, and much more disastrous here than it would be there. The trees are brown and autumnal, and English turf and hedgerows not at all as poets have sung them. Often the hedges are actually dead. As we drove up to this little hotel, we saw Judge Seth Shepard and his new wife coming out, and in our artless Texas fashion called to them as if we had been on the prairies. It is very pleasant to have them for playmates for a few days. I must do some shopping and J. gets rather tired of my program in London which he says is "Liberty's or death" every day. Now he and the Judge go off to the "brawling purlieus of the law," Inns of Court, and such mannish places, and Mrs. S. and I go to Liberty's. There cannot be another shop as colorful, warm and quiet. We have each bought an all-enveloping black satin burnous, hers lined with pale blue, as becomes a bride blushing for the second time, and mine gray to suit a settled married woman. I also bought a silk scarf of old fady blue and Oriental rose which I hope to have the moral force to give away, but how can I part from it?

When we join the Porters in Paris we can find so many better things to do than shopping, and in Rome, especially, it would be sinful to have clothes on one's mind.[7]

J. got invitations for the Shepards to go with us to see a session of Parliament, but the speakers' gallery, where Mrs. Shepard and I sat and peeped through the bars, was so dark and stuffy that I didn't enjoy it except for the mere satisfaction of knowing I was there. J. and Judge Shepard were in the Distinguished Strangers' section, which they said was quite comfortable.

A man named Ramsay MacDonald, a gaunt, intense, bitter Labourite, was heaping invective upon Austen Chamberlain, and I was told later that the very pretty woman with a picture hat sitting next us was C.'s wife. She didn't seem to mind at all.

I wonder if English women really dress worse than any others or if the way they carry themselves makes them look worse in their clothes. So often the bases of their spines recede, and their skirts run up in front. Their feet are large, too, and their shoes and stockings so heavy even with quite

[7] The Interparliamentary Union was to meet in Rome in October, but just before the members were to start, they had official notice that there was an outbreak of cholera. Almost too opportune to be true, it seemed, when the day the I.P.U. was to have assembled, Italy declared war on Tripoli. To have a world arbitration meeting on their hands at such a time might have embarrassed even the supple Italians.—E.M.S., 1925.

light clothes. The present style of short skimpy skirt and rather low-necked blouses you think is the most unbecoming to them until one appears complacently arrayed in the full pleated skirt and long coat of yesteryear. They criticize American women for extravagance, changing with every season, but they don't understand that we wear our old clothes with a difference. We make them over into new ones. There's nothing righteous or admirable that I can see in emphasizing their original vintage.

The street music this year is a hideous mixture of bad American and misunderstood Mexican—an echo of the revolution, no doubt. I heard a barrel organ playing "Good morning, Carrie," which took me straight to the Kerrville fair, and later "Meet me in San Anto-ni-o," which took me anywhere to get out of hearing of it. One evening at Stratford a band played "Sobre las Olas," leaving out all the dreamy Mexican feeling and phrasing it in stout English fashion as if one had dressed up a Mexican serenader in tweeds and English boots.

August 25

The day at Weardale Manor down in Kent was an experience to live in the memory but rather oppressive at the time. So many bowing footmen, who embarrass me, and Countess Tolstoi (though she consents to be called Lady Weardale now that our dear old friend, her husband, is a lord) to show me to my room. She left me to freshen up before lunch, and come down when I chose, and I got lost, of course, and have no idea what sacred places and secret passages I invaded before I found the stairs.

Lunch was good and interesting with portraits of Pitts and Chesterfields keeping watch over us, and I drank barley water for the first and, I rather think, the last time. They have it in English books and I wanted to try it. We had coffee on the terrace, and Lady W. and I walked in the garden and inspected the "herbaceous borders," also as they do in English books. I did my prettiest, but Russian countesses and I are just not *simpática*.

London, September 30

When Italy turned back the I.P.U. so that she could go on comfortably with her war in Tripoli, we were rather at a loss what to do with ourselves for another month. Having gotten as far as Geneva, we went on to Lausanne hoping to see Mr. and Mrs. Díaz, but found they had just left, so we made a dash for the high Alps to enjoy the scenery. We had one heavenly day by diligence from Brigue to Gletsch, but over the rest of the trip I like to draw a veil. Indeed, the veil was drawn for us by the heaviest snowfall we ever saw, and we were thankful to hurry back to Brussels and rejoin the Porters.

On our way to Ostend we went aside to Swevegem près Courtrai to visit the Van de Vennes. The old Senator was as gay as ever and J. slightly embarrassed at madame's kissing him roundly as she met us at the door. Marthe, the lovely little girl and our special friend (she calls us aunt and uncle), is quite a young lady and was presented at court last winter. How I wish our girls could get her sort of education. She speaks four languages, knows English literature, as I can testify, and no doubt several other literatures of which I know nothing, and yet she has had none of what we call "advantages." She is an only child and never went to a "finishing school," but just had lessons, and was taught the love, not the mechanical business, of learning. The house was full of pretty things, old Flanders carvings and Dutch marquetry, and a whole room, oak-paneled and shelved, built especially to fit the largest and most beautiful collection of old Delft that I ever saw outside the Dresden museum.

Three weeks to spend in London as we please! Could anything be nicer, except Rome? I find it hard to forgive those Italians.

October 17

Mr. and Mrs. Díaz are here for the wedding of one of those lovely Algara girls, and we hope to see them. They say that Don Porfirio is possessed by a demon of restlessness that drives him hither and yon without reason. A hard life for Doña Carmen.

Washington, November 20

Sitting at ease in Zion with Mrs. Porter while my own house was being put in order was very good fun, but Aunt Lucy has come in from the country, and I have to stay here and keep her company. It is miserably lonesome without J. I was inviting the old woman's sympathy, and she said, "Dat's de truth, Miz Slayden. You en I is in de same fix ezackly. Dat ole nigger o' mine ain't no 'count in dis world, *neither*, and yit I can't take no pleasure keepin' house widout him." I wrote J. of her estimate of him and "ole Turner" and hope it will hurry him on.

Mother has come, and we went to see Burton Holmes's pictures of Spain. As an extra he showed some marvels of motion photography of flowers—hyacinths, roses and lilies—the growth of three or four days in fewer minutes. They are beautiful with a sort of divine intelligence. Mother said they looked like angels. There was a significant political incident, too. Holmes said that Spain had benefited by the Spanish-American War and was relieved by the removal of "that troublesome appendix, the Philippines." He added, "Indeed, America is now a candidate for that operation," and there was loud applause.

Mrs. W. H. Holmes (wife of the artist-scientist), a woman so soundly intellectual that I marvel at my audacity in calling her friend, met me today and stopped to talk. She asked what I was doing this winter, what was my "fad," and I said, "My mother, at present." She said it was "a high and holy calling," and then became suddenly sad and told me with tears in her eyes how little she had seen of her mother the winter before her death because of some club work she was doing. It made me feel near to her and strengthened my resolution to resign from the Congressional Club so as to give myself more time for Mother and J.

Mrs. Pinchot's tea for her daughter, Lady Johnstone, was as charming as everything in her house—Lady Johnstone herself being the only one who seemed quite indifferent to the company, going through it as if just to humor her mother's little fancy. I could not reconcile her type to Mrs. Pinchot, who is my ideal of what an oldish lady of the best society should be. Her clothes never look new, and the exquisite lace ruffles that adorn the front and the long string of jewels look as if she had put them on just because she enjoyed wearing pretty things, and not at all to be dressed up. She is stately and gracious, but absolutely direct and unpretentious. Lady Johnstone is tall, athletic and handsome in an unfinished sort of way. She belongs, I think, to the ever-hoydenish Roosevelt school, taking enough up to twenty-five years, or so very little longer, but confusing socially when it extends into the thirties. When I left she was sitting on a little double-deck table by the dining-room door talking to Tom Page, and was not swinging her feet, but looked as if she might swing them at any moment. Her husband is British Minister to the Netherlands. The Netherlands Minister to the United States was there, and we had some pleasant talk about Mexico, where we met a year ago at the Centennial, poor Mexico's noon of glory.

A new M.C.'s wife, Mrs. William Kent of California, was a pleasant find. She talked well on woman suffrage, but her radicalism on that and some other woman questions left me shivering on the brink. I am never willing to venture into very deep water, unless some men are going with me.

Mrs. Pinchot's hatred of the Administration is an obsession. She talked about "Progressives," "Insurgents," and such political shades and plans until I pictured her and Gifford as a pair of deep conspirators with Jimmy Garfield stepping softly in front carrying a dark lantern.

Christmas Eve

The loneliest Christmas Eve we ever spent in Washington. Our best friends are out of town, and it has rained all day. We have invitations out for an eggnog party next Friday night for eighty people, and they are all developing miscellaneous relatives that complicate the situation. "Can I bring sister?" "Dear Father is with me," etc. I know they are all fat, and this house is so small. J. and I have read together as we always do on Christmas Eve "O Little Town of Bethlehem," and "Christmas Hymn," in which we find new beauties every year, and now "God bless us every one."

CHAPTER SIXTEEN

1912

January 20

Sometimes it seems as if the difference between big men and the herd is not so much what the big ones know as what they want to know, the consciousness, often increasing with the years, of "the little known, the unknown vast." Mr. Adams, old in years and honors, is a striking example of it. This letter came from him today:

> 1701 Massachusetts Ave.
> Jan. 20, 1912
>
> My dear Mr. Slayden:
>   Thanks for your note of the other day and the enclosure.
>   As to the enclosure it is only suggestive of one thought to my mind,— to wit, how long would I last, or be above ground, if I were in President Taft's place? I am in my 77th year, and naturally of a somewhat high-strung disposition. My impression is that if I were in Taft's place, by the third day I would cease to sleep, by the end of the first week it would get thoroughly on my nerves, and by the end of the first month, like the late lamented Wm. Henry Harrison—at a period of life then years younger than that at which I have now arrived—I should be carried forth from the White House feet foremost.
>   Turning, however, from these immaterial matters, may I ask if you know anything of the Association mentioned in this letter? You have been giving some attention to the subject of roads, and I suspect that this organization is simply one designed to get money out of the United States. If such is the fact I do not care to have anything to do with it.
>   I remain, etc.
>   Charles F. Adams

The enclosure was one suggesting Mr. A.'s own fitness for the presidential office, and J. says his suspicions of the organization mentioned were entirely correct. He is always alert to protect the taxpayer from such schemes and his scorn of the pension grabber is open and biting.

We often go to the Adamses' and our evenings there are in some respects more rewarding than any other social experience we have. Their house is a trifling distance from ours, but it is a far cry from our simple little home to their stately one. It is big and quiet, and entering it you feel as if you had shut out all that is small, sordid, and superficial. The general impression of the rooms is of soft but plentiful light, dark, heavy, red brocade hangings and good easy chairs for people to sit, not lounge, in. There are big wood fires in the drawing room upstairs, and the dining room on the first floor; and good pictures that are neither ancient nor modern. There is a vivid portrait of John Adams, by Stuart, I believe, and at dinners there from my seat by Mr. Adams I have been able to compare the two faces. If Mr. A. wore no mustache, and was older, it might be his portrait, only, I think, he will never look that old; he is so rosy and muscular, hardly a wrinkle on his face. There is no resemblance to the portrait of his father, C.F.A., Sr. No one could smile at the claims of long descent (of the right kind) with this group for an example of its results. The dinners are good and much less showy than some we go to. Everything is subordinate to the talk. Even the silver candelabra that at most tables dazzle your eyes and obscure your vis-à-vis are raised up on ebony blocks so that the lights are quite above your head, and the conversation moves easily around and across the table. There are rarely more than eight—the perfect company.

Another pleasant thing is the way they treat their servants as if they were trusted friends, not a hint of the scornful remoteness of the newly rich. Mr. A. says to the old butler, "Bring me a cigar, if you please," and the service is rendered with almost tender solicitude. I had begun to doubt if conversation as a means of entertainment survived anywhere in our country, but we have found it again at the Adamses', not so sparkling perhaps as in the old days in Virginia, but a bit more sound. They never talk small personalities, but there is much discussion of public men and measures, and the figures of history. Just now Mr. A. is going over his father's papers and is full of stories and reminiscences of a time too recent to be gotten at in books.

He has a slightly wheezy way of speaking, more English than American—and when he has been listening for a while and is going to speak again and bring the conversation back where he wants it, there is a funny little preliminary grinding in his throat like an old-fashioned clock in damp weather. He practically controls and directs the talk—not because he wants to monopolize it, you always wish he would talk more—but because there are subjects he has planned to discuss with the people then present (his invitations often specify), and he will not let them drift away.

The result usually justifies his system, but last night I saw him baffled. The only guest besides ourselves was a youngish lawyer with the typical oratorical voice of the Lower Virginian and opinions complete and unalterable on art, literature, and politics inherited from the sixties. All his admirations were superlative, and his talk so persistent that Mr. Adams grew smaller and smaller, sinking helplessly down in his chair.

Back in the drawing room the talk turned to the poets, and the Virginian declared "Childe Harold" the greatest poem in the English language and was about to dissect it by cantos when I introduced Browning and found him obviously unprepared to follow.

I know that Browning is Mr. A.'s first choice of poets, as he is my own, and he welcomed the diversion with a lively story of hearing Browning once in Florence swearing in anything but poetic language at Walter Savage Landor's bad manners.

We met the Adamses lately at a dinner at the Misses Putnam, and they had to go on to a musicale as did Secretary and Mrs. Fisher. Deploring the necessity, Mr. A. said that to him music was "only a disagreeable sound." I liked his honesty, but saw him in a new light. I cannot understand a developed soul that doesn't *need* music. Everyone had something to say of his unusual taste or want of it, but he never modified his first concise statement. I asked if he had not been inspired by martial music during the war, and he said, "Not at all, not at all. I never heard a band when in action in my life, no one ever did. They were put to better use caring for the wounded." Then commenting on the story that Pickett's charge at Gettysburg was with drums and fifes in the lead, he said, "I would have hated to be with them."

January 30

Could any other capital on earth present such a unique social spectacle as that at Congress Hall this afternoon? Mr. Arthur Jeffrey Parsons has asked me so often to take him to see it that I was sorry he wasn't with me. It was the first of the regular receptions of the forty-two Congressional women, wives, daughters, sisters of members of the House and Senate, who live in that great hive. In order of precedence they stood in line with their backs to the wall along two sides of the wide gallery overlooking the lobby for nearly three hours while hundreds of other women and an occasional man filed past and shook their hands. It was like playing "Thimble." Where we got out of the elevator there was a table with forty-two little baskets, all exactly alike, each tied with a bow of pink ribbon and a visiting card. A crowd of women hung over it like a bargain counter, trying in the dim light to read the names on the cards and leave their own cards on the right one. I followed the line of least resistance, and dropped a card into every basket I could reach. Then I went down the line, shaking hands with all the women with the same impartiality. At the end we were rewarded with cakes, punch, tea, and sandwiches dispensed by lovely young girls in evening dress. (It always grieves me that there are no young men, or almost none.) Children were weaving in and out of the crowd, and one infant of two months was being handed around for inspection. It was hot, noisy, and utterly provincial, but why shouldn't it be? Provincialism is only the custom of a country, and this is America's way. It serves the good purpose, too, of promoting friendly relations between the people from different sections of our far-flung Union. The overdressed lady from the Mississippi Valley said kindly she was "just a-wishin' I would come" and a Middle Westerner in a cloth street suit asked me energetically to come and "sit right down and visit with her." One from New York City was so inexperienced that her hands were shaking with nervousness, and another from Kansas had a voice like music and grace beyond one's utmost expectations. And so the life of Washington educates us out of our prejudices, and we stop generalizing about people from different sections. Still, I am glad I don't live at Congress Hall.

Poor Mrs. Champ Clark is finding her formal, wife-of-the-Speaker receptions almost too great a burden. She is constitutionally incapable of conforming to the conventionalities that make such things go smoothly, and Genevieve is too young to take hold. Mrs. C. will not "stay put." With the kindest feelings for everyone she forgets the crowd and talks with some special friend on the subject that interests her at the moment. In her apartment at 1509 16th Street she has a large drawing room well suited to her place, but when Mrs. Porter and I went to see her, she received us in the little vestibule where she had come to tell someone good-by. Neil, the Speaker's messenger, and a servant of large social experience, was there with his card tray and kept nervously hopping around almost begging me to take Mrs. Clark back to the big room, but there she remained entertaining us with quaint and amusing talk. When we finally insisted that we wanted to see the crowd inside, she protested in her funny hesitating voice, "But I want to discuss this with you *all!*"

Since the Ozark "houn-dawg" verses have been adopted—heaven knows how or why—for the Champ Clark campaign song, Mrs. C.'s rooms are overflowing with every size and shape of little houn-dawg with spiral wire tails sent by Clark supporters. They are not very attractive toys, especially when mounted on a cake or a baked ham, but on a par with the song:

> *Makes no dif'unce if he is a houn'*
> *You gotta quit kickin' my dawg aroun'.*

March 24

J., always an early bird, insists that he has seen some green leaves, but I have not. My soul longs for them, it has been such a bitter winter.

We took lunch today with the Lynden Evanses. Mr. E. looked and talked like John Randolph of Roanoke, except when saying a long Latin grace. I doubt if J.R. of R. ever went that far. The other guests were Senator and Mrs. Pomerene (there's a fortune in that name on a cold cream jar, "Try our new Pomerene, or Apple Cream."), a Mr. Bancroft, historically inclined, of course, and a Miss Waller. Mrs. Evans always has beautiful things to eat, and we talked woman suffrage and Roosevelt—there is no escaping either. I was the only defender of the former, and Roosevelt had none. Everyone claims to be "sick of him," but he will not down.

A late experience involving Governor Harmon almost paralyzed my interest in his candidacy, though he was not to blame. It is funny to look back on and has given our friends a world of amusement. At Christmas J. told me that Harmon was to be here sometime this winter, and that he wanted to have him and a number of men from different parts of the country to dine here. I reminded him that a "number" at our table meant eight, but he insisted it must be ten, including ourselves. I had to be present, a dinner was awkward without me, etc.—flattering, but not common sense in this household, though that is never my Texas colonel's strong point. It seemed rather far off, so what was my horror to come in from a party at twelve o'clock Monday night and have J. genially inform me that Harmon was here and would breakfast with us Wednesday at 8:30. My Tuesday reception was looming large, I had a cold, and my funny old cook is not exactly an emergency servant. I asked who was coming, but he was too sleepy to remember, just said, "Only eight, you know them all."

Mother and I were up early Wednesday morning and everything looked propitious when I went to speak to the guests. It never occurred to me to count them, but my small dining room never looked quite so small as when I stood at my place at the head of the table, and they filed past on either side. As they were about to sit down I felt something wrong, and found standing beside me a man who seemed to my terrified imagination at least ten feet high. I glanced at J. and his face was a pale green, and I felt faint, but the thought flashed through me, "This is a test of breeding; keep cool." It wasn't a test of conscience, though. I never told a lie so glibly, nor felt so proud of it. I lifted the coffee percolator, and remarking, "The maid has made a mistake, this does not belong here," I gave my seat to Johnson of Kentucky, and served the coffee from the sideboard as if it had been ordained from the beginning. And not one of those stupid men ever guessed that anything was wrong. Frank Harrison of New York, to whom I told the story afterwards, said he had no idea of it, and anyway it was the best coffee he ever tasted, and Governor Harmon has written to us and several other friends that it was a good breakfast. If he is elected, all will be forgiven. My poor J. is a picture of penitence—he "forgot to count Tim Ansberry."

March 25

Mr. Adams is having another topical dinner. His note is before me waiting for J. to come home and answer it. It says, "Mr. Redfield, your associate from Brooklyn, in the House, is going to dine with me tomorrow evening, in company with various other gentlemen whom I have invited in order that I may obtain enlightenment on the pension business. . . . I would be very much pleased if you could be one of my guests." I can't quite picture Mr. Adams and Redfield together, they belong to such different orders of mince. Mr. R. is all for uplifting and Mr. A. would probably express himself as not caring a damn for any of the altruistic vagaries.

March 27

Oscar Underwood, my old friend of university days who still calls me "Miss Ellen" with the most perfect Southern intonation, is coming to the front as a presidential possibility—a splendid one if Bryan's dog-in-the-manger tactics prevent Harmon's success. The University of Virginia Glee Club is to sing here for the benefit of the Confederate Home, and Mrs. Butler (President of the United Daughters of the Confederacy) and I are engaged to make the occasion an Underwood boom. He is to sit in a conspicuous box; we will have a picture of him and Woodrow Wilson, another alumnus and old acquaintance of mine, thrown on the screen, then we will call on Underwood for a speech, and the university alumni and the boys will do the rest to show that Underwood is their choice.

A day of strange quietness, a spiritual numbness, a sense of mysterious horror at the loss of the *Titanic*. There has been no loud display of grief, nor crowding around telegraph offices even among those who knew that their loved ones were on the great leviathan, but people moving softly and speaking low as if at a funeral. It is as if the world were shocked by some stupendous natural phenomenon, an earthquake or a tidal wave against which there could be no outcry or complaint—"no natural outlet or relief in groan or sigh or tear."

Monday morning brought news of the disaster, but terrifying as it was, people said, "Isn't the wireless wonderful? but for it so many lives might have been lost," or "Of course these great ships with their systems of watertight compartments will float indefinitely, but what a horrid experience." The usual hard optimism of our mechanical age.

We felt some apprehension but much more curiosity to hear the particulars. During the day J. called me up from the Capitol to say that all the news was good, passengers taken off by the *Virginian*, *Titanic* in tow but under her own steam making for Halifax. (Who could have invented such lies!) Then we wondered if such a sea monster could be docked and repaired at Halifax—our faith and pride in mere size still to the fore—and thought of the loss to the owners and the summer's trade. What mockery it sounds now.

All day there were "extras," but no news. Last night J., Emma Thom and I went to the opening of a part of the Freer Collection at the Smithsonian and had a quietly pleasant evening, laughing as we drove home at the varying cries of "Extry," "Extree" and "E-C-extry" that had redoubled but never thought of buying one. The papers cry "Wolf" too often, and extras are a common catchpenny device.

All night I was wakeful, and about six I went down for the paper and waked J. to tell him the incredibly awful facts.

F. D. Millet is the one we knew best on board. I could see his genial smile, his expression so full of wisdom, fun and goodness. At breakfast we recalled his bright talk one day last year when he said that of all things he liked "a Christian family breakfast" where people began the day with common interest and good fellowship.

Later at Rigg's market my faith in the brotherhood of man was renewed. Usually a noisy, sociable place, it was noticeably quiet. Even errand boys spoke gently. Two Serbians, usually unpleasant specimens of the bumptious foreign peasant, were different; his head was buried in a newspaper and she had tears in her bold eyes. In the afternoon there were groups on the streets, not only the kind that usually show collective interest in great events, but small-shop people, schoolgirls with plaited hair, and boys in knickers intent on the evening papers, trying to understand the plan of the ship from the pictures.

April 29

Nothing, not even Roosevelt and the deplorable spectacle of a President and an ex-President hurling accusations against one another from the stump, diverts our thoughts or talk from the *Titanic*. Every company is shadowed by it. The senatorial investigation is a farce and a horror combined. The chairman, who doesn't know the rudiments of marine science or travel, has insisted on knowing why the passengers were not in the watertight compartments and made the survivors describe the shrieks of the drowning. I have not been to the hearings, but must try to go once for the historical interest and "the experience that shall live in the memory"—the motive that so often impels me. At dinner at the Adamses' last night, Mr. A. leaned over to J. and said of one of the committee, "X. is a damned ass! A damned ass!" and seemed to feel better afterwards.

Admiral Stockton gave an interesting technical talk about the ship, sustaining my unwavering belief that speeding was the cause of the accident, too much luxury and dissipation, and the captain not on the bridge in time of danger.

May

Abdul Baha, "The Comforter," "The Beloved One," etc. etc., of the Bahaists has come and gone, and considering how interested I was in his coming, I am shamefully indifferent to his departure. I helped at the afternoon meetings for him in Mrs. Parsons' beautiful home for three successive days, and Saturday evening at a reception for five hundred people, and never got a moment of spiritual exaltation. He was just a *nice old man* who might sit in an Oriental market place and expound platitudes to his heart's content, like the good Pasha in the Arabian Nights, but his doctrines and his way of presenting them are too elementary for this wicked and perverse generation. He was followed by crowds, he talked and answered questions from five o'clock A.M. till midnight, and must have been weary beyond telling though his followers assured me he could not feel fatigue because he was sustained by the spirit. But none of these things proved his divinity nor even his special apostleship to me. I think it is the turban, the long white robe and slippers, the patriarchal wagging of his long gray beard and the mystery of the Persian tongue that attracts people who reverence anything that is priestlike and unusual. When he sat in a large chair and said oracularly, his interpreter repeating, "I love all humanity. All men are brothers. There is only one good. Sorrows must come, but every night has a day, every day has a night, every spring has an autumn, every autumn has a spring," his followers listened eagerly and wrote it into their notebooks, but in spite of a certain hypnotic quality it came dangerously near being ridiculous. If he had worn a sack suit and spoken English, no one would have listened. He is undoubtedly sincere, kind, and unworldly, but it is absurd for such moral milk for babes to be administered to justices of the Supreme Court, scholars, and public officials who accepted Mrs. Parsons' invitations to hear him.

Yesterday I told my new maid to remember that we had early dinner on Sunday and she said she "sure would" because she was president of "The True, Formers of the Rosebud" and had to go to the lodge.

May 26

This has been a month of company, all loved and welcome. The pleasure would have been unalloyed if they had brought fewer clothes, and in something besides the new wardrobe trunks that are gotten upstairs with difficulty—furniture has to be moved and all pictures on the landing taken down each time.

While Rena, Agnes and Mrs. Maxey were here I gave a large tea, the usual five-to-seven affair, sandwiches, punch and frappé. It was a lovely afternoon; flowers, big pink peonies, were plentiful, and the furniture all in white was cool and refined looking. The invitations read, "To meet some of the Regents of Mount Vernon." Mrs. Maxey, Mrs. Barrett, Mrs. Rathbone, and Miss King received, and several other members came. It was a pretty and agreeable little party but I have given so many little parties in this same house that looking backward I cannot tell one from the other. Different flowers—I always try to use the flowers in season— and different people to help me make the only variety. This time Mrs. Gregg, and Mrs. Ballivian (daughter of Mr. Calderón, Bolivian Minister) sat at the table, Elena Calderón and Agnes served punch, Mrs. Porter and Mrs. Ainsworth kept the company moving. I asked about one hundred and fifty people, and as usual some of the invitations went astray and led to embarrassment later. Our local postal service is the worst, but one can't help sympathizing with the postal employees. Such myriads of little card envelopes flying about must affect them like leaves blowing through the air.

Most people like to meet the Regents, some from human interest in nice old ladies, many from curiosity or respect for their position, which is more and more being considered the greatest social achievement for an American woman. They are so sincerely, almost religiously devoted to Mount Vernon and to teaching reverence for the character of Washington that they never give themselves airs—except one or two who are accidents and not entitled by birth or breeding to such good company.

The greatest difficulty I, and others with whom I have talked, find in entertaining these women's organizations is their tendency to hold post-mortem caucuses. They get their heads together and talk over the latest Council, and the blueblooded Regents did not differ in that particular from the U.D.C.s and the D.A.R.s. It was not always easy to break in and present their guests to them. Fortunately the interest of the company was divided between them and the three possible White House mistresses, Mrs. Harmon, Mrs. Underwood, and Mrs. Foss of Massachusetts. Mrs. Clark should have been there, but told me some days later that "*Your* friend Genevieve" forgot to give her the invitation. I was sorry for she is sweet, and people like to meet her. She is handsome, energetic, and well dressed, and has a social aplomb that none of the others possess. Mrs. Underwood is refined, nice to look at, and very cultivated, but so frail that you cannot think of her taking an active part in life. Mrs. Foss was pretty, pleasant, and wore lovely new clothes.

A politico-social outburst known as the Dolly Madison Breakfast had brought all these Democratic stars together. It has kept us alive with interest and laughter for weeks, and the women promoters of it are so pleased with themselves and the newspaper display that they propose to make it an annual festival. If they do, it is well to record its genesis. It began with a rooster made of electric lights! Mrs. Wickliffe of Louisiana, a young woman who has social zeal without too much knowledge, gave a luncheon and had the emblem of democracy in electricity for a table decoration. Someone suggested selecting a patron saint for the party, and Dolly Madison was chosen. The brilliance of the idea was thought to be only exceeded by the rooster so both were sent to Mrs. Champ Clark, who was too ill to be present. Mrs. Clark, who is a mine of historical facts, remembered that Dolly's birthday was May 20, and proposed that they celebrate it with a breakfast for Democratic women.

At first it was to be composed of the wives of Democratic officials here, then they added prominent women outside—Mrs. Cleveland and others—and finally the highways and hedges were raked until four hundred gathered at Ranscher's on a boiling hot day, in raiment to dim the luster of the Queen of Sheba, and reveled in oratory from noon till 5:00 P.M. Mrs. Clark presided. The luncheon was five dollars a plate, and for a book of biographies of Democratic Congressmen's wives, the story of your life and "a voluntary contribution of fifty cents" was requested.

Early in the action I was asked to serve on a committee but innocently declined, never dreaming of the wrath to come. I couldn't see any fun in it. It was very hot weather, and one would go a long way to escape hearing all those women speak. Of course I couldn't tell them so, and here I became involved in that tangled web we weave when first we practice to deceive. I was assailed on every side to know why I would not take part. "Your husband is one of our leading Democrats, one of the oldest in point of service," etc. Mrs. Clark and Mrs. Underwood told me that at the first meeting I was proposed as toastmaster (I would have died first) and here I was "not even going."

I had no polite reason to give; I was not going because I didn't want to be bored, and so I dodged and joked and tried to elude the questioners, finally settling down to the reason that I had so many things to do with five dollars, which was the truth but not the whole truth.

Then came the question of the biographies, and I felt that I had a right to decline having my career exploited on a menu card. The Texans met at Mrs. Gregg's apartment and declined to send biographies—for once we were unanimous—but I got the blame. Mrs. Clark told me later that "everyone knew who was responsible for it." Perhaps I should have gone into the thing just as a political amenity, but J. and I agreed long ago never to sacrifice our dignity, our social life, or our privacy for political success. When it came to that, the game was not worth the candle. I asked his advice about the breakfast, and he answered airily, "Do as you darned please. It's a free country." But is it?

The most interesting thing about this affair was the mob psychology. Of fifty or more women with whom I talked not six wanted to go. Many thought it foolish, more thought it would be a bore, and yet each one said, "I feel as if I have to; so many are going; I might be criticized."

Thanks, I fear, to the difficulty of finding Democratic women away from the breakfast, Mrs. George White of Ohio, whom I had only met once at dinner with Jim Cox, asked me to pour tea for her that afternoon at a reception for Mrs. Harmon. I was delighted to do it (Mrs. W. is very pleasant) and found myself at five o'clock in a strange house rapidly filling with guests who were thirsty, nervous and tired, and no hostess in sight.

But Mrs. Harmon, quite self-possessed, was soon in her place in the drawing room, and poor Mrs. White, tired out, introduced me to the dining room where she had ordered hot tea and frappé.

Guests were streaming in all begging for a little water to cool their tongues and the servants too confused to bring it. I flung frappé into glasses, and Mrs. Hitchcock at the other end of the table sent away the tea, and served frappé instead for mere mercy's sake. They were a bedraggled crowd. The pretty clothes were wilted, and huge summer hats hung sideways over limp hair. Even Mrs. Perry Belmont, usually fresh from a bandbox, was red in the face and looked moist. Many were enthusiastic over the success of the day, but others admitted that there were too many speeches, and resented Mrs. Martin Littleton's talking for forty-five minutes in a voice not audible ten feet away. Mrs. Hitchcock said one of the speakers was going strong when she left, and she doubted when she could stop herself. Mrs. Culberson, who is always ill, was a wreck, and wondered why she "hadn't had sense enough to stay out of the thing."

We were due at dinnertime at Dr. Simon Wolf's and I dressed in such haste that I forgot my gloves, but the guests were not of the kind to make one care for such lapses. The table was most lovely, but the company was the thing. Secretary and Mrs. Nagel, always clever, unpretentious, and interesting, were the guests of honor. The fine, bright talk was a tonic after so much of Dolly Madison. On the way home we stopped at Henry Clayton's to pay our respects to Mrs. Bryan and some other "leading women Democrats" receiving there, but the party was practically over. The leading ladies were sitting around eating ice cream with an air of conscious rectitude and a day well spent. I am afraid I do not value the solid Democratic qualities in society as I should. Dr. Wolf is a Republican but he puts more spice into life. We went home surfeited with Mrs. Presidential possibilities.

June 23

A week full of interest. Here it is quiet and dull, but with eyes fixed on Chicago every newspaper is an epic, and there are extras every hour. We seem to be seeing the last of Roosevelt, but he goes out tumultuously shouting prize-ring vulgarity in support of his utterly selfish ambition. His antics this week have brought us in the eyes of the world to the level of Latin-American republics. I am thankful that after routing him the convention could close with good humor and dignity. But will T.R. stay down? His real qualities, which even his enemies admit, and his gift for attracting the noisy rabble are so remarkable that no one would be surprised to see him heading some party again in six months. Now he has a bare handful of followers, most of them Rough Riderish specimens who have no political dignity to lose. The real Republicans say they will not follow him out of the party.

The Pinchots and Jimmy Garfield are still with him, and I am sorry for Mrs. Pinchot; she believes so sincerely that he will come back into power. We shall miss her charming political salon next winter. It was too obviously in T.R.'s interest to survive his downfall. Still, she and Gifford at one time were coquetting with other candidates, LaFollette principally. This was while T.R. was vowing he would ne'er consent, but after he had consented, as everyone knew he would, Gifford repudiated everyone else. T.R.'s coyness with nominations is proverbial.

And now it looks as if Bryan would precipitate a row in our convention next week. His delicate political sensibilities cannot stand Alton Parker for chairman. I wish I could never hear the words "reactionary" and "progressive" again, and I would throw out "uplift" and "reform" for good measure. Old Marse Henry Watterson says to the press today, "What the Democrats need is the pooling of issues, not the raising of disturbance." I pray that Bryan may see the wisdom of the suggestion, but it would not be like him.

June 24

Political events are moving too fast for my slow wits. We had barely finished the story of how the steam roller had crushed T.R. beyond recognition when news came that he was leading a new party organized immediately after Taft and Sherman were nominated. Not "bolters" at all, but just a few righteous men to save Sodom, I presume, and elect any old Democrat that we want to put up.

The women of the Congressional Club, especially the wives of some of the new Democratic majority in the House, have been perniciously active this year. I resigned last fall, so I should not criticize, but I like the club and hate to see it lose dignity by entertaining for people who don't appreciate the hospitality. Besides the usual teas for high officials, they have given receptions to diplomats who sometimes did not take the trouble to come and recently a countess who came from over the seas, and half seas over. Why should we run after such people?

A branch of the Woman's Welfare Association has been organized that is not confined to club members. When notified that my name was at the head of the executive committee, courtesy compelled me to go to a meeting, and I found myself in a strange gallery. Mrs. John Hays Hammond presided with a patronizing, cheering tone as if trying to encourage children or invalids, and some of the women were obviously "climbers," but it was a move in the right direction and has already resulted in some pleasant and informing effort. I renewed my favorite idea (in which I so signally failed in the club) to have the women learn something of the scientific departments of the government, and we are to have days with the Department of Agriculture, the Bureau of Standards, and the two Surveys. Dr. Holmes has given us an illuminating talk on safety and rescue work in mining, and we made a gay picnic of a visit to the George Junior Republic. We saw the junior citizens elect a president with more dignity than their elders, and then ate our lunch sitting on the grass in a grove of oaks, breathing the scent of sweet clover fields beyond. The picnic made an opportunity to study the social bent of people from different parts of the country—not the least of the interests Washington affords. A far Norr-rthern woman brought two tiny sandwiches in her handbag, another doesn't eat lunch, so she brought nothing, while the Western women and Mrs. Porter and I brought enough for three or four so as to be sociable.

My mind wanders from my sewing to Roosevelt and his bolting convention, and to wonder how things are marching in Baltimore. Bryan has arrived with his superior-conscience, and no doubt there'll be "wigs on the green" before he is through, but there were "broken noses and cracked crowns" in Chicago, so honors are easy. And in days to come when American youth is reviewing the history of our times, what will it make of this item? "The train carrying the St. Louis Democrats is known as 'The Houn-Dawg Special,' and it was planned to bring several hundred real houndawgs along. The plans were changed at the last minute, however, and they will get their dogs in Baltimore."

June 25

After staying here for the purpose it looks now as if we might not get to the convention at all. The tickets are distributed late and warily. Mine did not come yesterday. Senator and Mrs. Hitchcock asked me to go with them today, but it was too dark and rainy to leave Mother alone.

The President is calling loudly for appropriations for the army. He may yet be sorry that he vetoed the army bill to save his dear General

Wood and kept Congress here so long. But for that he could have had his money, and we could have gone home by the first of July.

July 3

I saw the Convention at last. Thursday Mr. and Mrs. Gregg, Mr. Harrison, Mrs. Porter and I started for Baltimore on the 10:00 A.M. electric car, Mr. H. looking grim disapproval of electric cars and the world in general because he had advised the train. We had the privilege of standing on the platform packed in a crowd of rough men as far as the District Line where we surrendered and meekly made our way back to the Union Station, Mr. H. walking in front with a triumph's evidence lighting his countenance.

At Baltimore we climbed almost perpendicular stairs to the street level and found ourselves at the door of the hall. Once through the dirty, paper-strewn entrance, the place was imposing, the good coloring a welcome innovation in our country. The vast arched ceiling of drab cheesecloth supported by yellow girders was like a London fog resting on arcs of sunshine. Below the vault like a frieze was a full valance of white with a yellow border that blew out in glorious big waving lines when the wind came in, as it did refreshingly now and then. Flags, shields, and emblems were better arranged than usual, and on three sides were pictures of Washington, Jefferson and Old Hickory with mottoes. The line with Jackson, "He never sold the truth to serve the hour," was a stone of stumbling for Bryan, who has tripped over several this week. In one of his speeches he ascribed it to the "hero of Monticello" and was instantly fallen upon by a pack of scholars asserting that it was from the "Ode on the Death of the Duke of Wellington" as if his error had been a moral offense. Bryan's followers have to be fanatics to offset the insane hatred of his opponents.

W.J.B. is much changed. His head is a shining bald crown with a fringe of dull, lank hair, and the fine, strong features that made him so handsome sixteen years ago have hardened and grown coarse—not the least sensual or vicious, just big. His neck is thick and his jaw has an iron rigidity. I still feel that he might be a power for good if he could ever believe that anyone but himself could be right. How singularly alike he and Roosevelt are in that respect.

Judge Parker, statesmanlike and modern if not "progressive," retired from the chair and gave place to Ollie James, a flabby giant, and the New York *Sun* says, "The enormous Mr. James of Kentucky, permanent chairman by grace of that sweet peace that fell briefly after the rollers had been put under Mr. Bryan, raised his hand, temporarily concealing a large section of the back gallery, and called the Convention to order at 4:15."

I was so bored, warm, tired, and disgusted with the noise, most of it mere sound and fury signifying nothing, that I said I wouldn't go again, but when they held on past Friday, with no indication of who would be nominated, the lure was too great, and we went again Saturday. Monday Nan Lightfoot had come and wanted to see it so we had another day of balloting, Wilson gaining two, two and a half, and then losing. The Texas delegation—such a queer set of carpetbaggers and political old fish to represent our solid democracy—voting for him *en bloc* every time.

Bryan had ruined Champ Clark's chances Saturday by a sensational announcement from the platform that he would vote for no man that New York supported, plainly implying that Clark was dealing corruptly with New York. Monday they brought in an immense scroll inscribed in big red letters, "I have known Champ Clark for 18 years and know that he is absolutely incorruptible," etc. (Signed "W. J. Bryan." It was carried around the hall, and at last almost wrapped around Bryan, but scarcely ruffled his self-complacency. In a fearful din of cheers, hisses and catcalls he walked coolly up to the platform steps and demanded to be heard on a question of personal privilege. There was a time when I would have been moved by it. He is always a brave figure, and he stood grimly facing us, head erect, jaws set, his very best ancient Roman manner, but these last few days are shaking my faith. Is it conscience, or a play for his own nomination? When the chairman ruled him out, he went as coolly back to his seat. Then it looked so like a Champ Clark stampede that a monstrous painting of Woodrow Wilson was produced and carried around creating such confusion that the chairman ruled that anyone bringing in another banner would be arrested.

The woman delegate from Washington interested me. She was large, stout and homely, the lower part of her face divided into three distinct chins, but her expression was intelligent and *good*. She wore an ill-made very blue dress without a trace of elegance. I would have given anything to talk to her, and find out the order of mind of a woman who felt equal to the rough and tumble of a political convention.

I didn't go again, but when I heard that Wilson was nominated the next day I was sorry I had been so lazy—sorry, too, that they had not selected someone like Harmon, Underwood, or Clark with a kinder face. I remember Wilson at the ripe age of twenty-three, and he was admired for his intellect then but never beloved at the dear old University of Virginia. We girls thought him too stuck on himself.

Last night chairs were at a premium in my small drawing room. I was glad to see the people, but it is confusing at this season when one doesn't expect company, and I am tired. We have guests to some meal every day, sometimes to all three as J. delights in company at breakfast. I am tired of Washington and want to get to some country at least as far from American politics as Spain or Mexico, but J. has offered himself for the campaign, and that will mean economy and discomfort for us both all summer. Being a congressman's wife involves many sacrifices.

Twin Lakes, July 27

And instead of Spain, I am in New England! Could there be a greater contrast? We can't even go home by sea. There is bubonic plague in Havana and Southern ports are good places to keep away from. But this place is pretty, and it is pleasant to be with J.'s family. J. went with Colonel Alexander Bacon (author of *The Woolly Horse,* a satire on Roosevelt) to see Wilson. He came back here for the weekend rather silent about it. When I questioned him he said, "Oh, yes, very pleasant," but there was no enthusiasm, nor is there any in the newspapers. Perhaps they feel as I do about a doctrinaire and a Calvinist believing himself foreordained from the beginning.

August 17

It is getting chilly here. We have a beautiful birchwood fire, and the gum and maple trees wave flaming branches to warn us that autumn is on the way, and yet my poor J. is still in the purgatorial heat of Washington. I am frantically homesick. I wouldn't give one stretch of sun-browned Texas prairie for all the pygmy mountains and smug rivers in Connecticut. The summer colony here is provincial New England, kind but so literal that my conscience restricts my conversation as never before. Their recording angel would have no tears to blot out my idle words—an awful thought to one given to levity.

Judge Roraback, a neighborhood magnate, is greatly worthwhile, and his family fine, lovable and broad-minded, but even they apologized for noticing that I said "gallery" for veranda, and "tote" for carry. Why couldn't they have teased me and let me tease back about some of the provincialisms and gotten on playful terms? No one plays conversationally. It isn't consistent with Puritan tradition. Their ancestors didn't joke with the tricksy witches. I would have preferred the witches to the deacons, and no doubt been burnt, as Miss B. would burn me today. She is a neighbor with a bungalow filled with things of "all centuries but this one and all countries but her own." She has traveled widely in Europe but knows only this northeastern corner of the United States, and yet has a habit of making nasty little dabs at the South and West. It began to irritate me, so when she asked me how I liked a history of Connecticut that I was reading, I answered lazily that so far its dead level and lack of romance suggested a stroll through a grove of wooden nutmegs. Her yellow eyes blazed, and I haven't been asked to tea at the bungalow since.

At eighty-five it is Mother's first experience of a country where there are neither negroes nor poverty. One day she came in with her blue eyes glowing and told me that she had seen "two pigs and a darky."

The millionairedom of Stockbridge and Lenox is beautiful, but "cottages" with fifty rooms will always look like hotels to me no matter how high the hedges around them. As a home I prefer Judge Roraback's nondescript house with the deep veranda where he asks the neighbors to sing hymns and hear a sermon. Yesterday a missionary to the "Southern mountain whites" described them (not inaccurately) as "the most ignorant and uncouth white people in America," and there was a ripple of fun later when Mother, looking like "a rose of yesterday," I, in my best frock, and a nice young navy officer from Asheville presented ourselves as specimens.

August 20

It has been pleasant here, but it is joyful to be starting home. J. will meet us in New York. He is there conferring with the Democratic Executive Committee on a plan he suggested to show up the iniquities of the Payne-Aldrich Tariff.

Pennsylvania R.R., August 23

In my dear old history of Rome there was a picture of Marius weeping amid the ruins of Carthage, and I felt just like him while we camped in our house waiting for this fifth longest Congress in history to adjourn. This afternoon we adjourned ourselves. Tomorrow the whole business comes to an end, more for want of a quorum than because the work has been well or wisely completed. Washington was a dreary spectacle. Insects have attacked the trees, and leaves are falling as if it were November. The Ainsworths and Calderóns were the only friends we had left in town. The whole country seems dull, strangely so for a campaign year. Roosevelt beats the air and shouts, "Liar, crook," etc.; Wilson continues a series of philosophical discourses, and Taft signs bills and plays golf. It looks as if nothing but an accident can prevent Wilson's election, not because the country wants him especially, but because of Roosevelt's madness in splitting the G.O.P.

August 25

We left St. Louis this morning under a magnificent dark-blue dome shot through every moment with wriggly lightning. Once we saw it strike on the rolling yellow breast of the Mississippi so close to us that the car crackled. This afternoon it is hot, dry, and just Arkansas—not inspiring now or ever. "What a background is the present, when we have the past to the fore!" I am so glad to have spent my life largely where the figures and events of history stir the dullest scene as in Virginia, San Antonio and Washington, which, if it has little history behind, is at least engaged in the daily manufacture of more.

San Antonio, Episcopal Residence, September 1

We are thankful to have this place for a few weeks, and dear Miss Mary Johnston has made it as pretty as such an old barn can be. What a rest it is to be just *at home*. When I waked and saw the soft, Gulf-cloudy sky, the long green wands of the hackberry trees in the park and heard the flute call of the blackbirds, my soul stretched itself and rested. It is fearfully hot, and I have to unpack, answer the telephone, and talk to countless people who "must see the Congressman at once," but I am happy as a bird. Mrs. Houston and Bessie next door are kindness itself, sending ice and figs, and above all, helping us to catch up with the local news. We are filled with horror at the divorces and at the marriages of much-divorced people, and wonder what will be the next phase of society so defiled and so indifferent.

Later I thought I saw one cause of it. We dined on the roof of the Travis Club and were entertained by two pairs of little girls about seven years old, made up with paint and powder, who danced ragtime and sang songs with such vile innuendo, leering knowingly at the company, that it made me sick. Their mothers stood by consenting to it and introduced me to the proprietor of a vaudeville theater who had taught them these choice accomplishments. Poor little babies! What will a divorce more or less mean to them later when their infant minds are poisoned with evil sneers at marriage and motherhood?

September 4

My birthday, and I always wonder at how long my little entity has gone on breathing, eating and sleeping without serious interruption. We go on living, no doubt, because there is some work for each one to do that concerns the whole creation movement though one may be the tiniest little bolt or screw in the Wheel of Things. Still, I cannot believe that I am destined to take a leading part in a tariff exhibit during the present campaign. A press clipping bureau that often tries to entice us into a subscription has deluged me with quite serious articles from the Northern papers giving me the credit of suggesting the tariff exhibit, and I am urged by wire to come and make speeches in New York and to send "a message to the working women" at some big meeting.

I did find sewing machines in Mexico costing much less than mine of the same make cost here, but the other stories are pure fiction. J. suggested the exhibit, which Woodrow Wilson opened with a flourish, and is to be one of the showmen if they put it on the road. I know as much of the tariff as I do of the multiplication table, but I am sorely tempted to have these articles copied into Texas papers to astonish some strenuous females who think they are politicians, and that I am only the eternal-womanly.

Good Housekeeping, too, asks for my picture to go with pictures of Jane Addams and other big women, but I can't accept glory on false pretenses.

September 5

We read that the Astronomical Society of Monterrey is unusually flourishing, with three hundred members. How like Mexicans! stargazing when their country is aflame with revolution. In the city the students are marching and shouting "Viva Díaz," as they vivaed Madero a while ago. If they set up Felix Díaz, it will be only the magic of a name for he has shown no quality or fitness for government. They ought to establish a monarchy. It would be a despotism tempered by revolution, but that is about the measure of their genius. There is much idle and worse than foolish talk here about "taking" Mexico, and a war of conquest under the name of intervention would be so popular that we wonder at Taft's forbearance in not riding back to the White House by that road.

Locally the Mexicans are taking us. The town is swarming with them, not only the usual cotton pickers, but prosperous ones who stroll on the plazas and revel at bargain counters. Fat, slipshod dueñas with black rebozas over their trailing starched lawn dresses guard bevies of pretty

brown girls in cheap silk dresses, piles of false hair and rhinestone ornaments. There are hundreds of young men, too, who if they love their
country ought to be there with guns on their lazy shoulders. Their patriotism spends itself in big talk and *juntas* out of range of federal or rebel
guns.

Apropos of the talk of intervention, J. had a reassuring note from
President Taft today. He is always so fine and dependable in his reverence
for law. It says, "I have carefully noted all that you say. You can rest
assured that I shall not intervene in Mexico until no other course is
possible, and then only by authority of Congress." The last phrase is added
with a pen in his own handwriting. Tomorrow we start on a campaign
trip through the district.

Kerrville, September 8

I have been out of Texas twenty-two months and see many changes. The
drought is terrible. Cypress Creek and the Guadalupe nearly dry, and
many of the big trees dying, and yet it doesn't look as it did in the old
days before we had windmills. Then the bare pastures were dotted with
dead cattle, and the smell of them sickened you. Today the cattle are in
fair condition and good milk and butter are common. Here at the St.
Charles I am the only one astonished at the white-enameled bathtub for
every room and the ice cream parlor across the street which has become a
"café" with hardwood floors and gray marble fittings just like New York,
more's the pity. Stranger still, the old German element is giving up
Kartoffel Salat, and all things vinegary. The loss of local color and variety
is more than atoned for by the safety to one's digestion. Wherever we go,
it is fried chicken, tomatoes and mayonnaise, rolls and delicious white wine.

Brady, September 20

A railroad train here is still a novelty—and conditions along the line like
the Texas of other days. It's a man's country, and the man is on horseback, not quite in the old cowboy style—his horse is too fat and well bred,
there are fewer ropes on his saddle, and he wears a smaller hat—but he
still likes to show off and dashes up to the moving train to hand a letter
deftly to someone on the rear coach.

Many things suggest the old frontier. The dust on "the square" is
deep and yellow, waiting horses are kicking and fretting at flies, and I
counted fifty men, and only three women—including myself. In the hideous

lobby of the Queen Hotel there are still more men, long-coated country lawyers, dapper commercial travelers, but the majority in shirt sleeves, with trousers tucked into high boots, and all waiting till Sunday to shave. I looked for the whiskey and pistol-toting badman but he has disappeared, gone to the ultimate frontier, pushed back by the electric lights, bathtubs and local option. He was outrageous, no doubt, but I am glad I saw him once.

Some leading Democrats called and entertained us with bright talk, two of them members of an old and distinguished New York family who have made good out here as horse and cattle men—all the essentials for heroes of a wild West romance. They stayed till late talking wistfully of the Wadsworths, Shaws, and Owen Wister, an old friend, who spent a month with them gathering material for *The Virginian,* among other things getting the story of the mixed-up babies.

Austin, September 23

We are making so many one-night stands that when I wake in the morning I can't remember where I am. It is a foolish feeling, but the towns are so alike, it makes no difference. The Capitol and Executive Mansion grounds here are parched brown, and there is wastepaper in every corner. The grotesque firemen's monument is a fit presiding genius for the scene. Governor Colquitt vetoed the appropriation for watering public places, but if I were Mrs. C. I would get out and sprinkle with a tin cup rather than live in such a setting. The Maxeys' place, green and fresh, shows what water can do even in a Texas drought.

Brownwood

The day of the month is lost but I know it is Sunday. At Lampasas we had a plunge in the splendid sulphur pool, and waiting for the train in the cool gray dawn, a small boy selling papers engaged us in conversation and said he "reckoned" he was "just a natural-born Methodist." He was so sweet I almost wished I was one too.

At Lometa we had one of Mrs. Pete Jackson's delicious breakfasts, chicken, hot cakes and honey with the scent of prairie flowers, and Pete stopped talking politics and Bob Ingersoll long enough to bring "thuh Cong'ussman" an invitation to speak at the Bank Corner before the train left. Shirt sleeves and scrubby beards predominated among farmers with an eye on teams hitched near, and troupes of fresh, well-dressed children stopped to hear J.'s appeal for money for the Wilson campaign before passing on their carefree way to school. Everyone was friendly, and it is good to get where a man's a man no matter what he wears and in whose lexicon there's no such word as snob.

In spite of the comic supplement the real old American joke crops up now and then. A waggish train conductor told me, apropos of the drought, that there were frogs in West Texas four years old that couldn't swim, and I read of a crop of watermelons at Ballinger: "They are a tribute to the success of dry farming as one man said his were raised on two cloudy days and a clap of thunder."

Today a year ago we were driving over the Furka Pass in a tremendous snowstorm, and now, with the mercury at 90 degrees in the shade, I am arrayed in my Washington clothes and must go to church with Mr. Harrison and behave ever so circumspectly though my poor face is aflame with sunburn.

San Antonio, October 3

J. is back in Washington and writes me, date 29th: "The *Post* has a scare story, from Hearst's *American* of yesterday, that Taft will call Congress together next week to ask authority to invade Mexico with arms. If it were in anything but a Hearst paper I should be alarmed." J. is going into the campaign again, beginning at a meeting with Governor Marshall in New York. He will speak in New Jersey, Delaware, and two other states and pay most of his own expenses, so I am not as enthusiastic as I might be.

Sunshine Ranch, October 15

This morning Rose, Jane and I were in the kitchen "worthily engaged" like Miss Edgeworth's heroines, when Mary came and said in her taciturn Maverick manner, "Papa telephones that Roosevelt was shot in Milwaukee yesterday.[1] He was not killed, and Arthur McCormick was captured by Mexican rebels and is held for ransom." The first story sickened us past interest in the second, which like most news from Mexico is probably not true. But what is the matter with our country? And how will it affect Wilson's candidacy? I hope T.R. will not die, but this gives him the prestige of a martyr.

---

[1] Theodore Roosevelt was shot in the chest by John Schrank, a lunatic, just before delivering a campaign speech in Milwaukee. The notes of the speech in his coat pocket prevented the bullet from inflicting a possibly fatal wound.

Later

They say he went on speaking after he was shot. "He's generally shammin' when he's dead," so it looks fishy and Rooseveltian. We had a good laugh when Mother said gravely, "I believe he had it done for effect."

San Antonio, Thanksgiving Day

Wilson's election was such a foregone conclusion that it was accepted without loud rejoicing. The evening of the election we saw Maude Adams in *Peter Pan* and later went to the office of the *Express* to hear the returns. All visitors had left, the staff was quietly eating supper, so we sent a few telegrams and went to bed feeling that a new political phase was unfolding that would bring many changes. And the next day it snowed, rained, hailed letters, telegrams, visitors pouring in on J., all asking for government jobs. I wouldn't have believed so many people wanted little $1,000 to $3,000 places not warranted to last more than four years. It is J.'s first experience on the side with something to give, and I dread it. I remember Jefferson's saying that for one friend you make with the gift of a government office you gain a hundred enemies.

Judging by the Texas press Wilson will select his entire Cabinet from this state. J. is nominated daily for secretary of war and oftener still, especially by those who want to keep peace with Mexico, for ambassador to that poor distracted country. The latter seems possible, but I am not letting my mind dwell upon it. J. was not an original Wilson man, and they are many and clamorous, and I doubt if Wilson is big enough to forgive anyone who failed to feel that he was predestined. I can't get over my early impression of him at the University of Virginia.

The Mexicans are outspoken in their wish to have J. sent to them, and Colonel Chapa, who is the spokesman here of many of their big men, said to me with his suavest smile, "I hope to call on you soon in Mexico."

General Anson Mills's card came up, and hurrying down I found the dear old gentleman bubbling over with a "secret." He had been "acting without orders," and wanted to know if I approved. I was really mystified until he explained that he was just in from El Paso, and that he and Turney, the Burgesses and all the big border lawyers were booming J. for ambassador. We took J. into our secret, he agreed that it would be very pleasant, and we went into definite consideration of ways and means. That night we dined at the St. Anthony with the General and Mrs. Mills, more beautiful and winning than ever. Miss Klein and Mr. Keblinger were there too and we had much fun over our plan—more I dare say than we would have if it materialized.

Mrs. Maxey writes: "The Judge and all your friends in Austin have gone right to work to see what can be done to make your Texas Colonel Ambassador to Mexico."

Washington, December 20

Few things I think indicate the quality of people more than notes on formal occasions which may with equal propriety be formal and noncommittal or have a touch of friendliness and sense of the individuality of the recipient. This from Mrs. Wilson, unless it is the work of an unusually good secretary, seems to me very promising. It is from Bermuda.

Glencove, Paget West, December 3, 1912.

My dear Mrs. Slayden,

It is hard to be forced to answer so very charming a letter as yours with a few hurried lines, but I am sure you will understand and pardon.

Your letter, showing as it does, how much we have in common in our point of view, etc., makes me look forward to meeting you with peculiar pleasure. I hope you will be a real friend to me in Washington—for "faith, I shall need them!" It is delightful to know that we have to begin with such good friends in common as the Seymour Thomases.

Mr. Wilson sends his very warm regards, truly you have found a word to conjure with when you speak to him of "The University."

With many thanks for your kind thought of me in writing, I am

Yours most cordially,
Ellen A. Wilson

The banquet given recently in Ranscher's ballroom by the Carnegie Endowment for Peace for the Baroness von Suttner[2] was rather dull. There were many bright people, but they were obscured in a system of seating past finding out, and the invitation list was made with an utter disregard of the interests of the Peace Movement—"Billy" Sulzer, and "Jeff" Levy, both big navy men, and far from interesting, anyway; numbers of the merely rich (always warlike), and a swarm of representatives of small countries, even the colorful Minister from Haiti. He sat a few seats away from me with Mrs. William Alden Smith beaming upon him, and obviously content with being in the inner circle of diplomacy. The inarticulate old Minister from Venezuela was next to the Baroness. My partner was good old Secretary Wilson, dotty and piping, but pleasantly renewing my acquaintance with Bur-rns. Next him, to my good fortune, were Mrs. John Sharp Williams and Senator Burton—talking distance if you like people and easy to let alone if you don't. To my left was the Minister from

---

[2] Bertha von Suttner (1843–1914) was an Austrian writer who took an active part in the movement for international peace. She founded the Austrian Society of Friends of Peace and was awarded the Nobel Peace Prize in 1905.

Nicaragua, bright and pleasant, and grateful for attention as his next neighbor was little Madame Chang who almost never speaks. My poor J. was on a desert island between two impossible Congressional women, one of whom told him an alleged joke playing upon the word "legacy," making it leg-I-see, and referring to her own stout extremities.

Being on the reception committee I had some talk with the Baroness before other guests arrived and found her sweet and easy to talk with but I could not fix my attention for trying to reconcile this stout, lame, sad-looking old woman with the young girl in the dissipated life she describes with such engaging frankness in her memoirs. Her face is still beautiful, and there was not a touch of make-up.

Both speakers who preceded her and James Brown Scott in his introduction dwelt regretfully on the Balkan War, but her voice had real tears in it. She saw and felt the horror and suffering. She said it was not a religious war, as it is being represented, but "a war like most others to gratify at any cost the ambitious designs of certain men." King Ferdinand was her friend and the last time she saw him he gave her a picture of himself with the word "Pax" written under it in Greek letters (I think peace is "Greek" to all Balkan kings). She told how the Balkan "rulers, leaders, and high military men" all gathered in a church and "gave God a lesson in geography." They prayed that the armies of Montenegro, Greece, Bulgaria and Serbia might be successful, and that God would take note of their little mountains and streams marking their boundaries "and on no account to permit his mercies to spill over into Turkey." She said Roosevelt had kept some of the promises he made her in 1904, but the arbitrations he proposed were "restricted." He reminded her of some lines from Faust— "I have two souls within my breast that draw me different ways"—and sometimes she thought he had served several souls within his breast. She spoke of his "innate roughriderdom" and thought perhaps the dove of peace would have found but an uneasy resting place between the horns of a bull moose. Some men, she said, kept up the war spirit because they feared woman suffrage, for in war alone could they prove their superiority to women. When asked what the world would do without war, she always asked, "What do you want in its place? What do you want in the place of rattlesnakes and tigers? Why not do without them?" For all her gay satire, it is easy to tell that she is acquainted with grief.

To drop from the Baroness von Suttner to Jeff Levy and Mrs. Martin Littleton is a sickening thud, but I must record, and with great pleasure, that Mrs. L.'s preposterous scheme to have the government pay Levy $3 million for poor old Monticello has been given its final quietus in the House and it will be a relief to hear no more about it and its promoters. No one would be more pleased than I to see Monticello taken out of the hands of the Philistines, but I don't doubt that Levy would gladly sell it for much less than a million. Except for the sentiment he would make a good thing at $250,000.

When Uncle Joe Cannon heard of Burleson's plan to pension ex-presidents and give them seats in the House with the right of debate, he said, "Why not put them in the Senate? I never had any use for that damned body."

December 23

I have been running like ole Br'er Rabbit, and every day J. tells me of new Texas people who must be called on—very pleasant often, but they stay at the biggest hotels, and it would disgrace me and ruin J. politically if I failed to appear in full canonicals. And every day letters come from fond "mommas" back in Texas saying that "little daughter" is at school here, and couldn't I "go to see her now and then." If Momma only knew how school and calling hours conflict, how far off many of the schools are, and how much real work there is to be done by the wife of a congressman with no income but his salary.

The weeks before Christmas are a nightmare of housecleaning and training green servants. Aunt Lucy came eight years ago to "try me for a week," and good old soul! she little knows in how many ways she has tried me ever since. She goes wild over the summer, forgets how to manage the cracked stove that always goes with a rented house here, and accuses the second servant of treason, stratagems and spoils.

At the annual dinner (at the Willard) of the Society for the Judicial Settlement of International Disputes all the speeches were interesting, though two were laughable misfits. Admiral Wainwright, trimly handsome, born for a uniform, advocated earnestly, even indignantly, a big navy as the only way to preserve peace, and Jim Mann, Minority leader, scorned the suggestion of arbitrating the Canal tolls because no other country would be just to us, and "the United States Congress alone can be trusted to decide the matter impartially."

CHAPTER SEVENTEEN

1913

January

This is the third year that the college women have asked me to speak at their annual banquet! What have I, who never went to a real school a day in my life, to tell these women who know all that textbooks and systems can teach them? I think I'll accept and tell them how I was not educated. Evidently, though, they have taken my measure and don't expect me to be profound. The note says (and, privately, I think I could write a better one), "A good many seem to think that our programs have been too serious, and several feel that no one can make a more brilliant speech than yourself." Who could resist that! I feel like the little woman who fell asleep on the King's Highway, and had to get her little dog to prove "if this be I."

January 29

The Democratic majority of the House Military Affairs Committee sent a letter to Wilson today asking him to make J. secretary of war. Of course Wilson is not going to do it, but the request was made without J.'s knowledge, and vanity and appreciation compel me to copy a part of it: "We regard him as authority on military affairs . . . of prepossessing appearance, at the zenith of his usefulness, active, energetic, a safe counselor, and favoring the reforms advocated by the Democratic party. We assure you that his appointment would be a most happy one."

J. would make a fine secretary, but stern officialdom is obviously not my milieu. The Carnegie Trustees invited me last week to act as a member of the committee at the reception to Dr. Inazo Nitobe, exchange professor of Japan, in the interests of International Peace. I accepted, went to the reception and had a beautiful time with learned and agreeable people, and never remembered that I was a receiving lady until just as I was leaving when something in Mrs. J. B. Scott's expression brought me to a conviction of sin.

January 30

Arthur Jeffrey Parsons, who always seems to me set apart from the crowd by his exquisite culture and sweetness, sends me a note jubilating over the passage of the Lincoln Monument bill. He gives J. the credit for it, and says, "The country will appreciate what he and his friends have done for the *beautification* of Washington. It is *bully,* and you must be very proud of him as a man and a husband." I am, so everyone is pleased. It has been J.'s darling project for so long that I went to hear the final vote, and afterwards waited at the office while he signed his letters for the day.

Two modest-looking men came in, bubbling with pleasure about the bill, and praising J. to the skies. I didn't catch their names until one addressed the other as "Guerin," and J. says I disgraced him by jumping up and exclaiming, "You? Jules Guerin!" They were Guerin the artist and Bacon the architect of the monument. Men who do great things take them so naturally. They were not half as cocksure about art as the art committee of a woman's club.

February

Hope for order in Mexico grows with the news that Felix Díaz is alive. They brought him from San Juan de Ulloa to the City where the students released him, and that little milk-and-water Madero should have taken warning and resigned. But the obstinacy of small men often makes more history than the wisdom of the wise. My dear old friend, Dr. Bibb of Saltillo, is a "regular" physician and has known "Crazy Pancho," as he calls Madero, all his life, and says, "He's a spiritualist, a socialist, a vegetarian, and a homeopathist. What can you expect?"

Today shells are pounding those big buildings between the Ciudadela and the Zuelo. I can almost hear them. If one should fall on the National Museum, it might destroy things worth more to the world than a legion of Felix D.s and Maderos. Each day we hope the worst is over, but madmen seem determined to force intervention. Everyone is praising Taft's wisdom and moderation. I think he deserves the Nobel Prize.

He has taken counsel with J. and other border members several times about Mexico, so J. asked an interview with him to say something in favor of recognizing Huerta as president *de facto*.[1] Huerta is not a saint, but he has some qualities of strength and firmness essential to success in governing those people. J. told Taft what he knew and thought. Once Taft said, "What you suggest seems to me the obvious and proper course, but a new President is coming soon, and I hardly think it courteous to take such an important step. His policy may be very different from mine." I wish Taft were less punctilious. Delays are dangerous with Mexicans. Promptness and decision they understand from us, but not temporizing.

March 2

The inauguration is two days off, and woman suffrage has the floor. The inaugural procession follows the suffrage parade in public interest as in fact. Suffrage headquarters, a basement shop on F street near 15th, looks the busiest place in town. It is stifling inside, and even this (Sunday) afternoon there were crowds of men and jaded, tense women at the desks handing out literature and yellow pennants. It is unbecoming work, and will be used against us by the antis, who plead ever so sweetly that we will "no longer be dainty." One said in the *Post* lately that "women were not made to vote but to be loved." Could the youngest Miss Pecksniff have made a sweeter argument? "The Pilgrims," a squad of enthusiasts who hiked from New York, are far from alluring in their dingy brown cloaks and heavy shoes. I admire their pluck but can't see what use there was in hiking.

Mrs. Porter, Mrs. Butler and I went to the anti rally at Belasco's, and I ask nothing better for our cause than the cheap sentimentality they poured over us. A tart old gentleman sitting by me said he came in undecided but was going out a convinced suffragist.

Representative and Mrs. McCall, Miss McCall, and R. U. Johnson of the *Century* breakfasted with us, and I enjoyed them in spite of conditions that might have given pause to a better housekeeper. My small butler was ill and a limp little yellow girl substituted, but Aunt Lucy gave us good corn bread, rolls, batter cakes and "trimmin's," and they all had good appetites. Mr. McCall had been through a night session but didn't look tired. He wavered between his taste for batter cakes and his talent for conversation,

---

[1] President Madero's regime was harried by revolutions led by Zapata in the south and Orozco and by Felix Díaz, nephew of the former president, in the north. Then on February 9, 1913, a revolution broke out in Mexico City. Victoriano Huerta, chief general, deserted and took the army with him, and Madero was overthrown, the Huerta government established. Madero met his death while being taken to prison on February 22, and it is generally believed that he was assassinated by Huerta guards. Huerta was provisional president of Mexico 1913–1914, but his regime was never recognized by the United States.

but cakes usually won, to Mr. Johnson's satisfaction, I believe, for he talks well and was full of his theme—the need of legislation for the American Academy of Fine Arts. J. was full of it too, and my usual twitter was hushed by their earnestness. I looked after the coffee urn and listened. Mr. Johnson had read Wilson's inaugural address and contrasted it with Poincaré's, which promised much to the cause of Art and Letters, while Wilson does not refer to them. "He seems to think such trifles can take care of themselves," he said. The air is full of surprises. I thought Wilson would be strong on those very things.

Now that they are leaving Washington, I regret having seen so little of the McCalls in all these years. J. admires Mr. McCall above measure, but I was afraid of her. She is so severe and clear cut, I feared to intrude my Southern effusiveness upon her Puritan calm. This morning, saying good-by, she reached over and drew my hair down a little on my forehead, and her tenderness startled me. There is nothing sweeter than a fine New England woman. She and Ruth praised too kindly my talk to the college women. It was light stuff about early education, or lack of it, in Virginia after the war, but it took wonderfully. "We speakers" sat on a platform overlooking an audience of 300 women (299 of them wearing spectacles), and my talk and I were sandwiched between the talks and persons of Julia Lathrop, of the Children's Bureau, and Mrs. Raymond Brown, who talked suffrage and wore a dress of blue and gold brocade so lovely that I forgot her theme in aesthetic delight in her beautiful lines and well-combed gray hair. No three people or three talks could have been more different, and I see the deep design of the college women in asking me so as to make the artistic and intellectual contrast more effective. Julia Lathrop has certainly found her right niche. She verges on old-maidenhood, but is like Jane Addams, a sort of Eve, a Mother of Mankind. She says she must get an astral body or a husband or something like that to keep her with her work.

Just forty-eight hours to the inauguration and several Cabinet places still unannounced. The Texans are sick over what has happened to them. Of all men, that one! and in the face of a petition signed by almost the whole delegation asking for Bob Henry—not because they love Bob more, but Burleson less. Obviously everything is going to original Wilson men, and they are selected by "the Veiled Prophet of Austin"—"Colonel" House. Mr. Redfield didn't know till yesterday that he was among the elect. There is a lot more gossip I might record, but I want to refresh my soul with Meredith's *Letters* until J. comes home. I hate these night sessions for him. He has been ill all winter, and there seems little hope of a rest in Europe or even Texas this summer. The Mexican plot thickens, and who knows the mind of Wilson—or his House.

March 3

Today Mattie and I stuffed eggs and made sandwiches enough for fifty people, and have everything ready for lunch in J.'s committee room tomorrow, then we hurried to the Gibson Building to see the suffrage parade. We almost fought our way to the room, which we found steaming hot and smelling of printer's ink, and then had almost to fight to stay there. Most of the space was rented to antis, and they thought it a part of our "unwomanliness" to keep one small grimy window open so we could breathe. It was a mild afternoon with bright sunshine, and we courteously suggested that if they kept on their furs and hats as we did, they wouldn't mind the air. Whereupon one of them told us we were not ladies, and no doubt still thinks so as we did not contradict her.

The crowd in the street appeared well dressed, good tempered and from the country, judging from the way they ignored the rule of the road and stampeded the two mounted men and five Boy Scouts doing their best to keep order in front of our building. There were wild stories of hoodlumism along the route. The suffragists claim that the police were inefficient or in sympathy with the mob. The crowd pressed so close that we could see only the heads of the marchers unless they were on floats, but as they went up the rise toward the Treasury, the line of colored flags and costumes was very fine. There were many distinguished women, some of whom I knew and others I wanted to see but couldn't identify because of the uniform caps and cloaks. I didn't know till after they had passed that the lonely figure in white sitting like a statue on a float with two tall cedars flanking her chair was Helen Keller. In spite of everything the parade was inspiring, and I was ashamed of the self-consciousness that kept me out of it—not to mention J.'s horror of my taking chances on foot in such a jam.

Ellie Polk Magill, the artist, carried the San Antonio banner for which I was responsible, and the little Texas flag fluttering gaily gave me quite a fullness of the heart and eyes. Why are we moved at sight of a little piece of cloth of a certain color and pattern? Maury Maverick,[2] who came in today with the V.M.I. cadets, tells me that he doesn't believe in war, and reasons about it seriously in the dormitory, but forgets it all

[2] Author's nephew.

and becomes pure pagan when the band plays and the flag waves on the parade ground—a good argument against the psychological effect of military schools.

The following piece of nonsense came to me anonymously. I suspect Senator Hitchcock; he always has something of the sort up his sleeve:

THE ELECTORAL VAMPIRE

A man there was and he cast his vote,
      Even as you and I,
'Til a suffragist came and "Got his goat,"
      Even as you and I.
Oh! the beers we taste
And the cheers we waste
On dear old election night
Belong to the woman who raves and rants
And sallies forth in her husband's pants
And makes herself a fright.

So the man is stripped to his very hide,
      Even as you and I,
While his wife struts forth with a mannish stride
And does the family voting beside,
      Even as you and I.
And it isn't the shame
And it isn't the blame
Of losing the vote that hurts,
It's seeing the woman you call your wife,
The female you swore to protect through life,
Wearing your pants and shirts.

                            J. L. S. Anon

We came home at dusk, and I put on my blue Liberty satin and went with J. to dine with the McCalls. The decorous Shoreham was as nearly noisy as it could be. R. U. Johnson was the other guest but talk was impossible in the din of voices and constant diversion seeing this or that distinguished visitor. There was a general consciousness of Wilson and Marshall being under the same roof with us, and after dinner we heard that Wilson was coming down to see a delegation waiting on 15th Street. We all went to the lobby, but J. was afraid of missing his vote on the navy bill and insisted on leaving. We took the new herdic up 16th, stopped at the Sweets' to pay our respects to the Governor of Michigan, and now J. has gone back to the Capitol.

We left home at 9:30 yesterday, our cab loaded with lunchboxes, china, and silver. The morning was gray but, for a wonder, not raining, and we found the plaza already crowded and streams of people still coming. At the committee room (northeast corner, 1st floor) I had Edward, J.'s messenger, arrange the table so that lunch could be served at any time, then put on a fur coat, and J. took me out to the stand. I was the first woman in the House section and felt a bit conspicuous until Mrs. Culberson and Mrs. Schluter joined me. They also had given away their Senate gallery cards—visiting constituents delight in them. The wind was cold, and Mrs. Culberson was so thinly clad. I tried to make my fur cover her, and we had a lot of fun during the long wait.

I hope the Vice-President is bigger than he looked as he tripped down the red-carpet path from the Rotunda. He wore the first cone-shaped silk hat I ever saw out of Wales.

When Champ Clark came, the crowd on the portico cheered a little; Bryan was applauded more, and Uncle Joe most.

I didn't see Wilson until he was quite close to us, and was struck with his youthful look, little changed since the old days at the University of Virginia when we marveled at the judges giving him only the debater's medal, when he aspired to the orator's. Taft was smiling as ever. Bryan, fat and much aged, stopped and shook hands with us cordially; then Burleson with his pink, hairless face (I'm afraid my congratulations to him were "from the lips outward," as the Mexicans say), and last Mr. Redfield, who is a good and sincere friend. He is a survival from the Victorian age, exactly like the heroes in Trollope's early novels, and, I believe, retains all their conventional integrity and propriety as well as their whiskers. J. is fond of him but says no man could be as wise as he looks. I ought not to laugh at Redfield's being a survival. Art Young, I think it was, published a cartoon of J. as "A Ouida Duke," and it was perfect.

Wilson took the oath and kissed the Bible in proper form. When he began to speak, it had grown so cold that most people on the stand went back into the Capitol, but he still had an audience of the Annapolis boys on his right, West Point on the left, the Culver Black Horse in front, not to mention a few tens of thousands packed in the plaza, on the roofs, the windows, and thick as blackbirds in the big trees nearby.

We went through the echoing tunnel to the committee room and found Mrs. Gregg already pouring coffee for Mr. and Mrs. John W. Davis and Mr. D.'s gracious and agreeable old father from Clarksburg. We had a gay crowd for an hour or more; then they went on to the avenue to see the sights, and the Lynden Evanses and ourselves were left alone. We stayed till five o'clock, sitting in the window facing the Capitol, intermittently interested in miles of troops that unknown to us had been parked all day back of the Library. My cup of content was full when the V.M.I. boys and the Richmond Blues came by. We leaned out and cheered, and clapped, and heard later that they were received that way all along the line.

March 6

This morning brought me an overwhelming sense of work to be done before we start to Texas Saturday. Liza, the serving woman, was mending and talking, and I was packing when it suddenly occurred to me that it would be amusing and wise to make the high official calls before we left. There has been so much talk of J.'s being in the Cabinet that we are sure to be suspected of disgruntlement if we fail in any nicety of custom. So I flew to the telephone, called up the White House and asked Miss Hagner for the earliest day we could come to pay our respects, and she said Friday at five o'clock, so that's settled, thank goodness!

March 7

To suit the era of democratic simplicity, I meant to walk to the White House, but time was so precious I ordered a cab and buttoned my gloves on the way. A colored man met us on the steps with a silver card tray, another opened the door, and a nice young officer checked us off in the hall and put us in the Green Room. Glancing at the clock I found we were fifteen minutes too early. And I had so much to do at home. We kept up one of those forced, self-conscious conversations with ourselves until General and Mrs. Leonard Wood came in. Her manner to me was remote, for which I can't blame her. I have not returned her two calls and an invitation to dinner, but how could I do it when they live at Fort Myer, and we have no carriage. He was lumberingly polite to both of us. Then Alice and Mr. Longworth came, she tossy and hoydenish, in a smart, short brown suit. She tossed me a "hotty-too" over her shoulder before she sat down on her foot beside Mrs. Wood and began whispering and snickering as she glanced at the filling room. The company was of all kinds, some earnest and dowdy, but many of the ultra smart who profess to scorn the Wilsons and anticipate a Wednesday-night-prayer-meeting social atmosphere. At last we were ushered into the Blue Room, ladies first, the men meekly following.

Mrs. Wilson, short, round-faced, round-pompadoured, red-cheeked and not becomingly dressed, gave each of us a limp hand and passed us on to Miss Wilson, blonde and chill, but refined and intelligent looking. Miss Hagner at her tea table in the corner was comforting by contrast. We took tea, settled into quiet little groups and gradually faded away. I don't question the Wilson breeding, but they certainly lack manner and cordiality.

At the Willard J. had to see about our tickets (or said he did), and the clerk told me to "go straight up to 101." I didn't know if it was Mrs. Bryan's bedroom or if she really wanted her visitors to come unannounced, but I walked miles of lonesome corridor until, hearing voices, I peeped into an anteroom and found Mrs. Bryan, but still no one to announce me. There were two pleasant men with her, and I never saw her so bright and vivacious. She told a funny story of seeing a man under her window during the suffrage parade fiercely guarding a baby carriage for hours with no mother in sight. When leaving I said, "Before I realize the solemnity of Mr. Bryan's being secretary of state, I want you to come and dine with us." She answered, "I am going to realize the solemnity only on rare occasions," and she really seemed the embodiment of kindness and simplicity. As I went out I heard her say, "Isn't she a cute little thing?" so I think we were mutually pleased, but it is bitter to be called "cute" at my age.

Constance Mills and Miss Klein were with J. in Peacock Alley gaily discussing the chance of his being sent to Mexico, but we had to hurry to the Shoreham to call on the Marshalls.

A bellboy brought a message for us to "come straight up," which sounded cordial, but we found the little V.-P. standing ruefully before his door feeling in all his pockets for the key. The boy produced a passkey, and Mr. M. bustled in with us following, past a wide-open bedroom door with Mrs. M.'s shoes occupying the center of the stage. She was out, but he urged us to wait, and we did for a reasonable time. He was unpretentious, but his interests seem bounded by Indiana. I spoke of his being related to Chief Justice Marshall's family, and he said, "Yes, but my family moved west in 1819, and I guess it's about rubbed off." I didn't *guess*, I knew it.

Anyway, we have made the calls and can tell the people in Texas about the new figures—not that I would dare to tell, nor would they believe, how odd and unpromising they are.

March 8

On train going south, and whistling "Dixie" from my full heart. The Democrats are whistling, too, and protesting almost too volubly that all is well for them with the best of all possible presidents, but they shrug their shoulders over the surprises in the Cabinet. I am reminded of a poem of the Revolution I read once in Old South Church, each verse ending, "Oh, my Washington, all is hazardous!" When the V.-P. said yesterday that our times were "troubulous" I wondered if our "troubules" were over or if he meant to be funny. He is inclined to that order of wit. J. says his inaugural address was "in ragtime with metaphors from the livery stable," but he seems honest and kind.

Later

We spent the day with friends and relatives at Charlottesville, and at night, waiting for the train, read in the New York *Sun* that J. was slated for Mexico. It was in the *Herald* too. What a change for us if it should come true, and another instance of "the wished-for come too late." More honor than comfort or pleasure as things are now in Mexico.

San Antonio, March 30

It is five years since we were here in the gay season—not even Holy Week was quiet. It is rather too gay for our nerves and digestion, but we are out of doors more, the nights are comfortable, and in the morning we hear the songs of mockingbirds instead of the vulgar chatter of sparrows. In Washington one forgets there are any birds but those vulgar little cockneys.

The brightest party was on Palm Sunday at Sunshine Ranch, about a hundred old friends, no smart element, and such good honest food—homemade bread, ham, salad and coffee. It was so much better than the overhandled and underseasoned stuff at the big new hotels, the St. Anthony and Gunter, which are considered the last word in elegance now.

House of Representatives, April 8, 12:50 P.M.

J. says I ought to write a careful account of the scene today when the President renews the custom—honored in the breach since Jefferson's time—of delivering his message to Congress in person. We have been here since 9:30. The galleries are packed, and every door, except that to the president's division, wide open and filled with people standing and reaching up to see over one another, but there is no excitement, no tension. I have seen much more at the prospect of an acrimonious debate. The crowd is curious rather than interested. Mrs. Porter and I are in left front row of the members' gallery. Mary Maverick, little, dark, and keenly observant, came up from Texas with me and is sitting on the aisle steps with Mrs. Percy Ash. There is a loud hum of talk. The lady Wilsons are all in place and all smiles—the family really has more than a fair share of teeth. The Senate has come in and taken the front seats. Clark has rapped for order; the chaplain has prayed, beginning, "O Thou," as usual, and Kern, Bacon, and Gallinger have gone out to escort Wilson from the Speaker's room.

Later

The hum of talk stopped suddenly. Wilson came in through the door to the Speaker's left, and the floor rose, and many people stood up and cheered. He was spick and span in very good clothes, the best I have seen in his family. He went up the steps to the Speaker's desk where Clark waited to receive him. They shook hands, and he spoke his speech in a concise, schoolmasterish fashion. There was nothing unexpected in it. The applause was enough but not enthusiastic. He lacks the warmth that holds one's attention. He made his bow and went out as he had come in. Talk became loud again; the Senate went out; the galleries emptied rapidly, and the House took up the previous question. The occasion has not been epoch making.

April 20

This Jeffersonian simplicity and intellectuality will drive me to drink or into the smart set. I sat by Secretary ———— at dinner last night, with only grape juice to stimulate our wits, and listened to a disquisition on the standardization of tin cups and the difficulty of estimating the amount of phosphorus in waste. I turned for relief to the Senator on my left, and he was describing in a sepulchral voice the horrors of the Dayton flood, little babes torn from their mothers' arms, perishing in the turbid torrent, etc. It was the devil or the deep sea for me.

Also the "refining influences" and "social uplift" strongly hinted at by the Wilsons appear to be, like the tariff, a local issue. Mrs. W. gave notice informally that there was to be no turkey trotting at the White House, but Mary tells me that at the Barracks hop the Misses W. were trotting nimbly and even doing the tango in an extreme style. The young ladies appear almost to forget themselves in social delights. I asked for an appointment for Mary to call on them, and when we arrived we met twenty or thirty young girls who had, of course, come by appointment. We were received kindly by Mrs. W., but a diligent search of the room failed to discover a single Miss Wilson. Finally I asked Miss Hagner where they were, and she explained apologetically that one was upstairs with a bad headache, one had gone to Baltimore, and another, at the last minute, had been persuaded by a lieutenant to go to the horse show. Mary enjoys my bewilderment. She says I told her she was here to learn good manners, and I think she is getting a few helpful hints—but by the Spartan method.

Wilson himself is not making friends nor measuring up as the Democrats had hoped. He is wise in his own conceits, always a schoolmaster, dogmatic and arbitrary. Colonel Cowart says he considers the Cabinet his "faculty." After declaring that the Cabinet officers were to select their own assistants, he has more than once overridden their decisions and gravely embarrassed them. Redfield selected Lynden Evans for commissioner of corporations, and while he (Evans) was in Chicago arranging to move here he was notified that the President had reconsidered—Mr. E. "was not in sympathy with the Progressive Movement." The papers say he wants a young radical.

Mrs. Evans took lunch with us today and told the story in full. When Redfield consulted the President, Wilson said it would be an ideal appointment, so the place was offered and accepted. But shortly afterwards he wrote Redfield that he had changed his mind, that Evans was "by constitution and temperament too conservative." The Evanses say they are not angry and, thinking they see a political storm ahead, are naturally glad not to have cut loose from Chicago interests, but if I were Wilson and wanted to build up my party or get re-elected (as he obviously does in spite of his platform promises), I wouldn't count on Evans' assistance. He doesn't look like Randolph of Roanoke for nothing, and his tongue is a two-edged sword. Some people think Redfield should have resigned, but that is asking a good deal even of early Victorian dignity.

May 16

At Mount Vernon yesterday the Regents were full of a visit they had had the day before from some of the new Administration. Mrs. Webb asked me many questions and said the South was hoping so much for them and she was "praying for them every day." I advised her to keep right on praying, it wouldn't come amiss. She said, "I wonder if they are *big* enough. The way they shake hands is not reassuring."

This very interesting week might make a longer, brighter story if I had not mistaken camphor for eyedrops an hour before I was due at Calumet Place to help Mrs. Bryan with her first reception. Feeling the Democrats socially on trial, it behooved us all (be we never so humble) to endure the occasion with what grace we might. So Mother helped me into my best flowered crepe frock, and completely blinded by pain and tears I went first to the oculist. With a bravely painted eye and white veil and Mary to guide me, we took our places on the lawn, Mrs. B. mercifully placing me under a big tree.

My nerves were a pulp, and I longed for coffee, but there was only chocolate and freezing grape juice in a battered yellow marble bowl that Mrs. Bryan said was from Monticello.[3] It was a heavy, ugly thing, like a deep jardiniere, and certainly the breath of Mr. Jefferson's honest rum punch didn't hang round it still. The ladle was another curio, from Peru, adorned with the sun of the Incas but suggesting the Kansas sunflower of prohibition. There was good ice cream, cake and sandwiches, but the caterer's men were indifferent and the service abominable. I put Nancy Johnson, Marie Sims and Mary at the punch bowl and told them to make the punch and the party *go,* and they routed the waiters and really served the stuff, but no one was either cheered or inebriated. In spite of the lawn in the glory of spring and the Marine Band tooting ragtime with an occasional blessed lapse into a Strauss waltz, it was like rolling a stone uphill to get things started. Mrs. B. had asked such an odd lot of women to assist (myself among them) and almost no men had come. The House was fighting hard over the tariff bill, and an army of new members' wives came without any husbands and stood around dumbly waiting, wondering, perhaps, at the worst-dressed company ever seen even in Washington. Not the least evil result of the Balkan War is the outbreak of "Bulgarian atrocities" in dress. Shapeless blouses have intrigued the fancy of the country dressmakers, and their development in Near Eastern mustard yellow, grass green and Turkey red adds to the grotesquerie—if I may coin a word which must be a good one because it came in response to a need.

At home at last J. sent me straight to bed where I might have stayed several days nursing my eyes but for a telegram from Lord Weardale saying he hopes to take lunch with us Sunday. It will be pleasant to have him and I try not to remember the contrast between Weardale Manor and 1631 R Street, which will intrude itself. I am comforted by knowing that he is not a snob even if I am.

---

[3] In 1921 I learned that it was the hominy mortar from the Monticello kitchen, bought by Mr. Thurman, a neighbor, at the sale of Jefferson's personalty, and sold many years afterwards by one of his family to Mr. Bryan.—E.M.S.

Lord Weardale more than justified my confidence, and the little luncheon exceeded my expectations as to both dishes and conversation. The Bryans, who don't usually go out on Sundays, came because it was "just a home affair"; Mr. and Mrs. Porter are always perfect for good talk, and Mary was thrown in for lagniappe. At first the talk was more anecdotal than I like, but it settled down at last to the peace question on which the four men talked well and sympathetically. The Porters lingered to tell me how they had enjoyed it, and said they had never believed me before when I said Bryan was a charming dinner guest.

Bryan repeated a story told by Sir Robert Reed at the Peace Dinner in New York. Sir Robert is enormously stout, and once while speaking to a great crowd on a peace measure of which he was the leading advocate, he said, "I may not live to see it. I may die and leave it"—when a voice in the rear of the hall called out with perfect gravity, "Then the fat *would* be in the fire."

The next day we took lunch with the whole Peace-of-Ghent party at Colonel Thompson's near Sheridan Circle. The house was new to me, though J. has been there often, and I found it charmingly spacious and light—I detest dark grandeur—and the Colonel and his wife are cordial and friendly to suit it. We were assembled in the large hall on the second floor when I beheld that aged courtier, Chauncey Depew, convoying down the broad staircase from the floor above three of the quaintest ladies imaginable, contrasted with our present long-drawn-out fashions. They were fairly pretty young women in enormous crinoline flowered chintz dresses with tight low-necked bodices and cameo breast pins. Their hair was plastered down at the sides, and hung in bag nets at the back. Nothing was burlesqued or overdone, they were just ladies of another time, Thackeray's women. One carried a small Irish harp and when they stopped at the foot of the stairs, she began to play on it, and the other two sang a ballad of Somerset, long and explicit as folk songs are. They sang without effort or evidence of the "voice teacher"—that person who has put an end to so much sweet and natural music in our time.

The Hon. Neil Primrose, a son of Lord Rosebery, presented himself to take me in. There was a semicircular table at each end of the big, well-lighted dining room leaving space in the center for the servants to pass and the Fuller sisters to stand and sing again. The tables were decorated with flat wreaths of coarse ferns interrupted by silver vases of roses and little standards flying the flags of all respectable nations: not at all pretty.

I felt sorry for the Primrose, under thirty and as pretty as his name, but his good British training made him appear oblivious of my gray hairs and pretend to find December as pleasant as May. Looking over the company, I was consoled by seeing that with the exception of pretty Mrs. Hobson, I was about as young as any petticoat present, and quite as good looking as Mrs. B.—into whose ear Lord Weardale was pouring gay little nothings, quite unaware that she is deaf on that side. Her eyes shot wicked lightnings at me when he looked over, laid his hand on his heart and drank my health.

Just before lunch Mr. Carnegie came to speak to me and took both my hands in his whereupon my stock rose visibly with several people, two or three of whom seized the first opportunity to ask me point-blank if I knew him well enough to ask for a contribution to this or that scheme. I naturally refused to advise, but teased one of them by telling her that I once asked him for something and got $50,000 by return mail, as did happen when he gave the library to San Antonio. People miss so much pleasure in Mr. Carnegie by thinking of him only in terms of dollars and cents. He is full of old-time poetry and romance—a quotation from the *Border Ballads* opens a floodgate of talk—and he is a delightful companion.

I asked him if he would go to the opening of the Peace Palace this summer, and he said quizzically, "I am not invited." I suggested trying to get him an invitation, but perhaps he would prefer shooting at Skibo about that time, and he said suddenly, as if it were a happy thought, "Why can't you come to see me there?" He wrote his address on his card and urged me to let him know if we came to Europe this summer. I hope we can go, but even if we cannot, I am henceforth a marked woman to the fashionable bystanders who heard the invitation.

June

No man is truly his own master, but a congressman is a slave to such small things. Dr. Morgan says J. must have a complete rest, and our going to Europe depends on the disposition of the post office in Fredericksburg, Texas. Captain von Hagen wants it, and J. wants it for him—he is such a staunch old Democrat—but perverse influences are at work on our nice new President. J. is to see him today, and if he gets his promise, we can sail when the navy bill goes to the Senate and get back by the time it returns to the House. If not—?

Later

J. reports the President "as icy as usual," but he did the decent thing. Of course he advised J. to "see my postmaster general," and, of course, J. refused—that is almost the rule in the delegation now—so the President said he could not promise him the office, but he would promise that no appointment should be made without advising him beforehand and he could go to Europe with an easy mind. It is a relief to know that the amenities are to be observed in spite of Burleson, and a congressman at least informed of appointments in his district. That is customary even when the president is of the opposite party. McKinley did it with Jim most punctiliously, and Taft always, I believe, but then, of all presidents I have known, Taft is the most perfect everyday gentleman.

London, June

Curiously enough, the noise of the militant suffragists is louder the farther off you are from the scene of their activities. At home we heard that women were excluded from St. Paul's and the Abbey and many public places, but we went into St. Paul's this morning without protest and a little later the whole vast floor was crowded with as many women as men. Having accepted the idea that churchgoing is out of fashion, I lost some of the service by gazing and wondering at the enormous crowd, and on an ordinary Sunday, too, when there was no festival or royalty to promote religious enthusiasm. J. from his commanding height was even more impressed, and leaned down several times to say to me, "The place is really *full*."

The Abbey in the afternoon was so crowded that we had to sit in the Poets' Corner. Our chairs nearly touched the names of Browning and Tennyson. We couldn't hear a word from the chancel, but I fed my soul with the music of that choir invisible which has made so much of the gladness of the world for me. When Boyd-Carpenter began his sermon we only knew it by the preliminary rustling of those in front of us as they settled down to listen, so we slipped off to the livelier scenes of Hyde Park.

Even there women were not in such dire disgrace as the conservative press would have us believe. We stood for an hour in a crowd around a yellow cart from which shaky rostrum Mrs. Pethick Lawrence demanded suffrage for women. Mrs. L. is handsome, and so well dressed that no anti could complain of a lack of "womanliness." There was no disorder, though the speakers were frequently interrupted in a brutal way. Such rude talk addressed to any woman speaker in America would precipitate a free fight. We missed "a jolly row" at the Pavilion where several women were knocked down, but the speaker, Mrs. Pankhurst, escaped unhurt. That woman must have nine lives, but otherwise is not as catty as some of her home-staying sisters.

Eight o'clock found us at the door of Thomas Lough, M.P., 14 Dean's Yard. It was broad daylight, but there was a solemn evening stillness under the tall elms enclosed by gray walls, that merged on the left into the somber mass of the Abbey. A friendly yellow cat blinking on the steps made us feel a little less like ghosts, and we were just laughing over the happy chance that had made us ring the visitors' bell instead of one marked "Servants" when a pretty maid opened the door into the oldest, homiest hall, took our wraps and showed us upstairs to a sober, comfortable drawing room.

What to wear to an informal Sunday tea had puzzled me, but Mrs. L.'s amethyst satin was quite as décolleté as my black lace over white, and nothing could have been more becoming to her clear skin, violet eyes, and wavy gray hair. Mr. L.'s niece from America, decorously clad in small-town, half-evening dress but very taking and clever, settled on a sofa with J. while Mrs. Lough and I rested on big chairs before the low windows looking out to "the Yard." She looked so Victorian I was surprised to find her a convinced suffragist, saying in effect that it was the brutality of Englishmen (the Loughs are Irish) and the medieval cruelty of English laws for women that had driven them to this rebellion. When Captain and Mrs. Pirie (old friends) came, we went down to dinner in the quaint, dim dining room—I wish people built as pretty houses now as they did in the time of Henry VIII. We had good talk, mostly political. Captain Pirie lives in France and represents Aberdeen—a strange system to us with whom residence in the district is obligatory, and even a long absence a political offense. No doubt J. is being criticized now for not taking his holiday under the burning sun of Texas. But our way is best for our vast country. What would a man from Maine know of the needs of Texas, or vice versa?

Monday

At tea on the terrace a few days ago, and again this afternoon with the Piries, I was distinctly conscious of being watched as a possible militant with a hatchet in my hip pocket. With many other women I cooled my heels on the benches outside while J. went freely into the lobby to find our host. Some man had to come out and identify each one of us, and those who emulated Caesar's wife as to militancy were personally conducted inside. But while waiting I enjoyed looking at the women's clothes and feeling a certain pride in Americans' sense of fitness—and fit. The first afternoon was cold and wet, and I wondered if I were the only well-dressed or the one ill-dressed woman there. I wore a tailored suit with a fussy lace blouse under the coat while the others had on pale wools and silks almost low-necked and no wraps. Later when the rain poured into our tea, I commended my own costume.

Today I Anglicized myself with a flowered crepe and carried a Liberty satin wrap. I was glad I had the courage of the calendar, for we were in a gay party with many well-dressed women. Tea was hardly served, the cake and buns circulating, and dear old Lord ———— fairly launched on the same story about the buns he had told me in the same place two years ago, when the floods descended. Each of us seized a teacup, the gentlemen rescued the cake and we crowded into the hall at the foot of the stairs, where we sat on a bench and put the tea things in a chair. They talked of the Queen, of her ill-made dresses "all little bows and elbows," and a hyphenated artist told a story, thought to be very risqué for Mary, of her saying to another artist who was painting her portrait, "Now that the women are wearing slit skirts, I shall have to wear my Garter (the order) on my leg."

With that triumph of hope over experience that makes the English great in spite of their climate, we returned to the terrace, had an entirely new tea served, and an entirely new shower. Later we found the ladies' gallery, as dark and stuffy as ever, and listened for a few minutes to a dreary discourse on liquor legislation for Scotland.

Captain Pirie had asked if we cared to hear the debate in the Lords for a while—the very thing we were most anxious to do and that dear old Lord Weardale after asking us had forgotten. Captain Pirie brought up Lord Fitz-Stephen, who asked the Black Rod—or something quite as medieval—who said there was a crowd; he would see what he could do. I had a chair on the floor to the right while J. *stood* back of me with several other gentlemen, among them young Gladstone, who is tall, has a nice face, and is said to be "promising." The room was a satisfying sight, so narrow and high, and richly brown, and in the steep, dim gallery a single row of brightly dressed women like a wreath for decoration. The Marquis of Lansdowne was conversing in a gentle, deprecatory fashion on the Irish question, and now and then the Lords would murmur, "Hear, hear," like people who rouse up and say, "I wasn't asleep; I heard every word you said." But it must have been worthwhile for the next day the *Daily Mail* had several columns of it. We stayed some time, then went to Heck's in Bond Street to try on the taupe silk in which I am to shine at the opening of the Peace Palace.

We called at the Consul General's and found that Mrs. Griffiths' was a society of magnificent distances. She has acquired the remote and casual British manner. No one was introduced, so we consorted with strangers while she nestled on a sofa with a friend who, she explained later, was Lady Somebody, "the wife of one of the greatest sporting men in England." A massive American woman fitted lightly into mustard-colored satin monopolized the tea table telling what she ate at the Savoy and how ridiculously cheap it was—only three pounds ten for dinner with two cocktails and two liqueurs, etc. Mr. Griffiths, a man whose charm of talk and manner does credit to all America, made no showing, so we flitted.

Scotland, July 16

So much society and sightseeing, it was only by packing till the small hours that we managed to get off yesterday morning on this trip to Skibo. We must be there for the fete, and Mr. Carnegie sent directions and schedules galore, but J.—American-manlike—prefers to find his own way. I only hope we shall not be embarrassed by arriving at the wrong time or place.

We stopped at "Pairth" for the night, or that brief spell of darkness preceding 5:00 A.M. when we had to get up. And now we are passing places familiar and beloved in Scotch history and poetry. The heather is purple, the gorse yellow, and there are great patches of snow on the hills about Drumtochty Pass. It is so strangely suggestive of the bleaker parts of Mexico—the cold pure air, the lovely graystone sheep folds, and the same sense of mournful aloofness from the world. We are shivering with cold and longing to reach Kingussie and breakfast.

Later

Two tea baskets with hot ham and eggs, marmalade and mustard, and slabs of awful bread have cheered us up, and a pretty girl and her mother, going to the Orkneys "to keep cool," are pleasant companions. The girl's frank talk is refreshing after English hesitancy and reserve. She says Mormons are getting numbers of girls from the Orkneys every year, and she's sure "there'll be a jolly bit of fighting in Ulster" when they get Home Rule, and she agrees with me that the scenery is better when not obstructed by signs of liver pills and malted milk as it is farther south.

July 20

In spite of J.'s trifling with British railway schedules, we did get to Bonar Bridge, and at the right time. A tall chauffeur (not in livery) was there to meet us and put us in a polished-oak car with a baggage compartment in the rear. Sitting in front with him was another passenger for Skibo, a meek little man with a bit of white paper pasted on his ear. He was so apologetic I wondered what manner of guest he was, but soon forgot him in pagan joy of the beautiful country under dancing sunshine. I think the sun dances here because it gets out so seldom. The long winding road was bordered with the tallest and riches plumes of broom I have ever seen. Our Virginia variety, brought over by Thomas Jefferson, is a weed by comparison. At last the towers of Skibo showed above the trees with the Stars and Stripes floating over them. (Later I was amused to find that the other side of the flag was the Union Jack—a canny fancy of the Laird's tenants who presented it.)

The entrance was rather small and stooping, but the hall satisfied my expectation for the moment we had to see it before Mrs. Carnegie came to give us a cordial, unaffected welcome. We liked her instantly. She is a pretty size, and walks lightly and well—that excellent and rare thing in a woman. She wore a tweed skirt with a thin white blouse, her iron-gray hair was simply arranged, and her eyes, also iron gray, were direct and kind. Her skin is clear, her mouth large, straight and firm. I could not think of a finer face. She couldn't understand our arriving at that hour when we had left London the morning before, and said, "Only Americans could have done it," which made J. very proud of himself. She introduced our anemic fellow traveler explaining that he was to try the organ; they had lost their organist, and Mr. Carnegie liked to have music every evening and hymns Sunday night. An elevator took us to the third floor, and she showed us our rooms. Mine was quite glorious, all rosy damask and white frilly things, but my glance went past it to the big windows framing a picture of the Firth of Dornoch—moor and meadow; white sheep browsing on emerald grass and shaggy Highland cattle resting under the trees, and over it all flocks of sea gulls wheeling and screaming foolishly. I think Mrs. C. heard my gasp of delight and entered into my joy, for she instantly pushed back a curtain and showed me the foreground of the picture, the castle part, the old walls and hedges, the graceful glass houses, fountains, swans and masses of flowers, without the least pride of possession but just pure sympathy in our enjoyment of it.

She told me to ring for a maid if I wanted one, showed J. his room next to mine, and left us feeling quite at home. On my dressing table J. and I noticed simultaneously a little manuscript note framed and set forward conspicuously, and as he read it aloud, we looked at one another and laughed and wondered. It said, "Your host and hostess beg that you will under no circumstances offer any gratuity to the attendants. They and their household have a perfect understanding on this matter and sincerely hope that you will respect their feelings." Of all the Carnegie philanthropies this seemed the most graceful! The problem of tips had haunted us. We didn't mind giving them, and had made ourselves a liberal allowance for the purpose, but accustomed as we are to the house with only a few servants, the question of when, what and to whom to give was bewildering, and here was the whole matter settled for us. Throughout our visit we felt that indescribable difference in the manner of servants where there is no sense of favors to come. The family's attitude to them was so pleasant, too. Everyone says good night and good morning and thanks them for the smallest service—as we were brought up to do—a pleasant contrast to the remote, unfriendly manner to "underlings" that one sees in England, and far too often in democratic America.

In the morning room we found Mrs. C. on a sofa by the Laird holding up a warning finger as she talked, so it made a cheerful opening for us to rescue him from a lecture. He was glad to see us. Mrs. C. wanted him to listen to the organ, but he wanted to talk about his golf; he had beaten Brookings, but sometimes these young men just let an old fellow beat them. Lunch was ready—and he went on talking and putting off the decision about the organist like a mischievous boy.

It is too bad that the Carnegie tartan is such big squares of gray, white, black, and yellow. It takes so few of them to make his coat, and fewer still for his trousers that met his heavy golf stockings at the knee.

After lunch, Margaret, wearing a big white apron, came to ask her mother if she might help the maids to prepare for the fete, and after a while we found her in the cavernous basement—dungeons once, no doubt—doing her full share packing immense hampers with bags of cake and buns.

A tall major-domo shook us all into warm Burberry coats (they seemed to have an inexhaustible supply of them) before we started on a trip to the salmon leaps.

We rode through the estate for fifteen long Scots miles, past clean villages with good schoolhouses and libraries, between deep-blue hills and wide moors covered with gorse and bell heather, and clover and sweet brier much redder and more fragrant than ours. At a steep turn that seemed the end of all things, we got out and walked down a wild ravine to the sound of roaring water, and suddenly came to a cliff where the stream looked through a narrow pass into a huge rocky bowl full of churning yellow foam. Just as we stopped to look, a big fish leaped straight up in an insane effort to reach the high level and swim upstream. Mr. Carnegie and I clapped our hands with delight, and soon we had counted 83 leaps, though the others exchanged incredulous glances when we told it.

Going back over the moors was even more beautiful than the road between the hills. Earth and sky were one deep solemn blue that made us quiet and meditative. Mrs. C. and I talked of books, and she seems to read *everything*. How does she find time with her varied interests and Mr. C.'s in which she participates with sympathy and comprehension?

Dinner at 7:30 hurried our dressing, and the peat fire in the hall was such a comfort to me that I clung like a kitten to the red-cushioned bench in front of it. The party had been augmented by a Mr. and a Dr. Morrison (the latter of Edinburgh Library) and their wives. The doctor was in kilt and sporran and a' quite at ease, and not as if in fancy dress, as it seemed to me while I eyed his white knees sympathetically wondering if they were as cold as my bare shoulders.

A wild skirl of bagpipes wound almost visibly through the hall, the Laird gave me his arm; the others fitly joined together dropped in behind us, and we marched to the door of the long corridor where the piper stood blowing like mad. There could not be a prouder figure as he strode ahead of us, his kilt swinging from side to side, his bonnet cocked over one ear, and a dozen tartan streamers fluttering from the pipes that were fairly deafening us. Nothing excites me like the sound of pipes, so I was treading on air. I heard the clans behind me; I was Dundee and Montrose and Rob Roy. I could have followed him all night, over the hills and far away, and murdered the base Sassenach in the morning, but instead we only marched once around the room to the Laird's chair, the pipes swung back down the corridor, the skirling died away, and I came back to earth and dinner. Very good dinner, too, with glorious roses, and strawberries big as teacups and the unpretentious talk of genuinely cultivated people.

In the drawing room Mr. C. took his forty winks on a sofa before the fire, then Mrs. C. ran some records of Scottish songs through a Victrola, and he hummed and enjoyed them. We were all in our rooms at 10:30 to rest for the fete tomorrow. What a sane, happy home it is. One forgets it is a castle.

In the morning I couldn't dress for running to the window to see the proud piper swing around the terrace playing first the Carnegie clan tune and then the ironical "Johnnie Cope, are ye waukin' yet?" to get us up.

(General Horace Porter told Mrs. Carnegie that pipers moved about when playing because they were trying to get away from the noise. Once she took the piper to New York as a butler, and sent the servants ahead of the family. When she arrived, she noticed that he had a severe cold, and asking him about it, he said, "Oh, madam, I always get a cold when I put on trousers.")

Going in to breakfast Mr. C. stopped to answer a question about the big stained-glass windows, one with a shadowy picture of the little white cottage where he has born and the other of Skibo; and he talked about his brave mother and the hardships of his early life. Mrs. C. came by, listened a minute, and said, "Oh, if Andrew is telling you that story, we are going on." He has a gift for saying things well and quickly, so I learned much history; he praised my knowledge of Scottish poetry and dialect, corrected my version of some lines from Sir Patrick Spens, and we had a fine talk.

Breakfast was very gay, too, with only one servant at the buffet and no one permitted to wait on anyone else. J. was so funny and helpless. He didn't know how he took his coffee and carried his plate as if he were afraid of it.

We went to Dornoch to see the cathedral, and some painters thinking us militants tried to keep us out, but at the name of Carnegie they almost fell off the ladders and laid their paintpots at our feet.

The mist became a steady rain and threatened to spoil the fete. Hundreds of red-cheeked children and farmers and their wives gathered about the castle door, and the Laird stood on a chair and made a speech of welcome, and then, with four pipers to lead us, we all marched down to the sopping sports field.

There was a killingly funny Punch and Judy show, "Tam o' Shanter Stands for Parliament," but few of the crowd even smiled, and there was no audible laughter but my own. I spoke of it to Mrs. C., and she said, "Oh, they will enjoy it immensely next winter when they've thought it over." Tea was served in a tent as big as Barnum's circus. There were 1,500 seats with a bag of cakes and a box of candy at each plate, and an army of servants with pitchers of tea and milk. Mr. C. and J. and several clergymen made brief speeches, and Margaret, the most sensible and unspoiled little girl imaginable, delivered the prizes. The lovely flowers on the tables were sent to the sick, and the day was over except for our comfortable and happy dinner party in the evening with a number of new guests.

The morning we left we were given the horn porridge spoons they keep for guests they want to come again, and we brought away besides the happiest memories of a family which, as Lowell says of the early Americans, "had better uses for wealth than merely to display it."

Wiesbaden, August

This is a deadly dull place, not even pretty, just stodgily German. But we have had one sensation, albeit an unpleasant one. J. has received his first batch of official mail, and we have been staring at one another, unbelieving, ever since. The President gave the Fredericksburg post office to the other man before we left America. J.'s secretary has reason to believe that he did it the very day J. saw him. Did the President tell a deliberate falsehood? Or is he to be just the tool of Burleson's spites and revenges? Surely Wilson will explain and make the *amende honorable* in some way. However, it still puts J. in an unpleasant position with regard to the patronage in his district; he cannot with dignity ask anything else and run the risk of being tricked and deceived again. Put not your trust in princes— nor professors!

One afternoon sitting in the Kurgarten listening to the music, I heard a strange roaring from the sky and, looking up, saw a monster Zeppelin coming over the trees so low that we could see the people in the car beneath, and so appallingly hideous that I stayed awake all night thinking of it. But we are getting used to them. Breakfasting on our high balcony every morning we see them lumbering about the sky like aerial walruses strayed from another world. J. laughs at me, but I hate and fear them.

Over at Mainz we saw the Kaiser review 15,000 picked troops, all "in shining armor" and strong and beautiful, but my heart ached knowing that such glorious youth may all be used as cannon fodder. Since reading *The Human Slaughter House,* which I bought in New York just as the Kaiser suppressed it here, I am convinced that the masses of Germany are opposed to this official militarism. A woman at a bookstore lamented the suppression of the book, telling me it was their best seller.

After the review we waited at a barrier to get a close view of the Kaiser. Hundreds of mounted officers came past, all so resplendent that I asked a German-American friend how we were to distinguish the "All Highest"? He answered confidently, "By the cheering." The procession ended, the barrier came down, and I asked again, "Where was the Kaiser? I heard no cheers." A man near me said sharply, "He passed some time ago. He is not liked here."

The Hague, Hôtel de Zalm, August 20

There were Japanese and many other outlanders at the station, and a typical peacemaking old gentleman invited me to ride here in his victoria instead of the crowded taxi with J. and our baggage. I am sorry I declined as he is more prepossessing than many others in this gloomy hotel. It has narrow corridors, brown paint and dull green paper, but we are fortunate because it is well situated, and every place is packed for this piping time of peace—the opening of the Palace, the Universal Peace Congress and the Interparliamentary Union one after another. Through my windows I get glimpses of the garden back of the Nordende Palace and hear a dismal and puzzling singing of hymns several times a day. The Queen is severely evangelical, but surely she doesn't have prayers at all hours.

Hall of the Knights

A picturesque crowd—Chinese, East Indians, red-fezzed Mohammedans, fisher folk and peasants, and many men in uniform wearing medals of honor and scars (practical converts to peace, no doubt)—moved toward this hall so steeped in history of wars, tumult and religious persecution, and now to see the beginning of a new chapter with a Universal Peace Congress. We passed battalions of little schoolboys with shining morning faces brought out to see the strangers, and were met at the door by Boy Scouts and cordial, well-dressed young ladies, one of whom, when we said we were Americans, asked anxiously, "But how many *are* there?" showing we are here in force. They are ready to speak any language needed, and I wondered sadly how many girls we could muster anywhere in our country for such a committee.

The appearance of the audience is reassuring; earnest, wise-looking men and women from many lands. The speakers—the Minister of State, La Fontaine, Weardale, Dr. David Starr Jordan, and others—are on the platform under the great baldachin of crimson velvet and gold embroidery, and back of them is the Queen's raised chair with the arms and the motto "Je maintiendrai" above it. The hall is stately and subdued in tone; the walls hung with Oriental prayer rugs, giving richness, warmth and color to the bleak medieval spaces; and the bare rafters are lost in darkness above glowing electroliers.

The more I see of medieval buildings the easier it is to understand the belligerence and restlessness of their times. People had to fight to keep warm. Perhaps the Crusaders themselves were drawn to Palestine more by the genial climate than by enthusiasm for the Holy Sepulchre. The hot-water pipes in here must make modern statesmen deliberate longer before cutting off one another's heads, or going to war, than their predecessors did in the brave days of old.

But the first leaflet handed to us makes me murderous. We are to be sung to by a group of "young men and maidens of the Raja Yoga," followers of Mrs. Tingley, of Point Loma, California, and they are already assembled in the gallery robed in pseudo-classical white cotton gowns with wreaths of pink paper roses. The songs are of Mrs. Tingley's "own composure"—deadly stuff—and the accompaniment a wheezy melodeon. Do any people on earth indulge in such banalities as provincial Americans!

Later

Tonight J. thought we ought to go to the official concert, but just as we were starting a welcome intervention of Providence appeared in the form of Dr. and Mrs. Jordan. Mrs. J. said they had come just for five minutes, but the way the doctor settled his gigantic figure into a big leather chair convinced me that we were saved from the long, cold ride to Scheveningen. Mrs. J. is bright and agreeable, but she is dead tired, as we all are, and the doctor was warmed up, and unwinding some of his peace theories to sympathetic listeners. She said "D-a-vid" several times, but he didn't hear her, until after half an hour or more she got up, shook hands with me, and said firmly, *"David Starr Jordan,* it is time to go," and David, like a big schoolboy, shook himself up and followed her.

August 22

The Peace Palace has no large auditorium, and the scarcity of seats is seriously embarrassing the management. Mrs. H. of the diamond D.A.R. insignia and the red shoes with diamond heels that startled Washington last winter demands a seat "in the name of half a million leading women of America." There are "leading clubwomen" and others, just humbugs and worse, determined to get in where there is not room for distinguished Parliamentarians. J. gave notice early that I would not be there as he positively will not beg for seats, but as he has a seat with the I.P.U., I am quite content. One of a family is enough.

August 26

Last night there was the quaintest party at Senator Van Houten's, just for our benefit, it appeared. It was a small company of clever people, artists and politicians, and we were shown beautiful pictures and intimate little souvenirs and sketches of modern Dutch artists. At ten o'clock a young daughter of the house and a young man brought in hot sugared waffles and wine which we took at the library table without even laying a cloth. Waffles on a chilly night are beautiful and fair. How I wish we dared to do such simple things in America.

Finding Lloyd Bryce, the United States Minister, a human and approachable person has been one of our pleasant surprises. His prompt call, followed by an invitation to dinner and a reception were all agreeable. Mrs. B., a beautiful woman for her age, is, I believe, a granddaughter of old Peter Cooper. Her dress and jewels were quite individual, and she entertained in the best old-fashioned manner introducing people as soon as they came in as far as possible. Even during the reception, she didn't seem to be nailed to the floor and left Mrs. Carnegie, the guest of honor, several times to look around the rooms and see if things were going comfortably.

It isn't always so with U.S. ambassadors. I recall with amusement and chagrin for my country the days of Wilson in Belgium, and Powell Clayton in Mexico, who proclaimed to a large company after we had had some pleasant talk with Díaz at the palace that "this little lady made an awful mash of the President."

August 28

All the bells are ringing hard as they can ring; the sun is shining gloriously, and there is a sound of distant cheering. The opening of the Peace Palace is bringing a message of joy to a war-worn world. I had to come in; it was so hot, and the crowd such a heavy one, sturdy folk from Scheveningen and the country, the women with the sweetest lace and gold headgear and solid with petticoats, knitting steadily as they walked and "jollied" one another, and the broad-based weather-beaten men. I wish we knew the art of decoration as the Dutch do. Their flags are of such good quality that the rain can pour on them without leaving the bedraggled misery of our cheap bunting and cotton streamers; and the wreaths festooned diagonally across the streets are hung with baskets of real, not paper flowers. The mass of clean, healthy people fills me with envy and admiration.

J. went off hours ago looking the usual sheepish American in evening clothes at noon, but he liked the orange-colored rose in his buttonhole. Men, women and children, horses and dogs are wearing a bit of orange color today. I knew he wouldn't wear an artificial flower, nor a marigold smelling like soup, so searching the florists on the Moelenstraat, I found a perfect rosebud, dyed, if you please, brilliant orange and very pretty. With white gloves and high hat, he looked much more *distingué* than the Prince Consort, who, the Dutch say, looks like "a German sergeant."

Later

J. came in all quills from heat and fatigue. He said the exercises were a bore, badly managed, and humiliating to his group because of the number of American pushers who were admitted because of their importunity when people of real worth were excluded. A certain mellow-voiced, always-in-earnest peace lady from Boston brought in five friends, took the seats reserved for the Queen and had to be asked to move.

When he had cooled down a bit, he remarked, "You are going to be asked to the palace. Are you ready?" I inquired casually, "When?" and when he replied, "Why, tonight, of course," I fairly leaped from the bed. It was 5:45; the shops were closed; I had no touch of orange color and had used my last pair of evening gloves! No doubt I had a wildish air as I sped to a little French shop where the family lives, and there was a chance of finding it open on a holiday. I flew back with the gloves and a huge, floppy, orange rose for my corsage. The "summons" to the palace had come—an octavo sheet of cardboard, a note scribbled on the margin from Mr. Bryce begging us to be prompt.

But my troubles were not over. The Lynden Evanses were not to be found, and I knew Mrs. E.'s dress had gone to be pressed. J. and Mr. E. had to go to a banquet at the Binrenhof and could only join us at the palace. But Mrs. E. and I were ready and our coach at the door in good time. The palace being just around the corner, we lingered talking to friends until the proprietor, with many apologies, suggested our starting. We protested, but he hinted at delays because of the crowds and, oh, how thankful we were to him afterwards! Difficulty number one was finding we must make a detour to get to Nordende Street, and then we kept on, and on, past familiar but distant places until we began to get nervous. Our knowledge of Dutch is the least possible, and the coachman only grunted and sputtered at our reiteration of "Nordende Palass" which was all we could think of to turn him in the other direction. Mrs. E. declares that I tried to coax him with baby talk. I would have chirruped and sung to him just as readily. When we realized that he was actually taking us to the Peace Palace miles away, we grew so frantic that we shouted to a traffic policeman to stop us. He spoke some English, so we poured out our troubles, and indicated haste by every sort of pantomime, and he asked to see our cards for the palace. Of course, we had never thought of bringing them, but over here everything is forgiven to Americans and lunatics. We were so manifestly both that he passed us on, and we arrived at the door breathless, only to be met with a stern demand for a blue ticket we had never even heard of.

Luckily some old I.P.U. friends recognized us, and we did get in. J., Mr. Bryce, and Mr. Evans met us in moods varying between rage and anxiety. With not a minute to spare we were marshaled to our places on the right of the audience room, the men on the left. Mrs. Bryce led the American group—pretty Miss Marburg, then myself, Mrs. Evans and Mrs. James Brown Scott.

At the upper end of the long room the big doors opened, and the Queen appeared with the fat German Prince, and my first thought was "Well! if I hadn't had a better frock, I wouldn't have come to the party." It was a dull, unbecoming mauve, years out of date, too long, and so full that it emphasized her typically Dutch figure distressingly. She went down the left side to speak to the men first while the Prince came over and spoke to us, and each of us stood up quite in the image of our Maker, and spoke back to him, except one willowy young American-born woman in the Dutch group who made him a sweeping stage curtsy, bowing almost to the floor. It looked silly and overdone to me. None of the Dutchwomen did anything of the kind, but it takes a free-born American to give royalty its due.

The Queen and Prince rejoined one another, changed places, and the Queen came down our side, speaking to each one in whatever language was needed. She is rather plain, and her expression more intellectual than amiable. After the audience we followed the Queen into one dining room and gradually scattered into several more. I never imagined so much or such substantial food for an evening party—ladies helped to broad slices of rare roast beef, for instance, and eating them too. I wondered what was to become of it all, but the unaffected Dutch didn't leave us long in doubt. They are amazing eaters, beginning with thick slabs of cheese for breakfast.

September

My faithful old friend, Lord Weardale, helped me, assisted by a new acquaintance, a dean of Worcester Cathedral, to lay a wreath upon the tomb of Grotius at Delft. Dr. Gobat stood on the pedestal of the statue of Grotius and talked until I thought I saw a Dutch girl growing faint and the American wreath she carried withering away. When the ceremony ended the carillon of the belfry, which had played in turn the hymn of each nation represented, pealed out gloriously "Oh, Susanna! don't you cry for me" under the impression no doubt that it was our national anthem. I wish it was, or something equally expressive of the genius of our people instead of the two we use—one doggerel and the other bombast.

I do like the sensible, kind Dutch custom of introducing guests to one another so that they can start talking without that stupid sparring for names or avoidance of them. The reception and garden party at the Peace Palace was so easy and gay because of it. J. enjoyed especially the clever and handsome Miss Bentinck, who acts as our sponsor. She speaks English so perfectly that he asked if she was related to the great English statesman, Bentinck, and she answered smartly, "No, he was related to me. His family went over with William and Mary. They are only English-born Dutch."

At the immense dinner Dr. Tydeman gave at Scheveningen, he and madame and their son introduced *all* the foreigners. I sat between two Dutch M.P.s whose frank and fearless talk about the Queen and affairs Dutch and European was like a breeze from the North Sea. I hate diplomats and love politicians—"one dry and one the living tree."

October 10

We had some delightful days down in Wales with our dear friends the Aeron Thomases near Swansea. Mr. T. has retired from Parliament and taken up "public work," and Mrs. T. and her clever daughter, Lena, are absorbed in humanitarian effort of every kind. It seems to me the women here *do* more and talk rather less than ours. They are not content with collecting money for their hospital, they go to the hospital and stay there certain days and hours of each week and get a closer interest in it. English land conditions give a wide-ranging Texan much to think of. There are thousands of blackened, undernourished children and smutty, bitter-looking men and women in the narrow streets of the Swansea, with never a tree nor a flower nor a blade of grass to make their world beautiful, and in walking distance 3,000 acres of land owned by one old woman! It is opened for a few weeks each year for her friends to shoot the deer and grouse that looked at us over the fence, so bored and tame they were. Mrs. Thomas told me she doubted if most of the children we saw, and we saw swarms of them, had ever rolled on the grass a moment in their lives. I want to go home and see our young barbarians at their play.

The Concord, Washington, November 25

Yesterday the wireless towers at Arlington caught the ticking of a clock in Paris! Such things can be, it seems, without especial wonder, as no one mentions it, but it opens such endless avenues to imagination and hope. Sometimes I feel a disgust for humanity in the aggregate. In New York last week there were such thousands upon thousands of people that I kept saying to myself, "What is man that Thou art mindful of him?" At least there is something godlike in our patient, farseeing scientists, but what of the rest of us, myself, for instance, with our endless whirling "like midges in the sun." And I am beginning another winter of it!

The "Cabinet Crisis," as it is laughingly called, threatens to rival the tempest over Mrs. Eaton in Jackson's time—women's wars, both of them. It began last spring, a couple of months after the inauguration of "the Foreordained." I first heard of it from Mrs. David Houston, who told me the Cabinet women had agreed not to call on the wives of members of the House. I like Mrs. Houston, and didn't want to see her make a mistake, so I mildly remonstrated, suggesting that it was bad politics, but she defended the plan so warmly that I said no more except to myself— declaring that I was then and there making my last call on that Cabinet. She did not see my fine irony when I said the members' wives would probably not notice their failure to call but might resent their publishing the fact that they did not intend to do so.

A few days later an article appeared in the *Post,* with large head- lines and evidently inspired by the Cabinet women, saying that in future they would limit their calling to "the Supreme Court, the Diplomatic Corps, and the Senate." The last was the fatal clause, a delicate distinction be- tween House and Senate. It attracted little attention a first; the House is a new one, and only a few of us older women and some politically observant citizens saw what it led to. A newspaperwoman interviewed me, but I refused to say anything except that I feared the Cabinet ladies lacked a sense of humor, were a bit hen-minded, in fact.

But when we got home from Europe the fight was on. During the long, tiresome session the House ladies had nursed their wrath to keep it warm. They were awake to the slight directed at their husbands and dis- cussed what "action" they should take. Some wanted to call a meeting of the Congressional Club; others, Mrs. Gregg and I especially, counseled playing the part of Br'er Fox, "layin' low and sayin' nothin'," but letting the Cabinet ladies alone. But the Cabinet men had been hearing things, and some sort of adjustment was becoming unavoidable.

One day I met Mrs. Houston at Woodward and Lothrop's—the scene of many grave conferences—and she said at once, "Mr. Houston and I are *very* anxious to see you and Mr. Slayden. Can you dine with us Sunday night?" We had another engagement, so she set another day, and I pleaded Mother's coming. She then said, "Well, when *can* you come?" Seeing that it had to be settled, I said, "Frankly, Mrs. Houston, I can't come to your house at all. You Cabinet ladies published a notice that you couldn't come to our houses, so you must see that we cannot with dignity accept your invitations." Whereupon we discussed the matter thoroughly, without any temper, and parted good friends, I hope, though I told her the plain truth that their calling on us was not the trouble, but their snobbish deference to the Senate in drawing a distinction between it and the House. They are not people of experience, so I think it was a new view to her. She asked if all the members' wives felt as I did, and I laughingly told her that only the Omniscient could know the minds of four hundred women, but I felt reasonably sure of the Texans. Later I called the six Texas women here, and each one said I had spoken for her.

It is too bad that this Administration, from which we poor Democrats hoped so much, with the President of Southern birth if not blood, should be made absurd by snobbery, for that is the whole secret. Most of the women of the official family are woefully provincial and consequently inflated with their high position.

At Mrs. Pinchot's recently several of them were in the receiving line, and their playful petulance with me indicated nervousness. Mrs. Bryan, always bland and slow, passed me on to Mrs. Houston, who said, "Here's the little thing who has gotten us into all this trouble." I blithely implied that the trouble was of their own making, and Mrs. Lane said she just felt like taking me up and spanking me. Farther on Mrs. Briggs, Senator Frye's daughter, with her kind, wise smile, said she had watched me running the gantlet, and I thanked her for saying that she knew the Texas delegation could be trusted to safeguard its dignity. Next day Mrs. Lane called up and asked me as naturally as possible to receive with her that afternoon. I answered teasingly, "O-oh, no, Mrs. Lane, not now. There was a time when I'd have come with pleasure." Then she simply besought me to suggest anything to save the Administration from a scandal. I think it is too late for that, but I promised to talk to some of the members' wives and see if they would discuss the matter with a view to compromise.

I called up several whose opinions are worthwhile, but, alas! things had grown worse. They are indignant over a newspaper article telling how the overburdened Cabinet women, though they could not call, intended to give "a series of intimate little dinners" where "the wives of members of the House are to be specially featured." I had to tell Mrs. Lane that there was "nothing doing." We might submit to rudeness but could not be patronized. It is public apology now, or nothing.

Sunday, December 7

Mother and I dined at the Porters'—they are among the few who have kept the old custom of midday dinner on Sunday—and we had pleasant company and talk till late in the afternoon when we left in an argument that lasted to the sidewalk, "Tod" Lowry of the New York *Evening Post* and I fairly pawing at each other to emphasize our different views of the Mexican situation. He is clever and a good fighter, but he regards Wilson as superman and, while admitting his genius for making enemies, defends him on the ground that he so compels mere normal beings to feel his superiority that they cannot help resenting it and disliking him. He outlined for me Wilson's Mexican policy, which he told me was "the grandest conception of the mind of man for the good of humanity." First: Huerta must go, though what or who is to follow him he didn't say. Next: foreign capitalists, concessionaires must go, not only from Mexico but from Central America. I asked him what made Mexico's economic greatness under Díaz, and he agreed that it was foreign capital. "But," he said solemnly, "do you know how many presidents Mexico has had since Díaz? And foreign capitalists have made all the trouble." I hurled after him, "And do you know how many presidents Mexico had before Díaz when there were no foreign capitalists?" But he would not stay for an answer, so I sent a note to tell him that in the fifty-six years preceding Díaz they had fifty-five presidents and a brace of emperors, so a paltry four in three years is moderate in these days of rapid transit and wireless telegraphy.

Wilson and his satellites are so pitifully ill-informed and incapable of seeing that they are trying to put down a dictator inside of Mexico by setting one up outside.

The New York *Evening Post,* too, has gone entirely mad. They profess to have discovered a military genius in the unspeakable Villa, call him a "sort of Robin Hood," and bracket him with our impeccable President as a savior of the country, though he has been known in his community as a common thief and fugitive from justice for many years. Patriotism, if not the last, is at least this scoundrel's latest refuge.

One gets tired of seeing, hearing and talking Wilsons. They are more before the public than any other White House family I have known. T.R.

personally never let the public forget him, but the ladies of his household
—until Alice took the center of the stage—preserved a well-bred privacy,
and Mrs. Taft was rarely heard of except officially.

The marriage of the youngest Miss W. was endlessly exploited, especially the wedding presents which every federal officer was encouraged
to give. I know several congressmen's wives who gave $10 toward the
diamond necklace (I didn't), who would be glad to have silver spoons
enough for daily use. There was a burst of sardonic laughter when the
papers announced that Mrs. Wilson and the altruistic elder daughter had
consented to be officers of the Society for the Prevention of Useless Giving.

Later

A wearing week! The National Suffrage Association was meeting here,
and I had to go when there were so many pleasanter things to do. I believe in suffrage for women in spite of the suffragists en masse; they bore
me to death. If my intercourse with them were confined to Jane Addams,
Dr. Shaw, Florence Kelley, and others of that type—too few, alas!—I
would ask no better company. But the coy, coquettish suffragist who
never lets you forget that she is a woman and therefore to be wooed, and
the strident dead-in-earnest *female,* or those—alas, too numerous—who
have ulterior motives, social or financial, shake my faith and paralyze my
efforts. I am national committeewoman from Texas, instructed, and openly
opposing their chief object—to demand a constitutional amendment giving
women the suffrage "all at once and nothing first" in utter disregard of
the common sense of leaving the question to the states. I don't believe
one woman in ten in Texas wants to vote, and if the right is thrust upon
them they will misuse or neglect it. When they waken to their need of it
they will work to get it and use it wisely. My strenuous sisters say otherwise, and mine is a small voice crying in the wilderness.

December

There is a recrudescence of that silly Cabinet squabble. A second acci-
dental interview between Mrs. Lane and me made the situation acute. I
had to tell her that the members' wives were more obdurate than ever
because of the sweet little piece about little dinners in precise rotation,
especially favoring us, and that, as the matter stood, they would accept
nothing less than a public apology, explanation or denial of the article
of May 25. It really is a harsh ultimatum, and she said it was "impossible,"
but once more the impossible has happened.

Mrs. L. said the *Post* belonged to Hearst (Californians would attribute an earthquake or eclipse of the sun to him) and that he had inspired the article just to embarrass the Administration. I told her the dignity of the House of Representatives had to be maintained whether Hearst was pleased or not and, besides, if he had inspired the article it would be all the easier for them to publish a simple denial of it. She told me confidentially that she and the Secretary had sent a denial—"even her colleagues did not know of it"—to the Associated Press, but it had not been published. That night the *Post* telephoned to ask if I knew who sent it and what effect I thought it would have on our side. Of course, I refused to tell who sent it but said that our side could not be placated by vague denials from anonymous Cabinet women, and that appeared the next morning with much elaboration along with the Associated Press notice.

Our position throughout has been passive, but I hear that at the club the decision not to make Cabinet calls is practically unanimous. Then the subtle Cabinet strategists planned a coup by which they expected to break down the opposition with one stroke. Such is, or was, their faith in the loftiness of their social position that they did not believe anyone, certainly not a mere congressman's wife, could refuse an invitation to the house of the Secretary of State, and good unsuspicious Mrs. Bryan was sent out to deliver it. It was an unpleasant half hour for me but would have been much worse if I had had a less just and truthful woman to deal with. Tuesday afternoon she arrived at my house in full canonicals, a very good hat, white furs, and altogether looking the part of high priestess of the sacred rite of official calling. Our thoughts on the weather having been disposed of, she said, "Mrs. Slayden, I came to ask you to receive with me one day next month." It was so direct and simple, so entirely a case for "Yea, yea," or "Nay, nay" that I was embarrassed for an instant, but I felt there had come the moment to decide, so I answered as sincerely as possible, for I really admire and respect her, "Mrs. Bryan, I would like very much to receive with you, but you know with the present misunderstanding between the House and the Cabinet I cannot accept your invitation." She looked as amazed as such an immobile face as hers could look on short notice and then expressed astonishment that we took the matter so seriously. I found what I had suspected before, that she had never heard the true story—the others had taken care to publish the offending article while she was away in May, and she had been given many crooked versions of it—and so I told it frankly and with as much detail as I dared when I knew that we might be interrupted any time by other visitors.

She is what the Scotch call "slow on the uptake," but the idea once gotten, she deals with it intelligently and honestly. Like the others she had missed the point, thought we were piqued because they would not call, instead of its being a question of the dignity of the House. She was shocked to hear that many members had told their wives that they must not leave a card at a Cabinet home, that we had had letters and humorous articles about it from all over the country, and that even in Europe I had been asked if it was true that a democratic Cabinet had drawn a social line between itself and the House. I asked, "What would you have done in such a case when Mr. Bryan was in the House?" and she said quietly, "Just as you are doing, I think." She justified my estimate of her by seeming to see only one way out of the muddle—to find the right and just thing to do, and then to do it. I told her that a denial, an explanation, or an apology was the only course, and she seemed to think the denial would be easy, but I thought privately that she was reckoning without her colleagues. Before she left, saying she would "talk it over with Will," she said, "And if it is all cleared up you will come to my house, won't you?" and I replied, "With the greatest pleasure."

A heavy gun on our side has come from an unexpected source. Senator Bacon gave an elaborate interview to the press on the whole question of official precedence, defining the places of the three branches of the government, and saying "all appointive officers, however dignified and important their offices, are necessarily of lower rank as their positions are created and can be abolished by Congress, and the creature cannot be greater than the creator." I am glad that was said with authority because I hear the ladies are especially bitter about a frivolous remark of mine that "Cabinet officers are only a superior variety of department clerk, anyway, and if they didn't be good we'd abolish 'em." I "hadn't ought to" have said it, perhaps, but it is pleasant to find that we maintained our rights knowingly.

Saturday about noon, after the women's cabinet meeting, an innovation of this Administration, Mrs. B. came to see me, not nearly so handsome and well looking as she was Tuesday. She looked jaded; a plain black suit and a black hat set down on her head like a cup were very trying. She held a sheet of paper in her hand and said the Cabinet ladies had told her to do what she thought best; she wanted me to see what she had written and to say if it was satisfactory.

I never admired her so much. She was not sustained as I was by the humor of the situation; she was doing what she thought was *right* and gave evidence of having gotten the consent of her colleagues none too easily. She might have dodged, prevaricated and played for time as some of them did, but instead she stuck honestly to the point. We went carefully over the note; I substituted "offended by an article in a local paper" for their misleading "annoyed by a rumor." I asked that she sign it, "Mrs. W. J. Bryan," so there could be no mistake, and this is the way it appeared. She thought she would try to get it in the society news, but I said it was too serious a matter for that and must be quite as conspicuously placed as the first article. Dear guileless soul that she is, she doubted if the *Post* would be willing to do that. (Later I pleaded with the *Post* by telephone not to make it too conspicuous, and the *Post's* answer the next morning was flaring headlines and more than a column of humorous comment. I couldn't blame the paper; it had such fine news value locally, and the ladies had not "toted fair" in blaming the reporter for the original article.)

Mrs. B. lingered to discuss minor particulars and the possible effect of the publication. She was sorry it had happened for I knew she and Will were not snobs; as I surely do. She hoped I would forget it, for she felt that I was one of her "old friends," and she kissed me in an old-fashioned, Sunday-school book way that touched me deeply. She wouldn't stay to lunch, so after seeing her to the elevator, I went back to my room and Stella Callaway, and said, "You won't have to decline your invitation to Mrs. Lane's. The trouble is over, and Mrs. B. and I have kissed and made friends." "You needn't tell me," she said laughingly, "I heard it in here."

She did decline the invitation, though, as she was technically ignorant of the capitulation and wanted to emphasize our position. I gave a "scoop" on it to a Texas paper, but no one knew it here till the next day. I spent the morning at the telephone receiving congratulations on our "famous victory," and later a reporter from the *World* came to get the complete story.

I wonder if the Cabinet women realize that they surrendered to a toy gun. If they had called my bluff, I had no authority back of me. A majority of the members' wives felt as I did, I know, but we never had a meeting and never appointed a spokesman. Obviously it was the Cabinet's fear of political consequences that brought them to terms. We understand that the men took an active interest and that even the Foreordained took part in the discussion. He wants the Cabinet admitted to the floor of the House in the English fashion, and this did not further the project.

We arrived late at the Boardmans' delightful annual evening party and were presented at once to a Mrs. Harriman. I thought she was the suffragist, Civic Federation, all-pervading Mrs. Borden H., but Jim told me later it was the many-millioned Mrs. Edward H. Harriman, and the string of diamond bullets around her neck justified his opinion. She is contributing largely, I believe, to the Red Cross Building that Miss Boardman is promoting so cleverly.

The Boardmans' parties are always agreeable; there are so many interesting people one never sees at teas and such generous, old-fashioned, well-served suppers. The Cabinet was largely represented, and the salutary effect of our recent little lesson to them is quite noticeable. They are as gentle as pussycats and evidently aim to please. Burleson crossed the room to speak to me—an unprecedented honor—and Garrison asked an introduction, and Mrs. Lane was as neutral and agreeable as she was before the inauguration. Simon Wolf was there, beaming with cynical humor as always. He said he wanted us to dine with him again this winter "to meet the new Administration." "But maybe they won't care to meet me," I said. "And we won't care a damn if they don't," he chuckled back. He held my hand as he leaned over to stage-whisper, "I have lived here fifty-two years; I have seen Cabinets come and Cabinets go, but I have never seen any as cheap, *cheap,* I say, as this one." Then he told an almost incredible story, but he could hardly have invented it just to amuse me. "I have been a Republican," he said, "I am known from one end of the country to the other as a Republican, and recently one of the Cabinet sent for me, consulted me at length on a Democratic measure, and when I left placed his hands on my shoulders (he leaned over and illustrated) and said, 'Oh, Mr. Wolf, it is good to talk to such a Democrat as you are!' " It is of a piece with Bryan's advising John Bassett Moore to read one of his own (Moore's) books on international law. If only Bryan would read Moore instead of the Pentateuch, how different the Mexican situation might be!

CHAPTER EIGHTEEN

1914

January 2

Poor Mrs. Bryan's easygoing housekeeping has brought on internal and perhaps international complications. Dr. Hardin had to see Mother today, and when he heard she had been to some Cabinet houses yesterday, he said laughingly, "I know what's the matter. You ate and drank too much." She answered seriously, "I didn't have anything at all." "Neither did some of the ambassadors at the diplomatic breakfast," he said. He had just been called to see two who were ill and furious because of the discomfort and the bad conduct of the servants at the Bryans'. One of them was met by a waiter who said, "There's nothing to eat here, sir, but plenty of grape juice," and slapping him on the shoulders said, "Come on and let's get some of that." No wonder the poor representative of his sovereign needed medical attention.

Those foreign caterers' men need a lot of suppressing, and Mrs. B. doesn't realize it. They are resentful and contemptuous because there is no wine, and hearing everyone else joke about it, they presume to do it too. Mrs. B. doesn't have servants enough either for the exigencies of the Washington free-for-all afternoons, where there may be fifty or five hundred people, one never knows. Belatedly one day, when I was to receive with her, I ran up to the door expecting it to open automatically, as the doors of well-regulated houses do when a reception is on, and stepping in hurriedly found that I had brushed past the wife of the Spanish Minister who was *letting herself out*. I bestowed my wraps under a sofa pillow in the hall and in the drawing room found Mrs. B. trying to take care of a big crowd with only the ponderous daughter of the Secretary of Labor to help her, and just one servant to open the front door and announce the guests! He is a well-trained old darky, but could not be in both places at once. It was uphill work anyway assisting in that gaunt house with the piratical face of John A. Logan staring at you from stained-glass windows, frescoes, canvases, and marble carvings. (Mrs. B. told me she had put out of sight as many portraits as she dared.)[1] I had bad luck too introducing Mrs. Miles Poindexter, who is proud of her Nez Percé ancestry, to a slightly queer old army officer who insisted on telling her how many "good Injuns" he had made in that tribe. By the time he got through she was as austere as one of Fenimore Cooper's heroes.

February 1

A marvelously proper note—gray paper with "The White House" in silver— came this morning to tell me that Mary Antin[2] would speak here on February 27 under the auspices of Friendship House, and saying, "I am very anxious that the lecture shall be a success, and I am writing to ask if you will let us use your name as patroness," signed "Eleanor R. Wilson." Of course I accepted. Mary Antin is one of the miracles of American civilization. She has learned better English in fifteen years than most of us have in fifty.

February 22

With Villa's murder of the Englishman Benton[3] the Mexican situation is to the last degree acute, and it looks as if we would have to intervene or surrender the precious Monroe Doctrine under fire. Everyone not too sorrowful over the chance of war is laughing at Wilson's declared policy of "watchful waiting." He has stolen the Mexicans' own plan of mañana, never do today what can be put off till tomorrow.

At Mrs. Pinchot's coffee reception last evening and at the British Embassy later we heard nothing but Mexico. Mrs. Pinchot (who is readjusting her admiration for Wilson) told us that at some big affair the night before she and a large group were discussing the Benton murder when Mrs. Bryan joined them. Someone asked, "And what do you think of the news from Mexico?" Mrs. B. asked, "What news?" and when they told her, said serenely, "Oh, I don't think there's anything much in tha-at."

[1] The Bryans lived in "Calumet Place," former home of Mrs. John A. Logan, who converted it into a shrine honoring her Civil War general husband after his death in 1886.

[2] Russian-born writer; author of *The Promised Land,* 1912.

[3] Scots-born William Benton, a cattle rancher with large landholdings in Chihuahua, was executed by Villa's firing squad after he angrily protested that Villa was stealing his cattle. His death became a *cause célèbre* in both the United States and England, but official protests were ignored by Villa.

February 26

J. has eight pages of jubilation today from Mrs. J. B. Henderson over his bill to move the Botanic Garden up to that fine unimproved area of Rock Creek Park, but I am afraid she does not realize how many owners of real estate in other directions will fight it; or, worse still, the number of men voting on it whose idea of a garden is a row of cabbages by the back fence with a lilac bush in the corner. She says, "How rejoiced I am that the greatest and largest and most beautiful National Botanic Garden is about to materialize, and largely owing to your common sense and sound judgment. The time will come when you will be very proud to have been the prime mover for it. Of course your statue or bust will sooner or later be seen there. . . . If your bill goes through, we must have a celebration—a jug of grape juice over some kind of festive board."

How fine to retain one's enthusiasm and care for the future to her age! Of course, there will be the usual cry that it is self-interest, but what has that to do with a right location for the Garden? And she is the only one of the big owners of real estate here who always backs her self-interest with splendid generosity.

March 8

At the Putnams' dinner Miss Ruth said she tried to put herself to sleep one night by counting the Presidents. That failed, so she tried the V.-P.s and found she could remember only five. She looked them up and decided to go write an essay entitled "Some Forgotten Vices. A Record of Compromise and Mediocrity." It was an agreeable dinner with Dr. Jameson of the Carnegie Institution, Professor and Mrs. Learned, she especially bright and a suffragist, and Louis Brandeis, always diabolically clever.

At a rather quiet dinner at the Hitchcocks' we were discussing the extraordinary revelations of the present fashions for women, and the Senator said in his gracious, pleasant way, "For generations women have been showing off their clothes, and now the clothes are reciprocating." At a dinner at the Sweets', he sat between me and good Mrs. ——— of the Cabinet. The same subject was up (it generally is unless the tango gets precedence) and he said that some people objected to the modern dress because it made women look shorter. "But," he added, "it makes the men look longer." Mrs. ——— said, "Ye-es," without the ghost of a smile, and went on eating bread and butter.

March 17

Announcement of Miss Eleanor Wilson's engagement to Secretary McAdoo was received with a sigh of weariness. Government officials are wondering if they have to "put up" for another bridal present, and I dread the damnable iteration in the papers of "Historical Weddings at the White House" and pictures of scenes there under Grant, Cleveland, etc. Mr. McAdoo's picture doesn't exactly present a subject for love's young dream.

Are we getting to be a less gracious and kindly society or just sophisticated and indifferent? It used not to be good form to criticize the powers that be in a company mixed politically, but today at a beautiful luncheon at Mrs. Porter's for Mrs. Benjamin Harrison we broke all precedent. Democratic women laughed with the rest at the melancholy society of the White House; the way some of the Cabinet couples address one another as "momma" and "poppa," and the V.-P.'s latest witticism in agreeing to make an address somewhere if they would just let him stand up on his hind legs and talk.

April 20

How strangely the agelong custom of war affects our thought and speech. Just now J. called up to tell me that the resolution had come into the House authorizing the President to use "all military and naval forces" to compel Mexico to salute our flag. J. does not approve of it and will probably vote against it. He wanted me to know that it was pretty sure to end his career in Congress, and was I willing. I hardly realized all it could mean to us so am not sure if it was a clear prompting of conscience, but I answered unhesitatingly, "Do what you think is right, dear. Stand to your guns whatever happens." Hanging up the receiver I had to laugh at the warlike expression I had used in the cause of peace.

We have dwelt in the midst of alarms for a week, and this is the climax—a declaration of war against a weak, half-barbarous neighbor who should look to us for help and, above all, example. If we only felt sure that Wilson was sincere or knew the truth about Mexico, but why has he let Villa and Carranza commit every horror with impunity and then be roused to indignation by a mere failure in punctilio from a drunken subordinate of Huerta's?[4] Is he consciously or unconsciously influenced by

[4] On April 9, 1914, an unarmed party from the U.S.S. *Dolphin* went ashore at Tampico to secure supplies. By error they entered a restricted area and were arrested by Huerta's troops on the charge of violating martial law. They were released promptly with apologies from a superior officer, but, without consulting Washington,

American businessmen, owners of vast tracts of land, whom we on the border have long suspected of scheming to annex the northern states of Mexico? Cleveland Dodge is his intimate friend, a large contributor to his campaign, and I cannot forget Mrs. John Hays Hammond saying to me once, "We *must* have Mexico. It is a very *rich* country."

I didn't go to hear the President address the joint Houses. Providentially it is a rainy day. Weather has so much to do with people's moods. Bright, cold air would have stimulated all the jingo and hurrah spirit, but the most unctuous patriot wilts under a warm spring rain and speaks of the United States flag instead of Old Glory.

Later

When J. came in he didn't call out for me as usual, but went quietly to his room and came to dinner so grave and preoccupied that we hesitated to question him. When we at last mentioned the absorbing subject of the President's message, he said, "I think it's the first time in history that a nation was asked to declare war on an individual." Still, we are assured that Wilson and Bryan are *peace* men, and they busy themselves mightily writing arbitration treaties with small countries too far off to bother us.

April 22

Today in the House Fitzgerald asked consideration of a bill appropriating $500,000 "for the relief of refugees." I hope no large part of it may be spent for coffins or marking the spots where Americans were killed. I can never forget a mob of *pelados* I watched one night through the iron window bars of Jennie Wheeler's pretty sala in the Presbyterian Mission at Saltillo until the horrible stench forced us to close the thick wooden shutters. The narrow street was bank-full of ragged, blanketed men with matted hair

---

Admiral Henry T. Mayo demanded that the port commander apologize formally, promise to punish the responsible officer, and hoist the American flag ashore, giving it a 21-gun salute. The Wilson administration felt that Mayo had to be supported to prevent Huerta's exploitation of the incident. Despite a warning that a refusal probably would result in intervention, Huerta succeeded in evading the salute. On April 22 Congress granted Wilson's request for permission to use force to uphold U.S. rights and secure redress of grievances. In the meantime, U.S. forces had already landed on Mexican soil. Having information that a German ship was approaching with munitions, Bryan advised Wilson to use the navy to prevent delivery. American forces bombarded Vera Cruz and entered the city on April 21, wherewith Huerta broke off diplomatic relations with the United States. The incident, which united Mexican opinion behind Huerta, brought the United States and Mexico close to war.

straggling about, their wild eyes under huge straw hats. They were celebrating an election of which they had no gleam of comprehension. These
are the people to whom Wilson wants to give "a free and full expression"
in an election. I am sorry enough for the Mexicans, heaven knows, but it
is bread and soap and a firm hand that they need, not the franchise.

It has been a tiresome, exacting winter socially—a great deal of *going*
without much pleasure. There is an atmosphere of bad temper, only the
most perfunctory entertainments at the White House, and the poor Cabinet
women doing double duty trying to drown the memory of their foolishness
in the beginning. One of them asked me to receive with her "to help take
care of the Congressional women." She evidently expected a great many,
and I had the onerous duty of presenting five.

April 24

What a difference there is in the public mind today and what it was sixteen years ago when we went to war with Spain. Then we were on edge
with excitement and enthusiasm. We marched instead of walking and
crowds cheered every trifling item on the bulletin board. We hummed "The
Star-Spangled Banner"; we saluted one another with "Viva Cuba Libre,"
and called our red hats and dresses by Cuban names. Were we really
aroused by the righteousness of the cause of Cuba or was it only that a
generation had grown up that knew not war? And is it the lesson we
learned then, the scandals, the trickery, and the ever increasing pension
list, that makes us so different, or so indifferent, today? No one seems to
want any war. I have not heard a shout nor a word of praise of the President and Bryan whose blundering and delays—and ignorance of Mexico—
have brought on this crisis, but there are jokes about the market price of
records of Bryan's oration on "The Prince of Peace."

J. was so interested in the comments in the market and the shops that
he had me come to his office and write the story for the *Evening Post*.
The young man from the *Courier Journal* was there and said he had
heard our views on Mexico from Tod Lowry, who had had a change of
heart, and I found his letter in the *Post* today on the same theme as mine
but much fuller. I telephoned him that all was forgiven, and his penitence
was frank and amusing, but he is still obsessed with the Villa myth.

The only real belligerents we have met are the grizzled veterans of
the D.A.R. holding their annual encampment at the New Willard. We went,
of course, to call on the Texas members and found them gloriously ap-

pareled, prancing with the rest in Peacock Alley. The ominous cry of "Extre-e" sounded from the street, and men in the lobby were reading the
smutty sheet with big headlines "Vera Cruz Bombarded. 4 Marines Killed,
12 Wounded," but our state regent struck an attitude and orated, "Our
organization is founded on war; we build monuments to heroes," etc., etc.—
such a stream of cant and stock phrases that we were glad to slip away.
Coming home we saw only small crowds at the bulletin boards and no
excitement.

The Marion Butlers' dinner to John Lind and his wife was one to be remembered. The Linds are excellent people, and he, no doubt, is intelligent
in his proper sphere of law and American politics, but for the President to
send him as his special emissary to Mexico was positively fantastic. There
cannot be one single point of sympathy or comprehension between him
and any Latin American living, and even on a strictly business mission one
should understand the people just a little. He has not traveled; he has stiff,
awkward manners, and his moral standards are fixed by the Swedish
Evangelical Church in Minnesota. In Mexico he must have been what the
Wall Street Journal calls Bryan as secretary of state, "a perfectly square
man in a perfectly round hole." At the dinner neither he nor his wife wore
evening dress. I doubt if they would think it consistent with grace. His face
did not light up, and he couldn't smile because when talking he pursed his
lower lip as if trying to hold something in his mouth. His solemnity would
be incredible if his wife were not a present proof that someone could be
solemner. She has two fervent enthusiasms happily combined in prohibition and Josephus Daniels.
    Over the coffee we discussed the growing custom of women smoking,
and I remarked that Austrian ladies did it very prettily and naturally, and
Lind said, "I never saw an Austrian lady," and went on to explain that he
didn't think an Austrian could be a lady.
    In seven months in Mexico he learned no Spanish, not even to pro-
nounce the names of the states, and knew no Mexican history except what
he "learned at school." (If J. was sent to a cannibal island, he would learn
some of their language and all their history before they had time to eat him.)
He never saw Villa or Carranza but gives opinions on them like a judge
on the bench. He assured us that our friends in Saltillo and San Luis would
be quite safe when Villa took the cities. "Yes," he added, "we have Villa's
word for it." When I said, "And, no doubt, Villa's word is as good as his
bond," he solemnly agreed. It is easy to believe the funny stories we hear
of his "observing" Mexico from an armchair and carpet slippers in Vera

Cruz. He speaks of the Administration as "we," just as fat little Tumulty[5] does; "we" are now open champions of Villa.

The State Department is issuing a biography of Villa to enlighten a prejudiced public, but if correct, it will not go far; the law forbidding obscene literature in the mail will stop its circulation. J. had the salient points of Villa's career sworn to by his neighbors of thirty years, decent Mexicans and Americans, and presented it at the State Department, but they would have none of it. A friend tells me she heard Secretary Lane (who must know better) stoutly defending Villa. He said he was "a pretty good fellow" and had "built a hospital costing $200,000." I told her I knew he had built several cemeteries, but I had not heard of the hospital, and I am not yet able to locate it.

May 6

The Marines so needlessly killed at Vera Cruz are being buried today, but the *Post* has a cheerful story of how the President went to the circus last night and was so delighted that he stayed for the Grand Concert afterwards. For days we have read how he was striving to save time to go to the funeral, and everyone else feels it an occasion to walk humbly before the Lord. The world isn't looking on us with approval just now, but the President—who in a fit of temper got up in the night and ordered the bombardment that caused the death of nineteen Marines and many Mexican women and children—is in the mood to go to the circus *and* the grand concert.

At a large luncheon given today by the Mississippi delegation to Mrs. John Sharp Williams I heard the words "shameful," "cold-blooded," and "disgusting" more than once. There was much gossip about the White House wedding. Neither the Champ Clarks nor the Jim Manns are invited. The Mexican opal the Burlesons were trying to get the Cabinet to buy from them was repudiated, so the B.s will be munificent and present it themselves, and the Cabinet give something else. It is all so common and sordid.

May 8

At dinner at the Crammond Kennedys', John Bassett Moore took Mrs. Porter in and sat between us. He was fairly bubbling with satisfaction at his escape into private life. For a man of his caliber to have been confined

[5] Joseph Tumulty, President Wilson's secretary.

to the State Department under Bryan is one of the ironies of democracy. When Wilson and House first began to explore the hitherto unsuspected mine of statesmanship in the Fourth Ward of Austin (Burleson, Houston, Gregory, *et al*) and finally appointed Thad Thomson, of whom I had never heard before, to the important post of Colombia, I asked a friend from Austin to tell me something about him. She said thoughtfully, "We-ell, if I had to buy a pair of mules, his advice would be invaluable." J. wouldn't let me tell it to Mr. Moore at the time, but last night when I dared, he said, "Now, that just shows your failure to comprehend the finesse of our work. Bogotá is very high up in the Andes, only approachable on mule back, so, *of course* the first requirement of a diplomat accredited there would be a thorough knowledge of mules." Our public men are so often pompous and ponderous that it is delightful to meet one with a light touch in his talk. Apropos of the influence of campaign contributions on diplomatic appointments (unctuously denied of late), Mr. Moore said he had discovered that "the New Freedom was very like the old slavery."

He said our present situation was unprecedented in history, but he proved most amusingly how Bryan might justify Villa's conduct by texts from the Old Testament, until Senator ———, a rubber-stamp Wilsonian, who has been my "steady company" at several dinners lately, turned from his usual tint of plain yellow laundry soap to green Cuticura with horror at our levity.

May 26

I am ashamed to confess that my joy at what promises a peaceful settlement of the Mexican mess is tempered by the thought that Wilson and Bryan will get a lot of praise that they don't deserve. If the ABC Conference succeeds, it will be a victory of peace forced by public opinion, in spite of supreme efforts of the Hearst and other iniquitous papers to inflame the country and create a demand for war.[6] But Wilson will say, "I did it with my little hatchet," and Bryan will tell Chautauqua audiences how his and W.'s righteousness exalted the nation. Both will forget that if they had tried this common-sense method a year ago they might have saved vast quantities of foreign property destroyed in Mexico and hundreds

---

[6] The offer by the ABC Powers (Argentina, Brazil and Chile) to mediate the dispute between the United States and Mexico was accepted by Wilson. At a meeting in Niagara Falls, Ontario, the mediators proposed the retirement of Huerta, the establishment of a provisional government in Mexico favoring agrarian and political reforms, and no indemnity to the United States for occupation costs at Vera Cruz. The plan was rejected by Mexico, but its moral effect was instrumental in forcing Huerta to leave office on July 15, 1914.

of Americans would not have been beggared and driven from happy homes, exiled, paradoxically, to their own country. Above all, those men so uselessly killed in Vera Cruz would be alive instead of having Wilson prate about "envying their glorious death," as he did at the funeral—the day after the circus.

May 28

The world could not show a more noble picture, I believe, than that I saw framed by the big west window of the Round Table Room at the Library of Congress last night. It had been a day of withering heat and humidity but the discomfort stole away as I rested my eyes on the dome of the Capitol, translucent, ethereal, against a background of fading rose, with one clear star quivering like a jewel above it. We were all sorry to turn away to sit down to what proved an unusually pleasant dinner given to the Executive Committee of the Library Association. It was the first evening entertainment Mr. Putnam has given there, and he promised to repeat it "in ten years," but I hope it will be sooner. He looks such a precise man, so associated with the card index that his grace as a host always surprises me a little. Last night it was especially evident in his skillful trick of moving his men around so that no one was talked out. I was a little panicky when I went up with Mr. Green (Superintendent of the Library) who is getting old and hard to entertain, but Mr. Anderson of the New York Library was on my other side, and then in succession Cravin of Pittsburgh, Bowker of Boston, with cool, polished talk of Oxford and Browning, and several others. As nearly all of them fed my vanity by telling me of J.'s invaluable services through his committee, I came home much in favor with myself, thinking I had been agreeable because the company was. It was so good to get away from politics and personalities. Today I tapered off delightfully at luncheon with the Misses Putnam and Mrs. Anderson. Miss Ruth read us some extracts from *Punch* on England's foreign policy during the Crimean War that with a change of names would apply equally well to ours today. It is meetings like this that make life in Washington so worthwhile, and thanks to J.'s standing and fitness for it, we have many of them.

May 31

My best hat was ruined as Mrs. Butler and I huddled under one small umbrella to keep off big drops from the awning and the ineffectual wisteria arbor, but it was a hat well lost in exchange for the scene at the memorial exercises at Arlington where the President played second fiddle to Champ Clark.

Last year, for the first time since Memorial Day was officially established, the President of the United States refused to address the G.A.R.—he went motoring instead. Some of the veterans were opposed to asking him this year, but thinking he had seen the error of his ways (as if he ever could), he was invited, and again refused, giving the flimsy excuse that it would be bad policy for him to discuss current politics, war especially, while the Mexican situation was so acute, and this in the face of his promise to speak the following Thursday at the unveiling of the Moses Ezekiel Confederate Monument. The G.A.R. members were furious and vowed they would not attend the Confederate unveiling, and that threw the Confederates into a panic as theirs was to be a spectacle of reunion, the Blue and Gray marching together, metaphorically weeping penitentially on one another's bosoms. The papers paraded the incident and applauded the G.A.R. for asking Champ Clark to take the President's place.

Mrs. Marion Butler, presiding genius at the U.D.C.s this year, and Colonel Hilary Herbert, their counselor, thought it would be courteous for them to appear at Arlington, and invited me to go, so, in my best white frock and the aforesaid hat, I went and am so glad that I was there to see.

Mr. Butler took us. Rather late and without tickets for seats, we stood in the dirt with the negroes, soldiers, and stray dogs as long as we could, and then, the program of tearful patriotic oratory, invocations and musical numbers promising to be endless, Mrs. B. and I slipped out and sat under the lovely trees enjoying jokes and giggles most unseemly for our environment of tombstones. We wanted to see Champ's reception, so hearing some clapping, we went back to the tent and were transfixed with astonishment to behold the President himself, spick and span, calm and cool, on the platform making one of his chaste and appropriate addresses. We stared at each other. "How had he got thar? Angels! . . . They had just swooped down and toted him to whar it was safe and warm."

Everyone was listening politely and applauding mildly as each rounded period rolled neatly into place. He talked of moral and physical courage, the self-forgetfulness of the soldier, all the usual things, and sat down with just enough applause to suit. Meantime we were invited to the speaker's stand and were given seats just back of him and Clark.

The G.A.R. man rose and said that there was one present who was "as pure as the mountain torrent; one who could *always* be relied on by *all* Americans; who had the courage of his beliefs at *all* times," etc., and Champ was brought forward in a suit of spotless white and looking really handsome and much of a man. And then came the blow for Wilson. The whole audience arose, clapping, shouting, throwing hats and handkerchiefs in the air, and refusing to be quiet. I said, "This is ghastly," and an Associated Press man standing by echoed, "It is ghastly, and it's the first gun for Clark for president next time." Champ was swelling visibly and still they shouted, "Glad to see you," "Ought to be in the White House," and many other things not pleasant for Wilson to hear.

When Champ could be heard, he said, "My friends, I thank you for the generosity of your reception," and after they laughed and cheered and clapped again, he went on the same way through a speech of musty anecdotes and commonplaces, really not half as good as Wilson's, but he said his say with a difference.

The thunder was rolling and C.C. left at once with the crowd still cheering, but Wilson stayed to the bitter end, through Smoot's talk, which couldn't be heard for the rain, and some lugubrious singing of the G.A.R. sadly reminiscent of our own Confederate reunions. Of course, we had to wait till his Majesty retired though we were almost soaking wet. As he went through the crowd, men lifted their hats respectfully, there was a faint handclap here and there, and no other demonstration. No one knows yet why he came. The Associated Press man told me that the G.A.R. gave him the chance to reconsider as late as ten o'clock last night, but he still refused, and so "they turned the story loose." About eleven they wired C.C., and his answer came back, "I will be there. C.C." He said it was the climax of Wilson's mistakes.

San Antonio, July 20

To stand and wait seems the only way I can serve in this unpleasant and unexpected campaign, and I am doing it now at our old friend Mitrovich's restaurant near the plaza, hoping J. will get time to take lunch with me. The mercury is a little over 100 degrees.

When J. met me at the station he looked so much better than he had in Washington that I thought he owed Slator a doctor's fee, as well as the licking he is going to give him on the 25th. But he is getting nervous and tired now, and though we don't put it into words, we feel that this is to be his last campaign for the House. We are dreaming dreams of serene old age with fruits and flowers, and cats and dogs and chickens and many homely joys, perhaps on my little farm in Virginia. San Antonio is losing its old-time picturesqueness and charm; its individuality being needlessly sacrificed to suit the taste of the Chamber of Commerce and boosters, with

all the sordid vulgarity that the latter name implies. The old society so elegant and simple is submerged and inarticulate under the flood of newcomers
who are merely rich. At present the town is swarming with Mexicans. All
those not actually cutting one another's throats on their native heath are
enjoying the movies here. I love many Mexicans, but what a people they
are as a whole; no real love of country, nor willingness to serve her, nothing
but a shallow patriotism spending itself in bombast and swagger—and
conspiracy. J. says there are enough able-bodied young Mexicans in Texas
loafing and declaiming about the revolution to turn the tide toward any one
of their leaders and settle the country if they would just agree and go home
and do it.

The New York *Evening Post* sees the resignation of Huerta as a triumph for Wilson, but we think the wily old Indian has played a practical
joke on our all-wise government and that soon there will be ten revolutions
growing where one grew before. But, *quién sabe?* There are things here
today that concern us more.

The campaign is vile. We have always trusted our early Victorian
domesticity to protect us from scandal, but now they are saying that we are
about to be divorced because one is a pro and the other an anti. I don't
know which is which. At a political picnic Slator spoke of my wealth, and
J. flew into a rage out of all proportion to the subject in hand. I am still
sitting on his coattails to keep him from doing something mannish and
absurd about it.

Last week while he was careering over the district making two or
three speeches a day in widely distant towns, I felt like a drone and a
parasite taking mine ease at the ranch with Jane. Our happiness was a little
tense, all of us feeling it one of those seasons of calm weather that never
last long on this queer voyage of life. The days were still except for the
pulsating earth sounds of growing things, the flitting of young mockingbirds,
scissortails and cardinals, and the deep and mournful undertone of doves.
At night we slept soundly in cots on the upper gallery until dawn roused
us to new joy in the wide-spreading valley, the wastes of green mesquite
and yellow stubble, and the distant town half drowned in purple mist, the
few high buildings very white and stately suggesting Venice.

July 24

I am standing guard over the telephone so J. can get an hour's rest. Last
night after his speech to a big crowd in New Braunfels, he started home,
was caught in a heavy rain, and the car ditched. They were towed back

to town, and at 2:00 A.M. he got to bed in a room with five men and two beds. At 8:30 he was here, tired to death. These are the things one pays for a seat in Congress that the average citizen firmly believes is all cakes and ale.

The fine Italian (black) hand of the Postmaster General is everywhere evident in the campaign. The last few days he has appeared in the open grossly assailing J.'s personal worth and influence in Congress. Bryan, Underwood, Secretary Garrison, and many congressmen of both parties have sent generous testimony in his defense, so I foresee the echoes of the fight will be heard in Washington next winter.

July 30

We are swamped with letters and telegrams of congratulation. J.'s majority was reduced by several thousand but for him to succeed at all against such odds is an evidence of people's personal affection for him that makes me tearfully proud.

Crockett Hotel, August 1

While I was resting this afternoon J. answered the telephone and gave an exclamation of such horror and grief that I was alarmed. Hurrying to listen in, I heard Mr. Clarkson telling him that Germany, the Kaiser, who has built up such a vast war machine to keep peace in Europe, has declared war on Russia! I am always amazed by the simple way that news of great world events comes to us. This cataclysm, the great European war that statesmen and financiers have dreaded or secretly hoped for according to the advantage to be gained, and which I feel should have been announced by all the trumpets of the sky, comes in a sleepy summer afternoon through a bedroom telephone.

I feel as if some black-winged monster had come between us and the sun, breathing poison over all the lovely green things upon the earth that should be praising God and magnifying Him forever. A little while ago I was grieved at the death of the Baroness von Suttner, and now I am glad she is not here to beat her breast and wring her hands as she would have done in despair over this hideous culmination of all her fears. She was more a sad woman than an old one, so gracious and so unself-conscious compared with many of the American "peace ladies" at The Hague last summer, who never forgot their lofty mission and were more or less inspired by the titled company in which they found themselves. I can hear her now as she spoke prophetically of the "great wah," which she would so gladly have died to avert. I trust she sees with clearer eyes than ours how good must be the final goal of ill. The opening up of the black depths of Russia is the only possible good that I can think of now.

Aboard the International and Great Northern to St. Louis, August 3
The Little Rock *Gazette* is made thrilling with news of Europe's madness. Germany invading France through Luxembourg without even the courtesy of a declaration of war—though why should savages regard courtesies? The paper has a cartoon, "As it was in the beginning," two hairy, apelike men attacking each other with stone hammers.

General and Mrs. Parker and other army people in the car are talking war, of course, but the point of view of the military mind is always incomprehensible to me. I ought to understand it for I know so many army people, and they are so alike. I think they put their minds in uniform (stiff and close fitting) just as they do their bodies, and one can tell in advance what most of them will say on public questions. Parker attributes the outbreak to "race hatred," and in the face of Germany's appalling preparation maintains that stupendous armament is the only way to ensure peace.

In spite of the intellectual atmosphere, the trip is not as bad as I feared. The heat is intense, but with oil-burning engines and an oiled roadbed there is no dust, and we keep quite clean and fresh.

Last Friday the mercury went to 106 degrees. We dined at General Tasker Bliss's that day with a half hour at the hop later watching the vigorous new dancing. The dinner was good, the company pleasant, and the table just the same that one sees at the formal dinners from Maine to Mexico. It never varies with place or season. It would have been cooler if the pink candles had been omitted, if there had been a few sprays of crape myrtle in the splendid silver bowl instead of an armful, and if the lovely flowers laid loosely on the cloth had not been withering before our eyes.

We are a nation of copycats, but there are signs of awakening independence in dress at any rate. When I was married, returning to Texas early in September, I wore a suit of golden brown camel's hair buttoned up to my chin, and finished with a stiff linen collar. I wonder I didn't go mad and run amuck. Today I am in white linen, cut low in the neck over a guimpe of white net, slippers, and silk gloves to meet elbow sleeves. Another encouraging sign of the times is the occasional disapproval of the so-called "popular" magazines. The Federation of Women's Clubs passed a resolution condemning them as "lowering to the moral tone of the home." I know so many homes with stacks of good books untouched and chairs and tables littered with magazines whose flamboyant covers are an index of the bad literature, bad art, and bad morals inside. I wish the clubs, or the police, would take charge of the music of the same character. The young people not only sing and dance it, but talk, read, think and chew gum in ragtime.

Washington, August 9

Back in Washington, war and "extras"! In less than two weeks the greatest war of the world is in full swing while the newspapers and special writers are still debating what it is about. Statesmen of many countries make oracular comments and no doubt look wise as if they knew it all but could not take the mere people into their confidence. Obviously it is just that the countries are tired of being "prepared" and not using their implements. Europe for years has been like a man with a new gun and a well-trained bird dog waiting for the season to open.

I am intrigued by the story (coming through France, however, and one of many) that the Crown Prince precipitated it by insolent messages to Russia during his father's absence in Norway. The Kaiser hurried home and their interview ended in blows, but the notes could not be withdrawn without loss of prestige—prestige is so much more important than truth, justice, and human suffering—so war was declared. J. and General Ainsworth say that I only believe it because of its picturesqueness, but why shouldn't it be true of two men of the blood of that old ruffian, the Elector of Brandenburg?

A few reasons to sustain my favorite theory of the ultimate good come to me like flashes of light in the general darkness. By its very immensity the war cannot last long, and the impoverished nations will be forced to limit their armament. Above all is the daily disproof of the militarists' choicest argument that the way to ensure peace is to prepare for war.

Thursday morning the *Post* announced that Mrs. Wilson was at the point of death of Bright's disease. With the rather meaningless secretiveness that characterizes the family, her illness was concealed so well that the first the country at large heard of it was when her death was announced the same afternoon. Poor lady! She never seemed to enjoy the greatness her husband had achieved; her manner was almost apologetic, her hands limp and cold. Seymour Thomas, the artist, who knew her well, said that she dreaded the White House unspeakably. War news overshadows everything so completely that there is much less effusion and gush than such events usually bring forth in Washington. After long discussion the family have determined to bury her in Georgia beside her mother, but today (Sunday) they are still waiting the coming of her brother. Champ Clark appointed a committee for the funeral on Monday, but adds to the notice, "If Mr. Axson fails to arrive, the whole matter will be put off for 24 hrs." "The whole matter" is a phrase typical of the cold, perfunctory nature of everything connected with it.

But the queerest thing is a story, also in the *Post,* of an all-night meeting at Mrs. Clark's "for intercession and prayer for peace in Europe." It sounds medieval, certainly like the circuit rider and revival period of our religious history. I know Mrs. C. was utterly sincere, and some of the women named were as pure and primitively religious as herself, but there were others, I am sure, who prayed not so much expecting favors from heaven as from the Speaker.

Monday

And it was all a lie out of whole cloth! What can the *Post* expect to gain by such base tricks of journalism? Today on an inside page there is a restrained and dignified note from Mrs. Clark contradicting the whole story. There was no meeting, no praying; the ladies mentioned were not at her house. The reporter who concocted the yarn did it with skill and knowledge of his characters, but if I had been the Speaker's wife my note would have been sharper and on the front page with an apology.

I asked Mrs. Clark to be patroness for a recital Charles Tittmann is giving for the Red Cross, and, as usual, her talk went far afield. She told me a funny story about Senator Bailey and the present Postmaster General. Dining once at the White House, she was seated between President Taft and Bailey, with Burleson opposite. Speaking of political tricks and obliquities, Bailey, with questionable taste, said, "Why, there is a man at this very table who ought to be hung, and would be if I had my way." "Would you show him no clemency at all?" Mrs. C. asked. "No," said Bailey, "I wouldn't wait for him to finish his supper. And that man is Albert Burleson." "And," Mrs. C. added, "I thought Taft would hurt himself laughing." One can easily imagine how a Republican president would enjoy beholding how these Democrats love one another.

This is the dullest place on earth in summer, no gardens, theaters, or music, and no driving except for the opulent. What little social exchange we have though is pleasanter than the heavy winter "functions," when I almost choke with my effort to be prudent and say nothing frivolous to or about the innumerable sacred cows of official life. The John W. Fosters are away, so Mrs. Robert Lansing has the house to herself, and she, Mrs. James Brown Scott, and I were having a delightfully intimate little luncheon in the arbor in the pretty garden. Of course, we were talking of Mrs. Wilson's death, of the pathetic isolation from all her friends, and the strange circumstance of her only unmarried daughter's being absent from her bedside. The others, I believe, are engaged in strengthening the succession. I said casually, "When the President marries again—" and Mrs. Lansing exclaimed, "Oh, Mrs. Slayden, how can you speak of such a thing!" I asked, "Why not? He is a youngish man, and we have reason to believe rather leans to the ladies." "*But*," Mrs. L. went on, horrified, "he wouldn't *dare* to marry again while he is in the White House; public opinion would not permit it." I reminded her that the public was having to reconcile itself to some worse things about him than marriage, and we argued the matter until we ended by betting five pounds of Huyler's—the usual stake these days—with Mrs. Scott the witness on condition that she will get some of the candy. My bet is that he will marry before leaving the White House. I expect to win, but Mrs. L. is so good and romantic that I think she was almost hurt at my levity.

September 19

The White House
    Washington.
My dear Mr. Slayden:
    I am, of course, very much in favor of the bill to grant an incorporation to the American Academy of Arts and Letters, but I am not writing now so much to press that matter as merely to beg that you will understand that this is quite distinct from the American Academy of Arts and Sciences of Boston, one of whose representatives, I believe, is to appear before your committee.
                    Cordially and sincerely yours,
                    Woodrow Wilson

    I wonder why he thinks J. might mix the babies up? A very ordinary intelligence could tell the difference between a society of one name in Boston and one of another name in New York. Just the incorrigible schoolmaster, I suppose, telling the children what to do. But he might even remember, with slight effort, that J. has been working to get the charter for the American Academy of Arts and Letters for several years without interest or moral support from him heretofore.

September 21

God the All-Merciful! Earth has forsaken
Thy ways of blessedness, slighted Thy word,
Bid not Thy wrath in its terrors awaken,
Give to us peace in our time, O Lord.

The hymn rings through my head. It is in our hymnal, but so far I have not heard it, or any other peace hymn, sung in church. The attitude of the clergy puzzles me. When there are famines or disasters they are not slow to enlist our sympathies or to warn us of the "visitation of God." I suspect they are so entirely on the side of England that they do not trust themselves to speak in face of the President's injunction to neutrality. I would like to believe England innocent, but it takes two to make a quarrel. A strong element in England has been talking war with Germany for a long time, and neutral "preparedness" is quite as dangerous as munitions.

Yesterday Mother and I went to see the clothes Miss Lucy Burleson would have us wear to help the cotton growers. The exhibits were not bad —though Mother, like a picture in her gray chiffon dress, and bonnet with wreath of tiny pink and blue flowers, attracted more attention than any of them—but it seemed like Mrs. Partington's mopping the Atlantic. What could the exhibition of a dozen ill-made dresses and some tables of cotton goods in the Red Room at the Willard do for a crop of fourteen million bales with the markets of Europe closed? Washington is threatened with death by suppressed amusement, too, as the handful of *very prominent* ladies promoting the show are notoriously ill dressed.

"Texans in a turmoil" would be a suitable headline for our present situation. With Houston and Burleson already selected from the Fourth Ward of Austin, Mr. House has hypnotized the President into making Watt Gregory attorney general. Riding with the Culbersons today, the Senator told me himself that so far from their being consulted, according to usage and courtesy, the first he and Senator Sheppard heard of the nomination was when it was sent to the Senate.

J. is deluged with requests to use his influence to have Judge Maxey succeed Shelby on the Circuit Bench, and he and Culberson have done their utmost, but neither House, Houston, Burleson nor Gregory—all the Judge's fellow townsmen and avowed friends—has lifted a finger. J. left a note on Gregory's desk congratulating him on his appointment and suggesting that they all pull together for the Judge, and it has not been acknowledged.

The horror goes on, and the shame of Louvain is dimmed by the greater shame of Rheims. Yesterday Antwerp fell. Today 150,000 people are dragging through the open country trying to reach Holland. October here was never more soft and sunny. Our windows are open; the leaves are tangible sunshine. In the hazy stillness of Indian summer the street noises seem muffled and far away, but I see nothing but the weary Antwerp folk dragging through wet fields in the searching autumn chill of Belgium. Will they lie down tonight and shiver under the gray mist or go on until the old and ill fall exhausted and welcome the vision of what their own Maeterlinck calls "the austere and peace-bestowing gate of death."

In September 1911 the Porters, J. and I spent some days in Bruges. We were in the pretty little Hôtel de l'Europe, well fed and warmly clad, but still so cold that we begged to stay in the gleaming kitchen, and at night our one hot-water bag went back and forth from Mrs. P.'s room to mine.

The streets were pools of icy water, and we laughed when the sleet whipped the bare legs of some brown-serge-clad monks singing through their noses in honor of a new figure of the Virgin over the door of the Hôtel de Ville. I hope the Germans will not molest her.

Before we sailed from Antwerp last year we walked about the busy, friendly town, and took perhaps a last look at the cathedral. I bought some lace, and the pretty girl who waited on me, in excess of courtesy, went with us to the glove shop joking gaily about coming to America. Have the Zeppelins rained their ghastly dew on those little shops and the clever, industrious women?—good citizens, even if they were subjects of King Albert. But if King Albert sustains his present record I would rather be his subject than that of any other king now trying to defend his divine right to rule wrong. Kings nowadays must wink at one another as they pass, tickled at their cleverness in fooling so many people so much of the time.

A letter from my good friend Mrs. Aeron Thomas, in Wales, gives a sketch of what conditions are over there. "Your sympathy cheered us in this terrible time of anxiety. Though we are free from the dreadful suffering that has befallen Belgium, that is brought home to us by the refugees. I hear that some children have come to Cardiff with their fingers cut off; another child is at Neath with both hands gone. There are some Belgian ladies from Malines at Lady Mond's, and it makes one ill to hear what they have suffered, and they are only a few of thousands." Then follow heartbreaking accounts of her only son going abroad, the death of his friend, a handsome young fellow I remember well, and such a picture of work in hospitals and camps, and the suffering of the poor that I cannot realize it is the same pleasant Swansea neighborhood I knew.

General Ainsworth, who is intensely pro-Ally but honest medical man first, says that the stories of mutilated children are "just damned lies." He says that children don't survive having both hands cut off unless they have the best medical attention, and Germans are not such fools as to carry doctors around to take care of their victims. I hope he is right. Anyway, a note of common sense is refreshing in the general hysteria.

Then here is the other side from Annie Giesecke of San Antonio, a nervous, delicate woman who landed in Bremen just as war broke out and is back after countless adventures and distress:

I wanted to stop in Washington and tell you all about it. My experiences thrilled and thralled me. They drained me of all physical and psychical strength. But the spell is broken now, and I am adjusting my opinions—they are not entirely from the German viewpoint any more. But it was magnificent. I shall always feel it is a privilege to have been there to witness the courage, the endurance, the sacrifice of a noble people.

New York, November 14

I wonder if it is war that makes New Yorkers lack their usual air of self-satisfaction and exuberant prosperity. Is it the indescribable ugliness of their clothes that makes the women seem less well dressed, or is there really less richness of silk and fur and feathers? Though resigned to being fashionable, maybe they just cannot enjoy spending money on a skirt only 40 inches wide, 9 inches from the ground, and usually slit up at least 9 inches more to show a flimsy petticoat of lace or chiffon or just plain legs. Above this single pantalette is a tunic, wide and ripply around the hips and narrow in the shoulders, and their heads are fitted into tight velvet caps with a single Mephisto feather darting skyward exactly in front.

New York, November 19

At the meeting of the American Academy of Arts and Letters today I was not armed with my trusty notebook, and it is the irony of fate that this was the occasion of all others when I wanted to use my patent little aids to memory. But a scrap of paper on the flat side of my handbag served. Mr. R. U. Johnson sent us invitations to this meeting of our new and ambitious organization, and J. and I decided we could do without new clothes or butter on our bread for the sake of seeing Howells and Cable in the flesh—so much of one and so little of the other—after loving their books for forty years. Cable's were the first books J. gave me before we were married.

Last week we were here at the meeting of Carnegie Trustees, and as befits a $10 million backing, we stayed at the Waldorf; now, though on pleasure bent, we are sheltered at the little Stratford on 32nd Street and, but for the weather, quite as comfortable.

We put on our best clothes early and went bravely out into the dull November drizzle. My London raincoat justified itself, and its ugly gray completely covered my taupe silk and ermine stole. We walked up to Aeolian Hall, and rain, ugly gray coats, and economy all faded into nothingness when we found our good central seats and saw the great men —most of them only great names on good books heretofore—assembling in a semicircle on the platform. They all looked their parts; none of them is commonplace.

Howells introduced Paul Brieux of France saying, "He has taught not Art for its own selfish sake, not Art for Beauty's sake, but Art for Truth's sake." Howells's voice is exactly what I wanted it to be, not a trace of Yankee twang and equally free from any sedulous aping of the English —just plain, sweet, best American. He doesn't look his age, and his face, even in repose, is luminous.

Brieux is smooth-faced, florid, almost English in appearance, but suggests robustness of spirit and full enjoyment of life rather than beef and beer. I wish I knew something of his writing besides that unpleasant medical treatise, *Damaged Goods*. He wore the French Academy uniform that Anatole France pokes fun at so delightfully, and, strange to say, it was decidedly becoming. An old lady near us, obviously a personage and conscious of it, remarked to a clever-looking man beside her, "I hope by next year our Academicians will have a distinctive dress of that kind," to which he replied, "Oh, no! I'm afraid we might look like the critics in *Fanny's First Play*." Then he had to go on and explain to her what *F.'s F. P.* was. Even personages don't know everything, it seems.

I picked out Hopkinson Smith—I have seen him often before; John Burroughs, whose white and straying beard and outdoorsy clothes were unmistakable; and Basil Gildersleeve, such a familiar figure at the University of Virginia when I was a child and where his witticisms still survive in neighborhood folklore. His hair and beard are a strange pewter-white. In the dear old Victorian days when people read *The Last Days of Pompeii,* we used to call him Arbaces the Egyptian and the stern black-bearded king with wolfish eyes. Now he looks like an astrologer.

Faith in my intuitions had the worst shock when Brander Matthews had to rise and straighten out the longest and thinnest legs and a figure distinctly "gangling." I had fancied him small and professorial like James Bryce, but his talk on "What Is Pure English?" justified my expectations. He pleaded for the growth of language, for the speech of everyday people in the sense of convenience and directness and praised specifically such valuable words as "loan shark," "windjammer," and "hen-minded"—that complete description of some women for which I've been thanking Howells for years. (Howells chuckled all over his comfortable person at the compliment.) He advocated prompt Americanization of French words such as "employee," and "garage," which he said should be made to rhyme with carriage. I wondered if he would commend the all-too-familiar speech of some well-dressed and bright-looking women sitting just in front of us. They greeted one another with the inevitable "Hello," and exclaimed, "Why, these seats are *dandy*, perfectly dandy."

We had a pleasant talk with Cass Gilbert after the meeting and with several others, all of whom had something kind to say of J.'s good offices in legislation for the Academy.

On train to Washington

Just before we left today we had an agreeable few minutes with George W. Cable, who was staying at our hotel. He looked like a little thin bird, an English sparrow, decidedly English but not Anglican. Presbyterian was felt rather than heard in all he said, and his eyes gleamed when J. recalled having met him in a Sunday school of that persuasion long ago in New Orleans. I wonder what J. was doing there? He said nothing notable but was friendly, courteous, and fidgety. I longed to thank him for making me an heir of pure delight in *Old Creole Days, The Grandissimes,* etc., but I am never sure that it's good form to talk shop with a *real* writer. Of course, the little fleas never forgive your failure to mention their achievements.

December

This 19-month session has upset all precedents, but chiefly it is the war that turns our thoughts from such futilities. The most fearless cannot fiddle with real zest while Rome is burning, albeit we are not in sight or hearing of the fire. The world has suddenly grown small, and St. Paul's dictum that we are all members of one body has taken on a new meaning.

Lately I have seen few Congressional women except those who come on Thursday to my small and selected Red Cross circle. The genesis of it is rather funny. In the early days of the war Miss Boardman came home with us from church one Sunday, stayed to dinner, and spent the afternoon telling us what she, as head of the Red Cross, was hearing privately of conditions in Europe. It was more difficult for us then than now to conceive of the horror—operations without anesthetics, wounds dressed with straw, the lack of antiseptics, medicines, clothing, everything that civilization has come to think essential and easy to get. She said the Red Cross needed help, that all America must contribute, and asked if I could not rouse my friends in Texas. I knew San Antonio had heard no such particulars, so I wrote a volume to Mrs. A. W. Houston, who is continually given to all good works. How her campaign aroused the whole state is another story.

Also at Miss Boardman's request I went to a meeting of "workers" at St. John's Church. I felt in a desperate hurry. I wanted to smother my agonized imagination and was ready to join them in the hardest physical labor. Instead I found a nice little meeting presided over by a nice little lady who prayed. I am not impious, but work is my favorite kind of prayer, and after the prayer they talked. They were pewholders at St. John's, with all that implies of ease and place, and obviously were not accustomed to serving. They had a lot of scraps of cretonne and wanted to make them into bags for Red Cross nurses going to the war zone, and they wondered whether we should sew at the parish house or at home, and seemed to think any time would do. Often in my earthly pilgrimage I have found myself in company too respectable for my taste, so I went boldly to the lady with the scraps and said I would take enough to make fifty bags. If I had offered to dig the Panama Canal, they could not have been more surprised, but I got the scraps, hurried home, and with dear Mrs. Gregg's help finished the flimsy things and took them back the next day. I saw with sorrow and amazement the trash that was to be put in them—cheap thimbles, spool cotton, and scissors that would hardly cut paper. God help the nurse who has to cut gauze or bloody clothing with such toys!

It occurred to me to save time, and maybe temper, by getting some friends to join me and sew at home with Mother, and my two big bright rooms have never seemed more cheerful. We have three sewing machines, a little fund to buy materials, and Mother, 87 years young and active, is in her element. She is like Cinderella's fairy who turned mice and pumpkins into horses and chariots. Miss Boardman, whose knowledge of shirts is entirely academic, sent us sixteen quite elaborate patterns and advised us to make the shirts in three sizes to fit Germans, English, and Frenchmen. Mother threw them aside and said, "Nonsense! the men need *shirts,*" and cut out a simple surgical shirt that we can make in much less than half the time. Miss Boardman sent directions for convalescent robes costing $4 apiece, but Mother said, "Bring me a pair of cotton blankets." They cost $1.25, and she contrived out of them two robes so pretty and complete that Mrs. Danforth of New York has borrowed one for the St. John's Guild to profit by. Mother was taught more than fifty years ago in the hard school of the Confederacy when they almost achieved bricks without straw. We have a pleasant time, too. Mrs. John W. Davis is a wonderful cutter, and never looks prettier than when she is busy over my dinner table piled high with unbleached cotton. Mrs. Ainsworth, Mrs. McCoy and I run the machines; Mrs. Hitchcock and Mrs. Green of Nebraska baste, and all of us talk not unworthily. At 12:30 my pretty, ladylike Lilian brings in coffee, or even eggnog, to reward us. At first we worked shamefacedly, feeling that perhaps we were unduly excited. But as the tale of horror grows we talk less and work feverishly. We sometimes send out more than fifty garments a week.

CHAPTER NINETEEN

1915

Auditorium of Carnegie Library, January 11

We paddled through the coldest rain to this meeting of single-tax cranks whom J. is to address on peace. A half hour past due, they are still straggling in, eminently peaceful-looking spinsters in out-of-date black and brown silks; shaggy old men with large, wet umbrellas, and pallid youths of a Jewish type with big eyes that seem to look beyond the stars.

At places like this how much research and oratory are spent on people already convinced of your theme. Perhaps it is well to strengthen the brethren, but it would be more interesting to round up a few militarists and reason with them. They wouldn't listen, of course, charmed we never so wisely. Our friend Bush-Brown, the sculptor, came in just now spick and span like a home-kept cat with pink ribbon in the strangest of garrets. He sat down by us and answered our whispered jeers by saying he was very much interested in such things. When it developed that he had landed at the wrong gathering—thought it was university extension—he seized his raincoat and fled like a startled fawn, but not before begging us to testify that he was sober.

A fluent young woman introducing J. has just declared, "If half the power that fills the world with terror," etc. It is inevitable at peace meetings along with our old friends the plowshares and pruning hooks, and the "Parliament of Man, the Federation of the World," but I have warned J. of dire domestic consequences if he mentions any of them.

Belva Lockwood is speaking at last, and she is always worth hearing. She says that on one occasion a Congressional committee was sent to see if our coast defenses were adequate, and, of course, reported that they were not and that it would cost millions to make them so. Whereupon the Detroit *Free Press* commented that no doubt it would, but it wouldn't cost us ten cents to mind our own business and keep out of war.

Belva is a tottering wheezy old woman now with a wretchedly bad hat. I remember her—oh, so many years ago!—a stout, confident Amazon with short hair and riding a tricycle, to the scandal of Washington. How our standards of propriety change! She has just said that she wished all congressmen had the mind and vision of Representative Slayden, which I think very handsome of her. She is 85 years old. How many of us at her age will have the courage and energy, the sincerity of belief in our cause to come out and testify to it on a night like this?

Later

I went this morning to the meeting following the mass meeting yesterday of the Women's Constructive Peace Movement. Jane Addams presided in her gently great way—she is always so much the biggest woman present— and Carrie Chapman Catt, Mrs. Fitzgerald, and pretty, concise Mrs. Louis Post took part in the discussion whenever they could stem the flood of Mrs. Kate Waller Barrett's irrelevant benevolence. Mrs. Henry Villard, full of vim and courage, wrote the resolution pledging us all to protest against further preparedness for war, and we may do some good if we are not swept off our feet by slushy sentiment or tangled up with woman suffrage politics. If we could get the women of the country to take as much interest in saving their sons from the shambles of war as they do in preventing everyone from taking an occasional drink, our influence might be tremendous. So few of them can see beyond the corner saloon, "which was the ruin of Uncle John."

January 18

Mrs. Porter, her sister Mrs. Llowndes, and I, and several hundred others accepted the Archaeological Society's invitation to hear Paul Wayland Bartlett describe the group he is making for the pediment of the east front of the House. It is not completely developed yet, but with the exception of one female figure to the right which I thought rather weak, the group as a whole is noble and interesting in spite of his lame and impotent exposition of it. Genius is not so rare that its eccentricities are not to some extent standardized, and one expects even a genius to respect conventionalities enough to stand up and speak to the ladies. But he was led across the stage like a culprit, made no bow or preliminary remarks, dropped into a chair, leaned his arm on a table, and talked through his hand. His voice is rather petulant and "foreign," and even people on front seats, as we were, heard him only in the high places. It was irritating because I wanted to know his ideas about it.

January 20

As I lay snugly in bed one morning skimming the *Post* for my shivering, shaving husband, I read to him about the arrival of the Sayre baby, the President's first grandchild, and J.'s reaction to the news was an expression of almost profane indifference. It looks as if he had unconsciously voiced the feeling of the community. I never knew a similar event connected with the White House to awaken so little interest. The Cleveland babies were first-page news all over the country, and "Baby McKee" in Harrison's administration was a political issue when "Private" John Allen in Congress recited his original verse ending,

> *Baby rules the White House*
> *And, damn it, there you are!*[1]

Concerning the baby's name, there has been a ripple of fun since the pedagogue grandpapa announced (in the *Post*'s Society News) that to be truly effective, to come trippingly to the tongue of the masses, a man's name should be composed of two spondees and a dactyl. No one had risen to dispute it, perhaps because, like myself, the masses are not acquainted with either party.

House of Representatives, January 28

J. is to make his speech on the navy bill today, and I early pre-empted my favorite seat—extreme left front in the members' gallery—and have waited for an hour. I sent down to him an editorial from the New York *Evening Post* on the tremendous part played by submarines in the late battle in the North Sea. It sustains his theory, and I can see his gleaming silver hair as he leans over nodding approval and fitting it into his manuscript.

January 29

Only four of us were here to sew this morning, Mrs. Green and Mrs. Hitchcock of Nebraska, Mrs. Fred Stevens of Minnesota and myself. We had

---

[1] "Private" John Mills Allen of Mississippi was elected to Congress in 1884, defeating a Confederate general. In a famous campaign speech he pointed out to the voters that during the Civil War he had stood on picket guard over the general "while he slept." Baby McKee was President Benjamin Harrison's grandson.

pleasant, quiet talk, and finished a great bale of pretty capes with hoods for little cold refugees and some big, ugly skirts for stout peasant women. Women talk better when their hands are occupied; my sewing day is pleasanter than my reception days.

January 31

Today, Sunday, Dr. and Mrs. James Brown Scott and Mr. Quezon, Philippine Commissioner, came to midday dinner. Dr. Scott was called away early, but Mrs. S. stayed on and told us some interesting stories she heard about the Wilsons when she and the doctor were in Princeton last week, as well as an item heard at a Cabinet dinner last night that is news indeed. Watt Gregory (Attorney General), joking with Mrs. David Houston, said that she ought to forgive him for some peccadilloes because they were going to send her cousin as the next special observer to Mexico. Mrs. Scott said they called him "Bud" something. Of course, it was easy for us to guess Duval (or "Bud") West, and we are delighted and surprised that Wilson should send one who not only knows the country's language and people but will tell the truth when he comes back. It will be a happy change from a blind guide like John Lind, excellent, but uninformed and incurious, or a questionable character like Philip Hale who, we hear privately, was not received by the decent Americans in the city in spite of his wearing the halo of presidential patronage.

J. telephoned at once to find out what the Texas correspondents thought of it, but it was their first news, so it looks as if we had a scoop. Funny for a Cabinet officer to be discussing it at a dinner party before it was announced.

February 8

We dined at Senator Bailey's one night last week in the grand new home on 16th Street. It is a superb establishment, and the dinner was pleasant but embarrassing at times as Bailey discussed Texans and Texas politics with his usual frankness, except when he digressed to pour hot shot into the Administration—with the Solicitor General one of the guests.

All the Texans made merry over the Garners' change of front toward the Burlesons. The Post Master General has treated poor little John perhaps even worse than other members of the delegation, and last year when the ladies' Cabinet row was on Mrs. Garner was especially bitter about Mrs. Burleson's part in it. So it was funny to hear of very gorgeous invitations from Mrs. Garner to a luncheon in honor of Mrs. Burleson. Of course, I am not invited. Mrs. W. R. Smith of the delegation, not usually given to joking, tells me that after writing her acceptance in due form she added to it, "Always reserving the right to ask how in the world it happened."

As to Bailey's ill-timed criticism of the President and his official family, everyone is reckless about that now. I have never known a time here when talk was so free. I wish I could reproduce the biting wit and sarcasm with which Mr. Adams last night treated Mr. House and his mission to Europe as the President's personal representative. I never heard the old man more scathing.

April 3

The weather really deserves mention. It has been cold, dry, and clear for a month. Last Sunday Mrs. Porter, Mrs. Butler, and I went down to Fairfax to pay our party calls and have a real lark together. A mild dissipation some people might think it, but we felt like birds uncaged and giggled like schoolgirls over nothing. We had what the landlord promised us, "a very fair dinner" at the Tavern—good turnip greens with a poached egg on top and pork roast with brittle skin as becomes a Virginia table in March. We made our calls and got home to supper.

Except where the branch had seeped into the road and made a bog that the limousine puffed through with difficulty, the dust was deep and the trees white and ghostly as in midsummer drought. Every day the weatherman predicts "Fair today, unsettled tonight," and each evening the sun sets like a ball of fire. This morning he was almost poetic in promises of fair skies and balmy breezes for Easter, but before we saw the paper the snow was pouring down or rather whizzing past us on the wings of a blizzard. It is still falling at five o'clock, almost the worst day of the winter.

Mother, Rena and I have sat around the radiator getting little things done for J.'s and my trip to Hawaii. It seems too good to be true. The Hawaiian government has invited a large Congressional party to come and see their Islands of the Blest and incidentally bless them still further with some federal appropriations. If left to me, I would forget the downtrodden taxpayer and give them anything they wanted in sheer gratitude for getting us away from Washington.

Montreal, April 18

Englishmen who come to New York expecting to gather bananas in Central Park are not further afield than I was when we alighted here yesterday. I expected a sleighful of furs to meet us, but there was never a sign of snow, and at the station the women made a brave show of spring hats. Alain de Lobinière, twirling his little swagger stick, had not even an overcoat over his khaki.[2]

His uniform brought the war to our minds more vividly, and it was never far off again during our visit. We hurried from breakfast to the "mil'try" service at the Armory, and from the narrow gallery crowded with sad-faced, nervous women watched the men down below looking so fine, erect, and fit—so much too fine for the hideous waste for which they are being prepared. A black-coated Scotch "meenister" looked absurdly out of place with a pyramid of drums for a lectern and a group of flags behind him but talked wonderfully well. The band played; we shouted the hymns, and when "God Save the King" was over the officers crowded upstairs to see their womenfolk. We found ourselves committed to a luncheon at the Hunt Club with the colonel's lady.

A clever Scotsman, McTeer, sat by me, crape on his sleeve for a brother killed in action ten days before and tears just hinted at in eyes and voice when he spoke of a young son in the trenches. I had more in common with him than with the purely mil'try-minded Colonel to my left. All of them questioned us about the feeling of our people toward the war —Were there any German sympathizers, and didn't we think that Americans would come in someday, some way? Their confidence of victory, or rather inability to conceive of defeat, was magnificent. Agnes mentioned incidentally that her uncle J. was "one of Carnegie's peace men," and the Colonel looked up from his plate as if he had heard that Guy Fawkes was under the table.

The next morning as we watched the regiment drilling on Fletcher's field, Mrs. de Lobinière, her only son marching past, kept saying, "What fine fellows! I'm sure if I were a man I would go with them." While Agnes, with thin, flushed cheeks and brimming eyes, said, "Are they not splendid? Doesn't Alain look smart in his uniform?" How fortunate that the routine of preparation has dulled these women's sense of what it all means! They were not born to the noise of the rolling drums as I was.

In the evening we had a pleasant dinner company of Agnes' special friends, and a lot of people afterwards. A tall, du Maurieresque young woman, Miss Yorke, lady in waiting to the Duchess of Connaught, I found quite pleasant. She said she was sorry we could not stay till the next evening as we were to dine with the Duke and Duchess. (It seemed funny to be told that you were coming, not asked to come, but that, I believe,

[2] Husband of Mr. Slayden's niece Agnes.

is royalty's little way.) I was sorry, too, for it would have been an interesting experience and Agnes and Alain say that the old people are very sweet, but the Congressional party is assembling in Chicago, and we have still another visit ahead of us.

Kansas, April 23

Our train is standing near a high, ugly structure rising abruptly out of the prairie and proclaiming itself in big red letters "The Mill on the Trail," St. John's, Kansas. The howling of wind surprises us as there are no trees or even bushes around the little white box houses to indicate that it is blowing, only endless still plains of vivid green. General Ainsworth warned me that to enjoy going through Kansas one must either be asleep or drunk, preferably both, but I find the rawness of the landscape and the hard, colorless sky strangely stimulating.

We spent two days in Chicago with our friends the Lynden Evanses, and my horizon is broadened, but such an atmosphere of civic energy would have exhausted me if we had stayed longer. Everyone had a purpose, a mission or a special interest. No one seemed to live, as I so often do, just for the pure pleasure of it. I would have enjoyed some time to browse and nibble in Mr. Evans' beautiful library.

Years ago Mrs. Evans heard me say that I thought there was little beauty in Chicago, and she seized the opportunity to prove me wrong. The university, the parks and the lake front made me proud of my country and ashamed of my ignorance. At a meeting of "The Fortnightly," of which she is a member by inheritance and grace, I met what I heard was the best socially and intellectually among the women and came away humbled, my sectional complacency oozing out at my finger ends. I missed something of the grace and gaiety of the women of the same class in the East. There were fewer well-corseted figures, more common-sense shoes, and voices a little harsher, though perhaps not so shrill, but they looked capable, and bravely fit to do the things they planned. I felt that my little vivacities were trivial and inadequate, like a canary strayed into a barnyard of pure-bred Plymouth Rocks. Mrs. Evans' special woman friends were antisuffragist almost to a man and looked their astonishment when they found that the much-heralded "Southerner" was among the perverted and unfeminine. They spoke as if conscience alone had whipped them to the polls, and I pictured them a sorrowful procession of veiled figures following the nun. Mr. and Mrs. Evans were even in despair of the future of the Peace party because the work had been taken up by that arch-feminist

Jane Addams. More than one person said regretfully that Miss Addams had lost much of her influence, but they generally attributed it to her following after strange gods with T.R. and the now almost extinct herd of Bull "Meese."

Last night we were nearly shaken out of our berths by the struggles of three engines that pushed and pulled us up to the plains of New Mexico. We waked at Las Vegas to the gay noise of college boys rah-rahing. A whole trainload of congressmen is rare in the West, and the glamour brightens over us every day.

We scrambled into our clothes, leaving undone many things that ought to be done in a morning toilet, and got out in time to have a few words with a good-looking and well-dressed crowd of people and get some intoxicating breaths of the thin, tingling desert air. All day my soul has "rolled itself out, a long pent scroll" in utter enjoyment of the measureless gray-brown, sagebrush-tufted plain, and beyond it the world's uttermost rim spiked with snow-capped peaks under banks of black cloud trailing thin skirts of rain. It is the peace of God after nearly two years of bricks and mortar, the noise and smell of automobiles, war talk, and political contention.

Mrs. J. Ham Lewis says "this scenery is perfectly great," and Mrs. Swagar Sherley gently concurs with her.

It is an odd company, so many shades of public opinion that by tacit consent nobody talks politics, but they all sing. Sometimes I wish they would talk politics. At this moment they are packed into the observation car, and above the roar of the train I hear lugubrious snatches of "The Old Oaken Bucket." I thought it was barred by statute of limitation. I lie in my snug stateroom, and when not looking out the window take a few pages of *Sense and Sensibility;* it supplies a rather obvious need. J. is busy on an article for the New York *Independent* on how to bring peace to Mexico. Heaven help him!

We have been taken about Albuquerque by pleasant people in good automobiles, and enjoyed the wide streets with arching trees, pretty homes and good public buildings, but the best to see and the best to praise was the new State University built and decorated like Zuñi cliff dwellings, making a wild harmonious whole of its site on the craggy mountainside. If the college work is as bold and original as the architectural scheme, it will surely be heard from. Bishop Howden met us and reminded me of a

New Year's Day callers at the White House during the Taft administration

"The Tafts have a gift for creating an easy, hospitable atmosphere."

President William Howard Taft

". . . sitting on the veranda facing the
golf links at the loveliest time of the
evening, we saw approaching us the
most appallingly fat man in shirt
sleeves. . . . he called out cheerily,
'Good evening, Mr. Slayden,' and behold it was the President. He ought to
play golf more and perhaps laugh less,
but his frequent chuckle is very pleasant to hear."

William Jennings Bryan

"When Bryan began to speak, I realized for the first time that he was a big man, not just a pleasant one. He has the most perfect voice I ever heard. . . . When he finished people swarmed around him, shaking his hands, touching his shoulders, almost kissing the hem of his garment."

Joseph Gurney Cannon,
Speaker of the
House of Representatives
1903-1911

"Uncle Joe Cannon has been the bright particular star of the trip; not because he has been in the public eye so long and is better advertised but because of a not uncertain charm in himself. He is a gay, companionable old bird, never oracular or playing the heavy states-man. . . ."

Preparedness parade,
Washington, 1916

"Wilson never looked more comme il faut—*white trousers, a short blue sack coat, and straw hat— and he walked with a swagger, not a vestige of the Presbyterian elder left about him. . . . Were not the eyes of his country and the new Mrs. Wilson upon him?"*

Suffrage parade,
Washington, 1913

*"In spite of everything the parade was inspiring,
and I was ashamed of the self-consciousness that
kept me out of it. . . . the San Antonio banner for
which I was responsible, and the little Texas flag
fluttering gaily gave me quite a fullness of the heart
and eyes."*

Mrs. William McKinley

"The first glimpse of Mrs. McKinley made me ashamed of coming. . . . Her color was ghastly. . . . Her poor relaxed hands . . . rested on her lap as if too weak to lift their weight of diamond rings, and her pretty gray hair is cut short as if she had had typhoid fever."

Alice Roosevelt

"The President has innumerable relatives, and some of them are so tacky that it really makes me like him better to see how frankly he parades them on occasion. Alice Roosevelt is getting to be almost pretty, but she has not quite arrived and still has bumptious, awkward manners."

Andrew Carnegie in his library
at Skibo Castle, Scotland,
where the Slaydens were his guests
in 1913

*"It is too bad that the Carnegie tartan
is such big squares of gray, white,
black, and yellow. It takes so few of
them to make his coat, and fewer still
for his trousers that met his heavy golf
stockings at the knee."*

Brown Brothers

Charles Francis Adams

*"He has a slightly wheezy way of speaking, more
English than American—and when he has been
listening for a while and is going to speak again
and bring the conversation back where he wants
it, there is a funny little preliminary grinding in
his throat like an old-fashioned clock in damp
weather."*

Addressing Congress February 3, 1917, President Wilson announced the severance of diplomatic relations with Germany

"It was two o'clock before the Senate and the President came in, and I didn't know I was excited until I stood up for their entrance and felt pulses throbbing in all the fingers of my clenched hands. The President never made a better impression. He was almost modest, not dogmatic and schoolmasterish but like a normal man seeking advice and help of other men in a moment of awful responsibility."

laughing prophecy I made for him when he was elected bishop of New Mexico. Hearing that his diocese extended to the Pecos River in Texas, I told him of Roy Bean, barkeeper, rough customer, and justice of the peace withal, who had a big sign over his saloon at Langtry, "Roy Bean, Law West of the Pecos." I suggested that he could run a rival show and become "Religion West of the Pecos." Since then Roy has been gathered to his fathers, the Bishop has gotten possession of the saloon and turned it into a chapel, and the sign retired to the junk heap. I wish it could be kept as a specimen of early Texas humor; the country does not produce such characters as Roy any more. I remember another sign at Devine—"We buy everything from a ratskin to a ranch."

San Francisco

The Exposition is like all the rest except that this one is colored and the others were white. Does the color make it rich or tawdry, I can't decide. The Tower of Jewels I have no doubt about. Maybe I lack imagination, but I hate it. And to think that wizard colorist, Jules Guerin, did it!

It has been a pleasure here to see some of our party gently but firmly rebuked for using that vulgarism "Frisco." The people resent it as we resent "Santone." San Francisco and San Antonio are two such fine, mouth-filling names with history back of them that they should not be cheapened by commercial travelers' short cuts.

S.S. SIERRA

The seasickness over the company begins to be noisy again. The young people have resumed their chewing gum, and some indefatigable ladies concoct a "program" for the evenings in the saloon. There are fair speeches from the men; Mrs. Brown of West Virginia (Isetta Jewell, that was) does some clever things left over from her actress days, always well and amiably; and invariably Mrs. J. Ham Lewis reels off a string of doggerel about the ship's company. It is an odd gift, so mechanical that it suggests the ticker in a Wall Street office. Fate cannot harm us, though. The sea is smooth, and getting warmer, and we have a table with our dear friends the Anthonys and Campbells of Kansas and a Mr. and Mrs. Rodenberg of Illinois, who are jolly and companionable. Mr. R. sits up o'nights, I believe, concocting yarns to disturb the ponderous dignity of Ollie James and Senator Overman. He has them in a thundering rage today. Ollie swears that he will go back home without leaving the ship rather than submit to being vaccinated on landing; and Senator Overman, who has brought four schoolgirls with him, and is canny, vows that to pay Spreckels $10 each for permits to bathe in the Pacific is an outrage, and he will introduce a bill next winter to put a stop to it.

Honolulu

I have learned on several trips like this that the meek shall inherit the best rooms eventually. I was drinking in the beauty of palms and banyans and self-conscious peacocks in the park while some of our party were asserting their right to rooms right here in the Moana and nowhere else when a slightly irritated member of the reception committee came and asked if we would mind very much staying in the Hustace Cottage. We would be delighted, of course, so through a little paradise of flowers we were led to the loveliest big ground-floor room, a bath of our own, and, best of all, back stairs going down into the very ocean itself where I can bathe and watch the surf riders, like bold merry mermen playing in the distance. Good little Mrs. B., who has a profound reverence for dignitaries and precedence, tells me that *even* Senator James has a small room on the third floor of the Moana, and no bath.

May 5

Last night I met my gastronomic Waterloo. I said I could eat anything that any other civilized people ate, but then I had not seen a luau! Eighteen hundred of us sat down to one in a vast park under awnings hung from one palm or banyan tree to the other, their trunks covered with big, lazy parasite vines, and strange bold flowers glowing under the electric lights. As a concession to our tastes the feast was spread on tables, but there were no knives and forks, and finger bowls appeared long after the inadequate paper napkin had become a greasy dab. I drew heavily on my sense of social duty and dipped my fingers twice into the bowl of poi and licked it off as well as I could. I opened a greasy ti leaf and got one sight and whiff of a triangle of hot, fat pork an inch thick, and then I surrendered and devoted myself to keeping down the bit of raw fish and some coconut glue I had swallowed earlier. When the floodgates of senatorial eloquence were opened J. and I slipped away and made for the seclusion of our cottage. Later I hunted a battered piece of chocolate in my hairpin box just to remind my poor little insides of better days.

The *Mauna Kea,* cleanest ship outside of Holland, purred her way over a
perfectly smooth sea all night and dropped anchor here this morning. When
we came out in the cool clear dawn, high fantastic mountains stood around
us, the little waves playfully slapping at their feet on the rim of the harbor.

We were taken possession of by a quick, efficient little man, Mr.
Wadsworth, once of Maine, and whirled in his automobile through miles
of misty, dim perfumed avenues, past fields of cane that we could almost
hear growing and trim American cottages pushing their familiar outlines
through a burden of tropical flowers. At Mr. Wadsworth's place there were
more flowers, an avenue of palms and a hedge of scarlet hibiscus. The
house was so gleamingly clean that I hated to go in with our travel-soiled
belongings. It was the essence of New England from the crisp white curtains
to the little china dog on the center table, but when madame came in she
kept me guessing: Hawaiian? Spanish? Brazilian? At last it turned out that
she was pure Portuguese and a member of the Episcopal Church!

Since our pretty breakfast with dainty linen, strawberries and cream,
bacon and eggs and Kona coffee, we have ridden far and wide or, rather,
high and low through the narrow, crooked gorge that they call the Iao
Valley. It begins in the garden of this house; at least the sharp ridges
and needle points of the mountains that form it hang threateningly over
my window, and the clouds that constantly curl in and out among them
seem almost in reach. The valley itself this morning had the glory and
the freshness of a dream, and some of the surprises too, and the sense of
falling from great heights and flying through space, as our Maine host drove
his machine up and down the corkscrew road with all the dash and abandon
of a Texas cowboy on a broncho. Still, the beauty made it worthwhile,
and we were safely back in our room that is cool as "a green thought
in a green shade," with time for a nap.

Our next drive was to the Kaiku pineapple cannery where we ate
incredible quantities of fruit and felt encouraged to eat a great deal more
in future by seeing how exquisitely it was handled. They trundled the ripe
pines in from the fields before us, put them into a machine that cut out
the core and took off the peeling and sent the yellow balls rolling down a
slide where pretty little Japanese women in blue kimonos and white rubber
gloves caught them and did the rest. During the luncheon, whenever
the orators ceased from troubling, there was lovely warm singing by
Hawaiian girls and later some wrestling by a squad of miniature Japanese
boys. It was wonderful work for such little brownies, and made me doubt
if I could whip them as easily as I have boasted I could to timid army

officers who whisper to me about the Japanese menace.

At the Puanini sugar mills we were entertained with a swimming contest, and saw Duke Kahanamoku, the world's champion, swim first in the ordinary fashion and then in his own stroke, twisting through the water like a bronze serpent. No matter what stroke he used in the contests he always came out first. A hideous old hula dancer writhed obscenely for our benefit, and Uncle Joe Cannon danced a reel, tripping it lightly for a man who is to celebrate his 79th birthday tomorrow.

May 7

The whole community joined us this morning on the Court Green. We were seated in the checkered shade of a glorious Monkeypod tree and were very gay. Uncle Joe standing in the sun on the courthouse steps had received many birthday greetings and odd presents. The congressmen were taking turns addressing us in rather a lighter vein than usual. J. spoke briefly and to my satisfaction, as he neither told an anecdote, made facetious remarks about "my wife" nor promised impossible things to our hosts—a marked departure from the style of most of the speeches on this trip. He struck an obviously welcome note to the islanders when he deplored the constant talk of war with other nations and warned against the power of suggestion. Later some of the men told me that they thought it the word fitly spoken more than any other talk that had been made. Just as Senator Warren began to speak, and everyone listening closely, a gentleman came up behind my chair and whispered to me that the *Lusitania* had been sunk. I felt as if my body had crumpled up all at once. My first thought was to try to keep the news secret; we seemed such impotent children laughing there in the sunshine with that black horror on the other side of the world, but the instant the Senator quit speaking someone got up and read the wireless aloud. The very sunlight grew dim; all the gaiety was gone, and the crowd became excited and distressful. Besides the general horror, there were several Honolulu people on the boat, and it meant sorrow for friends and neighbors. The lunch was a failure, and the singing of the inevitable "Aloha-oe" sounded more like "Ay de mi." None of our party doubted that we would be called home at once to declare war.

Lahaina

A Mr. and Mrs. Nelson who brought us over here were so pleasant that they almost compensated us for the loss of the Wadsworths, but there ought to be another verse to the song about what little boys are made of to explain what little Americans are made of. Mrs. N. is twenty-four and very handsome. Her mother, who was killed by natives on a South Sea island twenty years ago, was of English and Chilean parentage, her father a German Pole; she was born on the high seas near Spain and has married a Swede. There are two little Nelsons born in Hawaii and very proud of being "Americans."

Later

Our next stop found us in a cheerful little bay where Captain Cook, the pirate par excellence of my youthful taste, had met the reward of his iniquities by being killed and partly eaten by the natives. Beyond a pile of lumber on the shore we could see the Christian homeliness of the monument erected to his memory.

On the dock we received the wreaths of welcome, made of aromatic bay blossoms, from the hands of very ancient crones in holokus; and yet one more school of Japanese-Chinese, Portuguese-Hawaiian children rolled their eyes obliquely to heaven and sang with fine irony:

> *Land where our fathers died*
> *Land of the Pilgrims' pride.*

Once more the class orator bade us welcome and asked for a return of the tariff on sugar. Then we were helped into magnificent automobiles, Pierce-Arrows, Packards, etc., and took the only trail for the volcano. At first it was up dry and grating mountainsides and then all sounds were muffled as we passed into dense plantations of coffee trees white with fragrant bloom.

The way luxurious tables are spread for us in the wilderness is like a fairy story. The coffee planters surprised us with one on the mountaintop just at a nice breakfasttime. The pleasure of it was spoiled somewhat by the inconsiderate impatience of some of our party to get seats and *grab* the dishes as if it were a twenty-minute-for-lunch place instead of hospitality offered by most refined and gracious friends. But I am going home a chastened patriot. Manners, particularly the kind involving the grace of leisure, are not our strong point—at least not if Congress is fairly representative of the people.

S.S. WILHELMINA

Except for the failure of a few of our party to appreciate and respond properly to all that has been done for us, there has not been the smallest fly in our ointment. I thought myself satiated and dreaded the farewell party at Prince Cupid's, but it was, as it was meant to be, the climax of beauty and interest in a social way. Going through the really stately house I had a glimpse of a room where poor old Queen Lil, very much aged and broken, sat enthroned, with men holding the tall feather standards on either side of her. Some of her loyal old subjects were approaching her on all fours, but I did not accept the invitation to go in; it seemed indelicate for a stranger to intermeddle with their joy in one of these last opportunities to show affection to their royal family and customs, so nearly extinguished under our overwhelming democracy.

Uncle Joe Cannon has been the bright particular star of the trip; not because he has been in the public eye so long and is better advertised but because of a not uncertain charm in himself. He is a gay, companionable old bird, never oracular or playing the heavy statesman, very restful by comparison with one much younger than himself who sits near us at table and who, from salad dressing to statesmanship, knows it *all*. What time the young man can spare from educating his wife in public he quarrels with or about the stewards and instructs the rest of us, beginning, "You *ought* to know" or "I will explain to you." I love to saw him off on a limb by changing the subject abruptly, and then he pouts and puffs for the rest of the meal, and the poor stewards have an awful time.

Uncle Joe was always willing to make things go. He was called on daily to speak or show himself some way and usually made the same talk about having been a pioneer on the Wabash, trading corn for sugar from New Orleans, and then forty years in Congress with two leaves of absence "for which I did not ask," which always gets a laugh even from us who have heard it so often. Frequently he ends with a negro walk-around, very quaint and early American. He says, "It is a song with a thousand verses of which I will only sing two":

> Ole Joe come to the gyarden gate,
> An' he couldn' git in kase he come too late.
> Ole Joe kickin' up ahind and afo'
> An' de yaller gal a-kickin' up ahind ole Joe.

"And," he adds, "the other verses are just like that." Then he does the walk-around as nimbly as a boy.

Jack London was with us much of the time, but I did not enjoy him. It was impossible to reconcile his manner and appearance with the best that is in his books or with a speech he made for world peace at one of the luaus. Few men can wear thin linen clothes without looking slovenly, and he is not one of them. His figure is broad and gross in spite of its muscular development; his hands are red and his face sleek and florid, and a greasy curl of fine brown hair is always flopping over his forehead. The present incumbent of his heart and home, for whom he is said to have deserted a wife and two children, was so perfectly the Hebe of a London tearoom that I did not think it worthwhile to address her. I knew she would duck, and answer, "Yees, meddum."

San Antonio, August 14

Mrs. Porter writes of the last few weeks in Washington:

I went to the Davises' dinner. It was given to Sect. and Mrs. Lansing who are having Cabinet honors and food thrust upon them vigorously in spite of the heat. The gentlemen, including the Sect. of State, were in spotless white. The table was very pretty; the conversation suffered from the weather.

Gov. and Mrs. Folk were there. . . . A good-looking, conventional young Assistant Secretary with his t's crossed and his i's dotted all properly sat by me, but I could rouse no enthusiasm in his flinty bosom. He has had some years experience in one of our Embassies, and it will color all his life. He ought to have the fact embroidered on a banner to be carried before him. . . . Mrs. Lansing was just the same, neither more nor less vivacious than when you saw her, and I do not think she is likely to lose her head. . . .

I think everyone is relieved to know that Lansing is secretary of state. He will not be spectacular, but he is a man of experience, a good lawyer and not inclined to surround himself with cheap, stage mystery like Mr. House who we all thought would surely get the place.

August 17

At a dance last night it was my unhappy fate to entertain half a dozen self-invited chaperons. They had probably heard that chaperons were the style in New York but did not know that they were superfluous when "little daughter" went to a private house. One of them evidently thought a congressman's wife, especially one who wrote "pieces" for the paper, was a person to talk up to, so she began on Mrs. Pennybacker and others prominent in club work. Finding that a blind lead, she tried me on favorite authors, but in the midst of it, preoccupied with little daughter's conquests, she glanced to the gallery where the young people had been "ragging" for a long time, and said, "I declare, those young people have got Tennyson's Brook *skinned*."

Tarpon Inn, August 24

A few days in the new Nueces Hotel in Corpus Christi was quite enough but very interesting. Everything "just like New York"—our highest ambition—even to a young girl of good family paid to dance in the dining room with a pimply-faced young vulgarian imported from New York for the purpose. There is nothing fast, nor bad, nor even gay, alas! It is just *business*. I wonder if we will ever develop any local pride or independence. There are so many quaint and pretty things we might have that would be "just like Texas" and so much better suited to our climate, our history and our comfort. We are such copycats, so inartistic. Our climate is more varied, our states as large as many of the countries of Europe, each one of which takes pride in being itself, while we are all trying to cut ourselves to the same pattern and succeeding to a deplorable extent.

I enjoyed watching the faint, gossamer women in filmy white dresses, with dainty hands and many jewels, and the hardy, brown men, sinewy and capable, without coats, and ties often missing, talking cattle, cotton, fruit farming and gardening in the newly opened "Valley." They make a world of money to be spent on and by these pretty women, who clamor at their clubs for "rights" and the ballot.

There is peace and quiet at this tumble-down inn with its trumpet flower shaded gallery, its collarless, coatless and, at present, fishless fishermen.

We would like to stay on but J. has a long-distance call to come and help to get the soldiers who were washed out at Texas City and Galveston sent to San Antonio instead of Dallas. It should be easy to keep them near the border, moving on as we seem to be inexorably toward war *in,* rather than *with*, Mexico.

September 13

Mrs. Champ Clark has taken up the cudgels for the American Academy of Arts and Letters, and if persistence and plain speech can help, J. will have an able assistant in his dearest project of getting the charter.

Mrs. C. writes from "Honeyshuck," her home in Missouri:

I am greatly interested in a bill which you introduced in the last Congress, which for want of a better name, I will call the Author's Bill. . . . I was at Pass Christian when the bill came up, and I met Mr. George W. Cable of New Orleans, and he told me of the failure of the bill to pass, and, as I told Bennett and Champ [her son and her husband] when I came home, if mortification could have killed anybody, I should have fallen dead. When I said that we were under such a debt of obligation to our authors, Mr. Cable exclaimed: "Well, then, Mrs. Clark, why in the world did Congress refuse to grant articles of incorporation to the Academy of Arts and Letters?" . . . Please send me all the literature you have on the subject so that all hands can work together and get the bill passed. I believe when the members understand the purport of it they will vote for it. They seem to have an idea that the bill was discriminating in favor of New England, but if I understand the matter the authors only ask the privilege of attending to their own affairs in their own way. . . . Several members I talked to couldn't remember whether they voted for or against it. . . . If you have your own speech in favor of the bill, please send it to me, along with any possible objection that any member had for voting against it.

September 15

Many excitable folk and some normal ones are fearing a Mexican uprising here and on the border tomorrow (Mexican Independence Day) and are taking precautions against being murdered in their little beds. I cannot get alarmed, except for the poor flustered Mexicans, many of whom have been killed along the Rio Grande lately with small show of reason. And how we shout and wave the flag and demand "punishment" when an American, no matter how blameworthy, is killed on the other side. I believe the whole ugly mess is the direct result of the blundering and vacillation that our bleak Executive has chosen to call his "Mexican policy" for the last two years.

Personally we have had a pleasant summer, a season of calm weather. It has never been as hot as it knows how to be since the coast storm, and our room and bath at the little Crockett have been comfortable. We had pleasant trips to several parts of the district, and while J. was off Chautauqua-ing I had two weeks at Sunshine Ranch with children and realities, and Jane and Rose in what Allie calls our annual jabberwork.

We have missed Harnisch's old café where for thirty years we had good food, well served. At first it was just a garden under big trees on the riverbank; then, as the town took on city airs, it moved into a big white sunroom with quantities of rare plants and pleasant little Mrs. Harnisch to preside. Henry always served us and talked politics. He was brought up in Dresden but is much better informed than born Americans of his class and a true democrat in being proud of his work and not ashamed of his place in the world. Today, just for Henry's sake, we went in behind the bar, which has taken the place of the soda fountain and German bridal favors, and took our lunch. There were very few people, and I said, "Henry, is business good? How is the place getting on?" And he said, "Oh, ja, Mrs.

Slayden. Dey haf beeg crowds at night. Only de respectable people come dis time of day, and dere ain't many of dem." Is Henry right?

Garfield Hospital, December 15

The first day they allowed me to read I opened my Prayer Book at a favorite hymn and found it in two lines that had never lodged in my consciousness before:

> *Through sleep and darkness safely brought,*
> *Restored to life and power and thought.*

Their meaning is very real now, and I am deeply thankful.

Doctors, nurses, friends have all been so good to me that now when the pain is nearly over I am really enjoying the experience. Dr. Stavely, my surgeon, is so gentle and good to look at; Dr. Hardin, my long-time friend as well as physician, is full of fun, and the nurses whisper the most thrilling gossip about the Wilson-Galt wedding and why it is so mysteriously postponed from day to day. Not a word of truth in the stories, perhaps, but they are full of excitement for one who has to gaze for many hours of each day out the window at a bit of sky, or at gray walls and a photograph of the Rev. Dr. Talmage.

CHAPTER TWENTY

1916

January 4

War madness is destroying American women's sense of humor and, I fear, to some extent their sincerity. Twice lately I have received envelopes with the letterhead "Relief in Belgium" and found inside no appeal for charity but a wild dissertation from "The Woman's Section of the Movement for Preparedness."

The names of the seven women signing it fairly reek with money so they don't carry conviction of sin to me when they declare that "we have been too long basking in the sun of our prosperity." I am not exactly sunburned from it. Then, whether with a lack of sense themselves or the hope that their readers will be fools, they compare the fate of poor little Belgium, Serbia, Armenia, and Greece with that of our United States when some nation decides to make war on us.

One can get several thrills of amusement though from their rhetoric. They say that we are "perilled and ensnared," and who wouldn't feel so when "standing on the rim of the whirlpool of death, under a leaden sky, across which is written 'Woe to the Nations.'" There is an impassioned appeal for the women of America to "join the weapon of knowledge to the proud courage of our forebears" and declare that "we assume the guardianship of both Americas." Surely they assume that all by themselves. Just a little application of the weapon of knowledge might have made them aware that the second Pan-American Conference is sitting here now and that in Mr. Root's address he said, "We desire no benefits which are not the benefits rendered by honorable equals to each other. We seek for no control that we are unwilling to concede to others."

January 6

Mrs. Lansing invited me to serve on her committee to entertain the Pan American Union meeting here now and being smothered with official and private festivities. Not being able to accept was almost the worst disappointment caused by my illness, but I am so much better that it is base ingratitude for me to complain. J. and I had been furbishing up our Spanish for months so as to enhance our pleasure and usefulness with the South Americans, but J. has been too busy to go often and now has to miss the grand affair for them in New York.

Nicholas Murray Butler writes: "While we should be most happy to see you on the 13th, when we receive our Pan-American friends, I quite understand your call to duty in Washington. . . . Like you, I see great advance in the development of Pan-American relationships. We have not been much helped, have we, by the Administration of the State Dept. recently? Nevertheless we are getting on, and I think that public opinion is more vigilant and intelligent on these subjects than heretofore."

February 6

It seems to me J. and Robert Underwood Johnson have been working for ten years to get the charter for the American Academy of Arts and Letters. The opposition to it is so puerile, so provincial, it makes one ashamed. It has been defeated several times because there were "no Western men" or "no Southern men" in the membership. Why can't they be proud just because they are Americans, and not complain of the Lord's wisdom in not placing an outstanding sculptor in Arkansas or a poet in Montana? Genius is not of one time or place. Mr. Johnson writes today: "I have just written Lodge about the charter bill as I get only stereotyped replies from O'Gorman. Watterson is in Florida, but my letter will be forwarded. I have written Mrs. Champ Clark and asked her to see you. I hope we shall make some progress in the Senate this coming week." I hope so too, but the Senate has been as dense about it as the House, and Vice-President Marshall was said to have thought it clever when some bright person suggested Jack Johnson the pugilist as a member.

Good Friday

Facing a war with Germany! An unnecessary war many people say who know infinitely more about it than I do who merely agree with them.

There is a great ebullition of patriotism, a sensitiveness to American honor and dignity on the part of the J. P. Morgans, Dodges, and other millionaires. Their millions are invested in bonds of the Entente Allies who are not marching to victory as fast as we wish them to. Who was it said,

"Scratch a war scare and you find a capitalist"? Then a President has to be elected this year, and the old shibboleth about not swapping horses in midstream might do yeoman service again.

It is a late, depressing spring; only a faint green showing yet on the ginkgo trees under my windows, and the Japanese magnolias and japonicas in the parks so behind time that they will have to hurry out of the way of summer flowers.

May 1

Waiting for J. to get home from a long drawn-out vote on Philippine Independence, I have been reading Charles Francis Adams' autobiography, which General Ainsworth, with splendid unselfishness, sent to me even before he had read it himself. It is wrought with a sad, a tragic sincerity, and it leaves one with aching pity for a man who walked through life in vast intellectual loneliness. Everything, everybody is analyzed, and behold! it is altogether vanity. He records his own, his family's and his friends' mistakes, and none of their successes. Reviling and deriding the New England conscience, blaming it for his father's and grandfather's coldness and conventionality, he is whipped and driven by it all his life, and constantly looks backward, not just regretting but bitterly blaming himself because he was not omniscient.

The impression of himself that it leaves on one's mind is just as I knew him, clear thinking, intolerant, impatient, except for the restraint of custom that lay upon him with a heavy weight. I never saw him but once show emotion that indicated tenderness and that was at the memorial meeting for F. D. Millet.

I remember one evening at dinner his turning suddenly and asking me from what part of Virginia I came. I answered promptly "From Albemarle County," and he almost snarled back, "Oh, you Virginians with your counties, your counties! What *place* are you from?" I was frightened at first, but recovered myself, and said like the persistent little girl in "Seven Are We," "From Albermarle County. In the country. My father didn't think it quite respectable to live in a town." He actually smiled, as he retorted something about Southern pride. He found the one woman of his generation fit to marry him, so beautiful, so self-possessed, so nearly his equal in every way.

May 7

At luncheon at the Winslows' today everyone was from Worcester, Massachusetts, except Colonel Dick Richardson and ourselves from Texas, and

Commander Gilmore from nowhere in particular, but very pleasant.

Mr. Adams' book can hardly be called a "popular" one, but it is discussed everywhere and was about all we talked of at the table. In the drawing room over coffee we took up the failure of the Red Cross in the "European cataclysm"—everybody else uses that fine phrase, so why shouldn't I?

The army and navy men were severely critical of Miss Boardman's attitude toward the memorial tablet that the friends of Clara Barton want to put in the new Red Cross building, and said that if Miss Boardman succeeded in preventing it, they would erect a statue of Clara Barton across the street with outstretched finger pointing, "Shame on you!" She did start the Red Cross in this country and bring it to a place of great usefulness. It seems rather petty to judge her now by the cash register standard of honesty and make no allowance for an old woman whose work had outgrown her physical strength and business capacity. When I recall how she stood day and night in the horrible slime and stench of Galveston after the great storm, working with her own hands, I feel that we owe her all admiration and gratitude even if she did waste some money.[1]

One of the ladies from Worcester was a clever, rather tense person in a short dress, pretty feet and legs much in evidence. While drinking a cocktail before lunch and smoking cigarettes afterwards she knitted rapidly on a gray sock for "one of my poor French soldiers." (The woman who hasn't a French or German soldier in the offing nowadays is poor indeed.) She had just had a letter from a German soldier to whom she had sent some clothes, which read, "Dear Madame, The same mail brought to me the Iron Cross of my beloved Kaiser and your esteemed drawers."

She was interested in the Woman's Service Camp at Chevy Chase. In telling her of it, I happened to remember that she was a strong antisuffragist, so I enjoyed a slight look of antagonism in her eyes when I said that the camp was useful and significant because it broke down the argument that women should not vote because they could not defend their country in time of war.

The camp is a popular resort in the afternoon when the gallant soldier girls leave the parade ground, drink tea and darn their silk stockings. The "hardening" is being done gradually so as not to shock their systems. The menu of the camp dinner yesterday was chicken and fresh asparagus, peas, strawberries, etc. To prevent real suffering Ranscher has put up a shed near

---

[1] Clara Barton, founder of the American Red Cross in 1881, was forced to resign as its president in 1904 after disputes over its management and an investigation by Congress.

the gate where ice cream, pastries and cold drinks may be had at any hour.

One of the grim sisters of the Navy League, which is promoting the camp, told us at luncheon at Mrs. Porter's yesterday that "these two invaluable weeks of training" cost the girls only $40 each over and above their uniforms and equipment. She had opposed having waiters for the mess but was overruled, and numerous big negroes were provided. She asked if I didn't think the camp was "a *wonderful* thing for the girls." I said certainly, but it was more wonderful still for us citizens who could lie down at night knowing they were on guard and that no Japanese or Germans would dare to attack us.

The Navy League press has stated repeatedly that Mrs. Lansing had joined the camp and goes on doing it in the face of her definite denial. Of course, the wife of the Secretary of State would be an invaluable asset, but no one who knows Mrs. Lansing's sweet, rather old-fashioned womanliness could imagine her kicking about in khaki.

The campers take themselves very seriously. The only bit of fun they have been guilty of is calling the place "Catsburg" to distinguish it from the men's camp, Plattsburg.

J. came home interested and amused at a vote on the army bill that he thought showed a curious influence of the Ford Peace Movement. Strange if a thing so shallow and fantastic should have done good after all. Perhaps the legislature heard by this means that there was such a thing as a peace movement. All news of it is systematically excluded from the press.

J. is at the Willard tonight celebrating Uncle Joe Cannon's 80th birthday at a dinner given by Copley of Illinois.

May 20

The Federation of Arts dinner last night was delightful but tired me so that I have to forgo a political luncheon today and Miss Kauffman's wedding reception at Airlie this afternoon. Alfred Noyes alone would have repaid me for sitting through the long banquet, although there was much besides. He was like his pictures, young, pink, smooth-faced with thin hair, a big mouth and big spectacles. He gently criticized *vers libre* and the realistic school that intrudes dirt and ugliness, quoting that horrid couplet about "Your worm shall be my worm" that I am glad I've forgotten. He said that in April 1914 he sent some May Day verses to market. The editor, like other editors, liked his spring poetry served in January but asked to keep the verses for the following year, so Noyes, "like the children of this world, took the check and let the editor take the chances." Long before the next May the Great War had destroyed the world's taste for spring poetry, so the verses were still unpublished. But he thought that by one of those prophetic impulses of the poet, the last lines were especially fit for the unforeseen conditions, promising hope and deeper faith to sustain us through the darkness. His face was transfigured as he recited the poem, making us almost see the wreathed flowers, the blossoms and dewdrops, the dancing youth, and thrill to the spiritual awakening of spring in the heart with the refrain:

> *He is risen! He is risen!*
> *And Love is Lord of all.*

June 4

J. and Robert Underwood Johnson were almost ready to sing "Nunc dimittis" when the charter for the American Academy of Arts and Letters was actually wrested from a curiously unwilling Congress. J. received today a letter from Mr. Johnson in which he says, "We are also indebted to Mrs. Slayden for her influence." There is also a glowing letter of appreciation from the Academy itself, which I shall be vain enough to have framed for J.'s study. I am foolishly pleased that both are dated on his birthday. The message from his new Academy on its new stationery says:

June 1, 1916

Dear Mr. Slayden:

At a recent meeting of the Academy, I was instructed by a unanimous vote to convey to you the appreciative thanks of the Academy for your long, devoted, and decisive labors in support of the bill, bearing your name, granting a National charter to this organization. We know that it is primarily to your persistence, tact, and judgment that the passage of this measure was due, and we have confidence that in years to come the whole fraternity of writers, artists, and composers will bear this service as we do, in grateful remembrance.

The Academy sends you its respectful and cordial greetings and good wishes, and I am, indeed, faithfully yours,

Robert Underwood Johnson
Permanent Secretary

Hon. James L. Slayden, M.C.

Sunday morning, June 11

I want to go to church this morning but also want to go to Fairfax this afternoon, and I am not strong enough yet to do both. I wonder if you acquire merit most by staying at home when you want to go to church or by going to church when you want to stay at home? Some crude person might ask "Why not give up Fairfax?" but that would disappoint my two best friends, and it is my one chance to pay three party calls down there. And then, there's Fairfax itself—the square, the courthouse, the red-brick houses standing in colonial complacency undisturbed except by a trolleycar every hour from Washington. Wasn't it General Washington's own baili-wick, and didn't the village Hampdens with dauntless breasts recently com-pel Pierpont Morgan to return Martha Washington's will, which was carried off by Federal soldiers during the war, or else face a suit as a receiver of stolen goods? The will is framed and hung now in the co'troom over a pile of firewood where the citizens can see it as they sit around the stove enjoy-ing their tobacco in various forms. Of course, it may be burnt up any time, but that is Fairfax's business and not J. P. Morgan's at all.

Oh! the changes and chances of Congressional life. J. has to go in a hurry to Texas for a campaign as unpleasant as it is unexpected. Two men have come out against him, neither one dangerous in himself, but by dividing the antiprohibition vote they may become so. I had hoped to go with him, but a campaign like this means expense, and it is cheaper for me to stay here. That settles it. He will turn an honest penny by some Chautauqua lectures en route.

About 2:00 P.M. yesterday I heard "Extre-e *Star*," and forgetting the pos-sible calamities of the Chicago convention, I imagined all sorts of horrors after the conditioning of nearly two years of war. But the five cents expended brought only a picture of the calm bewhiskered Buddha, Hughes, nominated on the first ballot. I wanted Burton of Ohio. We know where he stands on war and many other burning questions, but who knows what opinions lurk beneath Hughes's primly parted hair. I have met him casually a few times and exchanged calls with his wife for several years without getting any-where, so I am not competent to judge of their fitness for the place. I often see him walking down New Hampshire Avenue, generally alone, as stiff as any tradesman's dummy and not unlike one with his whiskers parted to a hair and his trousers knife-creased, but I believe he is a more sincere man and a broader one than the present incumbent. It is funny how often the expression "a pig in the poke" is being used, and after the Wilson experi-ment there is no enthusiasm for another.

There is said to be deep gloom at the White House over Roosevelt's refusal to accept the Progressive party nomination and split the party again, and the Democratic Campaign Committee is childishly complaining that

Hughes's "To the President" in his resignation contrasts poorly with Wilson's "My Dear Mr. Hughes."

Hughes's pronouncement on public questions disappoints me, but even such as impeccable creature as he must play to win. One little phrase about "efficient administration of the army and navy" may hold the germ of trouble in the present situation. Just suppose he should suggest finding out how the millions already appropriated have been spent before more is given out?

At luncheon at Mrs. Butler's lately Mrs. Marietta Minnigerode Andrews told us a story of Mrs. Hughes that doesn't indicate tact exactly. At a reception shortly after she came here, Mrs. Barbour Walker, principal of the National Cathedral School, was under discussion. Several representative Southern women were present—Justice White's wife, Mrs. Micou, and Mrs. Andrews herself—when Mrs. H. remarked in her most precise manner, "I like Mrs. Walker; she combines the cordiality of the South with the culture of the North."

June 17

At five o'clock the morning of the preparedness parade, I was wide awake, and remembering a bowl of seeded cherries in the kitchen, decided to do my part in that "industrial preparedness" which the paid patriots tell us daily is only second in importance to building battleships and buying powder from Hudson Maxim. Before seven I had a fine row of sealed jars and went back to bed for a nap thinking, "Many daughters have done virtuously, but thou excellest them all."

The parade was not as "great" as the papers report, although it was a clear, fresh day, Washington at its best. Indeed what most impressed me was the cheerful irresponsibility of nearly all the paraders, from the President in the forefront switching a little flag like a drum major's baton to the fat negro women (always in the rear of departmental divisions) who carried the flag as if they were totin' a bundle. Department clerks were given a holiday but with a notice to march or lose their jobs.

Wilson never looked more *comme il faut*—white trousers, a short blue sack coat, and straw hat—and he walked with a swagger, not a vestige of the Presbyterian elder left about him. It was a great opportunity. Were not the eyes of his country and the new Mrs. Wilson upon him? He would never have to enlist nor would one in twenty of these following him, so why shouldn't they parade as a rebuke unto the foolish, unpreparing "slobs," as they call us, who sat in windows and looked on while "our country is menaced by enemies on every side." This is the favorite bogie of the preparedness preachers, and I don't believe them. Neither nations nor individuals have many enemies if they behave with decent fairness and courtesy to others, and we are never unfair—to anyone our own size.

The parade was monotonous, just everyday people with little flags, and we soon tired of our perch on a high counter. About noon Madame Panaretoff, one of our window party, seized the opportunity to escape by offering most kindly to bring Nan, Bess and me home in her electric car. Down in the street it had become very hot, and as we wormed our way through the crowd my eyes were aching from stripes. Every woman is wearing them; narrow and dull for the elderly and conservative, broad and brilliant for the young, in shades of rose, green, purple and every possible tone of yellow from canary to the quarantine flag. The young people are almost in a uniform of a striped sweater with plain skirt, or vice versa.

June 25

I am trying to hold my tongue (what a safety valve this notebook is!), but, as at present advised, it seems to me that in the brush at Carrizal, Mexico, the other day our officers were more foolhardy than brave, and two of them, poor fellows, were killed for their folly. If their commander had read just a little Texas and Mexican history, they would not have left their horses while they "parleyed" with Mexican officers nor let Mexican soldiers make a semicircle around them. Our officers need some preparedness not included in the War Department's estimates. A course with the San Antonio Boy Scouts would have saved them from disaster.

There is a tempest in the teapots of the Washington Club. Some of the members object to having Hugh Benson's *Confessions of a Convert* put in the library because it is "an attack on the Anglican Church." Mrs. Porter sent me the book, and after eighty pages I am so tired of ecclesiastical millinery I don't believe I can finish it. If he were to go swimming and have his clothes stolen, he wouldn't know what branch of the church he belonged to. His chortling over an Anglican archbishop's wearing a gold skullcap at the Queen's Jubilee and having his cassock "adapted to the Roman cut" is positively childish. I wonder how Christ's simple robe woven without seam would fit any of them, Anglican or Roman.

July 14

Going to Dr. Wilmer's this morning, I met only two people between here and Dupont Circle and not more than six houses were open. The heat is terrific; most of my close friends are gone, so I rarely leave my flat and my little balcony in the treetops where I have breakfast and dinner and stay till bedtime.

J. is having a tiresome campaign, a victim, he writes me, of "Harrison's ability to see ghosts." Mr. Harrison really has an extraordinary gift as an alarmist—the preparedness people ought to hire him. Even in face of the facts J. writes me, I cannot help feeling apprehensive when Mr. Harrison reminds me of the general apathy of the voters and that J.'s opponent has a perniciously active Ford automobile. While I feel morally certain that J. will not run for Congress again one doesn't want to be defeated just by negligence.

Neither war nor politics stirs this deadly calm of summer. Mobilization of the National Guard made barely a ripple that I could see. One can visit a different camp every day, and Sunday Mrs. Porter and I motored out to Radis and found it sordid and depressing, without a spark of glory firing anybody. It was hot and rainy, and the poor National Guardsmen were steaming with black ponchos over their khaki. Except for a few worthy women and some striped-sweater girls around the Y.M.C.A. there wasn't a sign of the social attention that made their progress through the country a May Queen procession. The citizens have "slopped over," meeting every train of Guardsmen with offerings of ice cream, coffee and sandwiches which "our leading society ladies sat up all night to prepare."

The poor old regulars who have borne the burden and heat of the day may go hungry and thirsty while these youths are glorified. The society ladies assume that the National Guard is composed entirely of millionaires and first families, and reading the Texas papers I get the impression that Mr. Vanderbilt, our young millionaire Guardsman, is defending the border all by himself like Roosevelt Alone in Cuba.

I keep an intelligence office for sweethearts and wives and anxious mothers of men in camp in Texas. One woman, who ought to have more sense as her husband knew the hardships of a Confederate soldier for four years, said tearfully, "Why, Mrs. Slayden, they have my Johnnie sleeping in a tent!" I assured her that in Texas at this season many people sleep in tents by preference. I assure them all that their Johnnies will come marching home sound and well. What I don't tell them is how much they will have learned of heat, and dust, and fleas, and red bugs, and of the breadth and significance of their own country. Mostly they are so provincial it will be a liberal education. They know nothing south of Washington or west of Pittsburgh.

The German U-boat, sneaking up all unbeknownst to our innocent neutral shores, has almost diverted attention from Mexico. Abominably as the Germans have behaved, they are clever, and someday when the Hohenzollerns are engaged in useful trades and Germany is a republic I shouldn't object to their dispensing a little of their Kultur to the rest of us.

July 15

England is reported as doing great things at last on the Western Front, but the condition of her embassy here gives one the impression of a country hard-pressed. It has been dingy and needing repairs for a long time but this summer it is dilapidated. The Spring-Rices are not the sort of people to care very much; they rather live in the clouds, I think. Some months ago Lady Spring-Rice planted a little garden under the trees on the U Street side that struggles pitifully to make an oasis in the desert of thin grass and big yellow toadstools around it. A struggling old althea bush almost in the front door displays a few dismal magenta blossoms. The windows all need washing and even on the drawing-room side are piled up with green paste-board boxes, letter files and the paraphernalia of an ill-kept office. This morning as I drove by one window of the Chancellery wore a festoon of dark-brown fringe torn from a half-raised shade, and a young man in shirt sleeves lounging in the front door gave the finishing touch of disorder and slovenliness.

July 16

Mrs. "Billy" Kent, with Mrs. Louis Post and Mrs. Danforth, came yesterday and took me to Dower House where we met some other nice people and had lunch, a refreshing break in the summer's dullness. Mrs. K. and Mrs. D. are Unitarians, Mrs. Post a Swedenborgian, so they had high discourse on the different forms of religious expression. Mrs. Post is not so much the cleverest woman present always, but she and her husband Louis Post, the sociologist (most people say socialist), are in complete sympathy and have much philosophical talk which makes her not only ready but exact, so her views were clear and worth hearing. Her religion and her theory and practice of democracy include all sorts and conditions of men in equal affection. Mrs. Danforth's eyes twinkled behind her pale-blue motor glasses in response to mine when she told us that the war was developing a pure and beautiful brotherhood of all classes. She established a friendship by messages between a young Canadian soldier and a most interesting colored girl, a graduate of Hampton, who graces her kitchen,

and she hopes to have them meet when the war is over. May I be there to
see! How that obsession of social intercourse clings to some truly good and
clever people in the North in defiance of the lessons of history.

July 24

This Cabinet took itself seriously from the first, but although my failure to
do them honor on their own terms in the early months of their service made
me, if not their Mordecai at the gate, at least the fly in their ointment, we
are good friends with some of them. I am still a cat privileged to look at,
even to joke with, a king, it seems. At a dinner a few evenings ago, which
was really very jolly, a bottle of wine was started around the table, and
Mr. Redfield to my right filled my glass too full, but seeing what he had
done, very gracefully contrived to exchange my glass for his. Someone
remarking on his considerateness, I said, "I'm not so sure it was consideration for me. He gets the most wine." And a lady near said, "My, how
saucy you are to the Secretary. How do you *dare?*" Whereupon he turned
on me the most benignant face imaginable and said, "Because she is an old
friend, and *knows that she may.*"

July 27

Over and over I make up my mind to believe nothing that I hear and only
half of what I see of public men, but in the heat of summer and a campaign
I forget and listen with credulity to the wildest campaign lies. No wilder
ones can ever have been told than those about Senator Vardaman of
Mississippi, and one can always find in Washington someone of the opposing camp to vouch personally for the truth of such things. Vardaman's
name has stood in my mind for a combination of a mountebank and a
murderer, so I was a little uneasy about the state of J.'s soul one day when
he remarked casually that he liked Vardaman. He went on to say that he
was useful as a senator and often did favors for Texas—Texas at present
being almost unrepresented in the Senate, poor Culberson so pitifully ill
and Morris Sheppard so obsessed with prohibition and Wilson. When at
last J. said he would like to have the alleged bogieman to dinner my
curiosity overcame my prejudice and the fried chicken and cream and
peaches were provided.

He arrived exactly on time—a good omen to a housekeeper—clad, as
so often reported during his campaign, in spotless white from top to toe.
The white sombrero, very hot and woolly it looked, too, was laid on the hall
table, and the scent of hair oil hung heavy on the ambient air. It was even

perceptible on the balcony where we waited while J. was dressing, and I couldn't keep my eyes from the thick, lank, jet-black hair lying several inches below his collar. It was clipped short in front of his ears, brushed straight back from his forehead, and generous oiling prevented the straying of a single hair. His skin was smooth and dark as an Indian's.

But he was not smug, nor the poseur he is reputed to be. His English was good, and his table manners better than those of "many a gent'man what wouldn't shake hands with him." His talk and compliments to me were so much of the old Southern school—liberal quotations from Moore and Byron—that I concluded he was not so much a humbug as an anachronism; his taste for white clothes, the eight yoke of white oxen, and all the spectacular features of his campaign were just a survival of some old far-off pastoral pomp, such as the shepherd kings of Israel might have indulged in. His treatment of public questions was sane and sincere, and his opinions of his political enemies much more courteously expressed than theirs of him. He didn't conceal his utter lack of faith in Wilson, but said he would campaign for him as a duty to the party at a crucial period. Very decent of him I thought considering Wilson's treatment of him—but, then, I am not a politician.

August 4

The unveiling of the sculpture in the pediment over the east portico of the House yesterday was quite the most classically beautiful ceremony I have ever seen. It was to be at 10:30, so I went with J. to his office where Herbert Putnam joined us and we strolled from there through the checkered shade of the plaza to join the party—not a large one—under the big elms immediately in front of the House wing. A pretty little speakers' stand, covered with white and festooned with green, and chairs in a semicircle facing the House were the only preparations. The Marine Band gave a touch of color near the wall a little south of us. There were no formal entrances, no uniforms, and the women were in simple summer frocks. Mr. Putnam presented me to a plump and pleasing woman with crinkly red hair and crinkly pink cheeks, Mrs. Paul Bartlett, wife of the sculptor; and she, Mrs. Danforth, Mrs. Jim Mann, Mrs. Clark and I had some pleasant general talk.

J., who was master of ceremonies, went up on the speakers' stand and made an excellent little talk. He reviewed the history of the sculpture from the inception of the idea by Mr. McCall, his predecessor on the Library Committee who got the appropriation, to its completion today under his chairmanship. He had invited Mr. McCall to come and speak but he could not leave his duties in Boston, so J. read a charming little note of regret from him.

Champ Clark made the formal address, and while it had nothing to do with the statuary, he was at his best, wise, humorous, and naïve, as when telling how near Seward came to being president, he added, "But not half as near as I did in 1912."

Paul Bartlett talked haltingly but well about his eight years of work and the meaning of the group, and then came the great moment of the unveiling. The air was cool, the wind fresh, and as the big flag rose on its staff above the House it seemed almost to exult in spreading itself against the dazzling sky. No flag could be found large enough, so the pediment was draped with immense white sail, and the figures seemed to be emerging one by one from the marble itself as the canvas fell in splendid folds down on the columns of the portico. The strains of "The Star-Spangled Banner" broke through the shining air, and the crowd watched in breathless silence.

Mrs. Clark was ecstatic over the beauty of the scene and the praise of her husband (how we all love it, be we feminist, suffragist or just *ewigweibliche*!) and like a child unwilling to end a happy day, made excuses to prolong it. She asked the company at large if we didn't think we ought to lunch with her to celebrate, but no one could accept with enthusiasm because she didn't specify which ones she wanted, and several who should have come drifted away in their embarrassment and were never recalled. At last Mrs. Mann and I who know her quaint ways accepted the implied invitation and helped her to define her plan. The Bartletts were quite touched at her friendly inclusion of Pichavelli, the stonecutter who did the actual work of carving the pediment. She asked us to wait under the trees while Mrs. White Busbey (wife of Uncle Joe's secretary and a born general) went with her to make arrangements for the lunch.

At one o'clock in the Speaker's Room Mrs. Busbey paired us off, and Mrs. C. had nothing to do but enjoy her party. To be sure she had forgotten several important people, Jim Mann for instance, but she cheerfully filled their places with friends she met in the corridor on our way downstairs.

Mrs. Bartlett was on the Speaker's right, I to his left, and Elliott Woods, Superintendent of Buildings and Grounds, next to me. At a hint from him and J., who was near, I talked up the idea of a tea place on the Capitol Terrace such as they have in Parliament House in England. Mrs. B. seconded me warmly, and I hope the seed lodged in the Speaker's mind, but like so many of our congressmen he has not traveled enough to realize that Washington could be improved.

Warming up with lunch he spoke out none too flatteringly of Wilson and told how, after months of insolent disregard, he had come like Nicodemus at night to beg his influence with Congress. He also said he had never heard the President make but one positive assertion. When as President-elect Wilson sent for him to discuss, as he supposed, the Democratic program, Clark quoted Wayne MacVeagh saying that if he were president he would, regardless of Civil Service rules, dismiss at least half of the postal inspectors and replace them with members of his own party. Wilson rubbed his long chin and said, "That would be very drastic."

That evening at dinner I asked J. why the President was not at the unveiling, and he said with the faintest twinkle in his blue eyes, "Why, I forgot to invite him."

San Antonio, October 16

We have been here three weeks and I have never seen the place more interesting—or hotter. Houston Street is solid with people like lower Broadway or Cheapside. More than half of them are Mexicans, all sorts and conditions, and Guardsmen fraternize with the Mexican men or flirt with the girls without a thought of the international crisis that brought them together. The army would intervene with less zest now than when they first came here. Then they thought of Mexicans as enemies; now there is friendliness.

Because of the suffrage agitation, I suppose I notice everywhere a kind of social ferment denoting change—whether among women for happiness or unhappiness it is too soon to tell. They have become inveterate public speakers, and to make opportunities for speaking society has abandoned the old tea, bridge and dinner parties and taken up luncheons instead. The spirit moves us apparently about noon, and we *have* to "testify." (I say "us" because I have become as incorrigibly loquacious as W. J. Bryan himself.) There are round-table luncheons at women's clubs; young girls' luncheons, where each one brings a current topic not connected with her social life (perish the thought that their social and intellectual life should touch elbows!), and a Pan-American luncheon where twenty-one women, taking the names of the American republics, enlighten one another with encyclopedic facts on geography, products and politics in their respective countries. A luncheon for Free Discussion among Advanced Women (that *might* be its name) was my undoing. Asked to tell what women were doing in Washington and not liking to give away the others, I devoted myself to my own experiences. My notes on the telephone banquet of the National Geographic Society last spring and the dinner of the Federation of Arts stood me in good stead. It was hard to talk with the eyes of some politically antagonistic ladies fixed on me looking their incredulity when I told about eight hundred of us hearing General Pershing talk from El Paso and about listening to the swish of waves in San Francisco Bay, but it must have pleased somebody for I have repeated it by request at the College Woman's Club, the Joske Department Store Club, at the Y.W.C.A. and at several schools. The Congressman's wife must always be responsive. Some years ago I remember regretting that American women, unlike Englishwomen, could not stand up and speak and now it seems to me they can hardly stand up without speaking. Many of them talk extremely well, and it may be said to their credit that they generally speak briefly. They rarely are humorous like men, but neither do they, as I heard Colonel Cowart describe some of our leading statesmen, "just wind up their mouths and go off and leave them."

High political refugees sojourn with us in expensive suites at the best hotels, Madame Huerta at the Menger, Madame Carranza and Francisco Madero's widow at the St. Anthony, as well as Hipolito Villa, his wife and some odds and ends of children of his brother, Pancho the Terrible. Hipolito looms up rather frightfully to me since an adventure we had last night. After dinner J. and I wandered across Travis Park as we often do to sit on the gallery with Mrs. Houston and Bessie. The house was ablaze with light, but no one answered the bell, so we sat down to wait. Presently the washer-woman came with the clothes and wanted to leave them, so I invited her in through a screen window and let her lay them out on one of the snow-white-beds. Shortly afterwards we tired of waiting and went home. This morning Bessie called to give us her "new address." Yesterday they had been tempted by a tremendous price to rent the house, furnished, to Hipolito Villa! It is midsummer madness to put such creatures into a decent house, but I kept thinking what would have happened if Hipolito had caught me there.

Last year at Juárez he was gambling concessionaire and receiver of loot (both highly remunerative jobs) for his brother Pancho. While we were in El Paso J. by some accident had to be introduced to him, and he has been washing his hands like Lady Macbeth ever since. And now he is lodged under the very drippings of the sanctuary, next door to St. Mark's Church. I wonder how he will amuse himself. His usual avocations would, on this side of the Rio Grande, bring him in conflict with the police. But maybe, as Gilbert and Sullivan said delightfully:

> *When the enterprising burglar's not a burgling*
> *And the cutthroat isn't occupied with crime*

Then he loves to hear the little brooks a gurgling
And he loves to hear the merry village chime.

Last week the whole town gave itself to promoting international good will and the calm neutrality that our calm President advises by helping with the Central Powers Red Cross bazaar at Beethoven Hall. We dined there every evening and I can speak with authority about the effect on the American internal economy of sauerkraut and bratwurst, kalter aufschnitt and pumpernickel, goulash and honey kuchen all washed down with beer to the tune of "Die Wacht am Rhein."

There were German, Austrian, Hungarian, Mexican booths, but the Texas historical—the Fredericksburg and Mason early settlers' log cabin—was far and away the best. The cedar logs wore their long strings of bark; the walls were hung with skins of beasts and obsolete firearms, and cruel Indian weapons hung from splendid antlers. The ladies in charge, daughters and granddaughters of Baron von Meusebach and Prince Solms' colonists, sacrificed their comfort to historical verisimilitude by wearing hideous butternut cotton dresses fastened with bone ornaments and the skin of a wildcat or fox across their backs. Stella Elmendorf, the artist, stained red and dressed like an Indian, sat on the ground and decorated big pieces of pottery, as detached in manner as if she had been alone in the desert.

The alarmists and the purely military-minded had predicted much embarrassment from this large assembling of the German element, but we saw nothing of it. J. was asked twice—once by Mrs. Hertzberg, a beautiful woman dressed as Louise of Austria—to sign the *Golden Book of von Hindenburg,* but when he laughingly refused, not another word was said.

The people of German descent came from far and near, humble farmers driving thirty and forty miles to see the fun and contribute their mite (the fair netted $20,000), but I haven't heard of one man—except those on leave from Germany and still in their service period—rushing away to fight for the Kaiser. It is quite different with the French, English and Italians who have flocked home in crowds.

CHAPTER TWENTY-ONE

1917

Washington, January 6

Mrs. Porter and I dropped in at a Serbian Relief meeting Wednesday afternoon more, I'm afraid, to see Mrs. Barrett Browning, the hostess, than from any new interest in the Serbians, whose woes are always ringing in our ears. It was a company of prominent women of the kind who wear shabby hats, loose clothes and ostentatiously flat shoes because everyone knows they can afford better ones. While Dr. Taylor Jones told well and modestly of her part in establishing a babies' hospital at Nish, I had a chance to study Mrs. Browning and found it hard to adjust her to my preconceived ideal of a poet's household. She is about medium height but almost double width, and a dress of alternate rounds of black satin and black chiffon was a peculiarly unfortunate selection for her figure. Her face is fine without being especially intellectual, and her manner was friendly and practical. The rooms were full of things, portraits, sketches and bibelots that I saw were connected with the other Brownings and longed to look at, but I never had a chance to ingratiate myself to that extent. Serbians had the floor, and we took home a quantity of wool for Mother to knit for them. I do my knitting by proxy. There is no use in adding mine to the other horrors of war, and Mother's is so beautiful.

February 1

Last night General and Mrs. Ainsworth were here when Mark Goodwin of the Dallas *News* called J. to tell him that Germany had announced a blockade of all the Entente countries, and General A. remarked, "It is only about what they've been doing, or trying to do."

This morning at breakfast J. asked me to give him a bite of lunch to take with him—he gets so tired of the House restaurant—so I made him three sandwiches, and now Stella Callaway and I are eating them while we wait to hear the President address the joint houses on the German situation. There is a mob around the doorkeepers and at the elevators, though they bear a placard "No admittance to galleries except by card."

Everybody is tense. This morning I called the Ainsworths to know what they had heard. The General had gone out for the papers, but Mrs. A.'s voice quivered with tears because the situation "meant war, and we are *utterly* unprepared, and we will just be *annihilated.*" I had never thought of that, and I hate the idea of being annihilated, but I asked how the Germans would go about it. She said, "Why, just come over in their ships and submarines and *do* it." It sounds simple enough that way, but I still don't believe that our annihilation will be labeled "Made in Germany."

We have a long time to wait in the gallery, but we owe our good seats and escape from the crowd to J.'s alertness. As soon as he reached the Capitol and heard the news he telephoned that if I wanted to witness a great historic occasion I must "decide instantly"—his favorite phrase with me—and he would come for me in the electric. Of course he was ahead of time, and Stella C. was not ready and says she feels like a ragbag, her new dress covers such a collection of half-adjusted lingerie. It is a wild day, brilliantly clear, with a furious biting gale tearing at signs and shutters, just the weather to put people's nerves on edge.

Later

It was two o'clock before the Senate and the President came in, and I didn't know I was excited until I stood up for their entrance and felt pulses throbbing in all the fingers of my clenched hands. The President never made a better impression. He was *almost* modest, not dogmatic and schoolmasterish but like a normal man seeking advice and help of other men in a moment of awful responsibility.[1]

But the most gratifying thing to an old observer like myself was the advance in dignity and restraint in the conduct of Congress in the nineteen years since the Spanish War. The quietness, even solemnity today compared

[1] On February 3, 1917, President Wilson went before Congress and announced that "all diplomatic relations between the United States and the German Empire are severed."

with the spread-eagle stuff, the "frantic boast and foolish word" of that time, should fill us with pride and hope for our people. We are aging rapidly. No one looking on now could think that Congress wanted war unless driven to it to maintain our self-respect.

I joined J. on the House floor, and as we stood on the portico help-lessly wondering how we could get our little car out of the crush of big machines, Attorney General Gregory and Solicitor General John Davis came up, and J. joyfully accepted their offer to take me home in what Representative Billy Kent calls a gov'ment hack. It was a handsome old-time coupé with two heavy elderly horses, and I enjoyed the clump-clump-ing of their hoofs, and at my door, the friendly courtesy of the old darky driver made me feel young again—even more than the pretty speeches of my two cavaliers.

J. had to go on to a luncheon at Congress Hall given for W. J. Bryan and expected him to talk about the war situation, but he said there was "something nearer his heart"—imagine it, today!—and held forth on pro-hibition. J. thinks he is hoping to ride into the presidency on that wave.

February 10

The town remains quiet, no display of flags except now and then from some army officer's house, little spread-eagle talk, and only three extras. Mass meetings for peace, arbitration and common sense are held daily in New York and other cities, but there is no news of them except in the New York *Evening Post*. The Washington *Post* is warlike and full of silly gossip, for instance, that the rumor of Germany's seeking negotiations is concocted by Bryan and Bernstorff in the interest of pacifists.

This afternoon we went to the Ebbitt to hear a major of the Marine Corps make a remarkably interesting talk against compulsory military service. For an officer to talk that way now takes much more than the courage of Julius Caesar.

All who are in sympathy were asked to come to the Union Station to-morrow morning to make a demonstration in force for a party of peace speakers coming from New York, Philadelphia and Baltimore to interview Congress and have a mass meeting at All Souls Church in the evening.

February 11

Stella Callaway and I went to the station and were led into the folly of letting our pictures be taken holding a huge scroll inscribed "War or peace?

Why not try a referendum?" We are none too happy about what our husbands will say when they hear of it or, worse still, see it.

> *The bells of hell go ting-aling-ling*
> *For you, but not for me.*
> *The Angel choirs they sing-aling-ling*
> *That's the goods for me.*
> *Oh, death where is thy sting-aling-ling*
> *Where grave thy victoree?*
> *When the bells of hell go ting-aling-ling*
> *For you but not for me.*

At a dinner at the Solicitor General's, Justice Holmes repeated those
lines in response to a plea of "Do, Mr. Justice. Do give us your favorite
poem" from a fatuous being, like so many in Washington who roll the words
"Mr. Justice" lovingly on the tongue. (I was forced to hold up a funeral
once by a friend who said she must tell me "what a lovely compliment Mr.
Justice ——— had paid me.") At the dinner Justice Holmes sat to Mrs.
Davis' right, and I next to him. He is extraordinarily handsome, clear cut,
humorous, and given to profanity in the old-fashioned aristocratic way that
is never cheap or offensive. A certain Mr. Secretary, opposite us, told in
a large manner how his son (a lad of eighteen in the navy) had "become an
absolute fatalist," and like a fond father he was going into particulars, but
Mr. Justice and I diverted him. Then he told how "the boys down there"—
officers at Hampton Roads, I believe—had sent a long telegram to the
joint Houses saying "Go as far as you please, old Prex. We are behind you."
It was followed, he said, by some verses which he couldn't remember but
they "were full of bad words."

When the Secretary came back from the smoking room he explained
that he had "asked the Justice's permission to leave ahead of him." Later
I heard the Justice express himself forcefully about people who put rules
of etiquette before common sense. He told me that W. J. Bryan did not
exist for him intellectually. He had built theories of government on phrases,
not phrases on theories. Bill James, he said, asked him why he didn't
join the Society for Psychical Research, and he retorted, "Why don't you
investigate the religion of Mohammed? Thousands are ready to die for it,
and yet you might go to its depth and care no more about it than when
you began, and that is the way I feel about psychical matters." He declared
that he wouldn't read a book written as much as twenty-five years ago. His
infinite jest is refreshing after the owlish solemnity of smaller men.

March came in like a lion, but a fluffy white one, with a coat of thick snow, too soft and lovely for the big black headlines of the *Post*—"German Plot to Conquer U.S. with Aid of Japan and Mexico Revealed." J. looked grave and sad over it, and said, "What fools to believe that poor war-wrecked Mexico could be of use to them!" We agreed that if Wilson had thought as much of American lives in Mexico as he now professes to think of them on the high seas the Germans would never have assumed that we were the cowards they think us now. We went to market and the prices looked as if we were already at war. Cabbage 12 cents a pound, onions 13 cents, and potatoes $4 a bushel.

The debate in the House on the President's being permitted to arm merchant ships, conduct a war by himself, and have a blank check for his expenses was very lively. The galleries were full, but compared to 1898 there was *no* excitement. A few speakers tried some warlike flights, but they gradually petered out, and asked to extend their remarks in the Record. That repository serves Congress as Hyde Park Corner serves the people of England—a place where they can ease their minds without boring others. Nearly every short speech began, "We do not want war."

History will record how Congress ended with a successful filibuster in the Senate, and I am not the only one glad the President was not given the power he asked for. The man who lifted the embargo on munitions of war into Mexico and got up in a fit of temper in the night and ordered the attack on Vera Cruz is not to be trusted with firearms.

The "twelve willful men," as he called the dissenting senators, have been excoriated by the press, burned in effigy in some places, and at a meeting of Navy League capitalists in New York, they cried out "Hang them." Will our people ever reawaken to the good old American belief that disagreeing with a President is not "treason"? Stratagems and spoils influence New York, I think. So much money lent to the Allies.

The truly Anglican rector of St. Thomas' Church echoed the President's phrases from the pulpit last Sunday and appeared in an interview insulting to every congressman who differed with him. After hearing from his own lips, over the telephone, that he "wrote every word of it," I said good-by to him and his fashionable sanctuary. He has called me up several times and written some expostulatory notes asking for "a chat," but I have no faith in the efficacy of chatting on differences so vital. I shall have to worship elsewhere or get on without benefit of clergy. I fear it will be the latter. The churches are wobbly; the doctrine of peace on earth doesn't pay in wartime. Dr. Panaretoff, the Bulgarian Minister, said sadly after a service at the Covenant that it seemed more like a recruiting station than a church.

What an unimportant thing an actual calendar date is. The event's the thing. I don't remember at all what day it was when I slipped out to the corridor as usual to get the morning paper and read the headlines saying that Russia had revolted; the Czar signed, with hardly a protest, a definite abdication; the Duma was in power, and the former things had passed away. It seemed the culmination of that far-off divine event toward which the whole *mind* of Russia had been moving for half a century.

How well I remember the stream of revolutionary books that thirty years ago came pouring out of Russia—they had to come out because they were read there at the risk of life and liberty. It seems to me that for some years we read little else, and yet I don't believe many of us thought of them as actually leading the Russians anywhere—except to Siberia—or imagined that conditions would be materially modified in our lifetime. The Russian intelligentsia (the word came into common use then) just seemed to be beating their devoted heads against a stone wall. This seems to prove that if only enough heads are beaten against it, even a stone wall falls at last. I went about my work all day singing "For in thy dark streets shineth the everlasting light—The hopes and fears of all the years are met in thee tonight."

The most amazing thing is how little there was of bloodshed and violence, and the great Orthodox Church is barely mentioned in dispatches. The Czar and his family are imprisoned in a commonplace, businesslike way, giving no opportunity for scenes of spectacular loyalty; the whole thing accomplished with almost German efficiency.

The morning the news came I went in to tell Mother, and it awakened her mind that has been so drowsy lately. She got up at once and dressed as if she had something important to do, and came in to breakfast saying "What a pity Tolstoi couldn't have lived to see it." She recalled his and other Russian books much more vividly than I did. Since then I have had no trouble in entertaining her if only there is news from Russia.

Something tremendous and epochal like this is good for our country just now. It may remind us of the beauty and benefit of a government by the people and for the people which we are inclined to forget while shouting "Stand by the President," as if he were a czar.

Flag waving becomes more frantic every day. Two years ago people were "just crazy about" the tango and the turkey trot, and now the same class has taken up patriotism. Much of the talk is the merest cant, more still the seething of small minds with the unaccustomed excitement of an idea. Worst of all is the inherited, almost conventional obligation to feel that every citizen of a country with which our country is in a dispute is an "enemy" whom you must traduce, abuse and imagine all manner of evil against.

The town is flaming with flags, very large ones generally on the outer walls of the houses of the "yellow rich" up in this fashionable district. They have spent their time and money largely in Europe and are enjoying the discovery of America just at this exciting crisis but are still not aware that it extends two hundred miles west of Newport.

The clergy, alas! are the worst. With very few exceptions they are war mad. According to them, our God has become tribal, a mere Lord of our far-flung battle line. Christ died only for us and the Entente Allies. The churches are bedizened with flags over the doors, in the vestibule, the chancel, and carried in the processional, and unctuous patriots bow as they pass.

J. Hampton Moore of Pennsylvania criticized Dr. McKim of Epiphany for his activities as a lobbyist, and Ernest Smith of St. Thomas—not noted for his affection for McKim heretofore—rushed into print taking the lofty attitude that a congressman has no right to mention a clergyman on the floor of the House. Smith is an Englishman and must be pardoned much. Having once begun to defend the war spirit he becomes more and more bellicose. He has put one flag in the church and now asks in the *Parish News* for "eleven more that have seen service." Can't be happy with less than a round dozen. Strange ornaments for the house of God and Father of *all*—even of the Central Powers.

Sunday, April 1

Everyone, myself included, is so bad tempered. There are as many opinions on the war as there are individuals, and each one maintains that his view is the "righteous" one. No meaner attitude is ever admitted. It was such a lovely morning, the earth appareled in celestial light, the little yellow-green buds making a sunny glow on the elm trees arched over New Hampshire Avenue, so, having no church to go to, I went with J. and Mother to ride. We stopped to pick up Rena, usually the most amiable person in the world, and before we had gone a mile she and J. were quarreling like bad children. Rena insisted that J. was pro-German because he said the British in the Boer War were as cruel as the Germans in Belgium and the war was indefensible. At the House Office Building, waiting for J., we talked to Mrs. Johnson of Kentucky and got deep into war again—spies this time—happily interrupted by J.'s return. Down on the Peninsula with the birds singing, the willows in full green, the river and Virginia hills one soft pastel of rose, blue and green, Rena and I argued so violently that people stared at us as we passed. I was glad to get home about twelve and find a note from Dr. David Starr Jordan saying that he would be up to lunch. His beliefs are just as "righteous" as anyone's, but he maintains them in such a big, humorous, humane way. I asked Mrs. Porter to come over, helped Annie set the table, evolved some flowers for the center and was ready to dress when Dr. Jordan arrived half an hour ahead of time.

When I went in he was sunk into a sofa with a whirl of newspapers all around him, so he didn't try to extricate himself, but just reached up a big paw to me like a friendly St. Bernard, and we went on talking where we had left off last summer. He wouldn't object to doing the conventional thing, but his mind is too full of larger matters for him to think of it. He looks tired. His gray hair doesn't show in front and needs brushing in the back, and his suit isn't pressed anywhere.

He has been east leading the Emergency Peace Committee's work, and amazed us with stories of things never mentioned in the papers, and the utter distortion of facts in those that were mentioned. He was *not* treated discourteously at Yale or Princeton; nothing was thrown at him, and there was no free fight at the Madison Square meeting of 12,000 people. A few hecklers around the door were notified that a recruiting officer was present if they wished to enlist, and they found business elsewhere.

Commenting on leading men he said he was waiting to see if Wilson would place himself on the level of Washington, John Adams and Lincoln or cuddle down in the niche beside Polk and McKinley.

While talking he ate the queerest lunch, two pieces of Virginia ham, some mushrooms and a quantity of salted pecans, ignoring peach pickles, salad, ice cream and coffee, but he never seems to know quite what he is eating.

Mrs. Butler came in full of enthusiasm, so glad to enroll herself in his party, and when he left he said, "I don't know when I've met three such nice women."

Mrs. Butler goes to help at the Emergency rooms tomorrow, and I ought to go, but cannot resist the Capitol when Congress convenes, and Miss Jeannette Rankin, the first Congresswoman, will be sworn in. Members have only one gallery card for these big days, and Rena is to have mine when the President addresses the joint Houses on the state of war.

April 2

Miss Rankin took her seat very prettily, but all other interests were obscured tonight when the President declared before the House and Senate that a state of war existed between us and Germany! I am such a foolish optimist; I never believe such hideous things can happen until I am stunned by the blow.

I did not hear his pronunciamento.

On the way to the Capitol this morning I stopped for a while with the Peace Federation working in a cramped little shop near the Munsey Building. Numbers of young men, women and girls were busy registering names of sympathizers, and handing out white armbands and badges printed large "Keep Out of War." Public opinion has certainly advanced since the Spanish War. A young man wearing such a thing then would have been mobbed.

At J.'s office I met some of the new Texas members; Smith's successor, who referred to himself and Mr. Smith as "him'n'I," not very hopeful; and the other, succeeding Callaway, a dark, slope-shouldered person, discouraging when compared with Callaway's big head and forceful carriage. I hear that the wife of one of them "elocutes."

We walked across the sunny plaza—the squirrels and robins very busy on the new grass—and up the steps of the House. There were many more policemen than usual. It was only eleven o'clock, and admission by card, but the galleries were already so full that I had to sit on the steps of the aisle. Soon Mrs. Clark came, and, finding one of her guests had failed, she took me into her seat. Her guests were Mrs. Mann, her Republican rival, Mrs. Claude Kitchin, wife of the Democratic floor leader, several distinguished strangers, and Mrs. Carrie Chapman Catt. The last-named interested me chiefly because of her late highhanded action in offering the entire Woman Suffrage party, of which she is president, for military service in case of war. She has been called down sharply for it and will probably be dropped from the list of honorary chairmen of the Woman's Peace Party at our next executive session. She is handsome and well dressed but, judging by her expression, is not in the same class spiritually with Jane Addams, Mrs. Post and others. There is more calculation in her eyes, less sweetness. Many kinds of strong women are coming to the front these days, but the bravest are still the tenderest. Jane Addams, Julia Lathrop, Mrs. Louis Post, Lucia Ames Mead, and keen, quizzical, homely Ella Flagg Young are to my mind the first ladies of the land, and all of them lovable, the kind of women you can joke with.

The chief interest of the morning—even exceeding that in the election of a Speaker, as Clark was a foregone conclusion—was the new Congress-woman. Not more than a year ago men would say when arguing against woman suffrage, "Next thing you'll be wanting women in Congress," as if that was the *reductio ad absurdum,* and here she was coming in, escorted by an elderly colleague, looking like a mature bride rather than a strong-minded female, and the men were clapping and cheering in the friendliest way. She wore a well-made dark-blue silk and chiffon suit, with open neck, and wide white crepe collar and cuffs; her skirt was a modest walking length, and she walked well and unself-consciously. Her hair is a commonplace brown and arranged in a rather too spreading pompadour shadowing her face. She carried a bouquet of yellow and purple flowers, given her at the suffrage breakfast.

She didn't look to right or left until she reached her seat, far back on the Republican side, but before she could sit down she was surrounded by men shaking hands with her. I rejoiced to see that she met each one with a big-mouthed, frank smile and shook hands cordially and unaffectedly. It would have been sickening if she had smirked or giggled or been coquet-tish; worse still if she had been masculine and hail-fellowish. She was just a sensible young woman going about her business. When her name was called the House cheered and rose, so that she had to rise and bow twice, which she did with entire self-possession. J. was among the first to speak to her and later volunteered to say that she was not pretty but had an intellectual face and a nice manner.

The etiquette of her position is puzzling. Mrs. Kent and I got our-selves into a tangle of conjecture as to what her legal status would be if she should marry a congressman from another state: could she represent a Montana district, or would she become automatically a citizen of her husband's state?

The galleries were in confusion over the President's arrival. A news-paperwoman whispered to me that he would come in the afternoon instead of the evening; another said we all had to go out and get pink tickets—much virtue in pink!—and then, at the behest of that fountain of wisdom and cheap mystery "a Secret Service man," they said all galleries were to be cleared. Still roll call voting for House officers went on and drearily on; everyone was tired and the air heavy with the odor of surreptitious ham sandwiches. At five o'clock there was a sudden and complete exodus from the Executive and Diplomatic galleries, so we, the commonality, knew nothing special was forthcoming, and we went too. The plaza was full of pacifists, police, sightseers, and a little later a troop of cavalry to guard the President when he should arrive.

April 3

Rena and Mrs. Porter went back at seven last night for the joint session and reported a great crowd in the House, the Cabinet ladies in evening dress as if for a gala occasion, and a Congress earnest and attentive but not "wildly enthusiastic," as the *Post* reports today.

J. took Mrs. Butler, Mary Lloyd Andrews and me to the mass meeting for peace in that awful old barn Convention Hall. It was fine to hear men speak who were inspired by a great moral purpose and with no material or political gain in view. Dr. Jordan spoke without a suggestion of bitterness and made no reference to the mob that broke up his meeting in Baltimore the night before, led, shameful to say, by professors of Johns Hopkins and students of that and other Baltimore educational institutions. I asked him if it was true that John Latane led the mob, and he said in his big, kind way, "The papers said so, but I can't believe it. Why, John Latane is a *gentleman* and we are both *teachers*."

The "state of war" message was brought in and read from the platform to a depressing accompaniment of high wind shrieking through the ventilators and rattling the tin roof. When we came out the place was surrounded by soldiers to prevent a repetition of the disgraceful scenes in Baltimore.

When poor old Chaplain Couden began his prayer at the opening of Congress yesterday, we all felt serious and listened reverently until he dropped into politics. When he said, "O Lord, diplomacy has failed us," I said *sotto voce* to Mrs. Clark that I didn't remember the Lord's ever advising us to put our trust in it. Then we both laughed and missed the rest of the argument. I am constantly realizing the wisdom of Congress in employing blind chaplains who can't see how many are not present or not listening.

This morning there was an advertisement in the *Post* for a gold cigarette case lost by Mrs. Augustus P. Gardner in the gallery of the House yesterday. She is Senator Lodge's daughter, a leading antisuffragist, a violent antipacifist, and an incessant smoker. I believe I would rather have a man's right to vote than his privilege of smoking.

April 15

As usual when there is the most to tell there is the least time in which to tell it, so my notes on the war vote must be very sketchy. I was not present when the actual vote was taken. Mother was not well enough for me to leave, but I knew J. was going to vote in the affirmative. I had not asked him not to; perhaps I should have done it to ease my own conscience, but it would have been a departure from our usual custom and it would have pained him to refuse me. He had said for some time that voting for or against the war was unimportant; the war was an accomplished fact, the President had plunged us into it long ago, and the only thing we could do now was to work to finish it as decently and promptly as possible. Voting against it was a fine gesture but left a member helpless to do any good afterwards. But my antiwar sisters gave me some evil moments during the next few days. A few of the unmarried ones held me personally responsible for J.'s vote, not knowing, dear things, that husbands sometimes have opinions of their own with which a wise wife intermeddleth not. Emily Green Balch got so bitter in her expression of disappointment about J. that it would have been embarrassing if dear old Dr. Jordan, whose right hand always carries gentle peace, had not joined in with, "I was sorry, too, that Slayden didn't vote with us, but he could not afford to lose all his usefulness in Congress."

J. says the stories of Miss Rankin's weeping and hysterics when she cast her vote are almost entirely apocryphal. He was quite near her and spoke to her immediately afterwards—he likes her very much. He said there was a sob in her voice—there were many men quite as much moved—but she made none of the heroic or sentimental speeches attributed to her. She simply said, "I love my country, but I cannot vote for war; I vote *No.*" It took a lot of courage and sincerity for her to vote as she did. Her brother and many political friends had been arguing with her for hours to make her vote the other way.

May 5

"Cinco de Mayo!" I wonder what form poor Mexico's madness is taking today. Her national holidays are always nervous times, making opportunities for mob outbreaks. Last week they inaugurated that old whiskerando, Carranza, and celebrated with a battle of flowers, but bullets will be next. Miss Wheeler writes me that our war prices have so increased the cost of living in Mexico that the people are hungrier than ever and ready for any violence.

Our excitement takes every form, but the latest is made logical by the government's frantic extravagance in the cause of war. Economy has become a raging fashion, and the richer you are the more you parade your thrift. We are invited almost daily to meetings at the biggest and most expensive hotels, with names of the biggest and most expensive women engraved on the cards, to discuss city gardening, conservation of food and household economics. Of course you are expected to join a club, send out more engraved cards to a still larger list of the humble poor and get the ball rolling by the time the expensive ladies go to their cottages in Newport and Lenox.

Josephus of the navy says in his newspaper that Southern people ought to eat corn bread because we know how, and the flour can be sent to Europe. Mrs. Butler observes that it is an excellent time for the Europeans to learn how, and she will eat what she pleases.

Mrs. Charles Hamlin, whose house is one of the most elegant and interesting in town, was led into publishing the menu of a "simple little three-course dinner" to show the rest of us how it could be done without loss of self-respect. The fact that it was given to the Secretary of State was supposed to make it especially daring and impressive. The menu as published was: Cream of oyster soup, filet of beef, fresh asparagus, fresh peas, fresh mushrooms, ice cream and fresh strawberries.

Mrs. Charles Francis Adams told me that she was shown the menu before the dinner came off and suggested that champagne was rather an expensive wine for a "simple dinner," so the wine, whatever it was, was not mentioned.

Dr. Julia Harrison, a scientific housekeeper, very watchful of markets and prices, sends me the following estimate of actual cost of food for the company of eighteen:

Creamed oysters	2.80
Fresh peas	7.00
Mushrooms	2.50
Asparagus	5.25
Filet of beef (not cold storage)	22.50
Cream in form	10.00
Cakes	2.40
Strawberries	2.75
Coffee, bread, and butter ⎫ Flowers and relishes ⎭	15.00
	70.20

Mrs. Porter tells me of a "very simple and informal luncheon" for twenty that she went to. There were three courses, all bad, and six men in livery between the front door and the drawing room.

May 12

At the presentation of the Red Cross building this afternoon Mrs. Porter and I had seats near the stage on the middle aisle, an excellent place to hear and see. There was a great array of flags, some held by "men-at-arms," a recent affectation. In the center of the stage were Taft and Wilson "side by each," Mrs. Wilson, looking less amiable than I ever saw her, the Spanish Ambassador, Josephus and the sweetly named Percy Silver—a fair young priest with a Raphael face, a voice like a fog horn, his speech the fog. There were many other worthies, J. among them, on the stage, but what gripped my interest was the President's speech. He said, "We have gone into this war with no special grievance of our own." Then why in the name of heaven go into it? Are we like an Irishman at a fair, just hunting a fight? He also said, "We are a united country and will never be troubled again by sectional or racial divisions"—a happy fiction and significant in view of the fact that Baker (said to be in favor of race equality) is opposed to separating negroes and whites in the army.

It was altogether the glummest performance, not a ray of real feeling throughout. Not even Taft could smile, and Wilson was the "grim Geneva minister" more than ever. Of course he is having an awful time, his responsibilities must be overwhelming, but if he met them with a little more heart and human sympathy—as Lincoln did, for instance—it would help him and the whole country. I read today of a man in the West being imprisoned for calling him a jellyfish. If he had said a starfish, hard, colorless, dry, and pointing all ways at once, it would have been nearer the truth.

We stayed to see him review the Red Cross workers. Mrs. Kent came up and gave me a sudden little squeeze with one arm around my shoulders —I turned impulsively to look at her, and her face was white and haggard. We watched together the jaunty parade of self-satisfied, fat-and-forty women in white with white caps, white with blue veils; gray with white, khaki, etc., with the red cross always cunningly disposed to be conspicuous and becoming. Mrs. Porter and Mrs. Kent had tears streaming down their cheeks. I didn't feel like weeping; I was just angry and contemptuous. No doubt many of the marchers are sincere, but I saw so many that I know are by no means given to all good works and love the limelight. It was so shallow. If they wanted to help why didn't they do it by trying to prevent the war, to keep down war talk, to "seek peace and ensue it"? When the kitchen division came by with a handsome young woman in white *posed* with one white arm over the black boiler, I cried too. I don't know why, unless in sheer rage at such misrepresentation. Is war a matter of white arms and freak draperies? Would any of them dare to pose a tableau of the real thing—filth, blood, human agony? Of course not, that is for the fighters to discover.

Another one of those preposterous appeals has come in, this time from the "Patriotic Economy League" urging me to simplify my manner of life to the end that we may have more money to give where money is needed, etc., and recommending "economy and simplicity in dress and a curtailment of purely social activities." They also ask me to sign three pledges to that effect, "for the duration of the war." The names of some of those sponsoring and signing this appeal are of women who, I have no doubt, spend more in a month than J.'s entire salary—Mrs. Medill McCormick, Mrs. William Corcoran Eustis, Mrs. Peter Goelet Genny, etc., etc.

I don't believe in pledges and would feel silly to see my name published in connection with these plutocrats, so I didn't go to the meeting. Of course it may be desirable for them to let their light so shine that other women may see their good works, but I can't imagine myself in such an arrogant role. Someone recalling J.'s magnificent salary of $7,500 a year might be moved to laughter.

June 4

I took Mother down to Amelia County and came back to Richmond for a little visit. The town obviously progresses commercially, and socially too, no doubt, in some circles, but apparently not at all among such rock-ribbed aristocrats as Lightfoots and Maurys. Nan invited a party of them to see me, an afternoon tea, and it might have been in Cranford. They often referred to "the war," but they meant the Civil War, and there was a kind of indignant hush when women suffrage threatened to intrude itself.

They told me family gossip (not scandal) more than fifty years old. Cousin Belle, in the softest black crepe and the creamiest lace ruffles, blushed like a girl when asked to tell what Henry James wrote about "the little lady in the Confederate Museum," but she repeated it verbatim. It was plainly one of the events of her chaste existence, and she is so *sui generis* that Henry James, of all people, couldn't have failed to see that she was "one of the three things best worth seeing in Richmond."

They shook their heads and would not discuss a current rumor that Dr. Russell Bowie, rector of St. Paul's, was not entirely sound on the Bible account of the Creation. His opinion of Adam and Eve doesn't concern me, but my hungry soul was fed by his simple morning service with no flags obscuring the chancel.

June 5

Registration Day, and thousands of battered, tottering old Confederate soldiers are here attending what will be for many of them their last reunion. The old warrior and the new; tonight over all the country ten million young men are signed up as soldiers, thousands still infants in the eyes of the law in all civil rights *conscripted* to be sent overseas to fight "that democracy may live," according to the President. Meantime England holds India, France, Algeria, Italy, Tripoli, and we the Philippines, Santo Domingo, and Haiti, not by "the consent of the governed"—the foundation of democracy—and without the least intention of surrendering them for all the pretty talk the warring nations are doing. The Russian Socialists demanding an end of secret treaties and a frank statement of the end of the war and the terms of peace seem to me about the most honest people involved in the melee.

Later

Our troubles and sorrows with the old Confederates began when we left Richmond on a train four hours late, crowded with veterans from Florida, Georgia and the Carolinas. They were tired and dirty, but all merry and full of old wartime jokes. Sometimes I wonder if war doesn't arrest the mental development of the average soldier. Throughout this heartbreaking week, entertaining, feeding, looking after the old men, nothing has impressed me so much as their childishness. Not greenness, like the one who enjoyed seeing the fountain at Union Station because he had "never seen one o' them artesian wells befo'," but just the simplicity of undeveloped children. The management has been unspeakably bad, inadequate shelter from the heavy rain, poor food and utter disorder. Many have been taken to hospitals, but I haven't heard a complaint. It isn't unreasonable to think in these days when we all talk psychology that three or four years of the horror and hardship of war might so dull the sensibilities of simple countrymen that the nerves would never react to anything less than the roar of cannons. General Miles said to me once that our Civil War was the decentest war ever fought; a pastoral affair, comparatively. If it affected the minds of the common soldiers to this extent, what must we look forward to for the millions of men who survive these years of hell, this combination of science and savagery in Europe?

June 14

Flag Day, and about noon we had one of the most awful storms I ever saw. It was too dark to read or sew. The wind didn't rave or lash, or do any of the describable things, but blew a steady roaring current like a blast furnace. The hail was deafening, and the rain a real flood. Annie, my cook, was frightened, so I had her come in my room, and when not too appalled by the lightning we stood by the window watching the water rise in the street. She was inclined to talk religion, as darkies do when uneasy, and surprised me with her plain reasoning when she asked how the Kaiser and others could believe in God and do as they were doing.

Yesterday evening J. and I went to see *Ingomar the Barbarian* played at the new Sylvan Theatre, and I noticed a temporary platform near the monument where the Foreordained was to speak today and tell the slightly fretful public why we are at war. At three o'clock it was still raining, and there must have been floods of water on the ground, but it shows the spirit of the people that thousands assembled and listened closely. I read the speech in the extra but can't say yet that I am sure what the war is about. It is so typical of us easygoing Americans that after war is declared, ten millions of men mobilized, and the Liberty Loan floated by Mr. McAdoo through the most approved patent medicine advertising methods, we are beginning to ask rather angrily what it is all about.

Secretary Houston says, "The war is the result of a combination of circumstances."

"O wise young judge!" who could dispute it? It explains not only the war but the universe.

June 16

Unseemly things are happening in the churches in the name of patriotism. The fashionable Church of the Covenant leads all the rest. The pastor, Mr. Wood, preached such an impassioned sermon on the "righteousness" of buying Liberty Bonds that Mr. Charles Henry Butler, a pillar of the church and the war, sprang from his seat and called out "I will buy five hundred dollars' worth. Who will be next?" A rich sister responded. It was about to become a stock exchange when Judge Peelle suggested "passing a hat or basket so that those making smaller purchases might not be embarrassed," and the hat was passed until Mr. McFarland urged the closing of the meeting with a prayer of thanksgiving.

After service there was lunch in the basement for twenty-five young men from Fort Myer and as many young women to entertain them, and there was such singing of ragtime that the neighbors had to close their windows. Mr. Wood from the pulpit urged the girls to go to the camps and "make it pleasant for the boys. It doesn't matter whether you know them or not." And the girls from that and other patriotic circles are doing it so enthusiastically as to be subjects of indignation to the mothers of the boys.

Senator Bailey's wife told me that while she was visiting Joseph, sitting outside in her machine, she saw a khaki-clad young woman come out of a tent, and Joseph said, "What business has that girl in there, I wonder? Those fellows are all undressed." Mrs. B. said severely that she didn't want her boy cheered up that way.

The young women with automobiles carry delicacies to the men guarding bridges in the woods and on lonely roads and stay to lunch with them. My respect for conventionalities is not exactly early Victorian, but this sort of thing seems to me late Roman.

Dr. and Mrs. Wallace Radcliffe are back from the great Presbyterian Assembly at Dallas, and she tells me that, next to the religious fervor, admiration, almost adoration, of Wilson was the dominant note of the meeting. She and the doctor share the view of, I think I may say, a majority of Washington people about the President, and she said they had to retreat to their rooms sometimes to relax their features after too long a strain of gravity when he was being lauded, applauded and given thanks for. His Christian graces became almost otherworldly, his Sabbaths had no end, according to the anecdotes told about him. One was that lately when some grave international question was put forward a gentleman who was "just strolling about the White House" opened a door and found the President and Lansing "on their knees praying for divine guidance."

These Presbyterian stories remind me that Louis Post told me that atheism was the vestibule through which he passed from Presbyterianism to Christianity.

June 28

Missions or commissions, as they are variously called, from our numerous allies have become so common that we no longer stand on the street corners to catch a glimpse of their uniforms as we did for the first one, good old Joffre. The day he arrived the schoolchildren were given a holiday and the gay peacefulness of the crowded streets must have been refreshing to the war-worn old man. A few days later when he made his formal visit to the War College we drove to the Barracks and saw a flash of blue uniforms and khaki in three rapidly driven machines, and had a very good look at Joffre, so exactly like his newspaper pictures that it was almost disappointing.

The French flag rolled grandly from the south front of the beautiful Henry White house on Crescent Place and was kept there to give the impression that the mission was still in residence until the cable told of the safe arrival of Joffre in France. I hope his enemies were fooled as I was.

In these days when America and England are gushing over one another one hears nothing but rapture over Mr. Balfour—his "beautiful English voice," his "gracious manner," etc. All true, no doubt, but I didn't like him. He is "foxy." His long, lank, slouching figure recalled so strongly Kaulbach's illustrations of "Reineke Fuchs" that I felt as if the stolen chicken were trailing behind him. All the lines of him were drooping except his mouth, where there lingered a shadow of the usual British sneer at all things American, although somewhat chastened by their present desperate need of our help. His trousers drooped because they didn't fit, each corner of his long-tailed coat seemed to have a weight in it, his narrow string tie was limp, and his turned-down collar so low that he might have worn a locket.

July 27

The step from the sublime to the ridiculous is an everyday occurrence. The latest instance is the $6 billion war fund and Mr. Hoover's suggestions of economies to offset it.

When the President summoned Mr. Hoover to come and save his country as food dictator, he came as the conqueror comes. We all stood on tiptoe waiting for Congress to give him authority to announce his system of food conservation which was to revolutionize our housekeeping and make a helpful patriot of every housewife in America—Congress was reviled, because by the law's delay we were going on in wasteful ignorance. At last Mr. Hoover's sense of duty overcame him. He would not wait for authority; he would divulge his system at once, and lo! the mountain brought forth a mouse. We were solemnly admonished to eat more fruit and vegetables and less meat, to use stale bread for toast and sour milk for cooking, and "not to take the fourth meal"—as if any American west or south of the afternoon tea belt ever did take a fourth meal! There was much of "meatless and wheatless days," of not buttering your potatoes in the kitchen, and cutting your bread at the table. For pledging ourselves on cards to do all these things, we can, by sending 10 cents, get a card with the American shield in a wreath of wheat to hang in our windows and show the neighbors that we are patriots; 5 cents will get a button for our lapels, and 85 cents an entire costume to wear while we conserve. I am going to spend my dollar on food and go on wearing my blue apron.

The papers are indulging in such ribald wit as "Use quill pens and save steel for the Allies," "Save your combings to make mattresses for the Serbians," and "Use old envelopes for sanitary drinking cups."

September 7

Yesterday Congress voted eleven billions to carry on the war, to kill the bravest and best young men of the race, while scientists say that one billion wisely expended would eradicate tuberculosis from the earth.

The Philippine Commissioner and Mrs. De Veyra and Mr. and Mrs. Louis Post dined with us last night. Mrs. Post and I counted up the poets alone (beginning with Rizal, the Filipino poet-patriot executed by the U. S. government as a "rebel" against our divine right of conquest) sacrificed to war in the last twenty years—Rupert Brooke, Alan Seeger, Francis Ledwidge. Think of the loss to the spiritual joy of the world, and for what? Mrs. De Veyra opened my provincial eyes. I had rather dreaded her and felt so silly afterwards. She looks decidely Chinese and must be descended from them, though she claims to be pure Filipino. This is her very first excursion from the islands, but she would have been a graceful and interesting addition to a dinner company anywhere. She was prettily dressed, her English was impeccable, and she talked with knowledge and vivacity on politics, especially, as well as books, Spanish and English, religion, the woman's movement and domestic science. She told a quick and good story and showed a keen and humorous sense of the prejudice she met here because of her race. She was not resentful, but evidently means to safeguard her dignity. De Veyra spoke so little English that J. had to take care of him almost entirely, but he said he was intelligent and a gentleman.

Austin, Texas, September 22

I have great luck in being here for dramatic occasions. Last fall we saw the installation of the president of the university, which the Governor refused to attend, and today we are seeing the impeachment of that same governor for unlawful acts of several kinds but chiefly connected with the university.

The quality of Governor James Ferguson is summed up in his declaration that the people are "just hog wild about higher education." He proves his lack of sympathy with it in many ways. I went with Mrs. Vinson, wife of the president of the university, a lovely woman, to see both ceremonies.

The Senate Chamber, when we went into the gallery facing the Speaker, was full of shaded morning sunshine and packed with people in light summer clothes. The floor was such a confusion of colors, form and motion that it was hard to believe it the meeting of a legislative body, much less one assembled for the most solemn crisis the state has ever suffered. The American flag back of the Speaker's chair with two large Texas flags draped roughly on either side made the one definite point of color. Around the room the row of very bad, dull-colored portraits of the early fathers seemed like so many policemen grimly regarding the tumult without trying to stop it. One of them wears full white trousers like a pirate of the Spanish Main, and the red has faded from the patrician face of Jeff Davis till he looks as if he were nauseated. A portrait of Sam Houston, undressed and clutching anxiously at a slippery toga, has gotten as far in its demotion as the rear wall of the press gallery, so near the door that I hope he will soon escape to the bathroom.

Under the galleries there were men, women, and children from six months up. A space of green carpet surrounded the brown chairs and desks of the Senate proper. The tables were littered with papers, women's hats and parasols, and many of the chairs were occupied by women and children. Not a few of the men had their feet on the tables. Two Ferguson supporters were smoking cigars. By each table was a large brown spittoon constantly being more or less carefully aimed at. There was a long table, lengthwise of the aisle in front of the Speaker's chair, and under the forward end of it a big zinc washtub for what purpose I cannot divine. There doesn't seem even a chance of its holding whitewash for Ferguson.

Senator Dean, the presiding officer, a pleasant-looking man in a gray suit, fidgeted in his chair, and chairs on either side of him were generally occupied by very young pages who sat on the back of their necks and threw their legs first over one chair arm and then the other. A respectable-looking old negro sprawled on the steps to the left and a young one in shirt sleeves on the right. Between the Speaker's platform and the right and left lobby doors men and boys sat on the floor, cross-legged, some squatting cowboy fashion, or with backs against the oak wainscoting and feet straight out.

The gallery reserved for negroes was quite full, many of the occupants asleep. Ferguson is very popular with them. He represents the power that keeps saloons open and is extraordinarily generous with pardons.

The course of the trial and its results will be matters of history. I am only recording the scene to refer to someday for purposes of comparison when this splendid empire of Texas has awakened to the dignity of keeping its public places clean and conducting its ceremonies decently and in order.[2]

Crane, attorney for the prosecution, turned a nice phrase in his closing argument. He said that the Governor knew the law, but in obeying it "wished to have a discretion commensurate with his imagination."

San Antonio, October 5

The drought is depressing, everything so ugly, no flowers, the trees almost leafless, early as it is.

Houston Street and the principal plazas are just moving columns of men in khaki, tired, bored, homesick, dusty. It only makes one more sorry for them to see how sober and patient they are. I almost wish they would be riotous, but they never are, and I have never seen a drunken one.

Some friends took me motoring through Camp Travis and I stayed awake in a horror of nerves all night. It was like the circles of hell, not the good old picturesque fire and brimstone place, but that deeper damnation where every finer instinct of the soul, the love of beauty, order, cleanliness, is eternally denied. As far as we could see were straight lines of two-story frame houses exactly alike, unpainted, and in every street swarming men marching, drilling, digging, hammering, to the harsh rattle of auto trucks, shrill whistles, and shouting, swearing foremen. Through and over it all the thick gray dust carried by a roaring north wind shut off even a glimpse of blue sky, not even that to prove that God's in His heaven. I think back to the preparedness days when Wood and Roosevelt shouted of the need of military training to "harden" our young men and "the splendid qualities developed by camp life," and this is it! Hardened they would have to be or they would "curse God and die."

Next to the press and the preachers, society is getting the most solid satisfaction out of the war. The little groups of foreign officers, observers, teachers, and the like are invaluable to build a tea around or for a pièce de résistance at dinner. The other day I went to a pretty tea at a pretty house to meet a young Frenchman. We waited and waited for a glimpse of his "horizon blue"—I mention his uniform because the women seemed more

[2] Ferguson was found guilty and removed from office.

interested in that than in the individual. At last the telephone rang and a message came from him. He was on his way, far out on the Fredericksburg Road, with a punctured tire. He couldn't possibly get to the tea, his grief was poignant. The company was solaced to some extent with very good refreshments, and on the way home I met friends who had been having a glorious time with the young officer at the Country Club, quite in the other direction from the Fredericksburg Road. What a multitude of sins are covered by punctured tires these days!

November 24

We have been keeping democracy alive the last few days by entertaining Miss Margaret Wilson with more pomp and circumstance than is usually shown to a princess of the blood royal in countries still sitting in the darkness of monarchy. Miss Wilson is on a concert tour for the War Relief Fund, and I think more money was spent entertaining her than was taken in at the crowded concert. Five rooms were reserved for her at the St. Anthony, a private dining room, etc. The merchants were asked to decorate the streets, and the schoolchildren were to be paraded for her inspection.

The Ladies' Luncheon Club had to limit its guests to three hundred. General Ruckman was to have a huge reception for her at the post and the chairman of the entertainment committee a dinner at the Country Club— all agreed to in writing beforehand by Miss W.'s secretary.

But who can count upon the caprices of a prima donna who is also a President's daughter? There were tears and bitter recriminations when Miss Wilson repudiated the whole program and spent the day visiting curio stores, and riding about in *Republican* automobiles, and calling on Miss B., a Republican, who has "not even bought a ticket for the concert."

The arrangement for the concert was most impressive and colorful. The stage had a background of huge flags hung smoothly straight up and down giving the effect of columns, and other flags drawn aside like curtains. Each box was draped with the colors, and filled with women draped like Venus rising from the foam. As the curtain went up two "heralds" with bugles strode down the right and left aisles blowing madly, and stepping up on either side of the stage, blew some sort of royal salute as Miss Wilson entered.

Seated in a row at the back of the stage were four French officers— such sad, tired-looking men—four British, and four Americans with palms tickling their necks if they leaned back. They led the applause through a program of twenty songs, and rose and stood at attention when Miss Wilson went or came. I had gooseflesh when I thought how they were laughing or raging at our crass provincialism in putting them in such a position.

The entertainment committee got a crumb of comfort from an interview Miss W. gave to the *Express* before she left. She praised the beautiful suite of rooms and wealth of flowers provided for her and said she could think of no sweeter place to spend a honeymoon.

I asked J. if he didn't think that appointing two major generals as military escorts for an unmarried woman without official rank was a solecism, and he retorted that it is "darned foolishness" which is "easier to spell than solecism."

November 26

After so much of the pomps and vanities a visit from old Captain Sansom, pioneer, Indian fighter, Texas Ranger, and soldier of the Civil War (Federal), was like a return to pork and beans after a prolonged season of olive sandwiches. He is 86 and so feeble that when he had to go I couldn't let him cross the plaza with the wild and whirling cars all alone, so I went with him. We walked around the front of the Alamo, and at every corner he stopped to tell me of some battle long ago that he had taken part in. He is a little wandering but I think he said it was on Alamo Plaza that Chief Barefoot's arrow took off a piece of his rifle butt at the same moment that his rifle ball struck Barefoot's heart. He came to San Antonio first in 1846 as bugler for General Tom Green with a horn that General G. had had a tinner make for him.

He stopped and looked over the roaring plaza, and said, "But I'm mighty lonesome now. I never see any of the boys I used to run with, and I've suffered from these wars I've been in." I expressed some sympathy, and he said, "No, I never had a serious wound, but war is murder; war is murder, nothing else, and it is for you women to stop it." He believes in woman suffrage because his mother, his wife and his daughter were all "better and smarter than their husbands."

I have done a little Red Cross work, but can't put my heart in it. There is so much, or maybe I should say there *seems* so much affectation, waste and sentimentality about it. One morning six of us able-bodied women spent three hours ripping little red crosses from the fronts of coarse yellow cotton nightshirts and sewing them on the pockets six inches away. Then I helped another woman fold them with great care so that the crosses showed and was told that they were now *ready for the laundry*.

Washington, December 15

Sometimes we almost forget the horrors in contemplating the absurdities of war.

Yesterday Mrs. Porter, because of the importunity of friends, went to a fashionable Red Cross resort on Connecticut Avenue and helped to fill little muslin baby socks with 3 dates, 2 walnuts, 1 ginger snap, 6 peanuts, and some popcorn. Once she put in 7 peanuts, and the manager rebuked her. Twenty thousand of them were to be sent to make a happy Christmas for enlisted men in camp.

Sums beyond the dreams of avarice are being spent to house and feed the enlisted man; he is clothed and given $30 per month—more, I believe, than any other soldier in the world receives. He is often a college graduate and frequently a man of ample means. I saw him often in San Antonio ordering his meals at the best hotels with epicurean care, and I am thinking how his soul will respond to that gift of a muslin sock and six peanuts. Commerce is seriously hampered by difficulties of transportation; coal is so scarce in some sections that people are freezing, and today's paper reports that nearly 400,000 children in New York are suffering seriously from undernourishment caused by war prices for food, and yet the trains are to be burdened with this trash. Of course "the fool women" will be blamed, and they do deserve some of it, but men have charge of the transportation.

Jane Addams here at dinner with us the other night told, at Harriet Thomas' suggestion, a story she had used recently in Chicago. Jane A. shrinks visibly from the excessive expressions of admiration and affection to which she is subjected, and recently she was introduced to an audience with a eulogy so overpowering that she was compelled to notice it. She said it reminded her of the funeral of one of her humble settlement people. The deceased was an Irishman noted for his bibulous habits, his profanity and other things not tolerated even in his class, but the young divine who preached the funeral sermon described him as a model father and husband, sober and thrifty, and finally told of how he never used bad language; whereupon an old woman leaned over to her son and said, "Hist, Jimmy, is there another corpse in the church?"

Another story was about Vice-President Jim Sherman's funeral. Taft and Roosevelt were both present, and when the service ended the people in charge of the ceremony could not decide who ought to go out first, the dead Vice-President or the President, and while they were debating Teddy hissed through his teeth so everyone could hear, "There seems to be precedence even between corpses."

If I permitted myself to gush I would probably be one of the worst about Jane Addams, but she is so big and sane and full of fun that anything like face-to-face flattery would die on my lips. I would know she was laughing at me.

The three days spent in Philadelphia at the meeting of the Woman's Peace party was a restful spiritual experience. Coming direct from San Antonio and Washington, my ears weary with the sounding brass of men and tinkling cymbals of women talking "patriotism" which they thought could be expressed only in military terms, our quiet meeting was like a poultice to heal the blows of sound. I didn't know till we had been there thirty-six hours that we were being "shadowed," that our hotel and the sweet old Quaker Meetinghouse had extra police guards to save us from a possible mob. Someone mentioned it, and we laughed and went on with what the War Department considers our privy conspiracy and rebellion.

Early the first morning I was there I went over to Wanamaker's for some trifle, and a pretty little shop girl in a sort of *Fille du Régiment* costume at the door handed me a booklet; "For the singing," she said. It contained a number of Christmas hymns and carols. Just then the splendid organ rolled out the opening chords of "It Came Upon the Midnight Clear." It was a beautiful thing to see and hear. Everyone, customers, clerks, janitors, pages, stopped and sang or listened. As high up as we could see, people leaned on the white balustrades of each story and sang. How much better the merchant Wanamaker understands the human heart than the preachers do.

Our executive committee met in Jane Addams' bedroom, just like a lot of elderly schoolgirls sitting on the bed and the trunk, and she with her feet wrapped up in a sweater to keep off the draft from a window we had to keep open, it was so close. We didn't seem the dangerous traitors the Military Intelligence Office accuses us of being. There was no "Madam President," no "Robert's Rules"; we just talked things over, sometimes laughing heartily at our poverty and at the whips and scorns directed at us by the subsidized press and the misinformed public.

The conferences were held in the old Quaker Meetinghouse around the corner from the Adelphia so I didn't get lost, as J., knowing my weakness, prophesied that I would when he let me come over here all alone.

The Friends, real ones they seemed, met us with the warmest, simplest hospitality. Jane Addams presided, and the meeting was opened with silent prayer, enlivened by the shouts of children at a school next door.

There were excellent talks by Jane A., of course, Mrs. Post, that stormy petrel Crystal Eastman, and several of the Quaker women. When it came my turn to report as chairman of the legislative committee, in the language of my childhood, I was "good 'n' scared," but to my amazement it "took," with the Quakers especially, several of whom asked me for a copy as if it were a real speech. I think the part they liked was a little peroration which I had hastily scribbled the night before:

For months I have been in an atmosphere and physical environment of such rampant militarism that it almost drove the hope of peace from my heart. To people enjoying the *profits* of great military camps the talk of peace is a stumblingblock, to those reveling in the excitement it is foolishness. To have called myself a pacifist would have convinced them that I wished to snatch the laurels from the brows of Guy Fawkes and Benedict Arnold.

So it is peculiarly pleasant to find myself here with sympathetic people in the Friends Meetinghouse, the abode of ancient peace, with the noise of the earthquake, the fire and the tempest shut out so that I can once more hear the still, small voice of God.

December 30

Early this morning good old General Anson Mills telephoned to ask us to lunch. The mercury is about zero and there is a horrid skim of ice on the ground, but the poor old man is so lonely since his wife's death that I couldn't refuse him. He said, "Miles is here too and wants to see you."

Bessie Pride's good Confederate nose took an added tilt as she lay back on her pillows (she is ill with a cold) when I told her where we were going. She said, "You all may enjoy sitting at the table with General Miles, but *I* wouldn't." "Because he put shackles on Jeff Davis?" I asked. *"Certainly,"* she answered, and sneezed with contempt.

We walked over to Dupont Circle, and it was sad to find the house so stiff and servant-kept, but the two old gentlemen were fairly snug in the study filled with General Mills's Indian trophies, books, and such queer pictures, guns, typewriters, and chairs much the worse for wear. At lunch I took the head of the table, and we had the funniest meal—a mild breakfast cereal, some muttonchops, peas, potatoes, and corn bread, followed by honey on the same plate. General Miles took several cups of tea with sugar and cream. General Mills drank buttermilk with sugar in it. It seemed like a meal at a home for aged gentlewomen rather than for two of the most noted old frontier warriors and Indian fighters of our time. Neither of them smokes, so they quite forgot to offer a cigar to J., who looked unhappy during the long session in the study after lunch, but we had some good talk.

Miles has a delightful voice and is a more than usually graceful talker with some quaint, old-fashioned pronunciations in places, like "men*ace*." He said the President missed the greatest opportunity that had come to a man in a thousand years by failing to demand a conference of neutral powers immediately after the sinking of the *Lusitania*. The Kaiser, he said, would have welcomed the opportunity to make peace at a time when he could have proved himself the greatest war lord the world had ever seen.

He told a funny story imitating very cleverly an Englishman who described Roosevelt as a combination of St. Paul and St. Vitus. He expressed himself as a strong pacifist, thought disarmament should follow the war, and said 50,000 men was army enough for this country, or even fewer if the other countries would agree on a basis of representation, so many soldiers to every one or two thousand citizens. He seemed sincere and sweet natured, not at all the peacocky old militarist I have thought him sometimes when in his panoply of war.

They had much to ask about Mr. House, the "man of mystery" who so often appears to direct the President's policies, and were amused when we told them how much more Mr. H. was heard of up here than he had ever been on his native heath. His publicity agent tells things of him in New York that would arouse Homeric laughter in Texas.

General Mills also is a serious pacifist; his plan is to accomplish peace by creating certain seas and straits free to all craft but fighting ships and making certain parts of the earth neutral zones, ideas involving more geography than I can comprehend. He tells me often that he intends to leave $10,000 in some form to the cause of world peace, and I try to hint gracefully to him to make it $100,000, which he could so easily do. But the old man lived so long in the school of adversity that he never realizes his vast fortune. He bases his belief in the ultimate abolition of war on the disappearance of the duel, which used to be held as sacred in personal affairs of honor as war is now in national.

It was a pleasant day, even including the tea and cereal, and an amusing contrast to the dinner we went to at good old Judge Howry's last night.

The Judge's young wife, who, after all, is not young enough to justify the pose, is a highflier. She gave us a fairly good dinner in a dining room the temperature of a potato cellar, the guests awkwardly seated—J. and I were together—and a wall of flowers down the middle of the table so you could only guess at the people across from you. Later we sat around a welcome open fire in the "back parlor," with Nottingham lace curtains, as befits the name, and discussed bridge. The lady averred that it was "the *only* way to get acquainted with *really* nice people." J. and I don't play, so like Br'er Fox we "laid low." She said Mrs. Leiter and Mrs. McLean took lessons at $25 a lesson and named several friends who made quite a good deal of money playing for stakes—from $2.50 to $5, *never* less. She and I did not smoke, but the other women were wreathed in it. One of them, *notoriously* rich, offered to buy the lovely Mexican shawl I was wearing that Jennie Wheeler gave me last summer. Poor J. was so bored, but I sat and enjoyed the contemplation of a society to which we are rarely admitted. The dear submerged old Judge was as ill at ease as such a well-bred man could be. No doubt he had asked for us—friends of his better days—to be invited, and she couldn't imagine why.

The following verses lend themselves to endless variations and are getting as tiresome as a popular song:

> *My Tuesdays are meatless,*
> *My Wednesdays are wheatless,*
> *I'm getting more eatless each day.*
> *My coffee is sweetless,*
> *My bed it is sheetless,*
> *All sent to the Y.M.C.A.*
>
> *The barrooms are treatless,*
> *My home it is heatless,*
> *Each day I grow poorer and wiser.*
> *My socks they are feetless,*
> *My trousers are seatless,*
> *Oh*—HOW I DO HATE THE KAISER.

CHAPTER TWENTY-TWO

1918

January 2

Our militant sisters, whose methods I heartily disapprove, are bringing a lot of trouble to the suffragists. Last night on the street in front of the White House they brought on a riot by burning copies of the President's speeches, denouncing him as a "false prophet" and doing a lot of spectacular things that do nothing that I can see but alienate dignified people from our cause. Five of them were arrested and taken to detective headquarters but were soon released. They announce that they intend to keep watch-fires burning until the Senate passes the suffrage amendment.

January 15

Years used to be such real things to me that to change the date was as difficult as remembering a new name for an old friend. Now they are swifter than a weaver's shuttle. I am hardly acquainted with one date before it must be changed for another. And in all the world's history can there ever have been such a sensational period as this last twelve months?

Added to the horrors of war there have been such freaks of weather— the mercury below zero here repeatedly in the last month; snow in the little town of Bethlehem; people freezing to death in Mexico City; skating on Alamo Plaza in San Antonio; and earthquakes in diverse places. Poor Guatemala City is a heap of sulphur-steaming ruins. Fortunately the sun has not darkened nor the moon turned into blood, else I should be constrained to join the millennial dawners and think the end of this little cycle of time was imminent and the thousand years of peace at hand. It would be a pleasant thought, but I keep hoping that the Lord will spare us a little till we recover our sanity. Christianity would make a miserably poor showing at the judgment seat just now. Practically all the white

"Christian" races are engaged in trying to exterminate one another, while the black and brown, the "backward" peoples, hold their sides with laughter and no doubt greet with loud guffaws our missionaries sent to "convert" them.

January 23

Political sensations even outdo the weather. The President's flying leap—or was it a double back handspring?—into woman suffrage by federal amendment has brought laughter or tears according to your enthusiasm for "the Cause" or your respect for the Constitution. I made a bet with Mrs. Allender five weeks ago that he would do it—he has so often, "vowing he would ne'er consent, consented." She said he couldn't. He had refused even to see the suffrage committee, because the question of suffrage was not mentioned in his platform and that must settle it for his administration. But she doesn't know how many spurs there are for his single-track mind to run out on for political gain.

It is fun to see his thick-and-thin followers, who a few weeks ago opposed the suffrage even by permission of the states, trying to adjust their positions. I love to stir them up by casually remarking, "Evidently the pickets knew what they were about; they brought the President to terms." For months past women have stood like wooden Indians, one on either side of the two White House gates. They never spoke unless spoken to, their appearance was irreproachable—except in the bitterest weather when poor Billy Kent said his wife had dressed them in his fur coats until he had nothing to wear. Mrs. Kent also had her servants bring at regular hours a wheelbarrow of hot bricks and build new platforms for them to stand on. We used to drive down to see it done, the servants, the pickets, and their friends perfectly silent, only rank outsiders making ribald remarks. The public never complained, but somehow they got on the President's nerves, and he ordered their arrest for obstructing traffic, and five or six of them were hustled off to the workhouse at Occoquan. They were all refined, intelligent women, so our horror increased daily as we heard how they were being treated. They were denied the simplest toilet articles of their own, dressed in filthy prison clothes, given beds that were unspeakable, and seated at the table with the lowest drunkards and prostitutes, black and white, arrested on the streets of Washington. The conditions at the place are so outrageous that the publicity this affair gave it may save many a poor wretch in future.

The suffragists, of course, and many not interested before in the cause became more and more indignant so that we were all ready to meet them with a grand demonstration and parade the day their sentence was up. But the President took alarm and ordered their release one day sooner. I was at headquarters when our culprits came in and could hardly believe my eyes. They looked ten years older, unkempt, dirty and ill for want of the commonest conveniences and decencies of life.

All this makes the President's flop more absurd. Administration papers and friends have been calling the pickets "traitors," "pro-Germans," etc. Only a week before his change of heart, I heard Secretary Redfield declaiming against them, saying they had "entered into a conspiracy to injure the honorable *gentleman* who kept the workhouse." His whiskers fairly shivered and shook as he declared that he "would not believe one of them on oath." And now the Foreordained is making common cause with them!

There is no social life. An occasional dinner or debutante's tea only emphasizes the general dullness and gives the superpatriot something to criticize. Mrs. Porter gave one of her beautiful luncheons in December and her heartless extravagance is still commented upon. "But," they whisper, "you know she is pro-German, anyway." This reproach is hurled at anyone who doesn't parade some form of hatred or pray with that blasphemous mountebank, Billy Sunday, "God damn the Germans' stinking hide." I have pious and apparently reasonable friends who go with vast crowds to his tabernacle out near Union Station to hear him every day even in this bitter weather. My good friend Mrs. Lansing has taken the British Ambassador and his wife to hear him, and she set the seal of Administration approval by inviting a hundred people to meet him at her house. Plump Mrs. Daniels comes tumbling after with a morning meeting for him in her drawing room. One of his "prayers" published lately, and not contradicted, I copy to show what the war has brought us to. A congressman who went to the special meeting Sunday held for the U.S. Congress tells J. that it is practically word for word what he said, that he was applauded, and after some antics flopped down and said it over:

O God, help the man on the ship who aims the cannon to send to hell a submarine every time one sticks its dirty stinking nose above the water. O God, damn Germany and Turkey and all that gang of thieves and cutthroats. O Lord, I don't want to bless them, and you can go ahead and damn them as soon as you get ready, as far as I am concerned; but, God, don't wait too long.

I wonder what posterity will think of us, calling ourselves "a Christian nation" so unctuously and applauding this sort of thing. And the regular clergy are almost as bad.

At least the war conditions are doing a little good in relaxing some of our rock-bound social customs. We could hardly believe we were in Washington when the first Tuesday of this month passed without an inroad of new congressmen's wives coming to call because they thought they had to. The Congressional Club is given over to Red Cross work and French classes, and Congress Hall has become a place of industry and pious meditation.

But even during a complete social moratorium the White House furnishes us with talk. Nothing but the unexpected happens there. We used to think Roosevelt excelled all other Presidents in his talent for astonishing the natives, but he didn't have the war for a background nor McAdoo for a son-in-law. Thanks, it appears, to differences of policy between the Secretary of War and the Secretary of the Interior, people in the East could not fill their coal cellars last summer, so the scarcity of coal, the prospect of actual famine has grown more fearful every day. Personally we have not suffered, apartment houses are among the favored ones, but every day we watch anxiously the unloading of a ton, or even half a ton, at our door, counting the ultimate lump. Our fireplaces are piled up with boxes and combustible trash because no one knows when such stuff may be our only resource. The winter has been one of almost unprecedented severity, only two days, I believe, since December 8 when the mercury went above freezing point, and snow every few days.

The President appointed Harry Garfield as fuel administrator, because he naturally thinks a college president is fit for any practical office, and hasn't Garfield written several scholarly articles on transportation? So the fuel administrator blamed the railroads; the practical coal men blamed the fuel administrator; the snow went deeper between us and the mines; and trainloads of coal make black lines across the country, but not a wheel turns to bring it to the cities.

Then came the President with the "Fuel Order." Without a word of warning the whole business of the East was to be paralyzed for 5 days, and for 10 Mondays thereafter, robbing thousands of working people of 15 days' income in two months. It was almost incredible; people were dumfounded.

The order seems to have been issued with the same insouciance as that to bombard Vera Cruz, but the shots fell closer home this time and some are still falling around the White House.

For a few hours the "psychological condition," as W.W. would say, was almost revolutionary. Downtown I noticed the streetcar crowds were humming with excitement, the drivers calling out to one another almost like the old horse-bus days in London. Clerks in the shops were gathered in excited groups, wondering what they would do. People believe the Senate's protest will make him think again, but one of his official family said to me with apparent pride in his master's stubbornness, "No, the President has set his jaw, and we have learned that he never changes."

Meantime the suffering of the poor drags at our spirits like a strong undertow. The poor negroes bring us pitiful tales of how they are permitted to buy only a bushel of coal at a time and have to get that home as best they can. Mrs. Porter's laundress, an excellent woman she has had for years, came weeping to ask her help to get enough coal to keep up her business and feed her family. Mrs. P. went in her beautiful limousine to see the coal merchant—limousines are often influential—and extending more than a block from the place she found a ragged crowd of women, white and black, with buckets, baskets, or just aprons, waiting for the few lumps they would receive if they could wait long enough in the cruel cold. A delicate, gentle colored woman, who comes to me often by the day, tells me that she and her children are living on cold canned food because they can't get enough coal to heat it.

The order works unevenly, too. The schools are closed and many churches but the theaters and movies are running full time, except on Tuesday. And above all, Billy Sunday's tabernacle is kept as warm as its construction makes possible.

February 3

Mrs. Porter and I were lured out one bitter day to hear Mrs. Josephus Daniels speak before the Society of Colonial Dames. I've forgotten what she was to speak about—Red Cross, Y.W.C.A., or something else of a patriotico-pious nature—but we wanted to hear her. She is so hen-minded that it would have been interesting to see her leave off crooning and mount the platform. But, alas! she got cold feet and didn't appear, and Mr. C. E. Parker substituted with a pertinent talk on coal. The Colonial Dames Club is closed for want of fuel, so they met at Mrs. Sam Spencer's palace on Massachusetts Avenue, and after the lecture we were asked into a splendid big dining room and given a Hooverized meal—bad coffee, bad chocolate, and four kinds of war bread and cake. I sampled three, and Mrs. P. vouched for the other. One kind of plain bread would have been as good and much less expensive. The horrors of war increase. I came home a raging pacifist.

February 7

A while ago I said in thankful mood to J. that we had not had an extra for a long time. He said, "There are few disasters great enough to shock us now, and the price of print paper is prohibitive for mere excitements." Last night at 12:30 I thought I was dreaming, but in a minute "Extry— *Post*" was unmistakable and I sprang out of bed. I couldn't make a newsboy hear me, so I went to the telephone and heard from the *Post* the cool words, "Transport sunk."[1] It was so little to know with the vast possibilities of sorrow for the country that I couldn't go to bed, so we waited until we heard General Ainsworth's imperious voice at the window below calling a boy. J. was up too, and ran to the hall to catch the General. Only the dim lights were on, and it was a weird company that crouched on the stairs and on our floor to hear the news. General A. in a long bathrobe, his hair very rumpled, had forgotten his glasses, so prim little Miss Heiberger in a pink kimono read aloud. My J. looked very gray and grim in a blue robe with bare ankles, and the banister was hung with half-dressed women, listening and weeping. There was little to hear, just the awful fact "transport sunk" on the bleak west coast of Scotland. There was no way of estimating the loss of life; the people on shore were helping all they could. We hardly commented or spoke to one another, just heavy sighs sounded down the halls as each slipped back to the rooms.

February 15

Since yesterday morning I have been four times down to the Speedway and the Peninsula to see the river, or rather the tumbled fields of ice where the river used to be. It is a wildish scene for this climate, and especially today when the sun sailed through a cloudless deep-blue sky. The ice was piled with wreckage of launches, skiffs and several tugboats. Yesterday there was no water visible above the highway bridge. Today there are great banks and boulders of clear ice piled on the sea wall, and in many places up to the driveway. The big willows have ice up to their necks, and many are broken off to the ground, and on the Peninsula the flowers along the sea wall must be totally ruined.

After the meeting of our Woman's Peace party at Mrs. Post's this morning, Mrs. Kent and I went in her tiny open electric, a sort of automobile pony, to see the river again. We sped like birds through the spring air with the hint of sap and warming earth in it. We could hardly

[1] United States transport *Tuscania* was torpedoed off the Irish coast on February 5, 1918. Loss: 101 lives.

force ourselves to come home to lunch, there was so much to see. Over in the polo field a very new-style airplane was threatening to go up every minute, but a high, rough wind got up first, and the plane was still there when I went back in the afternoon with Mrs. P. and Mother.

Mrs. Kent and I talked regretfully of the death yesterday of Sir Cecil Spring-Rice, agreeing that he was a very fine and unusual type of ambassador and we were so sorry to hear that the last part of his life had been harassed and much injustice done him by another diplomat. We hoped that one good result of the war would be to remove the halos from the heads of ambassadors in general, and thought that if the Bolsheviks had done nothing else to justify themselves the publication of the secret treaties should be counted unto them for righteousness. We wondered why ambassadors were so sacrosanct, anyway, and laughed over some of our friends who say "diplomat" and seem to feel it more worshipful than the plain American word. I know well at present only one diplomat, good old "Daddy" Calderón of Bolivia. Sometimes I forget and call him "Daddy" to his face when Elena is with him, and he smiles as kindly as if he were not a diplomat at all.

February 22

The Champ Clarks asked us to the Capitol today to lunch with "Colonel" and Mrs. George Harvey[2] and some New York friends of theirs. The New York friends must belong among the appallingly rich; they seemed so indifferent to us of mere political caste and wore clothes far in advance of any fashions here. One of the women, quite tall and lithe, was slipped into a black satin case spotted just here and there with brilliant embroidered disks as big as dinner plates. But the gods send nuts to those who have no teeth. There were all the materials for a pleasant party, and the Clarks were preoccupied and forgot to use them. They failed to introduce the guests of honor, so several of us introduced ourselves, but the less enterprising held back. We straggled down to the lunchroom, the seating was not thought out, and some of the women drew their own husbands. I wish I had had such good luck. Harvey didn't scintillate and looked snappish later when I asked him why. He stares through big shell-rimmed glasses like a cynical Persian kitten, and neither he nor his wife was the least

---

[2] George B. M. Harvey, long-time editor of *North American Review* and *Harper's Weekly* and president of Harper & Brothers, was an early supporter of Wilson, but as the war in Europe progressed he became an outspoken critic of the President's policies. In January, 1918, he began publication of *Harvey's Weekly*, using it as a vehicle of criticism and satire against Wilsonian officialdom.

bit *simpático* at any time. Obviously we were not worthy of their steel.

While I would have liked to see Clark president, it is perhaps fortunate that Mrs. C. never reached the White House. The life would have been a terrific strain on her uncertain nerves, and strangers, foreigners especially, would have seen only her surface eccentricities without any chance to discover the rarely noble and generous soul beneath them.

Last week she announced in the society columns that she would be at home Wednesday afternoon and would make a talk on "Religion in Wartimes." Mrs. Porter, Mrs. Montague of Virginia, and I went together, and arriving late found fifty or sixty women seated around the edge of the mezzanine balcony at Congress Hall, with Mrs. Clark in front of them talking about David and Jonathan. After a while I asked a friend what she had said about the war, and she whispered, "Not much, but she talked very cleverly about Hardy's novels."

Mrs. Butler down on the plantation in North Carolina writes that the flowers were frozen in her greenhouse this year for the first time in thirty years. But I think she must be making things warm there now. She said, "There is no war spirit down here except among the preachers and the women Red Cross workers. I went to Warsaw to buy covers for my tobacco beds, and was talking to my cousin on the train when an impudent man joined in and said something about Wilson, Democracy, and Christ. I asked him how he dared to mention Christ in connection with Wilson and this war? that if Christ were on earth he would drive Wilson out of the White House as he drove the other money changers from the Temple."

But then, she's a Republican and has three sons in the service. She'll be "shadowed" if she doesn't watch out.

February 28

Such spooky things happen sometimes. Mother has been too ill for me to read to her, so I was returning to the library the new *Life and Letters of Edward Everett Hale,* feeling it rather selfish to keep it any longer. The second volume fell out of my hand open at page 237 and the name "San Antonio" caught my eye. The letter was dated 1876, and at the end of it was a bracketed note evidently by Miss Nellie: "Everybody was kind to us in the town, and outside of it at the Military Post. But I find myself regretting that our very best San Antonio friends of later years could by no possibility have been living there then. Mr. and Mrs. Slayden would have made any wilderness a garden of pleasure. What would they not have made of a paradise like San Antonio in 1876?"

I liked it so much. The value of a compliment lies so entirely in the quality of the person who pays it, and praise from the Hales is praise indeed.

March 3

Mr. Wilson is not the only person who resents a difference of opinion on the war question. People I have known here for twenty years and counted as friends—not intimates, of course, but good, everyday friends—I find quite remote in manner; and one family with whom we have exchanged invitations every year I find had a large Christmas party and did not invite us because we were "pacifists." So stupid! They are pleasant people, and we have much in common, and I am vain enough to think they will miss us as much as we do them.

Today's paper announces the resignation of Professor Ellery Stowell from Columbia because Nicholas Murray Butler objects to his views on the international situation. He is the fifth to go for the same reason. Truly they are making our universities "safe for hypocrisy." Even the conservative old University of Virginia has driven a young man out with whips of scorpions for "unpatriotic (that is, pacifist) expressions" reported by the lady principal of a girl's school where he had been invited to make an address. In this line I believe "the female of the species is more deadly than the male." When they have sons at the front I can forgive them anything, but the spinster patriot—and she is ubiquitous—is intolerable.

April 12

This morning there are two inches of hard sleety snow on the ground, icicles on the tiny buds of the trees, and their brown branches outlined with ice. Snow fell yesterday afternoon as steadily as the wind would let it. The sparrows came back to Mother's window for breakfast (they don't know the price of crackers) and a robin sat on a bough near my bedroom and pouted. I don't blame him; there will be no cherries, nor much other fruit, this summer. The peaches are killed in the Valley and the Piedmont country too, and I was planning a perfect riot of conservation! Brandy peaches will henceforth, I suppose, be only a tradition of the elders since the prohibitionists boast that they have gotten Washington "bone dry." Apropos of flour substitutes, meatless meals and other wartime fads, General Ainsworth sent me up a verse this morning:

OMAR IN WARTIME

A jug of grape juice underneath a bough—
A hod of coal, a corn-meal loaf—and Thou
Beside me, mixing meatless things—
Oh, well, we've got some sugar anyhow!

Despite the bitter cold, I hear people are wearing spring hats. I have just tumbled my confections of yesteryear out of the boxes and found only one available, and it looks like the kind an Englishwoman would contrive for a tour in Palestine, and say, "It is ra-ather smart now, isn't it?"

April 25

Yesterday Mrs. Post, Mrs. Kent, Mrs. Burch and I, a committee from the Women's International League, had an interview with our miniature Secretary of War. I believe he is honestly trying to be a big little man, but the situation is such that he may easily overdo it and share the fate of the frog in the fable.

It is so many years since I have been in the "State-War-and-Navy" that I thought of it as it was in old half-forgotten days of peace—a place of vast empty spaces and echoing footfalls—so it was startling to find it surging with men and women all on business bent, running into one another without pausing to apologize, demanding information of distracted or merely rude janitors, complaining loudly or boasting (the women of course) of how "lovely" some official had been to them. It interested me so much that I was sorry when a patronizing negro ushered us into the Secretary's anteroom. There such impressive stillness prevailed that another negro had placed us neatly in a row of large chairs against the wall before Mrs. Kent and I began to talk again. In other chairs around the four sides of the room were men and women, young and old, rich and poor, "Jews, Turks, Greeks, and Samaritans, and strangers from Mesopotamia," all looking as if they were *planted* and meant, like the frog footman in *Alice,* to sit there for days and days together. Officers, high and low, bustled or strode through according to their rank or the length of their acquaintance with the uniform, but took no notice of anybody. Suddenly there appeared in the hall door, some of the chairs obscuring all but the upper part of her figure, a woman I felt sure represented one of the war's tragedies. Voluminous folds of rich dark-blue veiling fell from her head over her shoulders, a broad white band turned back from her face, and a dark coat was buttoned tightly up to her chin. She was a picture of stern grief. "Some poor war widow," I said, as she made her way past the crowd back of the desk and came out on our side. And behold! the dark costume reached very little below the knees of a pair of millpost legs in transparent white stockings and white shoes tied with big ribbon bows. She thumped down flat in her chair, not sideways as we early Victorians were trained to do, planted her large feet wide apart, and throwing open her coat displayed a red cross on her ample white front so large that it seemed like a target inviting a shot in her country's cause—obviously one of our fashionable charity leaders. She kept her eyes on the Secretary's door and waited with evident irritation until he appeared. But he stopped first to greet an oily little foreigner of some sort and then came straight to us, whereupon the dark lady of the stockings got up and banged out of the room.

Baker reminded me of "Little Breeches"—"peart an' chipper an' sassy," but courteous and well meaning. We told him of our errand which was to ask that the department provide some insignia, a brassard, a badge, or even the ubiquitous button, for young men of draft age engaged in productive work quite as essential for winning the war as purely military service but not recognized or requited by the public with the same enthusiasm. While they run ranches, wheat farms and dairies they are being insulted as "slackers." Society gives entertainments for men in uniform only, and preachers want in their churches only the man in khaki. The Secretary even expressed sympathy with our contention that it was unjust and referred us, as usual in the departments, to another man. We are to see Assistant Secretary Keppel, who "has charge of all such matters." Of course the war will be over before anything is done about it, but we have done our best and angels can do no more.

April 29

Keppel is quite the opposite of Baker—large, muscular, intellectual, or rather, professional looking. He questioned us, not unpleasantly but as if we had come to matriculate and must be classified. Truly this is a government of professors, by professors, for professors, but perhaps, with the war on, they may have a steadying effect on the purely military minded. *"La guerre est trop sérieuse pour la laisser aux militaires."*

June 2

Mother's desperate illness lately and the social conditions that grow stranger every day have so detached me from the world that I am surprised when anyone calls or I have an invitation. The old arbitrary Washington custom of calling has lapsed entirely, and I lay a wreath on its grave without regret, but it leaves us rather at loose ends. We have evolved no system yet by which to carry on any social life, and it is awkward at times. Another curious thing, not altogether lamentable, is the disappearance of the ultrasmart and noisy rich set in their usual roles of freak dinners, hunt breakfasts, and suppers of which the particulars are told in whispers. It isn't good form for patriots to give parties, and while, no doubt, some are given by stealth, they must lack zest when they cannot be blazoned in the society columns.

The city was never so full of rich people. "Dollar-a-year men, earning fully 99 cts. of it," as the papers say, are everywhere. I am told, too, by a government official who has to sign vouchers, that many of them are drawing expense accounts larger than the incomes they had before they offered themselves to their country. But charity's the thing, and every entertainment must have the excuse of something to sell or to be subscribed to.

The becomingness of the Red Cross costume—which can be worn to all charity functions—as compared to the season's fashions easily explains its popularity. There are two extremes of it, the soft veiled kind, very womanly, and the ultramasculine, overseas cap, tweed coat and boots. I was invited to join some sort of "corps" and was told as a recommendation of it that they had adopted a charming little costume that cost only $85. Early one morning at Rigg's Market I waited at the dairy for a long time behind what seemed a "sort of a bloomin' hermaphrodite," a woman in a long-skirted and belted coat, khaki trousers, leather leggings, and boots planted wide apart. The cap of a Red Cross ambulance driver half covered a crisped coiffure dyed fiery red. When she finally stopped laying down the law to the poor meek old clerk, she turned toward me; her face was chalked and cheeks and lips painted like a clown's, the queerest combination of grenadier and courtesan.

July 3

We have a brand-new devotional exercise established by the clergy and that great spiritual institution, the Chamber of Commerce. It is called the "Noonday Angelus." When the clock strikes twelve everyone is to stop short for two minutes and pray for victory—for the Entente Allies, of course. But suppose some treacherous German or, worse still, "pro-German" seizes the opportunity to pray for the Central Powers. How it will

mix things up, and what are we going to do about it? It is all very confusing. Can we pray by the alarm clock, or even by a notice so impressive
as the blowing of a siren from the top of the Washington Monument which
the Chamber of Commerce hopes to install? I remember a warning against
those who "love to pray standing in the corners of the streets that they may
be seen of men," but suppose the Angelus should catch you not even at the
corner but in the middle of the street with automobiles and streetcars
crowding around, and the drivers not stopping to pray? Neither my mind
nor body is nimble enough to strike the right attitude and pray for victory
under those circumstances.

I have not caught the effect in the street yet, but one day Mrs. Gregg
and I were buying some curtains from a sallow, dejected old clerk at Woodward and Lothrop's when he suddenly raised one hand and dropped his
head down on the other. We thought he was ill, and in our solicitude for
him the two minutes were over before we knew that it was prayer and
not vertigo.

The question of food is so absorbing now that market lists for "balanced"
meals require as much attention as my engagement book used to. Meatless
days have no terrors for me. My family smiles unreproachfully when they
have macaroni à l'Italienne, cream of asparagus or black bean soup. This
more restrained and sensible eating is the one thing for which I can really
thank the war. We are constantly confronted with the poster "Food Will
Win the War," so yesterday when I had made, labeled, paraffined and set in
a row fifteen glasses of currant jelly, the Kaiser couldn't have felt prouder
of the latest grandchild come to perpetuate the Hohenzollerns. Of course
we seek out many inventions to make our tables appear as usual to company. My niece, Nan Lightfoot, writes me of an incident in her house,
worthy of Sir Philip Sidney's "Thy need is greater than mine." They sat
down to dinner very much *en famille* and she, knowing there was only one
slice of ham, deftly slipped it on her husband's plate. Just then the door
bell rang, and while she went to answer it, her husband noticed the ham
and slipped it onto her plate. She brought in an old friend who had
dropped in to dine with them, and while her husband was greeting him
she put the ham on the guest's plate. That evening she noticed that their
grocery bill was addressed to "Mr. John B. Lightfood."

J. is down in Texas fighting for his political life. His opponent, a young
man well within the draft age, is running on a platform of flaming patriotism, accusing J. of "disloyalty" and "pacifism." He reiterates, "Mr. Slayden

voted *reluctantly* for the war"—as if any sane man would vote for a war any other way. With the military spirit more rampant than ever in San Antonio, an almost new district, and women voting in the primaries, the issue is extremely doubtful. The *Express* is against J. too. It opened its campaign for the other man with a list of accusations concerning J.'s votes, etc., so foolishly untruthful that we attributed it to mere ignorance. But when J. contradicted them with chapter and verse from the Congressional Record, they refused to print it except at advertising rates, showing that the misrepresentation was deliberate. It surprises me a little with the vastly moral pose of the present manager, but the poor little man has the prohibitionist order of mind, and J. is an anti.

No doubt I am subconsciously nervous over it—we are very well placed here, and have no desire to disturb the *status quo*—but so far I have lost no sleep. Thank God for "the years that bring the philosophic mind." I should have been much more perturbed when I was younger.

July 6

J. is having to prop up his character as an honest American and not hand in glove with the Kaiser by witnesses from here. Champ Clark testified to it in a fine hearty letter, so brief that it was a model. I telephoned to Mrs. C. to say how I appreciated it, and after expressing her indignation at such treatment of "a good and true American" and offering to write a letter for him herself, she branched off to say, "I have stopped going to church or any other place of amusement, because," she explained, "I was afraid the impulse to debate with these militant preachers would be too much for me." Knowing that she was quite capable of it, I commended her decision. She told me she had left the gallery when the President made his warlike speech for fear she should rise up and tell what she thought of his opinions. Wouldn't it have made a picturesque episode in American history?

July 11

I confess to a superstition about the new moon imbibed, no doubt, early in life from negroes and perpetuated by two or three painful coincidents of late years. Last night while I was putting Mother to bed I looked out the window and saw just one half of the red crescent showing above the black roof of a house beyond our pretty vacant lot, where in the morning the sweet clover and cornflowers draw swarms of yellow butterflies. It was almost an ugly thing like a piece of shiny stage property stuck on a box, but it has haunted me all day. J.'s letter today was rather anxious, and Mr. Harrison had a telegram saying that that organization of vocal patriots, the Security League, had denounced J. in the evening paper. General Ainsworth, Mr. Harrison and I were busy all morning getting the Security League's record, and it is a black one, but what's the good? I was convinced long ago of the futility of contradicting deliberate political lies. The newspapers and the public prefer them to the truth.

This afternoon I actually went to a tea party Mrs. Radcliffe gave at the Washington Club for a bevy of Michigan war brides and feel refreshed by the change after such long monotony. I told her I knew how Rip Van Winkle would have felt if someone had been good enough to wake him and invite him to a party, and she answered in her quick, pretty way, "But you are Rip van *Twinkle* and never need to be waked up."

July 25

The impish little half-moon stuck on the roof portended a political crisis for us as grotesque as it was unexpected. This morning my letter from J. was longer than usual. He said the campaign was "hard, dirty, and expensive," but his main opponent's character and methods were beginning to disgust people, and the support for the third candidate, Burleson's brother-in-law, was negligible. I came in from market serene of mind. As I took off my hat I saw the yellow edge of a telegram with my other mail, opened it quickly and read, "In view of Woody's telegram withdrawal seems advisable. Tell Harrison."

I hardly remember how I felt except that my first idea was not to let Mother know. She is so ill, and it would distress her needlessly. Then I called Mr. Harrison and said, "I have a bombshell." He answered, "So have I," and went on to tell me how he was being besieged by newspapermen. The Texas correspondents had gotten the news early and thought it a fake, not believing that even this President could send a message to a Republican paper taking sides between two men of his own party. They asked at the White House, and the answer came at once—he did. I begged Mr. Harrison not to talk (he is so extreme) nor to give any interviews. He wanted me to join him in a telegram to J. begging him not to withdraw, but the situation is so unprecedented and I am so afraid of offending against the ethics of good sport and good political taste that I insisted on waiting until I had consulted our wise and experienced friend, General Ainsworth.

The General was out when I called him but came in a few minutes, and I shall not soon forget his face when he read the message. Indignation, bewilderment, personal regret—for I think we are almost his closest friends—turned him a queer sallow color. He thought, as Mr. Harrison and I did, that the question of withdrawal was still open, so we concocted a telegram urging J. to fight it out, and then he went downstairs, as he said, "to do his swearing." Mr. H. sent the message, and several other friends advised the same, Senator Bailey among them, but by four o'clock J.'s answer came saying that the matter was settled last night.

The *Evening Star* has the President's telegram in full: "Your letter received. The administration as between candidates equally loyal never takes part. But in the light of Mr. Slayden's record, no one can claim that he has given support to the administration." There also is a part of J.'s brief answer. "No matter how false the statements made to the President that procured this telegram, my continued candidacy for Congress in view of it will appear to put me in opposition to those charged with the prosecution of the war. I therefore announce my withdrawal from the race for Congress."

Of course I am sorry J. is out, but I am proud of the way he took the President's insult—picking up his glove and throwing it back in his face. It was a *man's* gesture, not that of a mere politician or one who wanted the job at any cost.

We know who did the lying, but why clutter up my notebook with his name? My business now is to look bravely down the vista of our new life, think how to travel it with the least regret for the many pleasures here, and make J. feel the least anger and resentment for the dirty trick played on him by a Democratic president, for whose election he worked, spending more money than we could afford, though he had committed the unpardonable sin of not wanting him nominated.

August 1

I was given little time to meditate. The telephone began to ring that evening, and ever since indignant friends, and even mere acquaintances, have been pouring out their astonishment, wrath and contempt. The comments caused me to wonder that we were not all arrested under the Espionage Act, especially as the telephone service has just been turned over to the Post Office Department.

The next day telegrams poured in and letters so fiery that I wonder the Postmaster General was not attracted to them by the smell of scorching mail pouches. One or two have suggested that the telegram was a forgery—"Our President *could* not have done such a contemptible thing"—but the majority have just damned him like freeborn Americans. It is good to know that still they live in spite of the Espionage Act, the censorship, and other paraphernalia imported from Russia "to keep Democracy alive."

A woman whose husband is quite close to the White House expressed her regret, and I had a lot of fun quoting some of the worst letters rather too violent and ill-judged to be set down here, but amusing. She turned pale all around the rouge on her cheeks, and said, "I didn't know anyone would *dare* to speak so of the President." "Oh," I answered with exaggerated gaiety, "Americans who *thought* such things said them of Washington and Lincoln, and Wilson is no better than his predecessors were, is he?" I think she expected fire from heaven to consume me.

August 22

Anyway the preachers and the Chamber of Commerce have got their siren going, and it is to sound every day at noon to remind us to pray for two minutes "against the Central Powers." Someday maybe we can spare a few minutes to pray against those older and more subtle enemies, pride, vainglory and hypocrisy, but almost at the beginning of the war we declared a moratorium on the Constitution and Christianity.

August 27

An awful thing seems to have happened yesterday. There were huge headlines on the front page of the *Herald,* "Baker Keeps President Waiting though They Had an Appointment." The paper tells that "three minutes later the Secretary came down the corridor at double quick." Was it Louis XIV or some later autocrat who said to a courtier who arrived only a few minutes before his appointment, "Sir, you almost kept me waiting"?

In a letter from my dear little great-niece and godchild "Tekka W.," she praises her uncle Slayden's prompt retort courteous to the President's telegram and ends naïvely, "and Grandma and I think it is better to be a gentleman than a congressman"—a slightly invidious distinction, I'm afraid.

Several days ago Mother was so much better that the doctor advised me to seize the opportunity to get her out of town. We hurried to Virginia, and I came back the next evening expecting J. the following morning.

I never remember feeling so lonely, so unattached in all my life—Mother left behind, J. not here, and the outlook not very radiant anyway. The train was late, and there was only one person I knew in the car—my distinguished fellow Virginian Secretary Carter Glass. When we got in about midnight he passed me with a nod, not even offering to see me to my cab. Not quite the old Virginian of tradition. When I let myself into the apartment, I was startled to see a man's hat on the hall table but guessed it was J., ahead of time as always. I rushed to the bedroom to find him sound asleep, so I did not hear till morning the Texas side of the episode Wilson. I am inclined to think that the men who concurred in his idea to withdraw from the race are not his wisest nor most sincere friends, but I doubt if they could have prevented it even if they had tried. He is "heady" where his dignity is involved, and this was certainly a case for prompt and unequivocal assertion of it. At any rate it is settled, and our next thought must be what to do with ourselves after March 4. Naturally we want to go back to Texas, but the finger of fate points very straight to my little orchard up in the Ragged Mountains where 1,200 apple trees may stand between us and poverty. We might be much worse off.

The local consequences of J.'s withdrawal are unique. His friends, indignant, of course, decided not to support the Prohibition candidate, who really had a chance of the nomination, but to vote almost en masse for Burleson's brother-in-law to make plain to the country the purpose of the telegram, and, as they express it, to let the President get what's coming to him. They predict that his satisfaction in the new member of the House will not be unmixed with embarrassment. It seems improbable that he will last more than one term, so the district cannot be much hurt, and J.'s friends will enjoy their political practical joke.

Billy Rodenberg of Illinois telephoned me today to come to the House to hear him speak on the President's pet phrase "politics is adjourned." He is to touch him up on his recent meddling in state elections—J., Hardwick of Georgia, Vardaman of Mississippi, and Huddleston of Alabama. Mr. R. says I gave him his best point by calling his attention to the President's, or rather Woodrow Wilson's, book on constitutional government in which he says that an executive can by his great prestige influence the election or defeat of a congressman, but that it is "deeply immoral." What a difference there is between Philip drunk (with the sense of power) and Philip sober! I used to enjoy Wilson's books long ago when I thought they were sincere. "He would have been thought capable of Empire had he never reigned."

Mr. Rodenberg's speech was clever in his own peculiar way, a lot of good sense and philosophy constantly lightened with humor. There was sound applause when he grew serious and asked, "Was politics adjourned when the President sent the telegram to injure Slayden of Texas and promote the political aspirations of his opponent, who, by a remarkable coincidence, happens to be the brother-in-law of the Postmaster General?"

September 1

It looks as if Secretary Baker were exerting an almost too paternal authority over the army. His published Index Expurgatorius for camp libraries suggests Russian prerevolutionary censorship rather than this war for democracy. The list of books is as amazing as the order, and the order is that they be "removed or destroyed." Of the fifteen, only four are by authors of German name and not one of them is sensational or the kind to become dangerously popular. It is odd that he should put on the black list a book by Fred C. Howe. He is the President's personal friend. He appointed him commissioner of immigration in New York, and the book is dedicated to the President and accepted by him. Oughtn't they to order a few carloads of "Elsie Dinsmore" and the "Little Colonel" series to fire the heart of the armies in the field?

September 3

Oh, joy! not even the headlines can overstate the truth of the Allies' move forward yesterday. If only it will go on quickly, *quickly,* and let us wake from this four years of nightmare! I often wonder how it will feel to get the morning paper and not read war news first, the lying, boasting headlines, and then the official communiqué for a sobering bit of truth.

Which way I fly is war; myself am war! The government ownership of everything is a constant irritation. Our food is measured out to us in standardized tin cups, and I have almost to sign away my rights as a citizen to get a few pounds of sugar. A ticket to visit Mother, which used to cost $2.90, is now $3.76 and extras; and as for the mail and telegraph service, they are unspeakable. I came back from Virginia on the 15th and sent a special delivery letter to my cook at once. Fortunately she came in a few minutes later, but the letter was delivered at her house by a uniformed messenger of the government on the 25th. A telegram took five days to reach me from South Carolina, and yet there are people proclaiming from the housetops that government ownership will bring the millennium.

September 6

The casualty lists are three and four columns long every day, but just as regularly the first item of the society news is to the effect that the President and Mrs. Wilson occupied their box at Keith's (or Poli's) last night, accompanied by Miss Bones, Professor Axson, and Mr. John R. Bolling— "the usual five," as *Harvey's Weekly* calls them. Sometimes they go four and five times a week.

September 7

The air is fine and snappy today and the streets rather interesting with the sprinkling of foreign soldiers, English, French and Italian. They are picturesque but depressing, because so many are lame, or scarred, and all of them weary eyed. The English especially are nearly all so hollow chested and tubercular I long to take them to West Texas and feed them eggs and milk. I wonder if it is only the cut of their uniforms or if the British youth is not made to square his shoulders and stand up. They are so slouchy and bent it seems as if their Sam Brownes were pressing in their stomachs. I have often noticed this hollow chest and wretched carriage among London shop people, men and women, too, but they surely can't have drawn many soldiers from that class. The English faces seem to me a little more finished than our boys', more "touched with race" instead of "races" like our mixed product, but somehow I feel as if the American boys had the cleaner tongue and fresher outlook—perhaps because they are "so largely educated by women," as Rudyard Kipling suggests in one of his late patronizing outbursts. Oh, Rudyard, why didn't you stick to your heaven-sent gift of story writing and let politics alone?

A great number of our boys have girls hanging to their arms, tottering on the high, "hourglass" heels of their slippers, their ears elaborately concealed under round, snail-shell coils of hair, and their flesh-colored silk stockings elaborately displayed to the knee. They look so gay and pleased with themselves. Poor children! "Sing while ye may, another day will bring enough of sorrow." Still the President has spoken consolingly lately. He hopes the war will be over by 1920.

September 18

Mr. Gregg thinks he has a fine joke on J. He heard some congressmen talking about his leaving, and one said, "I am sorry to lose Slayden, he is one of the few old, courteous, ante bellum men that we have left in the

House." J. doesn't enjoy being mistaken for an old Confederate—he was seven years old when the war began—but I am rather proud of all that it implies.

September 19

Sometimes I think I believe in suffrage for women in spite of the woman suffragists. Their ethics are so peculiar. J. tells me that the same committee of members' wives, who ought not to embarrass their husbands' colleagues, has been at his office three or four times to ask him to change his vote when the suffrage comes up again. I have never dared to ask him but once. He explained to them the first time that his vote was a matter of conscience, but they seemed to think that a trifle light as air. A senator tells me that Secretary Baker's wife has been lobbying through the Senate Office Building for some of her pet measures and greatly embarrassing the men. It is awkward to refuse the wife of a secretary—exactly what she counted on for her success, no doubt. Many women have lost their sense of proportion and dignity and are becoming pests. Pretty little Mrs. Jessie MacKaye (Percy MacKaye's sister-in-law) rushed up to me one night on the street, her face all lined with nervous strain, and told me with delight that she had been arrested three times last week. They go out from the headquarters on Jackson Place every night, make speeches and wave banners till they get themselves arrested, and march off to jail, handbags packed in advance with toothbrush and nightie, to revel in martyrdom. The next day there is a spectacular trial at the police court, conspiracies of silence, threats of hunger strikes, and irritated husbands pleading "Mother, come home." They say they are doing it "to influence the Senate." Now, as Adamson of Georgia remarked, "Having revised the tariff downward we are doing the same for the Senate." I can't believe it will succumb to such childish methods.

September 20

When I saw that a company of the Foreign Legion—imported o'purpose to stimulate our interest in Victory Bonds—was to be received by the Senate this morning I went up there at once. It is the one war exhibit I have cared to see. The Legion is a "port of missing men," full of romance and mystery. The policeman sitting on the table at the Senate entrance stopped jollying the telephone man long enough to say, "Ain't comin' up here; be at Treasury one o'clock." So back I went to the Treasury. It was a sharp, cold day for the season, glaring sunlight alternating with stormy gray from big clouds rolled by a rough wind, but pouring down every path to the south portico were streams of women, overworked young geniuses that the government had given a holiday to help the Liberty Loan and welcome the foreign soldiers. En route they were practicing their welcome on everything in trousers.

There are said to be 30,000 of these department girls, drawn here from all over the country by McAdoo's advertisements in small papers. None of them, I understand, receives a salary of less than $1,100 but generally more, which must be out of all proportion to the value of their services. Two whom I happen to know were stock girls at my milliner's last year, sorting artificial flowers and delivering boxes at $10 a week. They are now drawing respectively $1,200 and $1,500. They all spend like drunken sailors, buying every sort of finery that the shops afford, a perfect orgy of extravagance. It is preparing a large class of women who, when the war ends and this inflation of wages collapses, will be as discontented as the taxpayers are now. Some church and Y. W. workers tell me that it has already led many of them into grave trouble. Village girls turned loose without guidance or responsibility are led into dangerous places and company every day. Notorious women from other cities have come here and opened "boardinghouses" with appalling results.

The faces of the Legionnaires were interesting but their poor bodies were so loaded with accouterment and walking with so little *élan* it made me ache in sympathy. They were of many types, but all had drawn, tired eyes. All the soldiers I have seen who had been in actual fighting have that look in their eyes that haunts me.

When McAdoo raised the flag of four stripes, the corners of his mouth turned up and the end of his nose pointing down, he was even more Mephistophelean than usual, so I came home without hearing the speech.

"Wonderful! Wonderful! Wonderful! beyond all whooping," is Mrs. Porter's comment in a letter today on the appointment of John Davis to the Court of St. James's. It was so utterly unexpected that I was stunned and at first felt only the negative satisfaction that it was not "Colonel" House. The New York *Evening Post* voices the feeling of most people, I believe, that "at this great crisis of history it would have been well to send a man better known internationally and of wider experience." But we can't have everything, and Mr. Davis is a gentleman born and bred, scholarly, refined, and good to look at, and acknowledged by everyone to be learned in the law. J. and I are more than content. The universal question is, where is the money to come from? The Davises have never had any, and how can they conduct an embassy in these days of high cost of living on $17,000?

Dr. David Starr Jordan's books today appear on the black list for the army. It is so ludicrous that one almost loses sight of the serious side of its interference with personal liberty. Were ever any people as much governed as we are? We are told what we shall eat and what we shan't drink and where withal we shall be clothed; and now we are told what we may read and when we must pray and what we must pray for. My delightful presentation copy of *Eric's Book of Beasts* will have to be put away. It might arouse dangerous thoughts in General Ainsworth's mind when he comes to visit us or lead nineteen-year-old Aleck Gregg to resign the first lieutenancy lately thrust upon him and go back to the nursery where he belongs. It would certainly be burned as seditious literature if the powers that be could see the couplet written in it about Woodrow Wilson by Dr. Jordan, at my suggestion on the page with the "Squidgy-cum-Squees who swallow themselves."

J. is convening this evening with the members from the cotton states who are up in arms over the President's benevolent "stabilizing" of cotton prices below the cost of production. The Southern members are shaking in their shoes. Those who haven't been defeated by the President's accusations of "disloyalty to my administration" were protesting their devotion and arguing that it is their duty to follow him blindly, and now they are confronted with the choice of loyalty to him or to the interests of their farmer constituents who *vote*. We begin to appreciate the sweet uses of adversity. Not a wave of trouble rolls across our peaceful breasts. The political grave is rather snug and comfortable.

October 1

Spanish influenza, a brand-new variety, looms large in the foreign news. As the war tension relaxes, the papers need a new sensation, and everyone is talking about it and creating a mob psychology to help it to do its worst if it gets across the ocean. Of course it could not be as virulent here as in Europe where millions of people are undernourished and nervously exhausted, making them susceptible to any epidemic that comes along. Madame Bryn, wife of the Norwegian Minister, told me a curious story about it. (Norwegian intonation running up and down the scale and ending on a high note always engages my ear so pleasantly that I often forget what they are talking about, and Madame B.'s voice is like a thin, Norse musical instrument.) She said her son, in some cadet corps in Norway, wrote that in a parade one morning eight men fell down simultaneously with influenza. He felt quite well until dancing in the evening he was taken so violently ill that he had to be carried to the barracks, and before morning almost the whole corps was down.

October 9

Next to censorship and espionage, government ownership of railways is the most maddening of our present tyrannies. The management admits its incompetence by such special pleading to the public as "Be a patriot and don't travel" and "Take only hand baggage when you travel," the result of the last suggestion being that our cars are as cluttered up with lumpy parcels as the cars in Merrie England on her merriest bank holiday. From having had an almost perfect baggage system we now have none at all. If your trunk comes in a week after you do, you are very fortunate. Rena arrived from Quebec last Monday, and expected to recheck her baggage for her next port of call on Saturday. I went to the counter with confidence born of long and happy experience of courtesy and efficiency, and was met by a ferocious female in khaki who ignored my good manners and the check and waving her hand toward the stairs said, "Take that down there." I went down, down, down into a vast sort of baggage purgatory where thousands of trunks waited for release. Another angry woman ordered me to go farther, which I did knowing I could not fare worse. A third one was meek and helpless and said tearfully if I could find the trunk I might have it. In the semidarkness I climbed over mountains of trunks and little hills of perambulators, got hung in a chain, and suffered from smells unspeakable, and at last was ordered upstairs again. I went gladly, but the khaki lioness ordered me back as if she were empowered to call out the full military and naval force of the United States to suppress me. This time I defied her, turned my back and went and hunted a *man*. He listened to my troubles, gave me a little paper to get the trunk when it came, and, above all, reassured me that good manners had not perished from the face of the earth. I am dead against government ownership, and fully persuaded that woman's sphere is the home and not the baggage room.

Friday, October 11

It is tiresome to be a prophet without honor even from one's self. A few days ago I set down some sententious views on why Europe was more devastated by influenza than we could be even if it got here. The news day by day is giving me a taste of a tragedy as defined by Huxley—"A perfect theory bowled over by a fact." Since Saturday there have been 7,046 cases *reported* in the District and a daily average of 50 deaths. In the army already 889 deaths are reported, God knows how many more concealed. The local death list has an added touch of pathos by so many on it being young girl war workers. Poor things! without home or friends, foolishly dressed, and living on trash, inviting death from any illness. Eight, I hear, have been buried in the potter's field because no one knew where they belonged. Sweet little Madame Koo, wife of the Chinese Minister, died of it yesterday. The District Commissioners began their protective and preventive campaign by closing the schools, which are warm and well ventilated. The theaters are left open so the children flock to the movies, which are rarely ventilated and by their very nature can never let the blessed sunshine in. Then the churches were closed and at last, regardless of the President's evening pleasure, the vaudeville theaters. Now they have forbidden the rights of assembly even to passionate patriots longing to subscribe to the Liberty Loan in public.

The powers called a solemn assembly and asked for volunteers, "thousands of them," who would ring people's doorbells at ten o'clock on Sunday and plead the cause of the Loan. They rang ours at four, but J. told the rather swaggering youth that he would subscribe through his home bank and not otherwise.

Our homes are no longer our castles. If it isn't loans, it is housing war workers. No one (but the very rich or those with political influence) may keep an empty room. If you leave your house overnight you are likely to find it full of gum-chewing young women in the morning. The Porters have returned indignantly ten days ahead of their plans and their servants, because their agent wrote that he could not keep the house from being commandeered unless it was occupied. It is all such irritating nonsense and sensationalism, too. What they need is not more room but fewer idle, overpaid people in town.

Sunday

Yesterday Mrs. James Brown Scott took us with her for a day at her country home on Weems Creek near Annapolis. It was a beautiful drive through "harvest happy farms," fields of shocked corn with scattered pumpkins "100% American," and every fencepost afire with Virginia creeper. No one could call these the melancholy days if color can bring joy. We had a picnic luncheon and hot coffee on the veranda, and while Mrs. S. went to visit her nephew—one of 1,200 ill of influenza at the Academy—we rested and enjoyed the lovely water view. I don't see how the Scotts can bear to stay in town at all. Maybe we could get the place commandeered for our use.

October 21

My forecast of the epidemic becomes more and more inept. Conditions today might be copied from a history of the plague in the Middle Ages, an average of 1,500 new cases and 95 deaths a day. Nurses and doctors are broken down and dying of it, hospitals overflowing so that many buildings have had to be commandeered for hospital use. Soldiers by hundreds are detailed to dig graves, and the demand for coffins is so much greater than the supply that cemetery chapels are filled with bodies waiting for burial. The suffering and deaths in army camps are frightful.

Mrs. Radcliffe, whose courage and efficiency thrive on difficulty, organized a temporary nursing home for convalescent girls turned out of the overcrowded hospitals before it is safe for them to go back to work or to their horrible lodging houses. Mrs. Porter and I are helping two or three days in the week. It is a horrid job and place, in that unknown country south of the avenue, but gives rare opportunity for the study of war workers. Eight or ten girls at a time are dumped on us several times a day, all sorts and conditions, from illiterate little shop girls to graduates of Smith and Wellesley. A part of my duty is to help them to bed, get their names and home addresses, and, if possible, to induce them to return there. My methods cannot be very persuasive, as I have not yet found one with the least sense of duty to home or parents, nor assigning any reason for coming here, except that she chose to. "Momma 'n' Poppa didn't want me to come." Several have told me that "Momma works awful hard," but there is no response to my suggestion that she could serve her country by helping at home as well as spending $100 or more a month here entirely on herself. In packing their handsome bags I find almost invariably very much filmy silk and lace underwear. When I put a thick outing gown on them they protest, but soon fall asleep. We keep them from three to five days, and feed them on the fat of the land, largely contributed from the homes of Mrs. Radcliffe's friends, but not one of them has offered to give a penny toward the upkeep of the hospital and those who are well enough to be up take a cab to go to their lodging houses for their mail. What is to become of them when the war is over? They love money and have no sense of duty to God or man.

I wrote Dr. Jordan a frivolous note about his books being excluded from camp libraries, and his answer makes me feel small. He *always* looks at things in a big way. He says "I am delighted to hear from you again. It is true that some prewar book of mine is, with Barbusse's 'Le Feu' and Bertrand Russell's 'Why Men Fight,' interdicted for the army. That is leaving me in good company, and maybe the soldiers will take time to read them when the war is over. It would seem that this may be soon. . . ."

Senator Bailey dropped in last night. He talked well, as always, on public matters, and it is refreshing to hear someone with firm convictions and political beliefs and the courage to express them. He advocated offering the old Springer Resolution against a third term to put the Democrats on record if nothing else, as he thinks they have forgotten the fundamentals. He said the President had destroyed the *principles* of the government as far as he could, and he wanted to see if he still clung to the traditions. "He (the President) has abrogated the Constitution, and we ought to see if he has left the bylaws."

November 7

This date will be marked with the biggest, whitest stone in all history's collection. I cannot realize yet that it means peace—peace to weary millions of men in trench and tent, to tens of millions of women and children all over the world borne down by sorrow and suffering. It is all too big and complicated to understand except that they ceased firing at nine o'clock this morning, they cannot kill any more. Selfishly I think first "Maury and George are safe,"[3] though M. is hideously wounded, and then of many other boys I love or feel an interest in for their parents' sake.

The morning paper said officers to sign the Armistice had left Berlin, but it meant little to me; papers say so many things. About one o'clock Rena and I were sitting in my room in a flood of sunshine. I was piecing up cuptowels from samples of Belgian linen sent to us in the fateful July of 1914 and R. was telling me how she cried hysterically as she sat in a quiet garden in Mexico when the bells rang to announce our declaration of war on Spain. Above the clatter of my sewing machine I heard a steam whistle, and then another, and another, unusual in this part of town. It was one o'clock and Annie came in to announce lunch. Her black face beamed as she asked, "Could they be peace whistles?" Just then the telephone rang, and it was Mrs. Gregg to tell us the news. She has one son in France, another waiting to go, and her voice was quivering. The *Post* had

[3] Mrs. Slayden's nephews, Maury and George Maverick.

telephoned Mr. Gregg that the Germans had surrendered. Rena and I laughed and cried in a foolish way, and said, "Why aren't we more excited? Oughtn't we to feel differently?" Then the telephone again, and Mrs. James Brown Scott was there to tell us that the surrender was complete; the Germans had walked out into no man's land carrying a white flag and signed the Armistice unconditionally.

Annie was as puzzled as we were at our lack of expression, and asked, "Oughtn't we to put our heads out o' the window and holler, or do *something?*" Soon we saw people putting out flags, and the newsboys were calling "Extree—War's over" at the top of their voices. Mrs. Gregg came in from the Capitol with a bag of fresh chocolates, to celebrate, and said the people up there were wild, congressmen romping like boys, officers and privates embracing and slapping one another on the back, and the streets so full that the cars were blocked repeatedly. People were carrying flags, shouting and singing, and long lines of young women with hands joined winding in and out of the crowds.

In the afternoon I longed to go to church—my favorite place in all great days of my life—but could not think where to go. For a year and a half I have been too much out of sympathy with my Episcopal brethren to find any comfort in their ministrations, so I decided on St. Paul's, where I have found peace and quiet several times. Passing St. Andrew's my Protestant conscience rather smote me and I was about to go in, but saw such an array of posters that I turned away. At St. Paul's there were posters outside, but none past the door. The church was almost dark, only a few sharp points of light about the altar, a scattering of people, and a little child toddling softly about the aisles. I stayed rapt, submerged in the stillness until I felt quite rested and ready to go home. On V Street I dropped in at the little Chapel of Perpetual Adoration and found more people, more lights and much incense, but the same heavenly peace and quiet. No one showed me to a seat or handed me a leaflet; there were no flags or posters, and when I came out, there was no supersolicitous church officer to shake hands with me and urge me to come again.

I wish Protestants could learn that lesson of quiet, a part of the peace that passeth understanding. I went into St. Andrew's, almost from a sense of duty, and found the vestibule covered with blood-curdling war posters and the chancel gay with flags. Coming home my old enemy, the crescent moon, peeped at me through the trees, and when I came in there was J. quietly reading the *Star,* which said the news of peace was all a mistake! All the same, I have had my hour of exaltation and am not disturbed because it was a few days ahead of time.

November 11

It has come at last! Since Thursday we have been like those who wait for the morning, and now there is news enough to satisfy the greediest.

General Wood addresses the soldiers and tells them the Armistice does not mean peace and they must keep on preparing. Teddy is not heard from yet but is no doubt preparing to rend the air in praise of war. They will both die hard. The Kaiser himself will not more unwillingly surrender his faith in battle and murder and sudden death.

It seems certain this evening that the Kaiser and the Crown Prince have run away to Holland with all the baggage they could carry and little kings all over Europe are hunting cover. Socialists are in power in Berlin, red cockades on soldiers' caps and a red flag on Cologne Cathedral. There are unpleasant symptoms here and there of Bolshevik barbarities, but I have faith in German capacity and love of order to keep that down. In some places soldiers have stopped saluting their officers—a childish sort of gratification, but think how tired they must be of saluting and all that it implies.

This afternoon there was a procession, a villagy performance with tawdry allegorical floats. We went to the Carnegie Peace Foundation (No. 2 Jackson Place) and had more fun getting through the crowd than in seeing the parade. I watched it from the shaky little balcony, and only the Y.M.C.A. and the Y.W. and the Salvation Army sections got much applause. The President reviewed it from the steps of the Executive office, quite a new place.

In the balcony party Mrs. D., large, pretty, bland as a rule, said she was provoked with the President for asking us so promptly to begin saving food for our enemies and a friend of hers had said that she "wouldn't save one single lump of sugar for those damned Germans." It is funny how many women now seem pleased with themselves when they use that short and ugly word.

I didn't know when the President made the request until we saw the evening paper. He read the terms of the Armistice to the two Houses, "after his ancient fashion," as he would say, but sprang it on them too late for people to know it outside of the Capitol.

November 13

Rena and Mrs. Gregg reviled me for saying there were many people sorry that the war was over and are shocked to find women more irreconcilable than men. At market yesterday I met pretty Mrs. F., whose husband,

Colonel F., has been a long time with the army in France. I gave her some joyful greeting about the peace, and her face fell perceptibly. She said, "We-ell, I'm afraid I am rather a vindictive nature. I am disappointed. I did want our army to get to Berlin."

Later General M.'s wife was indignant with my cowardly attitude, and said she would have agreed to nothing but Berlin and a devastated Germany. Saturday, before the Armistice, I made another unfortunate speech by asking a Cabinet friend in my most exuberant tone, "Isn't the news splendid?" A look of bewilderment, almost offense, came over her face, and I realized that news of the dire disaster of the elections rather than peace was on her mind. I had to hasten to talk of the Armistice and reassure her. It would have been rather bad taste for me to make merry to a Cabinet lady over the worst blow that has befallen Wilson's administration. After his and Burleson's touching appeal to the country for an all-Democratic Congress, to be slapped in the face with such a tremendous Republican majority must make them wonder where they're at. In my secret heart perhaps I am not as sorry as a good Democrat ought to be.

December 1

John Bright said he never knew a bishop to express disapproval of a war but once, and that was of a war to put down the slave trade, but we shall have to make exceptions in favor of Bishop Gore of Oxford and, I am glad to say, of a few bishops in the Episcopal Church in the United States.

Bishop Gore, despised and rejected by the Established Church and the war party in England and scorned by the Episcopal Church in this country, goes quietly along saying what he thinks about the war and the people who upheld it. We have heard him twice, once at the New York Avenue Presbyterian church where, except for Bishop Lawrence on the platform, there was only one Episcopal clergyman present, and lately at the Congregational church where I think there were two or three clergymen. Perhaps they didn't want to hear him say in his gentle way, more in sorrow than anger, "I am ashamed of the clergy." I wish they could take lessons from him in English pronunciation even though they scorn his broad humanity.

Last winter a prayer for all the warring nations was issued under his name and had considerable influence in giving pause to the militant preachers until the story arose that it was insidious German propaganda and that the Bishop did not own it. I was determined to find out, so after his speech on the League of Nations, when J. and many of the other solid men present went up to speak to him, I went too. While I held his nice slim old hand, I said, "Bishop, will you tell me if you wrote the prayer for all warring nations published over your name?" He answered instantly, "I am sorry to say I cannot claim it. I issued it and commended it to my people, but I do not know who wrote it. I wish I did." I was satisfied and obliterated myself as soon as possible.

We heard Dr. Charles Aked today at the Congressional church plead for a League of Nations and, incidentally, for $30 million for relief work in Mesopotamia. How this war has drawn together the round world and they that dwell therein. Who ever thought of Mesopotamia except as a place in the Bible, and here it is beating on our doors for bread. Dr. Aked always burns a few phrases into your mind. For the League he said "World league or world anarchy, take your choice." He spoke of war as "civilization eating her own children." An ordinary speaker would have said "devouring" and weakened the picture.

Members' Gallery, December 2

We are waiting to hear the President address the joint Houses before he sails away on his amazing trip to Europe, preparations for which exceed in grandeur those for the Field of the Cloth of Gold or the Queen of Sheba's visit to King Solomon. The apes and peacocks alone are lacking, and there are people unkind enough to say that even they will go along in one form or another.

The performance is so unprecedented that all other interests are subordinate. I quite forgot that this was the reassembling of the Sixty-fifth Congress for its last session and couldn't think why Champ Clark was so tumultuously applauded when he went up to the Speaker's seat. Thanks to Mr. Wilson's appeal to the Democrats, when the next House assembles a Republican will have taken Clark's place. I hope it will be Jim Mann. I love to see a long ambition gratified when the effort to attain it has been made without trickery or meanness. One always feels that Mann is *straight* though his Scotch bluntness antagonizes many people.

It is perhaps my last opportunity to be here for a great occasion while J. is still a member, so there is a bit of sentiment in it as well as the intrinsic interest, and I am glad to have my old seat in the front row to the left of the Speaker's section. The criticism of Wilson for going at all, for not informing or consulting the Senate, and for his insolent silence in general has been tremendous, but I feel sure that he will coin a phrase

to catch the public taste and fool some more of the people some more of
the time.

                                                                    Later

He came in escorted by senators and representatives, some of whom I
knew could have found more congenial tasks. He tripped lightly up the
steps, reached over the desk and shook Clark's hand with a fine imitation
of cordiality, then turned to the House showing his long teeth in that
muscular contraction that passes for a smile.

House and galleries had risen respectfully when he entered, and a
few noisy Democrats, like Heflin, added some whooping to the otherwise
dignified applause, but we had hardly settled back in our seats before it
was evident that something was happening, someone was being disciplined.
He began with the war, the platitudes, and "sob stuff" of the last eighteen
months, but he lacked his usual amazing grace of expression. Also, he
was hoarse.

Some Democrats, not all by any means, seized the first excuse to
applaud, and the next and the next, before I realized that the Republicans
across the aisles were frozen in their seats. They did not move a finger
until praise of our gallant and glorious army and navy compelled a politic
approval. Then they stiffened again. It became really funny; their eyes were
set in their heads, their bodies rigid. Iris Hawley sat next to me and I
asked her, "Haven't you Republicans *got* any hands?" *"Not for today,"*
she said with a twinkle.

The President began to feel it. He stumbled a bit, coughed, hesitated,
and even seemed in want of a word now and then. I made a mental note
of "devastate" which I had not heard him use before. He spoke as usual of
"disservice" but forgot the bland sweetness of "ancient counsel," generally
used on these befooling occasions. Perhaps the icy stare of the Senate,
with which he had failed to take either ancient or modern counsel, froze
that pet phrase on his lips.

When with a slight change of voice he began with the phrase, "May
I not"—which like Roosevelt's "dee-lighted" has become a joke—there
was a faint ripple over the company and a look of expectancy. Everyone
thought the time had come for him to tell why he was going abroad, but
we were treated to more abstractions and even fewer facts. His presence
was "ardently desired by all the Allied countries," though he didn't divulge
the form of their importunities. He felt it his "duty" to go, and he felt
sure of being "followed by the prayers and good wishes of a united

country"; he would come home as soon as consistent with duty and with the demands being made for his counsel and the elucidation of his Fourteen Points "already accepted as the basis of peace settlements." It became almost a plea for sympathy as the coldness of the audience was made more manifest. At last he stopped. There was polite applause; he was escorted out, and everyone looked at his neighbor as if to say, "We know no more than we did before." There had been a rumor that he would be interrupted by some straight questions from "certain willful men," but no gathering of the legislators was ever conducted with more decency and order.

December 8

The last few days have been full of gossip about the sailing of the *George Washington,* and who was to go. Many knew positively that Mother Bolling, Miss Bertha Bolling, and John Randolph B. were going, but "the usual five" are separated for once.

It is a real relief for the ship to be gone; one gets so tired of public men and measures, the futile discussion and repetition. I remember when the name of Roosevelt in all its forms—Teddy, T.R., etc.—beat on my ears with the irritation of a child's tick-tack. I hope Wilson will succeed in his professed wish to devise a lasting peace, but I am afraid he is not being "followed by the prayers of a united people." The Senate is contemptuous and the papers are excoriating him. I am tired too of hearing people talk as if Wilson had invented the League of Nations. It is referred to so often in the *Iliad;* Joshua even had one in working order, and the good old American Peace Society has had the idea nailed to its masthead for fifty years.

Democracy will have to be kept alive by artificial respiration if something isn't done to offset the class distinctions prevailing on the *George Washington.* The company of about 1,300 "hand picked" assistants that Wilson is taking over with him are divided into three distinct classes. He and Mrs. Wilson are quite cut off from the vulgar herd by having a separate dining room and promenade deck; Mr. and Mrs. House, their daughters and sons-in-law and a select few others have still another dining room; while "the masses," college professors, every variety of expert and professional man the occasion is thought to require, are herded together quite apart from "the classes" in just a common ship's dining saloon. Still, all alike have the benefit of chefs, musicians, and entertainment specialists from big New York hotels taken over with large salaries to keep up the morale of the peacemakers.

December 20

Thanks to a meeting of the Carnegie Endowment for Peace we have had a pleasant, inexpensive two days in New York. The weather was bright, the streets aflutter overhead with innumerable flags to remind us of the Red Cross drive, and the sidewalks and hotel lobbies surging with returned soldiers. Some, of course, are wounded, and many wear clothes showing stains of the trenches, but they are all touchingly responsive to a friendly word. There is not much laughter, or fun, even among the groups of well ones. More and more I am impressed with the sobering effect of a time overseas, even on the men who never got to the front. The *Leviathan* bringing 9,000 men docked while we were there. I would rather have seen the landing than any other sight the town afforded, but to get a pass was so nearly impossible that we didn't even try.

We found waiting for us an invitation to dine with the Robert Underwood Johnsons but had to decline it for a much less interesting engagement, so they suggested tea instead and we had an hour of good talk.

J. and Mr. Johnson naturally dropped into politics, and Mrs. Johnson and I frankly gossiped. She said there was no news in New York, and she wanted to hear all there was in Washington—impossible in one brief hour, but I did my best. Later we all wondered what had become of the dear old book-shaped magazines, *Harper's, Scribners, Century,* that used to fill such big places in our reading lives. Were they in themselves less interesting or had the tension of the war unfitted us for anything but the brevities of small square-paged weeklies, the *Literary Digest,* the *Nation,* the *New Republic?* Mrs. Johnson looked askance at the last-named, and said, "Isn't it rather radical?" She said J. would feel as lost for a while after being forced out of Congress as her husband felt when he was forced out of *Century,* to which he had given his life, but Mr. Johnson seems to be reveling in his work as chairman of the organization of American poets for the relief of Italy.

Never in my life have I felt such gross delight at being asked out to dinner. My Annie is sick and three weeks of my own cooking have almost persuaded me to join one of these nut-and-raw-carrot health schools. I jumped at the invitation to Mrs. John B. Henderson's last Sunday in spite of J.'s objection to peanut chops and cereal entrees, and what was our amusement when we arrived to find that the party was planned to celebrate the passing of the Prohibition Amendment, which J. has fought tooth and nail. Senator Morris Sheppard, the "Texarkana Titan," as the *Sun* calls him, was the pièce de résistance and so happy over the consummation of his dearest hopes that we all enjoyed ourselves in sympathy with him. Mrs. Henderson was not at her spiciest—a word she would no doubt resent, as spices are not in her lexicon.

I had Senator France of Maryland on one side of me and that ever youthful professional diner-out, Dr. Swisher, on the other. J. was opposite to me beside a grim female with a large hat secured by an elastic band under her chin in the fashion of the 60s. She had a wide mouth and sharp teeth that snapped when she talked. Obviously a woman with a mission.

Mrs. Henderson set the ball rolling by asking J. what he thought of the amendment, and he answered facetiously that it wouldn't do for him to express his opinion in such a select company. While the others gave the laugh his little witticism was entitled to, the lady beside him glared. In answer to a question of mine about her latest book of recipes, Mrs. Henderson said she was compelled to revise it, that now being rid of animal foods and alcohol she was opposed to salt, pepper and all the baking powders. The dinner was devised according to her latest prejudice, and a succession of dishes, beautiful to the eye, were apples of Sodom to the taste. At last we welcomed almost audibly a mold of ice cream knowing that its merits were not dependent upon either salt, pepper or baking powder, and one sip brought me a glow of delight—it was soaked with rum. A caterer had had his little joke. Shy looks of pleasure went around the table of twenty or more guests, and when I started to say something, Dr. Swisher laid his hand on my arm and said, "Oh, please don't tell her; she'll take it away from us." Nobody commented, and Mrs. H. and the Senator talked about proteins as they ate the last spoonful of their portions without knowing that they were destroying their efficiency and digging early graves for themselves.

After dinner, when the gentlemen went off to smoke, it came out that the lady with the elastic under her chin represented a Boston society for the suppression of the cultivation and use of tobacco. When everyone gets his or her favorite law to work how good we will be—or what hypocrites and lawbreakers.

CHAPTER TWENTY-THREE

1919

January 6

An hour ago, while I was enjoying my daily telephone gossip with Mrs. Porter, two plumbers came in to make repairs in the bathroom, and one inquired casually of J. if he had heard that Roosevelt was found dead in bed this morning. The receiver almost fell from my hand. My first thought was that a great reservoir of energy and activity had passed into nothingness as far as this old earth was concerned. I never admired him unqualifiedly as many people do, but he was bold, dynamic, and greatly versatile. He kept the political pot always at boiling point and compelled people to think, if, unfortunately, only on violently partisan lines.

I called General Ainsworth at once, and he said, "No-o? Heart disease, perhaps—or did someone pi'son him? It removes a storm center, doesn't it? It is hard to realize doing without him."

J. had gone back to writing on his Congressional swan song, as he calls it, and when I came in, he said, "This removes Wilson's greatest asset. If Roosevelt had run against him, it would have been one third-termer against another; now there's only Taft, and he hasn't a following to make him dangerous. Wilson will be sorry."

An extra is being called now, and even the President's triumphal progress through Europe will have second place for a while. Mrs. Wilson's gowns, "Made in America" of course, the diamond pins she is receiving, are details so important that our government has taken over the cables apparently for the express purpose of reporting them. Even the long-drawn-out casualty lists have been excluded. For several days we will hear of Roosevelt, and then no more until the historians begin on him. "Some little talk awhile of Me and Thee there was—and then no more of Thee and Me."

I must write this story down before I forget the actual words. I said them to myself over and over on the way home. This morning I went down to Cornwell's to get some little delicacy for Mother, and at the cake counter met Mrs. Franklin K. Lane. We had some pleasant talk, chiefly about her pretty daughter, Nancy, a blonde, Trilby-looking girl, and Mrs. Lane evidently enjoyed my quite sincere admiration of her. I went to another counter but presently came back for my package and found Mrs. L. still there. After a little talk she started away, took a few steps, turned, hesitated a moment, then walked straight up to me and said, "Perhaps I ought not to say it, but I think that thing was outrageous," then warming to the subject, repeated, "Yes, *outrageous!* There is no other word for it." I didn't pretend not to understand that she referred to Wilson's treatment of J. and said, "Yes, it was, but you know Mr. Slayden was not an original Wilson man—any more," I added maliciously, "than John Davis was." "Well," she went on, "you know that that thing came up in the Cabinet, don't you?" I said laughingly, "Indeed, no! No one knows less of the Cabinet than I do." She ignored my remark and went on, "And the President said, 'Mr. Burleson, you put one over on me.' Burleson turned very red, and said he knew nothing at all about it, and the President said, 'I have seen the telegram in your own handwriting.'" She did not say that the President appeared to resent Burleson's action or to feel himself tricked, but added, "It was the very first time he has ever shown any comprehension of the kind of man Burleson is," and that "Burleson said Tumulty asked him to write the telegram, but, of course, everyone knew that he had told Tumulty to send it." I told her I had ascribed the incident to the President's own dislike of Mr. Slayden, and she explained, "He is just a neurasthenic man who cannot bear to be opposed by anyone. The people around him have to get what they want by apparent submission to his wishes." I started to say that that accounted for the notorious feebleness of his Cabinet, but tempered it by telling her that a distinguished Californian had said to me lately that they were proud to feel that Lane was the only strong man in it. "Yes," she said rather sadly, "he is a strong man, but he is growing cynical, and feels bitter about how all these things are obscuring or bringing disaster to the really big things the Administration has accomplished and making hopeless the position of the party—there is no chance for the Democrats to have power again in twenty years." I laughed rather derisively and said, "Never, I'm afraid."

She reiterated her and Mr. Lane's admiration of J.'s dignity in withdrawing as he did and leaving the President to explain; said again that it was outrageous and that the oldest and best element of the party was being estranged.

With a sudden access of prudence she came back for a postscript and said, "Now, please don't tell this as coming from me, though I know positively it is true, as I heard it discussed by two or three Cabinet men.— If you *should* tell it, say that a Cabinet officer's wife heard the conversation." She praised J.'s position of unassailable dignity, and I said, "But there was nothing for a gentleman to do but withdraw. He could not *tell* the President he lied, so he could only let him know unequivocally that he *thought* so."

Of course I shall not tell the story to any but a few close and prudent friends. It was unwise for her to tell it, just an impulse of friendliness to us, and might do her and her husband a lot of harm. They say that Lane is having hard sledding with the Cabinet as it is. Burleson has been trying to oust him. He is rather too big and outspoken for such cringing company.

January 30

Mrs. Gregg said it sounded like the Dark Ages, but in spite of her jeers Mrs. Porter and I made the Cabinet calls yesterday and had a good deal of fun—chiefly by using up what we took with us. The receptions were dingy, very few people, and no flowers except at one place a bouquet of dried thistles, very dusty and depressing. A few electric lights, or even a pocket flashlight, would have cheered our lonely way, but the ladies are still conserving, trying to get even on those billion-dollar appropriations. No one offered us so much as a cracker to eat. There was a poor but honest tea table at the Bakers', but it was not suggested that we do more than look at it. Mrs. Baker in her early official days was stiff and a little afraid of herself, but she has become almost too animated. She meets her guests in the hall, and talks louder and louder about the hardships of her position, sometimes writing letters till three o'clock in the morning, many of them really the business of the War Department. I suggested a secretary, but she said many of the letters were from "heartbroken mothers" and had to have her personal attention. Baker's paternal attitude to the army, its morals, its literature, etc., has been a novelty in our government, but that the army has a mother too is a stranger innovation still.

Good, creamy Mrs. Daniels—one always thinks of dairy products when she is around for all she has become so *empressée*—usually has a bright house with a lot of young girls receiving, but she too was dusky and colorless yesterday. During our conversation she told me how Mr.

Daniels would never "sell his brain," how he often excluded valuable advertising matter because he wanted to "fill his paper with his own ideas." They felt the paper was "something sacred" (the Raleigh *News and Observer* in a new light).

We rounded off the afternoon at the Colonial Dames Club, dark there, too, so dark one could almost hear the ghosts of the ancestors flapping about. I like aristocrats individually, and have often thought of joining the C.D.s, but could I stand aristocrats en masse? It doesn't stand to reason that people are congenial because they had ancestors engaged in a certain work two hundred years ago. There is a strain of plebeian in me that would drive me outside to sit on a grassy bank with the grand old gardener and his wife, and not smile but laugh aloud at the dames of long descent.

January 31

Mrs. Henderson almost persuadeth me to be a vegetarian and a total abstainer! I might even forgo tea, coffee, salt, pepper and baking powder if I thought it would result in such radiant health and usefulness as hers at her age. They say she is eighty or more—she was called an old lady when I came here twenty-two years ago, but she still looks just the same. I sat by her at the Congressional Club last night and noticed how thick and soft her hair was, and her skin clear and rosy. She could never have been strictly pretty, but she is so pleasant to look upon. She does nothing to efface the marks of age, they just aren't there, and she talks as if she were playing a game with time, counting quite frankly every point she gains or loses. She said, "I like to sit in front, for I *am* getting a little deaf. I hate to lose any faculty, one oughtn't to."

The occasion was Taft's address to the Congressional Club on the League of Nations, and he was never more debonair. He professed to be embarrassed at addressing a woman's club, and I believe he really was, but he spoke of it as his opportunity to "address a message to Congress in person, a recent departure from the Jeffersonian plan of written messages." He believed in it, was glad the custom had been revived, but could not help thinking what "agonies of eloquence" it would have brought forth if he or Roosevelt had done it. On the League of Nations he laughed away our fears of "supersovereignty" as well as the old bugbear of "entangling foreign alliances," though that has not troubled me for a long time. The alliances have come almost in the course of nature, and I think it rests with us to see whether they shall be entangling or merely neighborly and altruistic. Taft's audible chuckle between sentences was almost like that of a professional monologist, infectiously merry and confidential. It reminded me of the cluck a whippoorwill gives, a laugh to himself, when he has been whistling with special vim and mischief.

February 3

We dined last night with Judge and Mrs. Watson of Virginia—J. thinks him one of the most scholarly and capable men in Congress—and he told us a bit of political news which will be epochal, perhaps catastrophic, if it comes true.

The Foreign Affairs Committee is preparing to bring in a resolution expressing our sympathy with Ireland's demands for a free government, self-determination, etc. It is said to be at the President's express suggestion, and the "incomparably greatest (paper) navy" is a stick to frighten Lloyd George, of whom he is jealous. It seems like midsummer madness, also like Wilson, to try such cheap political tricks just now when the League of Nations and the plan of a better world seem almost in our grasp. And what of the Philippines? If we got rid of that in our own eye, mightn't we see more clearly to remove the mote from England's?

"Bolsheviki" is such a porcupinish word, so foreign and bristling that it is used to describe all sorts of objectionable ideas and people, from plain tramps to the reddest anarchists. I was rather glad yesterday at a meeting at Poli's theater to learn that it only means "majority," and the reviled Soviet government is only "representatives of the majority."

Albert Rhys Williams and a leggy, undeveloped young woman, Louise Bryant, author of *Six Red Months in Russia,* were advertised to tell us "The Truth about Russia," and as J. and I are glad to hear the truth about anything we went to hear them. The majority of the audience was distinctly foreign, woolly and radical looking, but there were many like ourselves, respectable married people with umbrellas, who came because they felt sure that the speakers knew more about Russia than they did and would not make red revolutionists of us in one afternoon. There was nothing the least anarchistic, unless it was their saying that the "capitalist press" was concealing the truth and publishing lies. From the way this morning's *Post* misrepresents the spirit of the meeting, I am inclined to think they were right. We had had enough and didn't stay to the questions following the meeting, but Representative Mason did and participated, and the papers are raising a hue and cry about it, saying the matter is to be investigated in the Senate.

We are getting much praise, not quite deserved in my case, for our serenity in the face of untoward circumstances—J.'s loss of place and uncertain future. With me it is no more than just a nature sloping to the Southern side. I am not sure whether I am emulating the Psalmist in waiting patiently upon the Lord or Mr. Micawber in expecting "something to turn up." But with J. it is a fine philosophy, keeping always in mind the fact that whoever goes into political life must be prepared for some such event sooner or later and have some spiritual and mental reserve to draw upon. Twenty-two years in the thick of things have broadened our horizons so that our lives can never be really circumscribed again. We have delightful friends and a rich store of happy memories. We have good health and have been ill often enough to realize its value; books are cheap, and a dignified old age in the country, with a garden, is rather an enticing picture. I can hear still my dear old grandfather's sweet piping voice singing:

> *In the downhill of life when I find I'm declining*
> *May my lot no less fortunate be,*
> *Than a snug elbow chair can afford for reclining,*
> *And a cot that o'erlooks the white sea.*

Our cot will overlook the Blue Ridge—"and the mountains also shall bring peace." To one who inherits a love of the soil, and one special spot on it as I do, it is not unpleasant to look forward to closing one's eyes on the same view of sky and earth on which they were opened.

Mrs. Barrett Browning is an inexplicable sort of person. All her ties and interests must be in Europe, so it is quite natural for her to work for the Serbians, Italians, etc., but how did she become interested in the "po' whites" of the Blue Ridge Mountains? There she was at a meeting of the auxiliary, held annually in Dr. W. C. Rives's charming library. They aren't very interesting meetings; exactly the same people come every year. I could go in blindfold and put my hand on Miss Mattie Tiffey, Miss Cox and Mr. Singleton, and we talk about the same things in the same way each time. We all say how brave and good and untiring Archdeacon Neve is, and, what is more, we all mean it; then some younger man tells about the work, and we take up a collection. It was at that stage that I found myself standing by Mrs. Browning. She was stouter than ever, and her clothes looked rough and badly worn—she must give to the ultimate penny. Like many other people, she seemed surprised to find me still in town and said she was sorry she hadn't invited me to her sale of Italian laces; she had made more than $800. "But I sold some of my silver, too," she said. "I cannot bear the thought of so much suffering, and why should I keep the silver? I want to go back to Italy to spend at least two years when conditions are better."

We were invited to the same pretty tea table in the next room presided over by the same patrician lady in black, and Mrs. Rives pressed upon us the pretty cake in pretty dishes just as she did at this time last year. Their library, next to the Pinchots', is the pleasantest one I know, and the whole house so genuine; nothing is new and nothing old enough to be shabby, nor the sort of thing that was considered pretty *once*. This is the proof of good ancestry that I enjoy, the things inherited, no matter how simple, proving good taste, fundamental refinement in those who passed them on.

February 14

Mrs. Louis Post telephoned that she and Jane Addams were doing a little committee work and wanted me to join them. I deserted a merely pleasant luncheon at the Cosmos Club quite early, and when Mrs. Post opened her door I saw in her tiny blue-print-curtained drawing room not only Miss Addams, but Anna Garlin Spencer (a Dresden china intellectual), Florence Kelley, Lucia Ames Mead and Jeannette Rankin. Miss R. doesn't appall me with her intellectuality, but why did the others want me in their council? I exclaimed what was my first thought, "If I had known there was such an assembly of the great, I'd have been afraid to come!" And Mrs. Post replied, "The idea of the wife of James L. Slayden being afraid in any company!" So, being only the wife of my husband, I took courage. We conferred over the possibility of getting General Anson Mills to trust our Woman's International League with some of the money he says he intends to give to the cause of peace, and Miss Addams and I finally took a cab and went to see him, but I fear it is hopeless. The poor old gentleman is getting very penurious and suspicious. He has so many strings to his gifts and makes such odd conditions that he will probably die before he makes up his mind when and where to give it. Perhaps his daughter will carry out his wishes someday.

The Victory Dinner was sandwiched between days of solemn conclave of hundreds of women from all parts of the country. In spite of its being historical and rather unusual, I dreaded it. In large gatherings women are apt to get too tense, too bitter, or foolishly joyful, and emphasize their mere womanishness, but this was quite different. I think I can see already the effect of our having the franchise in a finer seriousness and dignity and a sense of responsibility for what we say. It was an inspiring sight, 750 women sitting down together in peace and harmony, no politics, no elections, no "Madam President" or "Robert's Rules." And they were so good looking too—strong, healthy, not over- or underdressed, and sane, intelligent faces. Of course the fact that "Babushka,"[1] the poor little "grandmother" of this and many other Russian revolutions, was to be there had brought a great many people, and just before we were seated the rumor went round that she had arrived. Like a great wave, we swept up to that end of the room and simply looked at her. There was nothing else to do, so many could not possibly speak to her, but the poor tired old soul has been through too much to be embarrassed by anything and seemed as unconscious of our stares as a soft old caged animal in a zoo. She is exactly like her pictures, only lacking the dark woolen shawl over her head. Her rather short gray hair was brushed straight back and held down on top with a piece of curved comb; her skin was clear, and a good color, but all her front teeth were gone, and the two long dog teeth on the side give her a slightly leonine look. Her small eyes are the wariest I ever saw. Still she looks as if she might have been pretty in her youth, and you wonder why, over here, at peace, and the center of loving attention, there was not some little tiny touch of womanly vanity, but her dress could not have been more severe. Her gown was rough and black and fastened at the wrists like a shirt. She wore a big white silk handkerchief around her neck and knotted and pinned down at her waist. Not a flower, a bit of lace, a jewel, or anything that she might not have worn in prison.

There were several good speeches, Julia Lathrop at her best, and a very handsome Canadian woman who stressed the point of loyalty to England while maintaining that Canada was entirely independent— "Daughter am I in my Mother's house, but mistress in my own." A slightly difficult thing to make clear, I thought. Baker also spoke.

When it was Babushka's time to speak the company rose spontaneously and applauded, but it is too late for her to speak to an American audience. She writes English, but cannot speak it. Her voice is tired and weak, her accent impenetrable, and her manner just childish and pleading rather than impressive. It was much just to see her, the "Russian Messiah," a delicately nurtured lady who has spent a greater part of her life in Siberia in prison or under restraint to serve the cause of freedom for her fellow countrymen.

[1] Catherine Breshkovsky.

February 20

I am making farewell calls but didn't refer to anything so sad as my departure when we went to see Mrs. Henderson yesterday. She always keeps the sunny side up in her talk and was so exhilarating that we would gladly have stayed longer, but one of Miss Nicolay and Miss Spofford's annual "days" called us onward and upward. After that came a huge tea at the Willard given by some New York women, Mrs. Calder, a pastel herself in pastel chiffon, and Mrs. Fairchild, always friendly and commonsensible. The rigidity of the new "Pro" law stiffens many companies. Who could be gay on grape juice punch, or even loganberry, no matter how spiked with White Rock?

In the evening we went apleasuring again to a meeting of the Archaeological Society at Mrs. Matthew T. Scott's grand new residence—it would be undue familiarity to call it a home. The reception rooms are like the first bare antechambers of Versailles, pale-cream walls, and the windows covered with white silk shades. A painted Italian ceiling kept me constantly staring upward while trying to sit still and look at ease with my poor little feet dangling six inches off the floor from one of those penitential gilt chairs used by the truly rich on all state occasions. How I hate 'em!— the chairs I mean, not the rich; they give me many pleasant times.

A professor from somewhere talked about mummies and looked like one who spoke with authority. There was a beautiful supper, and Helen Wright, Representative Merrill Moores, Miss de Graffenreid and ourselves were a congenial talking party. Miss de G. tries to maintain her attitude of admiration and approval of Wilson and all that pertains to him but actually joined in the laugh at the current joke. "How fast does the *George Washington* travel when conveying the President to and from Europe?" The answer is, "Fully twenty-one may-I-nots an hour."

February 21

The lame duck dinner at the McKinleys' last night was like "the good old days befo' the war, suh," in the way of things to drink. There were cocktails to begin with. I dislike them extremely but took a sip of mine just as a symbol of liberty, and I enjoyed the sherry and champagne in their proper places at the table. The old days of laying by something for a rainy day have given place to providing something for the approaching drought, and there was much talk of trips to Baltimore and truckloads of liquids coming over today, which is the end of the open season. They say that the Prohibition Amendment is to be carried to Boston to get the President's signature as soon as he lands. It would be appropriate to have it signed on Plymouth Rock, as it is the fine flower of Puritanism, fought for in the very same spirit of intolerance of any opinion but your own that characterized those Pilgrims who, Joseph Choate said, "fell first on their knees and then on the aborigines."

Senator and Mrs. Weeks, the Fairchilds of New York, J. and I, and the Swagar Sherleys are all lame ducks, but to keep us from feeling like a company of pariahs Mr. McKinley had kindly added some other people. They must have been edified at the general satisfaction, not to say joy, with which Weeks, Sherley and Fairchild were retiring. One even wondered why they had all endured such strenuous campaigns and spent thousands of dollars getting themselves elected to serve an ungrateful country when the one thing they longed for was home. J. exercised his really charming gift of laughing away the question and didn't commit himself, while I injected a harsh note into the unctuous atmosphere by telling the truth: "I am *dreadfully* sorry to go, and would be delighted to come back." I believe the Fairchilds really are willing to go, but the others—

February 23

The effort to decorate the city for the President's return is rather listless. Streets and buildings are hung with the tattered and faded bunting of yesteryear, and the dull misty weather makes it even more dingy and forlorn. The returned soldiers are included in the welcome, but most of the advertising is for the President. He likes to be welcomed promptly as he returns to his duties in Europe on March 5 or 6. Just running over to see that we were all right, I presume. Perhaps he heard George Harvey's warning that if he didn't hurry home he might find that the United States had declared itself a republic.

February 26

I expected to be sad and sentimental over leaving Washington, but I am too tired to have any emotions left. Our friends are making the most of our time, and as the proper care of my house and packing might easily take all of it, it is like trying to be in two places at once. We made a flying trip to Virginia to say good-by to Mother and got home in time to dress for supper at the Ainsworths'—the General's usual chafing dish of the best oysters in the world but with the unexpected extras of cocktails and sparkling Burgundy in our honor.

The next evening we dined with Helen Wright at the new Arts Club, and I was glad to see the place, such a restrained old private house. It brought me a tender *souvenir d'enfance* of evenings at Piedmont with "a clear fire, a clean hearth and the vigor of the game." Not that I ever did more than look on at the game; I detested cards then as I do now. The dinner was simple and good and even with this bachelor maid we had good sauterne and brandy peaches.

Tuesday morning I had a séance with a dressmaker, a rush to the Washington Club to hear Charlie Tittmann sing—a pleasure I never miss at any cost—and then a luncheon at the Cosmos Club with good talk. "Oh, the dalliance and the wit!" How I shall miss them when we are settled in some small place with small talk and a fixed horizon.

That evening we had dinner at Justice McCoy's and more champagne. They said it was the first time they had ever served it at their table.

We have even found time for a twice-deferred dinner at Ranscher's for Dr. and Mrs. Panaretoff. The other guests were Judge and Mrs. Watson of Virginia, Mrs. Porter, and Charles Moore, chairman of the Federal Arts Commission, J.'s darling project which he thinks has already saved the country from many atrocities committed in the name of art. How fortunate that the commission got into running order before our fiery untamed patriots begin to vent their feelings in statuary and soldiers' monuments. If J. had done nothing else in Congress he would deserve his country's gratitude for getting the Lincoln Memorial in its present form, instead of a highway to Gettysburg, and for firmly establishing the Arts Commission. No one unfamiliar with the work of the Library Committee would believe the horrors that are proposed for the government to build every day, and the Commission represents the angel with the flaming sword to scare them off. These two achievements of his committee and his long and at last successful fight for the American Academy of Arts and Letters give him a comfortable sense of something accomplished, something done, even if his career has not satisfied the element in San Antonio that neither knows nor can understand a representative's interest in anything outside of his own district. Packing, moving and shipping goes on relentlessly around me.

2:30 P.M.

The air is throbbing with the sound of airplanes—and now and then a strain of martial music comes on the south breeze. I cannot spare time to see the parade though Julia Harrison tempted me almost beyond my strength with the promise of good company in her drawing-room windows. In spite of the confusion around me I am really resting while I add these few lines to my notebook, to the last few blank pages of it. Everything connected with our life here seems to be "coming out even." Monday when J. resigned the chairmanship of the American Group of the Inter-parliamentary Union, he was so pleased to have Mr. McKinley elected to succeed him. He thinks Mr. McK. so capable and such a sincere and practical peace man. Then J. and Representative Moores of Indiana were appointed delegates to the meeting of the Union this fall—the first since the war began—and my head is full of dreams of going to some new place in Europe. I hope it will be Sweden. We might be merry there, but in one of the battle-torn countries, could we forget? How gay we were in Brussels, and all the time the conferees were planning how Europe could be saved from "the next war," the awful thing they foresaw with clearer eyes than ours. Sometimes we thought them just obsessed with an idea, but they knew the signs of the times. The hideous menacing thump of airplanes at this moment reminds me that those earnest, anxious men knew whereof they spoke, and it makes the sneers and sarcasm about the League of Nations by war lovers like Senator Lodge seem so cheap and shallow.

The morning *Post* implies delicately that the President last night at a meeting of the Democratic National Committee, in speaking of the senators who are opposing him, used some language unfit to print. It makes me almost wish I had been there. "His long wooden face," as a French paper described it, must be so funny when he forgets himself.

Sunday

After a hard morning of packing and letter writing we went to lunch with our old and dear friends the Calderóns of Bolivia. "Daddy" put his arm around my shoulders and patted me in such a dignified Spanish way when he said how sorry he was to lose us, and dear pretty, coquettish Elena made fretful little mouths of distress over the separation. There was a delicious luncheon as always under dear Madame Calderón's ministrations. And under the protection of the Bolivian flag we enjoyed it with good sherry and Château Yquem without a tremor of conscience or fear of the law. How fine to live in a free country!

I find myself rather tragically enumerating the things I enjoy that I cannot have elsewhere. The gray dome of the Capitol, for instance, on misty days, itself a cloud, a bubble; and I love to walk up S Street trying to forget the Masonic Temple so that turning to 16th I may be transported once more with the splendor of the sky between the three columns of the southwest corner. Why are columns so much the most beautiful and satisfying things in all architecture? And if I were on the Potomac Drive this afternoon I would hold my breath waiting to catch the glimpse of the Monument framed for an instant at the end through the north colonnade of the Lincoln Memorial. These are things that I can find nowhere but in Washington, and, oh, some friends, some friends! I cannot even write their names, for it is with feelings as with waters; the shallows murmur and the deeps are dumb.

March 3, 3:30 P.M.

Twenty-two years of service here are finished, and we are in a Pullman section on the Pennsylvania Railroad train on our way to Texas. We have gone through these motions of getting away so many times when it meant only the end of a session or the beginning of a pleasant journey that I cannot realize that this is the end of an epoch for us. As Mr. Harrison brought us to the station in his car the city looked brilliant and springlike under a spotless sky. None of us referred to its being a last ride together; instead we talked of the meeting of the Texas Club so cleverly arranged to give J. a graceful and warm farewell and of the slim chances of our finding a room in Fort Worth, where we have to spend a night. The oil boomers have possession of everything. I watched J. furtively to see if he cast one longing, lingering look behind at the flags still fluttering over the House and Senate, but he was cumbered with much hand baggage, and so far the only word of regret he has spoken was about leaving his old brier pipe, and he cannot get a new one till we reach St. Louis.

March 4

I slept soundly all night and till late this morning. After breakfast we found some pleasant men, old acquaintances and new, and were having a bright talk when I suddenly remembered the date and asked J. if he were still a member of Congress. He took out his watch, looked at it and said slowly, "No-o, I became an ex one hour ago."

INDEX

ABC Conference, 238, 238n.
Abdul Baha (Bahaists), 172-73
Adams, Charles Francis, Sr., 166
Adams, Charles Francis, 86, 114; *Autobiography*, 275, 276; characteristics, 275; on Emancipation, 117-18; entertaining, 166-67, 170; House, criticism of, 259; presidency, fitness for, 165; "A Reflex Light from Africa," 86; Slaydens, 165-67, 172
Adams, Mrs. Charles Francis, 302
Adams, John, 166, 297; in White House, 46
Adams, Maude, 188
Adamson, William C. (Representative from Georgia), 339
Addams, Jane, 225, 256, 298, 314, 315-316, 360; Peace party, 261-62
African, assimilation of, 87
Afro-American problem, 118 (*See* Negroes, race problem)
Ainsworth, Fred C., 44, 156, 245, 250, 261, 275, 290, 291, 324, 327, 341, 354; entertaining, 363; Slayden campaign, 333-34
Ainsworth, Mrs. Fred C., 156, 173, 254, 290, 291
Albert, King of Belgium, 249
Alger, Russell A. (Secretary of War, 1897-1899, Senator from Michigan), 17, 17n.
Algeria, 305
Allen, Frederick Lewis, xvi
Allen, John Mills (Representative from Mississippi), 257, 257n.
Allender, Mrs. 320
Ambassadors, salaries, 341
America: ambassadors, 218; beauties of, 262; Benton case, 231n.; Congressional representation, 208; –Cuba relations, 38-39 (*see* Spanish-American War); English in, 289; French in, 289; Germans in, 289 (*see also under* Texas); independence in dress, 244; Italians in, 289; manners, 21; millionaires, 274-75;

music, 126; patriotism, 274 (*see also* Patriotism); possessions, 305; provincialism, 168, 217, 223, 313; soldiers, 338; women, 288 (*see also* Women); World War (*see under* United States)
American (Hearst paper), 187
American Academy of Arts and Letters: Charter, 274, 278; Mrs. Champ Clark, 270-71; New York meeting (1914), 250-52; Slayden and, 247, 274, 364
American Academy of Fine Arts, 195
American Association for the Advancement of Science, 48
American Expeditionary Force, 67n.
American Forestry Congress, 64
American Peace Society, x, 351
American Red Cross (*see* Red Cross)
American Revolution, 35
Anderson, Mr., 239
Anderson, Mrs., 239
Andrews, Marietta Minnigerode, 280
Andrews, Mary Lloyd, 300
Andrews, Wynne, 1
Anglo-American Joint High Commission, 24
Annapolis, 198, 344
Annual Conference on International Arbitration, 84
Ansberry, Timothy T. (Representative from Ohio), 170
Anthony, Daniel R., Jr. (Representative from Kansas), 263
Anthony, Mrs. Daniel R., Jr., 263
Anti-Imperialist League, 102
Antin, Mary, 231; *The Promised Land*, 231n.
Apponyi, Albert Gyärgy, 57, 73, 75, 89
Argentina, 238n.
Arlington National Cemetery, 110, 124, 240
Armenia, World War I, 273
Army and Navy Journal, 32
Ash, Mrs. Percy, 202
Association of Historians and Scientists, 114

St. Louis Exposition (1904), 55, 57, 58, 59
Sampson, William T., 19, 19n., 41
San Antonio, 183; Alamo, 313; Central
  Powers Red Cross bazaar, 289; change
  in, 241-42; library, 22-23, 23n., 206;
  military spirit, 332; representative atti-
  tude toward, 89, 364; Roosevelt in, 71;
  Rough Riders, 20; Security League,
  333; weather, 110, 287
San Antonio *Express,* xiii, 111, 123, 156,
  188, 332
San Francisco Exposition (1915), 263
San Giuliano, Marchese di, 57
Sansom, Captain, 313
Santiago, Cuba, naval victory, 19n.
Santo Domingo, 305
Santo Domingo (ship), 26
Sayers, Joseph D. (Representative from
  Texas, Governor of Texas, 1899-1903),
  6
Sayers, Mrs. Joseph D., 6
Schley, Winfield Scott, 19, 19n., 24
Schluter, Mrs., 198
Schrank, John, 187n.
Schurz, Carl, 154
Scotland, 210-14
Scott, James Brown (Trustee and Secre-
  tary, Carnegie Endowment for Inter-
  national Peace), 190, 258
Scott, Mrs. James Brown, 193, 220, 247,
  258, 343-44, 346
Scott, Julia Green (Mrs. Matthew T.),
  362
Scribner's, 352
Seawell, Molly Elliot, 28-29
Seeger, Alan, 309
Senate (*see* U. S. Senate)
Sepulveda, Conchita (Mrs.), 140
Serbia, World War I, 273, 290
Seward, William H., 286
Shafter, William R., 24
Sharp, William G. (Representative from
  Ohio, Ambassador to France, 1914-
  1919), 151
Shaw, Anna Howard, 225
Shelby, David D., 248
Shepard, Seth (Associate Justice of Court
  of Appeals of District of Columbia,
  1893-1905, Chief Justice, 1905-1917),
  49, 50, 90, 160
Shepard, Mrs. Seth, 50, 160
Sheppard, Morris (Representative and
  Senator from Texas), 248, 284, 352-53
Sheridan, Mrs. Philip, 29
Sherley, Joseph Swagar (Representative
  from Kentucky), 363
Sherley, Mrs. Joseph Swagar, 262, 363

Sherman, James S. (Representative from
  New York, Vice President, 1909-
  1912), 108, 120, 177; funeral, 314
Sherman, Mrs. James S., 108, 123, 152
Sherman, John (Representative and
  Senator from Ohio, Secretary of the
  Treasury, 1877-1881, Secretary of
  State, 1897-1898), 17
Sherman, William T., 23n.
Siberia, 295, 361
Sickles, Daniel E., 37
Sigsbee, Charles D., 14, 14n.
Silver, H. Percy, 303
Sims, Marie, 204
Singleton, Mr., 359
Skibo Castle, Scotland, 206, 210-14
Slaughter, Rosalie, 62
Slayden, Agnes (niece), 150, 152, 153,
  154, 173, 260n. (*see also* Lobinière,
  Agnes)
Slayden, Clarkson, and Robards (cotton
  brokers), x
Slayden, Ellen Maury: aristocrats, 357;
  biography, 367; on breeding, 2; cam-
  paigning, 110-11; church, 296 (*see also*
  Clergy); Civil War, 260; clubwoman,
  120, 149; compliments, 327; conventionalities, 307; dress, 47, 48, 113,
  208-9; education, xiii, 192; entertaining,
  12, 13-14, 62, 64, 93-94, 115, 151-52,
  156, 164, 166, 169-70, 173-76, 194-95;
  father, 9-10; on friendship, 127; grave,
  ix; health, 272, 274, 278; hero-worshiper, 144; hobbies, xiii-xv, 7, 108,
  109, 167, 192, 195, 262, 269, 364
  (*see also* travels); –husband relation-
  ship, 117, 236, 301; on husbands, 82;
  influenza epidemic, 344; intellectual-
  ism, 163; journal, xv-xvi, xviii-xxi;
  Maury Maverick, xviii; National
  Committeewoman (Texas), 225; pacifist, 327; peace work, 315-16; protocol,
  317; publicity, aversion to, 123-24;
  Red Cross, 253-54, 257-58, 313; Roosevelt, T., 51-54, 55; servants, 10, 12, 15,
  17, 30, 66, 90, 106, 133, 152, 162, 191,
  194, 199, 254, 297, 306, 345, 346,
  352; on slavery, 118; social arrogance,
  xii, xiv-xv, 204; Spain, 43, 84, 108,
  112; taste, 109; travels, 41-42, 71-80,
  153, 159-62, 207-21, 249, 259-69,
  365; war, terror of, 14, 16, 18; Washington life, xv, 9-10, 27, 36, 94-95,
  113, on leaving, 363-66; wealth, 242;
  weather, effect on, 29; Wilson (*see
  under* Wilson); (*see also under*
  Mexico *and* Woman suffrage)

ABOUT THE AUTHOR

Ellen Maury Slayden was born in 1860, at Piedmont, ancestral home of the Maurys in Charlottesville, Virginia, now a part of the campus of the University of Virginia. She did not attend a real school, but at times the Maury children had tutors from neighboring families even more impoverished than they were during the aftermath of the Civil War. They had books, and they were surrounded by the culture and the youth of the university. Early in life Ellen Maury formed the habit of keeping notebooks.

In 1883 she married James Luther Slayden, a cotton broker and ranchman, and went to live in San Antonio, Texas. The Slaydens traveled widely, in Europe and in Mexico, and Ellen Slayden wrote accounts of their travels for the *Century* and other leading periodicals of her day. She also was the first society editor of the San Antonio *Express*.

When her husband was elected to Congress, where he served from 1897 to 1919, Ellen Slayden turned her reportorial and writing talents to recording in notebooks the Washington scene and the major historical events of the time. Before her death in San Antonio in 1926, she put the journal in final manuscript form. The Slaydens had no children. Ellen Slayden gave her manuscript to her nephew, Maury Maverick. It has remained in his family until this publication.

Format by Betty Anderson
Set in Linotype Times Roman
Composed, printed and bound by The Haddon Craftsmen, Inc.
HARPER & ROW, PUBLISHERS, INCORPORATED

Fort Washington, Indiana.

New York, N.Y. xxxx xxxxx

Composed, printed and bound by The Haddon Craftsmen, Inc.

Harper & Row, Publishers, INCORPORATED